Human Rights

Alan Gewirth

Human Rights
Essays on Justification and Applications

The University of Chicago Press
Chicago and London

ALAN GEWIRTH is the Edward Carson Waller Distinguished
Service Professor of Philosophy at the University of Chicago.

The University of Chicago Press, Chicago 60637
The University of Chicago Press, Ltd., London

©1982 by The University of Chicago
All rights reserved. Published 1982
Printed in the United States of America
88 87 86 85 84 83 82   5 4 3 2 1

Library of Congress Cataloging in Publication Data

Gewirth, Alan.
  Human rights.

  Includes index.
    1. Civil rights—Addresses, essays, lectures.
2. Civil rights—Moral and ethical aspects—Ad-
dresses, essays, lectures. I. Title.
JC571.G44   172'.1   81-21933
ISBN 0-226-28877-3   AACR2
ISBN 0-226-28878-1 (pbk.)

To the memory of my Mother and Father
and
to Aunt Rebecca and Cousin Libby
who as young emigrants from Czarist Russia
knew the importance of human rights

Contents

Preface

The idea of human rights has been central to some of the most far-reaching developments of modern times. The English, American, and French revolutions of the seventeenth and eighteenth centuries were proclaimed and conducted in its name, as was the struggle against slavery. Especially since the genocide perpetrated by the Nazis in World War II, renewed concern for human rights has been a pervasive feature of political and legal thought and action. The impact of the idea continues in the contemporary movements for civil rights and against violations of human rights by oppressive regimes in many parts of the world.

At bottom, the idea of human rights is a moral one. It becomes a legal and political idea only because of its supreme moral importance. Hence, while the idea has been fruitfully studied by political scientists, legal theorists, theologians, and others, it has been a constant and continually increasing field of inquiry for philosophers of ethics, politics, and law.

Philosophers, like other persons, have been involved in the struggle to expose and remove the crimes and evils that constitute violations of human rights. The distinctive contribution of philosophy, however, ideally takes the form of a comprehensive theory, analytical and normative, that focuses on the most basic and general questions about human rights. The theory should explain what rights are, how they are related to other sorts of norms or values, how human rights differ from other moral rights, why human rights are of supreme importance, what are their contents, what are the orders of priority among them, how conflicts between them and between rights and other values should be resolved, how rights are related to duties and responsibilities, including political obligations, how it can be established that all persons do indeed have human rights and have them equally, and similar questions. Together with other, more empirical disciplines, philosophy can also contribute to the understanding of what are the chief kinds and causes of the violations of human rights and how the rights can be made more secure against these violations.

The present volume is presented as a contribution to the development of such a comprehensive theory. In my preceding book, *Reason and Morality,* I tried to lay the foundations of the theory of human rights in a systematic analysis of the rational basis of morality. During the past generation, indeed, there have been many books by philosophers and other writers bearing the title Human Rights. Most of them, however, are collections of essays by many different authors, and while this has given them a valuable diversity, it has also meant that they have not developed a consecutive line of argument from first principles to practical applications. In addition, they have often left unresolved certain basic problems about human rights, especially problems of justification.

This book is also a collection of essays, all previously published or scheduled for early publication. Their dates of publication range from 1970 to 1982; eight of them have appeared since the publication of *Reason and Morality* in 1978. Nevertheless, the essays are unified not only by author but also by the fact that I pursue, throughout, certain central objectives. Among the questions mentioned above, these objectives include especially the detailed presentation of a justificatory argument which establishes, on the basis of a rationally grounded moral principle, that there are indeed human rights and what are their contents. I also undertake to work out the applications of the principle of human rights to some of the most important issues of human life, including the relief of starvation, the prevention of cancer, the basis of political obligation, and the democratic effectiveness of civil liberties. As these examples indicate, I regard human rights as extending to social and economic objects as well as to political and civil ones, because human rights are derived from the necessary conditions of human action. The doctrine that human rights are so derived is the most distinctive thesis of this book. Since there may be variations in the degree of necessity of the conditions of human action, there are corresponding variations in the stringency of human rights, so that orders of priority must be developed. These and related questions are discussed in various of the essays.

The conception of human rights presented here is based on the Principle of Generic Consistency, the moral principle elaborated in *Reason and Morality.* While the essays can be understood independently of that book, the reader who is interested in further analyses of relevant issues is referred to my treatment of them in *Reason and Morality.* In the Introduction, written especially for this volume, I try to indicate more fully the central themes that unify the essays, and I present in summary form the main argument for the moral principle of human rights that figures in all the essays.

As with all my other writings, I wish to express my deepest gratitude to my wife, Marcella, for her encouragement, support, and wise counsel. Most of the essays collected here were delivered as lectures at universities and conferences, and I am glad to acknowledge both the stimulus of the invitations and the enlightenment I received from audience responses. I thank the various editors for permission to reproduce these essays here. A note of appreciation is also due to the secretaries in the Department of Philosophy at the University of Chicago, who, during the past decade, have produced fine typescripts while coping efficiently with my often difficult handwriting and my deadlines.

Acknowledgments

Essay 1, "The Basis and Content of Human Rights," is reprinted by permission of New York University Press from *Nomos XXIII: Human Rights*, edited by J. Roland Pennock and John W. Chapman. Copyright © 1981 by New York University.

Essay 2, "Must One Play the Moral Language Game?" is reprinted by permission from the *American Philosophical Quarterly*, volume 7 (April 1970), pages 107–18.

Essay 3, "The 'Is-Ought' Problem Resolved," is reprinted by permission from the *Proceedings and Addresses of the American Philosophical Association*, volume 47 (1974), pages 34–61.

Essay 4, "The Golden Rule Rationalized," is reprinted by permission from *Midwest Studies in Philosophy*, volume 3 (1978), pages 133–47.

Essay 5, "Can Utilitarianism Justify Any Moral Rights?" is reprinted by permission of New York University Press from *Nomos XXIV: Ethics, Economics, and the Law*, edited by J. Roland Pennock and John W. Chapman. Copyright © 1982 by New York University.

Essay 6, "The Future of Ethics: The Moral Powers of Reason," is reprinted by permission from *Nous*, volume 15 (1981), pages 15–30.

Essay 7, "Human Rights and the Prevention of Cancer," is reprinted by permission from the *American Philosophical Quarterly*, volume 17 (1980), pages 117–25.

Essay 8, "Starvation and Human Rights," is reprinted by permission from *Ethics and Problems of the 21st Century*, edited by Kenneth M. Sayre and Kenneth E. Goodpaster (Notre Dame, Ind.: University of Notre Dame Press, 1979).

Essay 9, "Are There Any Absolute Rights?" is reprinted by permission from *The Philosophical Quarterly*, volume 31 (1981), pages 1–16.

Essay 10, "Individual Rights and Political-Military Obligations," will appear in *Morality and Military Service: Essays on the All-Volunteer Force and Its Alternatives*, edited by Robert K. Fullinwider—a volume in the *Maryland Studies in Public Philosophy*. It is printed here by permission.

Essay 11, "Obligation: Political, Legal, Moral," appeared first in *Nomos XII: Political and Legal Obligation*, edited by J. Roland Pennock and John W. Chapman (New York: Atherton Press, 1970), pages 55–88. It is reprinted here by permission of the publishers, Lieber-Atherton, Incorporated.

Essay 12, "Civil Disobedience, Law, and Morality," is reprinted by permission from *The Monist*, volume 54 (1970), pages 536–55.

Essay 13, "Civil Liberties as Effective Powers," is reprinted by permission from *Moral Values in Contemporary Public Life*, edited by Robert B. Ashmore and Lee C. Rice (Milwaukee, Wis.: Marquette University, Department of Philosophy, 1975), pages 3–10.

Essay 14, "Reasons and Conscience: The Claims of the Selective Conscientious Objector," is reprinted by permission from *Philosophy, Morality, and International Affairs*, edited by Virginia Held, Sidney Morgenbesser, and Thomas Nagel (New York: Oxford University Press, 1974), pages 89–117.

Introduction

The fourteen essays collected in this volume fall into two groups. The first six deal primarily with the problems of justifying the moral principle that all humans equally have certain rights; the remaining eight deal primarily with applications of the principle to some important issues of human life, society, and government. This division is only approximate, for the justificatory essays also touch on problems of application, and in some of the applicative essays I sketch in outline the justification of the principle on which the applications depend. Nevertheless, the main emphases of the essays in each group are as stated.

My aim in this Introduction is to indicate certain distinctive themes that unify the essays, to explicate further some of their main concepts and premises, and to give a very brief sketch of each essay in order to show its place in the overall sequence. It should also be noted that many of the concepts whose import is assumed in this Introduction are discussed in Essay 1 and more fully in my book *Reason and Morality*.

I. The Concept of Human Rights

Human rights are a species of moral rights: they are moral rights which all persons equally have simply because they are human. To call them "moral" is to say that they are based upon or justifiable through a valid moral principle. To call a principle "moral," in turn, is to indicate that it sets forth as categorically obligatory certain requirements for action that are addressed at least in part to all actual or prospective agents and that are concerned with furthering the interests, especially the most important interests, of persons or recipients other than or in addition to the agent or the speaker. Since human rights have the egalitarian universality mentioned above, the moral principle through which they are justified must also require that the interests subserved by the rights be those of all persons equally.

There are other rights besides moral ones, including legal, prudential, and intellectual rights. The differences among these stem primarily from the different kinds of principles or criteria that serve to ground or justify the rights. This is most obvious in the case of legal rights, which are based on statutes and other laws. Hence, on the one hand, it is important not to confuse these various kinds of rights with one another and to attribute to rights in general features that pertain to only one kind of right—to moral rights, for example. But, on the other hand, all kinds of rights have certain features in common insofar as they are rights. Philosophers have tried, with considerable difficulty, to analyze what these common features are. The difficulties include the dangers of circularity and of using expressions that are at least as opaque as the concept of a right itself.

In what follows I shall confine myself to what Hohfeld called "claims," or claim-rights,[1] in contrast to liberties, powers, and immunities. For the human rights are entirely or mainly kinds of claim-rights. The initial way of distinguishing claim-rights from other rights is not, as in the preceding classification, in terms of their diverse justificatory criteria but, rather, in terms of their logically implied correlatives. A claim-right of one person entails a correlative duty of some other person or persons to act or to refrain from acting in ways required for the first person's having that to which he has a right. The reason why the human rights are claim-rights is not only that many of them require enforcement or protection by government, for this aspect also pertains to others of Hohfeld's kinds of rights. The essential reason is that human rights are rights to certain especially important objects or goods, and for any person to have these objects it is necessary that all other persons at least refrain from interfering with his (or her) having the objects and also, in certain circumstances, that other persons or groups assist him to have or acquire these objects. The latter requirement often involves a framework of institutional, especially governmental, rules. These necessities or requirements constitute duties that are hence correlative with the rights.

It will be helpful for understanding this and related aspects of human rights if we note that the full structure of a claim-right is given by the following formula:

A has a right to X against B by virtue of Y.

There are five main elements here: first, the *Subject* (A) of the right, the person who has it; second, the *Nature* of the right; third, the *Object* (X) of the right, what it is a right to; fourth, the *Respondent* (B) of the right, the person or persons who have the correlative duty; and fifth, the *Justifying Basis* or *Ground* (Y) of the right. (I capitalize each of these elements for the sake of emphasis and for easier recognition in what follows.) It will be convenient henceforth to use this terminology in discussing the various components of human rights.

The primary thesis of the following essays is that human rights are of supreme importance, and are central to all other moral considerations, because they are rights of every human being to the necessary conditions of human action, i.e., those conditions that must be fulfilled if human action is to be possible either at all or with general chances of success in achieving the purposes for which humans act. Because they are such rights, they must be respected by every human being, and the primary justification of governments is that they serve to secure these rights. Thus the Subjects as well as the Respondents of human rights are all human beings; the Objects of the rights are the aforesaid necessary conditions of human action and of successful action in general; and the Justifying Basis of the rights is the moral principle which establishes that all humans are equally entitled to have these necessary conditions, to fulfill the general needs of human agency.

It is the universality of these four elements, together with the equality of the Subjects and the necessity of the Justifying Ground, that serves to differentiate human rights from other moral rights, including those standard kinds of claim-rights whose Justifying Basis is some specific transaction or relation among a restricted number of Subjects and Respondents. And the exceptional mandatoriness of human rights derives both from the overriding importance of their Objects and from the rational necessity of the moral principle that provides the Justifying Basis of the rights. The principle I have developed for this purpose is the Principle of Generic Consistency *(PGC)*. Addressed to every actual or prospective agent, it says: Act in accord with the generic rights of your recipients as well as of yourself. (The generic rights are rights to the generic features of action— freedom and well-being—which constitute its necessary conditions.) The content and justification of this principle are discussed more fully below.

Many philosophers who have tried to explain the value of rights have implicitly assumed that they are had by all humans and by all humans equally.[2] But such egalitarian universalism is not a part of the concept of a right as such. There have indeed been many societies that effectively had the concept of rights, but the rights they acknowledged were had by, or were distributed among, only a small group of persons, so that they were not universal. And even when rights have been universally distributed, they have often not been had equally. In the feudal era, for example, both lords and vassals had rights, but they were not equal, because the lords' rights were superior to those of their vassals both as to their Objects and as to their Nature, in that the lords could enforce their rights in ways that were closed to the vassals. Hence, the concept of a right, as such, is compatible with various kinds of particularism and inegalitarian universalism as well as with egalitarian universalism.

If, then, one wishes to maintain that there are human rights in the sense of egalitarian universalism, that is, rights that are had equally by all human beings, a justificatory argument must be given which conclusively supports this alternative as against its rivals. Before discussing such an argument, however, let us consider further certain aspects of the primary thesis.

The Objects and Justifying Basis of Human Rights

The most distinctive feature of the theory of human rights presented in the following essays bears on both the Objects and the Justifying Basis of human rights. Their Objects, as I have already said, are the necessary conditions of purposive human action, and their primary justification consists in the fact that these conditions are their Objects. Because of this, for every actual or prospective agent the Objects of human rights are necessary goods—goods that he or she must have in order to be able to act either at all or with general chances of success in fulfilling the purposes for which he acts.

The connection of rights with goods derives in the first instance from the generic purposive feature of human action: that persons act for purposes they regard as good. But the Objects of rights are not these particular apparent goods but rather the freedom and well-being which are, respectively, the procedural and substantive necessary conditions of acting for any purposes either at all or with general chances of success. Because every agent regards his purposes as good, he must regard as necessary goods the freedom and well-being which are the necessary conditions of his acting for any of his purposes.

As we shall see, there are degrees of necessity of these goods, so that the Objects of some rights are more necessary for action than are the Objects of other rights. An example is the relation between being alive and having promises to oneself kept. But these degrees, to be explicated more fully below, do not remove the general point or Justifying Basis of human rights in the generic necessary goods of action.

To hold, as I do, that the Objects of human rights are the necessary conditions of purposive action is to make a decision of theory. It stands in partial contrast to theories that base human rights on human dignity, on the needs of human "flourishing," on the choices of persons to control the actions of other persons, and so forth. The contrast to these other theories is only partial, however, because my theory can accommodate these others.

My main reasons for basing human rights on the necessary conditions of human action are the following. First, these conditions are undeniably of supreme importance. They indicate at once why every actual or prospective agent must be concerned with human rights, and they indicate also why these rights must take precedence over all other practical criteria or requirements, including those that bear on objects or conditions of action that are of lesser stringency. Second, to tie human rights to the necessary conditions of action is to connect the rights directly with morality, since action is the common subject matter of all moralities. Third, the necessary conditions of action have more specific and less disputable contents than may be attributed to concepts like "dignity" and "flourishing."

A fourth very important reason for grounding human rights in the necessary conditions of human action is that this serves to emphasize that the ultimate purpose of the rights is to secure for each person a certain fundamental moral status. All the human rights, those of well-being as well as of freedom, have as their aim that each person have rational autonomy in the sense of being a self-controlling, self-developing agent who can relate to other persons on a basis of mutual respect and cooperation, in contrast to being a dependent, passive recipient of the agency of others. Even when the rights require positive assistance from other persons, their point is not to reinforce or increase dependence but rather to give support that enables persons to be agents, that is, to control their own lives and effectively pursue and sustain their own purposes without being subjected to domination and harms from others. In this way, agency is both the metaphysical and the moral basis of human dignity. Consequently, when the human rights are held to have as their Objects the necessary conditions of action, the connection of the rights with human dignity is not merely asserted but is explicated in terms of the autonomous rational agency that grounds this dignity. I shall return to this connection below.

A fifth reason for holding that human rights have as their Objects the necessary conditions of human action is that this provides a way of giving a rigorous proof or justification that there are such rights. The proof proceeds by showing that every agent, on pain of contradiction, must hold that he has rights to freedom and well-being as the necessary conditions of his action. Other candidates for being the Objects or the Nature of human rights do not admit of such proofs that the rights exist, as I indicate briefly in Essay 1 (pp. 43–44). Especially important here is the modal point that the human rights involve requirements or claims of necessary conduct on the part of other persons or groups; that is, the correlative "oughts" of human rights are practical-prescriptive "musts" addressed to other persons or groups, and these "musts" can be logically derived only from antecedents that themselves are similarly necessary. The necessary goods of human action fulfill this condition; other proposed Objects and Justifying Bases of human rights either do not do so at all or do so less directly and explicitly.

This normative necessity is a distinctive feature of human rights that gives them a more stringent modality than other moral or valuational concepts. Goods are worth having; virtues are good to have and indeed admirable; what is right is at least permissible and may also be justified by some relevant rule. Human rights, however, are normative relations to Objects which one must have in order to be an agent. It is for this reason that human rights are uniquely and centrally important among moral concepts: they are the necessary basis and focal point of all morality, since no morality, together with the goods, virtues, and rules emphasized in diverse moralities, is possible without the necessary goods of action which are the Objects of human rights.

This central and fundamental character of human rights does not mean that all such rights are absolute. But when a human right is overridden, it must be by another human right, especially when the latter's Object is more necessary for action than the former's. Even when a right is overridden by considerations of the general welfare, the latter criterion, to be genuinely overriding, must be composed of the rights of individuals. For example, the national defense or even the rules of the road involve the rights of individuals to security from attack and to safety.

The unique importance of human rights among moral concepts also does not mean that the concept of a right is self-explanatory or self-justifying, for the rights are based on certain necessary goods as their Objects. And the moral basis of the sequence from necessary goods to human rights also includes a requirement about the necessary equal distribution of these goods.

The grounding of human rights in the necessary goods of action gives these rights a status different from that of other moral claim-rights. This difference is parallel to the distinction between contingent and necessary obligatoriness. Moral claim-rights that are based on specific transactions and relations (which Hart called "special rights")[3] are only contingently obligatory in that they take the form: *If* a certain promise has been made (or *if* some other specific transaction or relation has occurred or been entered into), *then* the promisee has a right that the promise be kept. That the promise must be kept by the promiser or Respondent, and hence that the right exists, is contingent on the making of the promise or other transaction; but there is no moral necessity, or practical necessity in relation to the general conditions of action, that the promise or other transaction itself be entered into.

Human rights, on the other hand, do not have such a contingent antecedent. Their form is: *Because* every human being must have certain goods if he is to be able to act either at all or with chances of success in general in achieving his purposes, *it follows that* he has rights to these necessary goods. The "because" and "if" in the antecedent are necessary in relation to the general conditions of action; they are not contingent on persons' variable choices or decisions, since they pertain to the very possibility of action and successful action. Hence, no person can rationally disavow either the necessary goods or the consequent human rights. Even the attempt to bring to an end all one's further actions (as by suicide) must itself use the necessary goods of action (see *Reason and Morality,* pages 166–69). The human rights are thus equivalent to "natural" rights in that they pertain to all humans by virtue of their nature as actual or prospective agents. This point applies even to the rights connected with promises; but these rights must now be viewed in the broader context of institutions serving the general needs of agency and not only as based on specific transactions for particular contingent ends.

Objections to the Linkage of Human Rights with Action

It must be kept in mind that the conceptual linkage here upheld between rights and needs obtains only when the rights are human rights and the needs are the necessary conditions of action. Thus the present thesis is not affected by the fact that neither of the following is self-contradictory:

(1)   "A has a right to X, but he doesn't need X"—where X may be, for example, the repayment of a debt.

(2)   "A needs X, but he doesn't have a right to X"—where X may be, for example, a bicycle that enables A to get around town more conveniently.

But the plausibility and apparent consistency of (1) and (2) do not remain when the rights in question are human rights and the needs are the necessary goods of action. Even with these qualifications, however, the argument from such needs to human rights goes through only when the dialectically necessary method is used, as I indicate later in this Introduction and also in Essay 1 (pp. 48–50).

Other questions may be raised, however, about the linkage of human rights with action. In particular, it may be contended that this linkage removes the rights' universal and equal distribution to all humans as their Subjects, since some humans (such as those in perpetual coma) are not capable of action at all, and others (such as children, the senile, and the insane) are capable of action only in severely reduced degrees. To cope with this difficulty, I have worked out a certain interpretation of what I call a Principle of Proportionality: When some quality Q justifies having certain rights R, and the possession of Q varies in degree in the respect that is relevant to Q's justifying the having of R, the degree to which R is had is proportional to or varies with the degree to which Q is had (*Reason and Morality*, p. 121).

My interpretation of this principle entails the following. All humans have the human rights in full to the extent that they are inherently capable of exercising them. This inherent capacity pertains to each human so long as he is a rational agent in the minimal sense of having purposes he wants to fulfill and being able to control his behavior accordingly while knowing the particular circumstances of his action. All such persons satisfy in an absolute or noncomparative way the requirements for having the human rights. It is only when humans are not rational in this minimal sense that their having the human rights varies in degree. This variation may obtain for one or both of two reasons. The humans in question may not be capable of exercising the rights either (1) at all (as in the case, for example, of the right to education for certain persons who have severe mental deficiency) or (2) without serious harm to themselves or others (as in the case, for example, of the right to freedom of movement for very young children). I have discussed this matter more fully in *Reason and Morality*, pages 119–27, 140–45, 316–17; see also Essay 1, pages 51–52, 54–55.

It remains, then, that the human rights pertain equally to all humans who have the minimal degree of rationality needed for action. It is difficult to see how the diminution of the possession, or at least the exercise, of rights below this minimal level can fail to be admitted by any theory of human rights.

The linkage of the human rights with the necessary conditions of action may also be criticized on the ground that the Objects of some of these rights have little or nothing to do with action. Examples are the rights to a fair trial, to emigration, to a nationality (United Nations Universal Declaration of Human Rights, 1948, articles 10, 13, 15). It must be noted in reply, however, that the human rights as worked out in the present theory involve two distinctions. One is between different degrees of necessity for action. Thus I distinguish between three levels of human rights: basic, nonsubtractive, and additive. Basic rights have as their Objects the essential preconditions of action, such as life, physical integrity, mental equilibrium. Nonsubtractive rights have as their Objects the abilities and conditions required for maintaining undiminished one's level of purpose-fulfillment and one's capabilities for particular actions. Additive rights have as their Objects the abilities and conditions required for increasing one's level of purpose-fulfillment and one's capabilities for particular actions. The Objects of the basic rights are the most necessary conditions of human action, while the Objects of the nonsubtractive and additive rights are progressively less necessary, although they are still needed for successful action in general. Being lied to, for example, tends to lower one's capabilities for success in actions affected by the lies, and receiving education tends to increase one's capabilities for successful action.

It is on these grounds that I include among human rights such nonsubtractive rights as not being lied to or suffering broken promises, and such additive rights as education and self-esteem. Not all of these rights, of course, have governments as their Respondents. Now the right to a fair trial is one of the nonsubtractive rights, and the rights to emigration and to a nationality are additive rights. Thus these rights are derived from the varyingly necessary conditions of human action.

Also relevant to this question is a second distinction: the distinction between direct and indirect applications of the Principle of Generic Consistency *(PGC)*, the moral principle that requires of every agent that he act in accord with his recipients' generic rights as well as his own. In the direct applications, the *PGC*'s requirements are imposed on the actions of individual agents; in the indirect applications, the principle's requirements are imposed in the first instance on social rules and institutions (see Essay 1, pages 60 ff.). In these indirect applications, governments are justified insofar as they recognize and help to secure the human rights justified in the direct applications, especially the basic rights. Because freedom is a basic human right, such governments must use certain democratic procedures and guarantee certain freedoms as well as certain components of well-being (see *Reason and Morality,* pages 304–11). It is in the context of these indirect applications that there emerges the connection between the necessary conditions of action and the political and civil rights, including not only the rights, mentioned above, to a fair trial, emigration, and nationality, but also the rights to the various civil liberties and political participation. All these human rights are either species of the generic right to freedom or components of the rights that must be guaranteed by governments that fulfill the justificatory requirements of the *PGC*. I have discussed in Essay 10 (pages 243–44) what should be done when governments fulfill some of these rights but not others.

The Nature of Human Rights

It is not easy to characterize claim-rights as such without reference to the other elements of rights. In fact, what underlies the disagreements over some of the most widely held "theories" of the Nature of claim-rights is that the theories select different elements as constitutive of this Nature. For example, the "will theory" maintains that for someone to have a right is for him to be in a position to determine by his will or choice how another person shall act.[4] Here the Nature of a right is defined by reference to a kind of authority or control possessed by Subjects over their Respondents. In contrast, the "beneficiary theory" defines the Nature of rights primarily in terms of their Objects, for it holds that to have a right is to be in a position to benefit from someone else's performance of a duty, so that rights have as their Objects certain goods or benefits.[5] Since each theory ties the Nature of a right to different elements in the structure of rights, the theories are not necessarily mutually exclusive. At the same time, however, neither theory as formulated up to the present is entirely satisfactory, for there are important kinds of claim-rights to which they fail to apply.

Is it possible to give a true general characterization of the Nature of every claim-right? Such rights have been variously defined as *entitlements,* as *justified* or *valid claims,* as advantages that are *due* to persons, as persons' *normative property.* These characterizations are good, but there are certain central features of claim-rights that they may fail to capture. Let us first note that the characterizations are at least in part equivalent. The equivalence leads to circularity when one expression is used to explicate another; but the circularity is not necessarily vicious, because the diverse phrases bring out different facets of the common notion. Thus the word "entitlement" suggests the idea of a "title" in the quasi-legal sense of a Justifying Basis which serves to allocate to a person some advantage or good as his property or his "due," such that it is not only not wrong for him (or her) to have that Object but it is wrong for other persons to deprive him of it without his consent. In this respect, an entitlement is the same as a justified or valid claim, where "claim" is used in a dispositional rather than an occurrent sense, as referring to what *could be* claimed rather than to what is *actually* claimed. For a person A to have a justified or valid claim to some Object X is thus for him to be in a position of being able to assert correctly that X belongs to him, where the assertion in question is intended to be prescriptive as well as descriptive. But insofar as the assertion is descriptively correct, it indicates that X does indeed belong to A, so that we are returned to the idea of a right as one's normative property.

A central and distinctive feature of human rights may not be sufficiently brought out by these familiar characterizations. The Nature of human rights follows from their having as Objects the necessary goods of human action. Human rights are normatively necessary, personally oriented moral requirements.

The point of these qualifications can be readily indicated by way of contrast. Utilitarianism presents stringent duties that are normatively necessary moral requirements, but they are not personally oriented; that is, they are not requirements owed to distinct Subjects or individuals as such for the good of those individuals. They are rather for the good of society as a whole, concerned with aggregating or maximizing utility regardless of necessary goods that may be owed to distinct individuals for their own sakes.

It is thus a mistake to say, as is sometimes done, that only human rights, or claim-rights generally, can justify strict duties as against loose, nonmandatory duties. This overlooks the way in which imperious and stable demands can be laid on persons for various collective goals, as in utilitarianism and other aggregative or collectivist moral and political theories. It is the personal orientation of strict duties correlative with personal rights that is missing from such theories. Even when utilitarianism uses the concept of moral rights, their ultimate Subject is not distinct individuals but a larger collective whole (see Essay 5).

On the other hand, various forms of libertarian altruism and related theories of moral virtue recommend actions and policies that are personally oriented, since they are for the good of individuals who are in need of help, but the recommendations are not presented as normatively necessary moral requirements. The recommended actions are, rather, loose duties of charity or love, so that, while these are indeed of very great value, they are at the option of the agent rather than strictly required of him; they normatively cannot be exacted from him as something owed to their recipients.

For a person to have human rights, then, is for him to be in a position to make morally justified stringent, effective demands on other persons that they not interfere with his having the necessary goods of action and that they also help him to attain these goods when he cannot do so by his own efforts. The latter, positive demand is usually to be embodied in appropriate laws and institutions. But these laws must be for the necessary goods of individuals as such, not for the maximizing of overall utility.

It follows from these considerations that the concept of human rights is both deontological and teleological. It is deontological in that the rights are correlative with strict duties to forbear or assist, so that performance of the duties can be demanded by all Subjects. It is teleological in that these duties are for the sake of persons' having certain goods. But this teleological feature is distinct from that found in standard teleological theories, in at least four respects. First, the goods in question are the necessary goods of action; they are not *all* goods or utilities, indiscriminately. Second, the requirement respecting these goods is not that they be maximized regardless of their distribution but that they be distributed equally among all prospective agents. Third, this distribution to each agent is owed to him, and for his own sake; it is not owed to him only as a consequence of more general social goals. Fourth, conflicts among rights are not to be resolved by considerations of quantity of goods produced, regardless of who has them, but rather by considerations of degrees of necessity for action. Basic goods of one individual cannot be outweighed by multiple nonsubtractive or additive goods of many other individuals; in cases of conflict, basic rights must be fulfilled before other rights.

Human Rights as Moral Requirements

To understand more fully the Nature of human rights as normatively necessary, personally oriented moral requirements, it is important to distinguish three different but related meanings of "requirement." First, human rights are requirements in the sense that their Objects are the fulfillment of objectively important needs. Here, "requirement" signifies a relation between the Subjects and the Objects of the rights, i.e., between agency and its necessary conditions. To say here that X requires Y is to say that Y is a necessary condition of X. These necessary conditions of action do not vary according to arbitrary wishes of agents or other persons. Because they are such necessary conditions, they constitute needs on the part of every agent: he must have the Objects of human rights if he is either to be an agent at all or to have general chances of success in achieving his purposes.

Second, human rights are requirements in the sense of entitlements. It has sometimes been held that the word "entitlement" does not help to clarify the Nature of a right, since it is as opaque as the term it is supposed to clarify. But, as I indicated above, "entitlement" suggests the idea of a "title" in the quasi-legal sense of a Justifying Basis which serves to allocate to a person some advantage or good as his property or his "due." In this regard, when it is said that human rights as entitlements are "requirements," this signifies a relation between the Objects of the rights as goods or advantages had by persons and their Justifying Basis: the former normatively follows from, is justified by, the latter, in that the Basis or principle justifies that the necessary goods of action be had by or be granted to all persons as their due.

Third, human rights are requirements in the sense of justified demands against other persons, the Respondents. These have the correlative duties at least not to interfere with the Subjects' having the necessary goods of action, and in certain circumstances they also have the correlative duties to assist or see to it that the Subjects have these goods. Here, "requirement" signifies a relation between the Subjects and the Respondents; the former, by virtue of the Justifying Basis, are in a justified position to demand of the latter that they perform or refrain from performing certain actions. In this respect, human rights are prescriptive.

It is important to distinguish these three different respects—in the sense of needs, entitlements, and interpersonal demands—in which the human rights are justified moral requirements. These three respects involve the relations, respectively, between the Subjects and the Objects of the rights, i.e., between action and its necessary conditions; between the Objects and the Justifying Basis of the rights, i.e., between the fulfillment of these conditions as persons' due and its Justifying Basis; and between the Subjects of the rights and their Respondents. In all these respects the human rights may also be characterized by the more familiar phrase "justified claims." But while this phrase can accommodate the distinction between claims to Objects and claims against Respondents that are embodied in the second and third relations distinguished above, it obscures the distinction between needs and entitlements. Human rights are both certain needs and entitlements to their fulfillment; the sense of "needs" is more readily conveyed by "requirements" than by "claims." In addition, "claims" does not convey the stringent modality of necessity that human rights involve and that the concept of a requirement directly signifies.

It is sometimes said that the chief importance of rights consists in their connection with "the activity of claiming," because this activity gives the claimant a sense of self-respect and dignity.[6] This view is close to the "will theory" of rights mentioned earlier; it puts chief emphasis on the relation between the Subject and his Respondent, whereby the former is in a position to choose to exact a certain duty from the latter. Now this relation is indeed important for the understanding of human rights; but it must be supplemented by the other two relations indicated above. If the Objects of human rights were not the necessary goods of action, or if they had no Justifying Basis in these Objects, the rights might still be claimed or demanded, but the claims would have little point or justification. Hence, all three of the relations specified above must be emphasized to understand the importance of human rights.

When it is said that for some person to have a human right to X means that there is a justified moral requirement that A have X, it is important to note that this requirement is not made on A himself, the Subject as such. While it is indeed normatively necessary that he have the Objects of the rights, the prescriptive aspect of the rights—the demand that his having them not only not be prevented but, if necessary, be assisted—is addressed to other persons, the Respondents. The senses in which the human rights are requirements, then, involve demands on or duties of Respondents for the fulfillment of Subjects' needs of agency, stemming from a certain Justifying Basis. As we shall also see, however, the Subjects of human rights are also the Respondents of other Subjects, and this is important for the social character of the rights.

The Redundancy Problem

I have said that the human rights are claim-rights in that they entail correlative duties of Respondents, and I have also propounded a version of the "benefit theory" of rights since I have held that their Objects are certain necessary interests or goods of Subjects. To such a theory it has been objected that "if to say that an individual has such a right means no more than that he is the intended beneficiary of a duty, then 'a right' in this sense may be an unnecessary, and perhaps confusing, term ... since all that can be said in a terminology of such rights can be and indeed is best said in the indispensable terminology of duty."[7] The concept of a right is thus "redundant"; it can be eliminated without loss in favor of the concept of duty.

The most direct answer to this objection is that the correlativity of human rights and strict duties still leaves the former prior to the latter in a certain crucial respect. In contrast to what Hohfeld seems to have thought, a claim-right is not exhaustively constituted by its correlative duty, at least so far as human rights are concerned. Rather (as I argue in Essay 5), Respondents have correlative duties *because* Subjects have certain rights, and not conversely; the duties are for the sake of the rights, and not conversely. This priority of claim-rights over duties in the order of justifying purpose or final causality is not antithetical to their being correlative to each other. Consider a somewhat parallel case. Parents are prior to their children in the order of efficient causality, yet the (past or present) existence of parents can be inferred from the existence of children, as well as conversely. Hence, the causal priority of parents to children is compatible with the two groups' being causally as well as conceptually correlative. The case is similar with rights and duties, except that the ordering relation between them is one of final rather than efficient causality, of justifying purpose rather than bringing-into-existence.

Since, then, rights are prior to duties in the order of final causality or purpose, it follows that the Nature of a claim-right is to some extent independent of its relation to the correlative duties. How this is so was suggested above, in the distinction between the first and the third senses in which the human rights are "requirements": as needs of agency and as demands on Respondents. It is because of these needs, to whose fulfillment all persons have rights, that the correlative duties arise: of respecting the rights by refraining from interfering with other persons' possession of these necessary conditions and, in suitable circumstances, by assisting them to possess these conditions. Hence, it is false that "all that can be said in a terminology of such rights can be and indeed is best said in the indispensable terminology of duty." To omit reference to rights would be to omit the Justifying Basis of the duties, so that the language of rights is not redundant.

Why Human Rights Include the Right to Freedom

The general Objects of the human rights are freedom and well-being, which are the necessary goods of human action. Some recent writers have denied that one or the other of this pair of goods is such an Object. Cranston and Nozick have argued that there are no social and economic rights to well-being, or at least that these are not human rights.[8] I have dealt with this objection in Essays 1 and 8, pages 64–65 and 211–14.

Dworkin and Fried have held that there is no general right to freedom.[9] Dworkin's main argument for this may be put as follows. If there is a general right to some X (in the strong, claim-right sense of "right"), then the having of X may not justifiably be denied or prohibited by the government on utilitarian grounds, that is, on the grounds that it is in the general interest that having X be prohibited. But the having of freedom or liberty may in certain cases be justifiably denied or prohibited by the government on utilitarian grounds; an example is the freedom to drive the wrong way on a one-way street. Hence there is no general right to freedom.

This argument does not, however, prove that there is not a general human right to freedom, so long as it is recognized that this right may be overridden on grounds that derive from the *PGC*, the principle of morality mentioned above. These grounds may at some points coincide extensionally with grounds based on utilitarianism, but their underlying rationale is different. Before going into this, the right to freedom must itself be elucidated.

There is a general human right to freedom because freedom is a necessary condition of human purposive action. The freedom in question consists in controlling one's behavior by one's unforced choice while having knowledge of relevant circumstances, with a view to achieving some purpose for which one acts. This freedom hence includes the negative freedom of not being interfered with by other persons, for such interference would remove the agent's control of his behavior. The right to such freedom is a claim-right and not merely a liberty-right (in Hohfeld's sense). It entails the correlative duty of other persons, as well as governments, to refrain from interfering with persons' control of their own behavior. Hence, the state or condition of each prospective agent whereby he is not interfered with in initiating and controlling his behavior must be maintained or continued without interference from other persons (see *Reason and Morality,* page 67).

It has been held that "freedom of action" must be distinguished from the "social freedom" which consists in persons' not preventing one another's actions. The argument for this distinction is that the two freedoms are structurally diverse, in that freedom of action involves "a relation between one actor and an action," while social freedom involves a relation between one actor and another actor.[10] But social or interpersonal freedom may also be construed, as here, as a specific sort of freedom of action: as one in which the agent's control of his own behavior is not removed or interfered with by other persons. For since freedom of action consists in controlling one's own behavior by one's unforced choice, an especially important kind of such freedom involves that one's control of one's own behavior not be prevented or interfered with by other persons.

Now it has long been recognized that there cannot be universal or completely unrestricted freedom. For if some persons are to be free to perform certain actions, then other persons must be prevented or restrained from interfering with them. Thus the freedom of potential interferers must be interfered with; for there to be freedom, there must be unfreedom, or interference with freedom. In this consists the so-called "paradox of freedom," which may have two versions, logical and causal, depending on how one interprets the "must" and the "if-then" connection stated above. In either version, however, the "paradox" must recognize the distinctions between occurrent and dispositional interferences with freedom and between cases where the "potential interferers" intend and do not intend to actually interfere with persons' performance of various actions.

Since there cannot be completely unrestricted freedom, it is no objection to there being a general right to freedom that certain freedoms must be restricted. Indeed, it is difficult to see how any human right, including the right to life, can be absolute in the sense of not being justifiably infringeable in any circumstances (see Essay 9). The important question about the right to freedom, then, is: When, and on what grounds, may any freedom be restricted? It will be noted that this question already suggests (although it does not prove) that there is a general right to freedom, for it implies that there is a general presumption in favor of freedom. This is, moreover, a strong presumption: it requires compliance on the part of all persons so that, without special justification, no one's freedom is to be restricted. There is no similar general presumption in favor of coercion or of unfreedom, except insofar as unfreedom is required for freedom (as the above-mentioned "paradox" suggests).

The presumption in favor of freedom is overridden only by certain considerations derived from the *PGC*. These considerations consist in the action-based rights of other persons. In general, the *PGC* requires that each person be left free to perform any actions he wishes so long as he does not threaten or violate other persons' rights to freedom (by coercing them) or to well-being (by harming them). The criteria of "harm" are quite definite. On the personal level, harm consists in removing or threatening the basic, nonsubtractive, or additive goods to which all persons have rights of well-being. On the sociopolitical level, harm consists in violating laws that provide for these goods, including the public goods whose benefits necessarily accrue to each and all of the members of a territorially circumscribed society.

These public goods are close to the utilitarian grounds of collective benefit or general interest; but it is preferable to construe them in terms of the *PGC*. For example, traffic regulations, like those which prohibit driving the wrong way on a one-way street, are laws that provide for public goods. These laws are a justifiable interference with freedom on the *PGC*'s grounds of helping to secure each person's right to well-being as embodied in a physically safe and predictable environment.[11]

The *PGC*'s justification of such laws does not, however, extend to laws prohibiting civil liberties and other freedoms that are vital to the necessary conditions of action and of successful action in general. Such laws cannot be justified in terms of preventing coercion or harm, where the latter is construed according to the *PGC*'s criteria. Hence, the fact that certain particular freedoms may be justifiably restricted according to the *PGC* does not refute the thesis that there is a general human right to freedom.

The presumption in favor of freedom remains even if it is insisted that utilitarian grounds alone may justify the overriding of certain freedoms. For example, the expenses needed for operating a public park may be obtained by taxes which remove persons' freedom to spend some of their money as they wish. But this particular freedom, so long as the amount of money involved is relatively slight for each person taxed, is only peripherally connected with the freedom to which there is a general right according to the *PGC*. For it must be kept in mind that the latter freedom is a necessary condition of action. A distinction must hence be drawn between freedoms that are essential for action in general and those that pertain to particular actions whose performance or nonperformance does not affect the general necessary conditions of action. In part, this is the distinction between dispositional and occurrent freedom, between having the continuing long-range effective ability to exercise control over one's behavior by one's unforced choice and exercising such control in particular situations. But the distinction also applies to particular exercises of freedom or control, in that the unrestricted ability to perform some actions is much more important for one's general status as a rational agent than is the ability to perform other actions. Prime examples of the former type, in each of these two distinctions, are the civil liberties, freedom of movement in general, and choices of ways of life. Utilitarian grounds, where these cannot be shown to coincide extensionally with criteria based on the rights needed for action and successful action, may not override any of these freedoms. Hence, there remains a general right to freedom as one of the necessary goods of action. The support of this right, and of basic well-being generally, where needed, is essential to the moral legitimacy of governments.

Human Rights, Egoism, and Social Solidarity

A traditional criticism of the concern with rights is that they are excessively individualistic and even egoistic. The young Marx, for example, wrote: "None of the supposed rights of man, therefore, go beyond the egoistic man, man as he is, as a member of civil society; that is, an individual separated from the community, withdrawn into himself, wholly preoccupied with his private interest and acting in accordance with his private caprice."[12] The emphasis on rights, it is held, entails the view that persons have rights but no duties toward others, that they are preoccupied only with claiming their own property and other goods and holding them to be inviolable, so that any attempts to enforce duties for the benefit of other persons or the general welfare are deemed morally wrong.

This criticism may be valid against some conceptions of rights but not against the theory of human rights based on the *PGC*. It is indeed true that the *PGC* is derived from each prospective agent's claiming for himself the necessary conditions of his agency, and these claims are shown to be rationally justified. But the *PGC* also shows that all prospective agents are the Respondents as well as the Subjects of human rights. Since each person has rights to freedom and well-being against all other persons, every other person also has these rights against him, so that he has correlative duties toward them. Thus the Respondents of human rights are all persons, not simply governments.

As previously indicated, the duties that are correlative with these universal human rights are both negative and positive. Each person must refrain from removing or interfering with the freedom and well-being of other persons. The positive duties are limited by the principle that "ought" implies "can." In interpersonal relations where one person's life or other components of basic well-being can be saved only by some other person's action at no comparable cost, the latter has the strict duty to perform such action, and the former has a basic right to be helped in this way. Obviously, conditions of physical proximity and related factors enter into the "can" of such duties. In broader social contexts, where basic well-being and equality of opportunity (which involves rights to additive goods) can be fostered only by collective action, the positive duties require advocacy of the basic rights of others and taking the necessary steps toward their support, including taxation. These requirements, which must be embodied in appropriate laws and institutions, are not violations of the Respondents' own rights to freedom (see Essay 8). In such ways the emphasis on human rights promotes social solidarity rather than exclusive preoccupation with private interest. The fact that the rights, as a matter of moral principle, must be universally distributed contributes to a greater awareness of the needs of others. And when appropriate steps are taken to meet these needs, the persons thus helped can recognize the justice of such efforts and can use the opportunities thus provided both to make their own contributions and to develop further a sense of common interests.

The indirect applications of the *PGC* also contribute to this social emphasis. According to these applications, social rules and institutions are justified when they are instrumental to securing persons' rights to freedom and well-being. The duties of each person to respect the rights of others are here extended to various aspects of political obligation. When a state is justified by the *PGC* as securing the rights of all its inhabitants, each person living in such a state has the duty to support it. This duty ranges from obeying its laws to contributing, by taxes, advocacy, and other relevant means, to the state's carrying out its justified functions (see Essay 10). More generally, the *PGC,* in requiring respect for the generic rights of each person, requires also support of the whole system of mutually sustaining rights and duties. In this way, the emphasis on individual rights is not only compatible with, but requires a conscientious concern for, the common good.

II. The Justification of Human Rights

For the understanding of human rights, it is important to see how their Justifying Basis in the necessary goods of action serves to prove or justify the moral principle that the rights are had equally by all humans. The sense of "are had" here is morally normative; the proof is not given by referring to what rights are actually recognized by societies and governments. In Essay 1 (pp. 43–44) I have briefly criticized five recent attempted proofs based on intuition, institutions, interests, dignity, and ideal contract.

The justificatory argument that I uphold for equal human rights has been presented extensively in *Reason and Morality,* chapters 2 and 3; it is summarized in various of the essays collected here, especially in Essay 1 (pp. 45–55) and its Addendum (pp. 67–68) and in the first section of Essay 8. I shall not now provide a further summary in similar detail. Instead, it will be sufficient for present purposes to note that the argument has four main steps, as follows. First, every agent holds that the purposes for which he acts are good on whatever criterion (not necessarily a moral one) enters into his purposes. Second, every actual or prospective agent logically must therefore hold or accept that freedom and well-being are necessary goods for him because they are the necessary conditions of his acting for any of his purposes; hence, he holds that he *must* have them. Third, he logically must therefore hold or accept that he has rights to freedom and well-being; for, if he were to deny this, he would have to accept that other persons may remove or interfere with his freedom and well-being, so that he *may not* have them; but this would contradict his belief that he *must* have them. Fourth, the sufficient reason on the basis of which each agent must claim these rights is that he is a prospective purposive agent, so that he logically must accept the conclusion that all prospective purposive agents, equally and as such, have rights to freedom and well-being. This conclusion is equivalent to the *PGC*.

In sum, then, my argument for the existence of human rights is that every agent logically must hold or accept that he and all other agents have these rights because their Objects are the necessary conditions of human action.

Many questions may be and have been raised about this argument. Some bear on specific substantive points in the sequence from necessary goods to equal rights; several of the more important of these I have discussed above, as well as in the places indicated in the preceding paragraph. I wish now to deal with certain questions of method that are especially relevant to understanding the justificatory path to human rights.

The Dialectically Necessary Method

My argument uses what I call a *dialectically necessary method*. The method is dialectical in that it begins from statements presented as being made or accepted by an agent; it proceeds from within his first-person conative standpoint, and it examines what his statements logically imply within this standpoint. The method is dialecticalhy necessary in that the statements logically must be made or accepted by every agent because they derive from the generic features of purposive action, including the conative standpoint common to all agents. Thus what my argument purports to prove, in the first instance, is not the *assertoric* proposition that every agent equally has rights to freedom and well-being but, rather, the *dialectically necessary* proposition that every agent logically must hold or accept that he and all other agents equally have these rights. Since, however, action is the general context of all morality, and all humans are actual, prospective, or potential agents, the fact that the thesis about equal rights is stated as being relative to what every agent logically must accept still allows the thesis to be restated as an assertoric, necessarily true moral principle of human rights. I have argued for this in some detail in *Reason and Morality,* pages 150–61.

It is important to note the sense in which it is said that every agent "logically must hold or accept" the various statements that culminate in the *PGC*. This sense is not an empirically or phenomenologically descriptive one; it does not refer to the conscious thought processes or explicit utterances of agents. It signifies rather what agents are logically committed to hold or accept insofar as they are rational in the sense of being able to follow out the implications of the concepts of action and agent. Denials of any of these implications are thus failures of rationality. The rationality here in question, however, like that to which I referred previously, in connection with the having and exercise of human rights, is a minimal one, of which all normal agents are capable. In *Reason and Morality,* pages 98–102, I have discussed and given evidence for the historical universality of the concept of rights. But it must also be recognized that throughout human history there have been agents who have rejected or not upheld the thesis of equal rights. This is to be explained mainly by the corrosive effects of unjust institutions. The fact that such agents have not exercised their rational powers in this context does not establish, however, either that the propositions in question are not rationally justified or that the agents did not possess the requisite rational powers.

The dialectically necessary method stands in contrast with two other kinds of method. An *assertoric method* proceeds throughout by statements about what is the case, as against statements about what persons think or say is the case, or statements presented as being made or accepted by certain persons. A *dialectically contingent* method begins from statements that happen to be made or accepted by certain persons, as against statements they are logically required to make or accept. I deal with some aspects of the distinction between dialectically necessary and

dialectically contingent methods in Essay 6 (pp. 168–78), where the dialectically necessary method is discussed in connection with "full
apodictic rationalism" and the dialectically contingent method is discussed in connection with both "probabilistic rationalism" and "partial
apodictic rationalism."

Why, in the justificatory argument for human rights, must the dialectically necessary method be used and not these other methods? My
answer is that the existence of human rights—that all persons equally
have certain moral rights—cannot be proved otherwise. One way to begin
to establish this would be to show that, and why, previous attempts at
proof, which use one of the other two methods, have failed. I have attempted some of this very briefly in Essay 1 (pages 43–44). I have also
indicated in that essay why it is only by the dialectically necessary method
that statements about necessary goods can be shown to entail certain
salient features of rights-judgments: prescriptiveness, entitlements, and
ascriptions of correlative duties (pages 48–50).

I shall here supplement the discussion in Essay 1 by presenting certain
more elemental aspects of the dialectically necessary method as it functions in my argument for human rights—aspects which show why the use
of this method is indispensable

The Dialectically Necessary Method, Agent-Relative Truths, and Prescriptiveness

Suppose an agent A does something X for some end or purpose E. Assume
that this doing is a genuine action in that it is a voluntary and purposive
behavior: A controls his behavior by his unforced choice while having
knowledge of relevant circumstances, with a view to attaining some goal.
Now we may truly say (1) "A does X for end or purpose E." This is an
assertoric statement, not a dialectical one. But from (1) we may infer the
dialectical statement (2) "A thinks or says, 'E is good.'" This is a dialectical statement because it states not merely that something is the case
but that A thinks or says that something is the case. The warrant for (2) is
that, since A aims or intends to attain E by his unforced choice, he thinks
E has sufficient value to merit his acting to attain it; the criterion of this
value varies with his purpose. Here, the component statement "E is
good" is true from A's own standpoint but not necessarily otherwise. It is
a relational truth in that, *for the agent A,* E is worth trying to get.

Suppose, next, we try from (1) to infer simply (3) "E is good." Here (3)
is stated assertorically, not as part of a dialectical statement, as in (2).
That (3) is true does not at all follow from (1), because (3) is not stated as
being relative to A's purposes or standpoint. That E is good is not true

simply because of A's conative attitude toward it; on the contrary, E might be very bad from many points of view. Rather, that A *thinks* E is good, or that E is good *relative to A's conation,* is true; but this truth is relational, not nonrelational. This, then, is one example, in my overall argument, of where a dialectical proposition can be proved but not its component assertoric proposition.

Consider, next, a further stage of my argument. From (4) "A needs freedom and well-being in order to act" (or "Freedom and well-being are necessary conditions of A's acting"), there does not follow (5) "A has rights to freedom and well-being." A person who accepts (4) may, without contradicting himself, reject (5); for example, he may not care about A's fulfilling his needs, so that the endorsement required for the statement of (5) would be absent. In (5) the rights-judgment is assertoric; it is stated as a nonrelational truth. On the other hand, from (6) "A regards his freedom and well-being as necessary goods" or (7) "A says or thinks, 'My freedom and well-being are necessary goods,'" there does follow, for reasons I have presented in detail, (8) "A rationally holds that he has rights to freedom and well-being" or (9) "A rationally says or thinks, 'I have rights to freedom and well-being.'" Here, (8) and (9), unlike (5), are dialectical, not assertoric; and the component statement "I have rights to freedom and well-being" is true relative to agent A's conative standpoint but not necessarily otherwise. This component statement, unlike (5), cannot be denied without contradiction by agent A; for, if he were to deny it, he would have to accept the permissibility of other persons' removing or interfering with his freedom and well-being; and this, in turn, would contradict his statement or belief, "I must have freedom and well-being," which every agent must accept for himself because it is equivalent to "My freedom and well-being are necessary goods." (See below, pages 50–51, 67–68). But in this whole argument the constituents are dialectical, not assertoric. What does not follow in the attempted inference from (4) to (5) does follow in the inference from (6) or (7) to (8) or (9), because the latter inference, unlike the former, proceeds from within the agent's conative standpoint, and its conclusion is true relative to that standpoint.

What is indicated by these considerations is that the existence of human rights can be proved only dialectically, within the context of agents' necessary claims, but not assertorically. From the assertoric statement that persons have certain needs that must be fulfilled if they are to be agents it does not follow that they have rights to the fulfillment of these needs. The consequent can be denied without denying the antecedent. For the statement that someone, A, has rights to X is prescriptive; it involves an endorsement or commitment on the part of the utterer to A's having X. But the assertoric statement that persons have certain needs is presented as being made by an external observer of the agent, not by the agent himself. Since the observer, as such, does not necessarily endorse, is not necessarily committed to, the agent's having what he needs, the observer does not necessarily hold that the agent has rights to the fulfillment of his needs. There is no necessary prescriptiveness or endorsement in the antecedent; hence, there is none in the consequent, so that the statement that the agent has rights does not follow.

On the other hand, from dialectical statements that agents themselves make or accept about their having these needs, as necessary goods they must have if they are to be agents, it does follow that they rationally must say or think they have rights to the needs' fulfillment. For, if they deny this rights-conclusion, then they logically must also deny their antecedent statement that they must have the necessary goods of action. But, as agents, they cannot deny this because they are committed to having these goods, to fulfilling their needs.

The Dialectically Necessary Method and Rational Necessity

Another relevant aspect of the dialectically necessary method is its connection with rationality. This bears especially on the method's necessity. It is sometimes objected against my argument that it unrealistically diverges from the kinds of paths agents actually take. Admittedly, agents act for purposes. But if some agent A acts for some end or purpose E, why should he be concerned with anything else, including the necessary conditions of his action? Why, from his own prudential standpoint, should he do anything other than act for his purposes? If he finds obstacles set by other agents, then he may prudentially arrange some sort of contract with them involving mutual forbearance. But as against the realistic grounding of such a contract in his actual desires, why should an agent follow the path set by my dialectically necessary argument, according to which he must consider the necessary conditions of his action and then claim rights to these conditions?

My reply to this line of questioning is as follows. The dialectically necessary method restricts the argument to what every agent is logically or rationally justified in claiming from within his conative standpoint in purposive action. The point of this restriction derives from the fact that morality is, or may be, the scene of severe dissensus, of conflicting claims and counterclaims about what is right and wrong, what ought to be done and not done, and so forth. These claims and counterclaims are, as such, quite inconclusive, because they reflect or rest on contingent, logically deniable, and sometimes seemingly arbitrary assumptions, beliefs, or principles. The problem of moral justification is: How is one rationally to adjudicate among these conflicting claims? The answer I offer is that what is needed is recourse to a context that is logically binding on every agent. Such is the context of action itself. For whatever the divergent purposes for which they may act or advocate acting, all agents are involved in the context of action. Hence, if there are any practical judgments that logically must be accepted by every agent from within his own perspective of purposive agency, then these judgments can serve as a firm, rationally ineluctable basis for evaluating whatever further judgments or actions he may want to pursue. In this way, then, the use of the dialectically necessary method yields valid criteria for morally right actions which every agent must accept on pain of self-contradiction. The method achieves a kind of rational necessity in the form of truths relevant to agency, including affirmations of rights, which no agent can deny without self-contradiction. Thus the initial moral dissensus is brought to a halt by truths that every agent logically must accept.

This same point may be put more directly in terms of agents themselves. Whatever other, variable descriptions may be true of the protagonists in morally relevant situations, it is necessarily true of all of them in the most typical cases that they are actual or prospective agents. For it is to such agents that all moral and other practical precepts are addressed. Hence, this description of being an actual or prospective agent is necessarily and universally connected with the context of morality and practice, so that this description has a rational necessity within the relevant context which is lacking to other, more restricted descriptions. For this reason, the universal description takes precedence over more particular descriptions, and there is a rational justification for restricting the argument to the necessary contents of action and agency as against the contingent and variable further contents that may enter into more particular descriptions of some agents and actions as opposed to others.

If, now, there are logical consequences that follow simply from being an actual or prospective agent, consequences that every agent must accept for himself on pain of self-contradiction, then these consequences are rationally justified to each agent. What I have tried to show is that every agent logically must in this way accept for himself certain moral obligations involving respect for the generic rights of all other prospective agents. For these obligations follow simply from the fact of being an agent and having thereby the conative features of voluntariness and purposiveness that lead to the necessity of accepting for oneself certain right-claims. Every agent, whatever his more particular, differential characteristics, must accept these obligations on pain of self-contradiction.

Hence in restricting the argument to the necessary contents of action and agency, the theory presented here has a rational justification, in the most stringent sense, that is lacking in other ethical theories either because they apply only probabilistic rational criteria or because the contents to which they apply their criteria are contingent rather than necessary.

Human Rights and "The Pain of Self-Contradiction"

A related question concerns the appeal to logical consistency in the justificatory argument leading to the *PGC* as the principle of human rights. Why is it so important to show that any agent who denies or violates the *PGC* must contradict himself? What is so "painful" about self-contradiction? Isn't such a consideration an arch example of a kind of rationalistic fallacy in ethics, whereby moral evil is reduced to logical error? After all, the morally bad person is not simply or primarily a person who commits logical mistakes; rather, he is a person who is viciously self-aggrandizing, not caring for other persons, lacking in sympathy and respect for them, treating them as mere means to his own ends, and so forth. What do these specifically moral considerations have to do with his falling into inconsistency or self-contradiction?

The chief answer to this question must recur to the consideration that the sphere of morality is one of great dissensus, of conflicting claims and counterclaims among competing criteria or principles of moral rightness. The claims and counterclaims bear on the substantive and distributive questions of morality: what interests of which persons should be supported or regarded as justified, and which ones not? Any answers one might give to these questions can always be countered by alternative and opposed answers. Now these conflicting claims can be rationally adjudicated in a nonquestion-begging way if we can show that one principle is such that logical inconsistency results from rejecting it, while this is not so with the other principles. For this provides a conclusive argument in favor of the first principle, since a proposition whose denial is self-contradictory is itself necessarily true. This, then, is the point of emphasizing the criterion of logical consistency: not that of *superseding* moral criteria that use specifically moral concepts of persons and their interests but, rather, that of providing a culminating structural argument where other arguments fail of conclusiveness. The appeal to consistency, then, is a second-order logical argument about first-order moral arguments, so that there is no confusion of types of criteria in justifying the supreme principle of morality and of human rights by showing that its denial or violation commits every agent to self-contradiction. This is another way of saying that principles or judgments that are self-contradictory are not rationally justifiable.

Human Dignity as the Basis of Human Rights

A widely upheld justificatory argument for human rights is that all humans are equal in dignity or worth. Thus the United Nations Declaration of Human Rights (1948), in its first Article, says: "All human beings are born free and equal in dignity and rights." It will be helpful to compare this doctrine with the justificatory argument I have presented here.

The doctrine may be understood in several ways. It may mean that all humans have rights simply in virtue of having dignity, or that they have rights because these are necessary to maintain or protect their dignity. In these two cases the rights would have, respectively, an intrinsic and an instrumental value in relation to dignity. In either case, the emphasis would fall on characteristics of humans as the Subjects of rights that justify their having rights.

In my above dialectically necessary argument, on the other hand, the emphasis was on the Objects of rights: the necessary goods needed for the existence and success of agency. Hence, it may be plausibly contended that my argument has to be completed by a further consideration. Even if these Objects—the necessary goods of action—are indeed needed by every agent, why does it follow that these needs ought to be satisfied? What is there about agents—what qualities do they have—that makes it justified and indeed mandatory or normatively necessary to fulfill their needs of action, so that they have rights to this fulfillment?

My dialectically necessary argument has tried to answer this question by recourse to the claims implicitly made or accepted by every agent from within his own conative standpoint. But it may be held that this agent-centered consideration is not sufficient, because agency is not self-justifying: it must be justified by an appeal to a value or criterion that goes beyond agency itself and validates its claims to fullfillment of its needs.

The difficulty with this contention, however, is one that has been emphasized above and also in Essay 1 (pp. 46–47). Since action is the general context of all morality and practice, what action-transcending criterion, apart from reason itself, can be used to justify fulfilling the needs of action?

It is possible, nevertheless, to bring together the two considerations— dignity and action—in a way that lets each illuminate the other as bases of human rights. To see this, we must first examine further what is meant by "dignity" and how it is related to rights.

When it is said that all human beings have dignity, what is presumably meant is not that dignity is an empirical characteristic in the way the having of interests or the capacity for feeling physical pain is empirically ascertainable. The sense of "dignity" in which all humans are said to have equal dignity is not the same as that in which it may be said of some person that he lacks dignity or that he behaves without dignity, where what is meant is that he is lacking in decorum, is too raucous or obsequious or is not "dignified." This kind of dignity is one that humans may occurrently exhibit, lack, or lose, whereas the dignity in which all humans are said to be equal is a characteristic that belongs permanently and inherently to every human as such.

One difficulty with the attempt to derive human rights from such inherent dignity is that the two expressions, "A has human rights" and "A has inherent dignity," may seem to be equivalent, so that the latter simply reduplicates the former. Thus, for example, Maritain wrote: "The dignity of the human person? The expression means nothing if it does not signify that, by virtue of natural law, the human person has the right to be respected, is the subject of rights, possesses rights."[13] If, however, the two expressions are thus equivalent in meaning, the attribution of dignity adds nothing substantial to the attribution of rights, and someone who is doubtful about the latter attribution will be equally doubtful about the former. Thus the argument for rights based on inherent dignity, so far, does not satisfy the requirement of noncircularity.

It is essential, then, to consider whether the attribution of inherent dignity can have a status independent of and logically prior to the attribution of rights. An important doctrine of this sort was set forth by Kant, who based his attribution of dignity *(Würde)* on the rational being's autonomy or freedom, his capacity for self-legislation, for acting according to laws he gives to himself.[14] Now Kant held that such autonomy is not an empirical characteristic, since it applies only to rational beings as things-in-themselves and hence as not subject to the deterministic laws of natural phenomena. This doctrine, however, involves all the difficulties of the distinction between phenomena and noumena, including the cognitive nonascertainability of the latter.

We may, however, abstract from this aspect of Kant's doctrine and reinterpret it along the lines of the conception of action presented in some of the essays in this volume and more fully in *Reason and Morality*, pages 26–42, 48–63. Human action, as an empirically ascertainable phenomenon, has the generic features of voluntariness (whereby the agent controls his behavior by his unforced choice with knowledge of relevant circumstances) and purposiveness (whereby he aims at certain goals he wants to attain and can reflect on his goals). By virtue of the voluntariness of his actions, the agent has a kind of autonomy or freedom. And by virtue of his actions' purposiveness, he regards his goals as good, as worth attaining. An ineluctable element of worth, then, is involved in the very concept and context of human purposive action. Such action is not merely an unordered set of episodes or events. Rather, it is ordered by its orientation to a goal which gives it its value, its point. This is so even if the action is done for its own sake, so that it is its own goal. In either case, the goal or end has worth for the agent as something to be reflectively chosen, aimed at, and achieved. And this worth is not merely instrumental; it characterizes at least some of the agent's ends themselves as he conceives and pursues them.

Now there is a direct route from the worth of the agent's ends to the worth or dignity of the agent himself. For he is both the general locus of all the particular ends he wants to attain and also the source of his attribution of worth to them. Because he is this locus and source, the worth he attributes to his ends pertains *a fortiori* to himself. They are *his* ends, and they are worth attaining because *he* is worth sustaining and fulfilling, so that he has a justified sense of self-esteem, of his own worth (see *Reason and Morality,* pp. 241–42). He pursues his ends, moreover, not as an uncontrolled reflex response to stimuli, but rather because he has chosen them after reflection on alternatives. Even if he does not always reflect, his choice can and sometimes, at least, does operate in this way. Every human agent, as such, is capable of this. Hence, the agent is an entity that, unlike other natural entities, is not, so far as he acts, subject only to external forces of nature; he can and does make his own decisions on the basis of his own reflective understanding. By virtue of these characteristics of his action, the agent has worth or dignity.

This attribution of dignity may be interpreted both dialectically and assertorically. Dialectically, the argument means that every agent must attribute worth or dignity to himself, since he is the locus and source of his attribution of worth to the purposes for which he acts. Assertorically, the argument means that, regardless of the specific worth or value of any of his particular purposes, every agent has worth or dignity because of his capacities for controlling his behavior and acting for ends he reflectively chooses.

The sequence from this dignity to rights can similarly be established in either of two ways. One is the dialectical way discussed above. By this method the agent simply augments his statement that freedom and well-being are the necessary goods of his action with the affirmation that he must have these goods not only as an agent but as a person who has dignity or worth by virtue of his agency. The argument, with this corroborating qualification, otherwise proceeds as previously indicated. Its conclusion is that every agent must act in accord with his recipients' rights as well as his own, so that he must respect his recipients as well as himself (*Reason and Morality,* pp. 137–38).

The other way is assertoric. Since every agent has dignity, his status as an agent ought to be maintained and protected. For dignity is an attribute or characteristic that, of itself, deserves respect and makes mandatory the support of the being that has it. This mandatoriness or "ought," moreover, is strict: it is correlative to an entitlement on the part of the agent who has dignity. In this way, dignity entails rights.

I think that the assertoric arguments incur somewhat greater problems than do the dialectical ones. Each mode of argument, however, is based on the connection between human action and human rights emphasized in this volume, and each serves to bring out an important element in the justification of human rights.

III. Themes of the Essays

Except for Essays 5 and 10 (scheduled for publication in 1982 and hence not yet published at the time of my writing this Introduction), all of the essays in this book have been reproduced, photographically or otherwise, from their original places of publication. This has meant that I have not been able to make any corrections, and various repetitions between some of the essays have had to remain. I apologize in advance to the reader who gets a justified sense of *déjà vu* when he reads the first part of Essay 8, as well as parts of some of the other essays.

In Essays 3 and 13, I state the Principle of Generic Consistency as follows: "Apply to your recipient the same generic features of action that you apply to yourself." And in Essay 11 I present the "Principle of Categorial Consistency" as saying: "Apply to your recipient the same categorial rules of action that you apply to yourself." These two statements are equivalent both to each other and to the *PGC* as I have stated it above ("Act in accord with the generic rights of your recipients as well as of yourself"). For the generic rights are rights to have the generic features of action characterize one's behavior; and the categorial rules of action are likewise these generic features viewed as norms that regulate the context of human action as such.[15] I shifted from "categorial" to "generic" because the former term was constantly confused with "categorical." And I shifted from "rules" to "features" because "rules" raises complex questions of interpretation—questions I felt an already complex doctrine could dispense with.

In general, whenever there are differences of doctrine or statement between earlier and later essays, the latter should be taken as reflecting my present views.

I shall now give a brief description of each of the essays included in this book.

Essay 1 ("The Basis and Content of Human Rights") presents some of
the main justificatory problems of human rights and shows how the *PGC*
as the principle of human rights is to be justified. I here spell out some of
my reasons for holding that the existence of moral rights cannot be
justified by any assertoric method, but only by a dialectically necessary
method (pages 48–50). This essay also distinguishes the main kinds of
human rights—basic, nonsubtractive, and additive—in terms of the different sorts of goods that are necessary for action. The criteria for resolving conflicts of rights are presented, as are some of the main applications of the *PGC* in both individual action and social policy. I show why
the Respondents of human rights cannot be restricted to governments, and
I answer objections to the view that the human rights include social and
economic rights to well-being as well as political and civil rights. This is a
synoptic essay that summarizes some of the main doctrines of *Reason and
Morality*. It was originally written for the annual meeting of the American
Society for Political and Legal Philosophy held in New York, September
1978. Versions of it have been presented as lectures at many universities
in the United States and Canada.

In the Addendum to Essay 1 I deal with some important criticisms of
the argument for the *PGC*. In reply to these criticisms, I argue that it
makes sense to refer to "prudential" rights, including the prudential
right-claims that figure in the agent's attribution to himself of rights to
freedom and well-being. I argue also that even an amoralist must make
"ought"-judgments and use rights-language. A further point taken up is
that the *PGC* is a principle of equal human rights despite the fact that
humans have the abilities of agency in differing degrees.

Essay 2 ("Must One Play the Moral Language Game?") argues that
every agent logically must accept certain moral "ought"-judgments of the
form "All persons who want to have *y* ought to do *z*." These are moral
judgments in that the person who makes them endorses other persons'
pursuing their purposes on the same basis as his endorses his own pursuits. He is therefore in the position of giving favorable consideration to
the interests of persons other than or in addition to himself. Although I
deal mainly with "ought"-judgments in this paper, I also indicate how the
agent's universalized judgments commit him to upholding a system of
mutual rights and duties.[16] This essay is a link in the chain of argument for
the *PGC* as set forth in Essay 1. For it may be objected to that argument
that an "amoralist" (with whom I deal more briefly in the Addendum to
Essay 1) may reject all "ought"-judgments, including those I adduce
when I trace the implications of an agent's denying that he has rights to
freedom and well-being (pp. 73–76). Essay 2 shows that no agent can

rationally support such a refusal to accept any "ought"-judgments at all.

The version of universalization presented in the third section of Essay 2 is less adequate than my subsequent version based on the use of "because" to indicate a sufficient justifying condition. And it may be a mistake to hold, as I do in this essay, as well as Essay 3, that, because one statement entails another, the prescriptiveness of the former logically must also characterize the latter. Although the issue is still somewhat controversial, I am no longer so sure that continuity of illocutionary force from antecedent to consequent is a necessary condition or a logical consequence of the former's entailing the latter.

Essay 3 ("The 'Is-Ought' Problem Resolved") goes beyond Essay 2 by showing that every agent logically must accept the *PGC* as an egalitarian universalist moral principle. The paper makes this point in the context of an overall discussion of the "is-ought" problem, and it shows how, from the "is" of the agent's statement "I do X for purpose E," there logically follow first his claim to certain rights and then the "ought" of the *PGC*. Thus, where Essay 2 argues that every agent logically must accept for himself certain moral "ought"-judgments which involve giving favorable consideration to the interests of at least some persons other than himself (with an implication of correlative rights on the part of these other persons), in Essay 3 I argue for the more extensive thesis that every agent must logically hold that he and all other prospective agents have rights to the necessary conditions of action. This essay was my presidential address to the meeting of the western division of the American Philosophical Association in April 1974, and it has received considerable discussion, including a symposium in *Ethics* (July 1976) and papers at all three divisional meetings of the American Philosophical Association.

In Essay 4 ("The Golden Rule Rationalized") I present some familiar difficulties of the Golden Rule as a general moral principle, and I argue that these difficulties can be resolved only if the "wants" referred to in the Rule are required to be rational ("Do unto others as you rationally want them to do unto you"). I then show how this Rational Golden Rule is logically equivalent to the *PGC*. The argument includes the point that rational wants or desires have as their objects the generic rights of both agents and their recipients. Thus, while the *PGC* has the universal mutuality of the traditional Golden Rule, it differs in that it refers not merely to wants but to rights whose Objects are the necessary goods of action: Do unto others in accordance with their generic rights as well as your own.

Essay 5 ("Can Utilitarianism Justify Any Moral Rights?") answers its question in the negative by distinguishing between "essential" and "accidental" justifications. This paper was written as an invited commentary on one by David Lyons; briefer versions of both papers were presented at the annual meeting of the American Society for Political and Legal Philosophy held in Phoenix, Arizona, in January 1980. My references to Lyons' paper are, I think, self-explanatory, so that my paper can be understood apart from his. By means of what I call the "utility-rights dilemma" I argue that the distinction between utilitarianism and theories upholding moral rights, which Lyons (as well as I and others) wants to maintain, requires a fuller theory of rights than his own (and, by implication, that of many other exponents of rights). I then try to show how the *PGC* incorporates such a theory. The last three paragraphs of this essay, as printed in this volume, have been added to the version published in *Nomos* XXIV.

Essay 6 ("The Future of Ethics: The Moral Powers of Reason") was presented in 1981 in a symposium at the annual western meeting of the American Philosophical Association. I argue that future progress in ethics requires a unified combination of normative ethics and metaethics, and I distinguish various versions of ethical rationalisms that try to pursue such a combination. Especially important is procedural ethical rationalism, which falls into two groups, probabilistic and apodictic. By an extended criticism of the recent book by my cosymposiast, Richard Brandt, I try to show why probabilistic rationalism is unsuccessful. The main point of the critique is that appeals to empirical facts and similar considerations are insufficient for resolving certain basic moral disagreements. I then argue that full apodictic rationalism (the position represented by the *PGC* and the essays in this volume) can successfully cope with the problems of moral philosophy. My discussion of the dialectically necessary method in the Introduction, especially where I deal with the method's relation to rationality and necessity (above, pp. 24–26), is complementary to this essay's treatment of full apodictic rationalism.

The remaining eight essays present applications of the principle of human rights to some controversial issues of individual action and social policy. In Essay 7 ("Human Rights and the Prevention of Cancer") I argue that there is a basic human right to the noninfliction of cancer and that the Respondents of this right include manufacturers and sellers of carcinogenic products as well as government officials. The right entails at least the negative duty to refrain from subjecting workers and consumers to carcinogenic dangers. I then discuss some problems about this attribution of responsibility, and I examine the ways in which the right to the noninfliction of cancer is an absolute right. This involves a consideration of two areas of probabilism, one concerning cause-effect relations in the production of cancer, the other concerning the weighing of certain values (by cost-benefit analysis and other means) in reacting to those probabilities. I conclude that these probabilistic considerations do not remove the absoluteness of the right to the noninfliction of cancer.

Essay 8 ("Starvation and Human Rights") shows how the *PGC* requires positive action to relieve the basic needs of persons who cannot fulfill these needs by their own efforts. Thus the *PGC* is a principle of positive rights as well as negative ones. I argue that the right to food sets strict duties in both interpersonal and international relations, and I discuss some of the complexities of the latter. Although several philosophers have upheld the duty to relieve starvation, my argument differs from theirs in basing this duty not on utilitarianism but on basic rights to well-being. I now think, however, that the positive duty to help other persons can be derived from the *PGC* more directly than by construing such help as "noninterference" with well-being. The point is that if the basic rights of one person or group can be fulfilled only by the help of another person or group, then, given certain further considerations (including those of comparable costs), the latter person or group has a strict duty to provide this help. In many circumstances such provision requires a context of institutional rules. I also show in this essay how certain conflicts of rights and duties involved in the provision of such help are to be resolved, including the conflict between the duty to provide such help and the provider's own right to freedom.

In Essay 9 ("Are There Any Absolute Rights?") I first try to clarify the concept of an absolute right, and I then discuss one of the main objections to absolute rights: that any right must be overridden if the consequences of fulfilling it are sufficiently disastrous. I argue that this objection cannot overcome the absoluteness of a certain test right: the right of a mother not to be tortured to death by her own son. After discussing some of the problems of this absoluteness in the face of a threatened nuclear explosion, I conclude by generalizing this right to the absolute right of every innocent person not to be made the intended victim of a homicidal project.

Essay 10 ("Individual Rights and Political-Military Obligations") shows how the obligation to obey one's government rests on the government's serving to protect the generic rights of persons. Since the *PGC* is the moral principle that requires respect for these rights, political obligation is a species of moral obligation. I then discuss the justifiability of military conscription as based on such obligation. One of the paper's contributions is, I think, quite important for understanding how a certain traditional criticism of the emphasis on rights is to be answered. The criticism is that rights are excessively individualistic and hence cannot account for the duty to contribute to the common good. The essay deals with this criticism by showing that, according to the *PGC*, moral duties are owed not only to each person but also to the whole mutually supportive system of equal rights to freedom and well-being. This essay was originally written for the Working Group on Voluntary vs. Involuntary Military Service, sponsored by the Center for Philosophy and Public Policy at the University of Maryland.

In Essay 11 ("Obligation: Political, Legal, Moral") I discuss the basis of political obligation more extensively. I first present a critique of the institutionalist view of moral obligation, a view that has figured in many discussions of the "is-ought" problem and in many attempts to justify rights based on promises and other transactions. I then argue that institutions themselves need justification by moral reasons and that the justification of these reasons, in turn, is that they are inherently rational. This involves an argument for the earlier version of the *PGC,* here called the "PCC" (for the "Principle of Categorial Consistency"). This principle sets the moral obligations of justice, requiring each agent to respect other persons' freedom and welfare as well as his own. I then show how this moral principle is to be used in evaluating institutional obligations, and I apply it to the institution of law and legal obligation, including the legal system of a constitutional democracy. I conclude by discussing how civil disobedience can be justified despite the general justification of political and legal obligation in a system of constitutional democracy that fulfills the requirements of the principle of morality. Although the essay is focused on obligations rather than rights, most of the discussion of moral and legal obligations is readily translatable into correlative statements about rights.

Essay 12 ("Civil Disobedience, Law, and Morality") continues my discussion of civil disobedience through an examination of the doctrine of former Supreme Court Justice Abe Fortas. I focus on the apparent conflict between his statement that morally wrong laws ought to be disobeyed and his statement that, nevertheless, the state does right in punishing persons who disobey those laws. I discuss and reject three possible defenses of his doctrine and conclude that his qualified defense of civil disobedience must be extended to take account of the degree to which government is responsive to basic needs. This requires a more affirmative notion of political rights, one that requires governments to positively assist submerged groups to press their claims in the democratic community.

Essay 13 ("Civil Liberties as Effective Powers") continues the argument of Essay 12 by maintaining that the rights to the civil liberties require positive governmental assistance in the political process for those groups who are too poor to participate effectively. I first distinguish between negative and positive freedom as, respectively, noninterference by other persons, and power or ability to act, and, within the latter, I distinguish between latent and effective power. A person has the effective power to do X if his doing X depends on his own unforced choice. I then define the civil liberties as effective powers to perform or engage in actions of speaking, publishing, associating with others, and so forth. Two different senses of such effective powers are then distinguished: conative and achievemental, the latter consisting in having the effective power to succeed in the aims of one's speaking, publishing, and so forth. I next argue that there is an unequal distribution of the civil liberties as effective achievemental powers in the political process and that this inequality is unjust for several reasons. Various modes of remedying this injustice are suggested, including positive governmental assistance to groups of the poor. The paper points to important problems of the democratic process, but it also recognizes the vast superiority of that process over the extensive prohibitions, in totalitarian states, of the civil liberties even as conative powers, that is, as the legally protected right to speak, associate, and otherwise participate in the political process and elsewhere without fear of punishment. There remain serious questions both about the way I have formulated the problem of unequal effective achievemental powers and about governmental intervention to help solve it. The essay was presented as a Mellon Foundation Lecture at Marquette University in April 1975.

In Essay 14 ("Reasons and Conscience: The Claims of the Selective Conscientious Objector") I discuss the question whether exemptions from military service should be granted to persons who conscientiously object, not to fighting in all wars, but to fighting in some particular war. I show that four variables are involved in this question and that one of these, the Conscience Variable, does not provide a conclusive basis for a right to exemption. I also argue that the Reason Variable is especially important in justifying an affirmative answer to the question. This Reason Variable is a species of the Justifying Basis, which I have distinguished as one of the five elements of rights. Although my discussion in this essay does not proceed explicitly in terms of rights, the "should" stated in the question can be interpreted so that it has rights as its correlative. In this way, the issue concerns the right to be a selective conscientious objector. I indicate a possible qualification of this right when the particular war to which one objects is being fought to protect basic rights of freedom and well-being. This essay was originally written for a meeting of the Society for Philosophy and Public Affairs, held in Saint Louis in May 1972.

Notes

1. See Wesley N. Hohfeld, *Fundamental Legal Conceptions* (New Haven: Yale University Press, 196?, p. 38.
2. See, for example, Joel Feinberg, "The Nature and Value of Rights," in *Rights, Justice, and the Bounds of Liberty* (Princeton N.J.: Princeton University Press, 1980), p. 143 ff.

3. See H. L. A. Hart, "Are There Any Natural Rights?" *Philosophical Review* 64 (1955): 183 ff.

4. See ibid., pp. 178, 181.

5. See David Lyons, "Rights, Claimants and Beneficiaries," *American Philosophical Quarterly* 6 (1969): 173 ff.

6. See, for example, Feinberg, "The Nature and Value of Rights," in *Rights, Justice and the Bounds of Liberty*, pp. 148–55.

7. H. L. A. Hart, "Bentham on Legal Rights," in *Oxford Essays in Jurisprudence*, 2d ser. ed. A. W. B. Simpson (Oxford: Clarendon Press, 1973), p. 190. See also Christopher Arnold, "Analyses of Right," in *Human Rights*, ed. Eugene Kamenka and Alice Erh-Soon Tay (New York: St. Martin's Press, 1978), pp. 77 ff.

8. Maurice Cranston, *What Are Human Rights?* (London: Bodley Head, 1973), pp. 66 ff.; see also his contribution to D. D. Raphael, ed., *Political Theory and the Rights of Man* (London: Macmillan, 1967), pp. 96 ff. Robert Nozick, *Anarchy, State, and Utopia* (New York: Basic Books, 1974), pp. 30–33, 150 ff., 170, 173, 179 n., 238.

9. Ronald Dworkin, *Taking Rights Seriously* (Cambridge, Mass.: Harvard University Press, 1977), pp. 268 ff.; Charles Fried, *Right and Wrong* (Cambridge, Mass.: Harvard University Press, 1978), p. 132.

10. Felix E. Oppenheim, *Political Concepts: A Reconstruction* (Chicago: University of Chicago Press, 1981), pp. 82 ff.

11. The distinction between utilitarian grounds and grounds based on individual rights is often unclear, as I point out in Essay 5. For example, Dworkin defines a presumably utilitarian "argument of policy" as one that justifies a political decision on the ground that it "advances or protects some collective goal of the community as a whole" (*Taking Rights Seriously*, p. 82). He gives as an example the "argument in favor of a subsidy for aircraft manufacturers that the subsidy will protect national defense." But if national defense is necessary for making secure the life and freedom of individual members of the community, then isn't the argument also based on individual rights to these necessary goods? It is, of course, important to distinguish between those Objects of rights that pertain to an individual separately and those Objects of rights that pertain to individuals collectively or as members of collectivities. But the distinction between arguments of principle based on individual rights and utilitarian arguments of policy is left obscure if the relation between their respective Objects is not specified. In particular, is the important difference between these two kinds of arguments simply that the former is distributive and the latter aggregative, or is it that the former, in being concerned with "some individual or group right," has an Object or purpose that is more important to the individual than is the object of an argument of policy? The former answer would be inadequate to ground Dworkin's support for the general superiority of "arguments of principle" over "arguments of policy"—of individual or group rights over collective goals—while the latter answer is false unless the Objects of rights are specified in some such terms as the necessary goods of action. The reader is referred to Essay 5 for my fuller discussion of this matter.

12. Karl Marx, "On the Jewish Question," in *The Marx-Engels Reader*, ed. Robert Tucker, 2d ed. (New York: W. W. Norton, 1978), p. 43.

13. Jacques Maritain, *The Rights of Man and Natural Law*, trans. D. Anson (New York: Charles Scribner's Sons, 1951), p. 65.

14. I. Kant, *Foundations of the Metaphysics of Morals*, sec. 2 (Akademie ed., pp. 434–36).

15. I have discussed this point in "Some Comments on Categorial Consistency," *Philosophical Quarterly* 20 (1970): 380–84, at 384.

16. Virginia Held (in "Rationality and Reasonable Cooperation," *Social Research* 44 [1977]: 708 ff.) has written that my argument in this paper does not refute egoism, construed

"as giving priority but not exclusivity to reasons of self-interest." Such priority might be expressed, in the symbolism of my essay, as the egoist's saying, "I ought to do z because I want to have y rather than w," where "y" is self-interested and "w" is not. But then the egoist logically must accept the universalization, "All persons who want to have y rather than w ought to do z." Here he would grant to other persons the same priority for *their* self-interested pursuits as he upholds for himself. This is a generalized egoism, but it is a moral position in that it involves the speaker's giving favorable consideration to the interests or pursuits of *other* persons as well as to his own. I also show in Essay 2, however, that acceptance of the universalized statement requires certain restrictions on the pursuit of self-interest.

Part I
Essays on Justification

1
The Basis and Content
of Human Rights

Despite the great practical importance of the idea of human rights, some of the most basic questions about them have not yet received adequate answers. We may assume, as true by definition, that human rights are rights that all persons have simply insofar as they are human. But are there any such rights? How, if at all, do we know that there are? What is their scope or content, and how are they related to one another? Are any of them absolute, or may each of them be overridden in certain circumstances?

I

These questions are primarily substantive or criterial rather than logical or conceptual. Recent moral philosophers, following on the work of legal thinkers,[1] have done much to clarify the concept of a right, but they have devoted considerably less attention to substantive arguments that try to prove or justify that persons have rights other than those grounded in positive law. Such arguments would indicate the criteria for there being human rights, including their scope or content, and would undertake to show why these criteria are correct or justified.

The conceptual and the substantive questions are, of course, related, but still they are distinct. If, for example, we know that for one person A to have a right to something X is for A to be entitled to X and also for some other person or persons to have a correlative duty to provide X for A as his due or to assist A's having X or at least to refrain from interfering with A's having X, still this does not tell us whether or why A is entitled to X and hence whether or why the other person or persons have such a correlative duty to A. Appeal to positive recognition is obviously insufficient for answering these substantive questions. The answer is not given, for example, by pointing out

that many governments have signed the United Nations Universal
Declaration of Human Rights of 1948 as well as later covenants. For
if the existence or having of human rights depended on such recognition, it would follow that prior to, or independent of, these positive
enactments no human rights existed.

The questions, "Are there any human rights?" or "Do persons have
any human rights?" may indeed be interpreted as asking whether the
rights receive positive recognition and legal enforcement. But in the
sense in which it is held that humans have rights (so that such rights
exist) even if they are not enforced, the existence in question is normative: it refers to what entitlements legal enactments and social regulations ought to recognize, not or not only to what they in fact recognize. Thus, the criterion for answering the question must not be
legal or conventional but moral. For human rights to exist there must
be valid moral criteria or principles that justify that all humans, qua
humans, have the rights and hence also the correlative duties. Human rights are rights or entitlements that belong to every person;
thus, they are universal moral rights. There may of course be other
moral rights as well, but only those that morally ought to be universally distributed among all humans are human rights.

This answer, however, seems to get us into more rather than less
difficulty. In order to ascertain whether there are legal rights we
need only look to the statute books; these, for present purposes, may
be held to supply the criteria for the existence of such rights. But if
for a moral or human right to exist is for it to satisfy valid moral criteria which justify or ground the right, where do we look for such criteria? What is the moral analogue of the statute books? If there were
a single set of universally accepted moral criteria, our task might be
somewhat easier, although even in this case we should still have to
take account of the distinction indicated above between positive social recognition and moral validity.

In fact, however, the field of moral criteria is full of controversy:
consider the competing substantive views epitomized by such thinkers
as Kant, Kierkegaard, Nietzsche, Mill, and Marx, who hold, respectively, that the criteria for having rights consist in or are determined
by reason, religion, power, utility, and economic class or history.
The disagreements among these thinkers do not respresent merely
different "second-order" analyses of a commonly accepted body of
"first-order" moral judgments, in the way philosophers may differ
about the analysis of knowledge while recognizing (except for some
borderline cases) a commonly accepted body of knowledge. In contrast to these, the divergences among moral philosophers are dis-

agreements of basic substantive first-order moral principle about what rights persons have, about how persons ought to regard and act toward one another, about what interests of which persons are worth pursuing and supporting, and the like. Considerable evidence also indicates that many contemporaries, both philosophers and nonphilosophers, would share (although perhaps less systematically) one or another of such divergent moral principles.

Nor does the difficulty end there. For in many fields of empirical science and of practice where the "authorities" or ordinary persons disagree, we have some common conception at least of the context or subject matter to which one must look as a kind of independent variable for testing their divergent assertions. Examples of these subject matters are natural or experimental phenomena in the case of natural science, physical health in the case of medicine, rates of inflation or unemployment in the case of economics. But it seems that the very context or subject matter to which one should look to resolve the disagreements of moral principle is itself involved in such disagreements. Obviously, we should already be taking sides on this issue of moral principle if we were to urge that religion or economic history or social utility or aesthetic sensibility be appealed to as the independent variable for this purpose. Although Thomas Jefferson, following a long tradition, wrote that "all men . . . are endowed by their Creator with certain unalienable rights," it does not seem true to say that persons are born having rights in the sense in which they are born having legs. At least their having legs is empirically confirmable, but this is not the case with their having rights. And whereas it is indeed possible to confirm empirically, although in a more complex way, that most persons are born having certain *legal* rights, this, as we have seen, is not sufficient to establish that they have *moral* or *human* rights.

These general difficulties about moral criteria are reinforced when we look at recent attempts of moral philosophers to answer the substantive questions of what are the specific criteria for having moral rights and how it can be known that humans have such rights. For even where the philosophers agree at least in part on the scope or content of the rights, they disagree as to how the existence of these rights can be established or justified. We may distinguish five different recent answers. The intuitionist answer that humans' possession of certain inalienable rights is self-evident, most famously expressed in the Declaration of Independence, is reiterated in Nozick's peremptory assertion that "Individuals have rights, and there are things no person or group may do to them (without violating their rights)."[2]

Like other intuitionist positions, this one is impotent in the face of
conflicting intuitions. The institutionalist answer that rights arise
from transactions grounded in formal or informal rules of institutions, such as promising,[3] incurs the difficulty that some institutions
may be morally wrong, so that an independent moral justification
must still be given for the institutional or transactional rules that are
held to ground the rights. A third answer is that persons have rights
because they have interests.[4] This, however, indicates at most a necessary condition for having rights, since there would be an enormous
and indeed unmanageable proliferation of rights if the having any
interest X were sufficient to generate a right to X. Even if "interests"
are restricted to basic or primary interests or needs, there still remain
both the logical question of how a normative conclusion about rights
can be derived from factual premises about empirically ascertainable
characteristics such as having interests, and also the substantive question of why moral rights are generated by characteristics that all humans have in common rather than by more restrictive, inegalitarian
characteristics that pertain only to some persons, or to persons in
varying degrees, such as expert knowledge or will to power or productive ability.

The fourth answer, that persons have moral rights because they
have intrinsic worth or dignity or are ends in themselves or children
of God,[5] may be held simply to reduplicate the doctrine to be justified. Such characterizations are directly or ultimately normative,
and if one is doubtful about whether persons have moral rights one
will be equally doubtful about the characterizations that were invoked to justify it. The fifth answer is Rawls's doctrine that if persons
were to choose the constitutional structure of their society from behind a veil of ignorance of all their particular qualities, they would
provide that each person must have certain basic rights.[6] Insofar,
however, as this doctrine is viewed as giving a justificatory answer to
the question whether humans have equal moral rights, it may be convicted of circularity. For the argument attains its egalitarian conclusion only by putting into its premises the egalitarianism of persons'
universal equal ignorance of all their particular qualities. This ignorance has no independent rational justification, since humans are not
in fact ignorant of all their particular qualities. Hence, apart from
an initial egalitarian moral outlook, why should any actual rational
informed persons accept the principle about equal moral rights that
stems from such ignorance?

It may be objected that all the above difficulties about moral or
human rights arise because I have taken too "cognitive" or "ontologi-

cal" a view of them. Thus, it may be held that moral rights are not something known or existent; the correct analysis of a rights-judgment is not "descriptive" but rather "prescriptive" or of some other noncognitivist sort. Rights-judgments are claims or demands made on other persons; they do not state that certain knowable facts exist; rather, they advocate, urge, or exhort that certain facts be brought into existence. Hence, questions of justification or validity are logically irrelevant to such judgments.

Now the prescriptivist interpretation of rights-judgments is partly true, but this does not remove the point of the justificatory questions I have asked. For one thing, as we have seen, different persons may make conflicting right-claims, so that the question still remains which of these claims is correct. Moreover, ascriptions of correctness or justification are intrinsic to rights-judgments: these consist not only in certain claims or demands but also in the implicit view, on the part of the persons who make them, that the claims have sound reasons in their support. If this were not so, discussion or debate about rights would consist only in vocal ejaculations or attempts at propagandistic manipulation; it would not have even potentially the aspects of rational argument or reflective appraisal of evidence that it in fact can and does display. In addition, the logical connections that hold among rights-judgments would be obscured or even left unexplained if the ejaculatory or manipulative interpretation were the sole or the main correct analysis of such judgments.

II

Let us now begin to develop answers to these questions about human rights. First, since these rights derive from a valid moral criterion or principle, we must consider what I have referred to as the context or subject matter of morality. We saw that although in many other fields their subject matters serve as independent variables for testing the correctness of conflicting judgments made within them, it was difficult to find such a non-question-begging subject matter for morality. Nevertheless, it does exist and can be found. To see what it is, we must consider the general concept of a morality. I have so far been using the words "moral" and "morality" without defining them. Amid the various divergent moralities with their conflicting substantive and distributive criteria, a certain core meaning may be elicited. According to this, a morality is a set of categorically obligatory requirements for action that are addressed at least in part to every actual or prospective agent, and that are intended to further the interests, especially the most important interests, of persons or recipients other than or in addition to the agent or the speaker.

As we have seen, moralities differ with regard to what interests of which persons they view as important and deserving of support. But amid these differences, all moralities have it in common that they are concerned with actions. For all moral judgments, including right-claims, consist directly or indirectly in precepts about how persons ought to act toward one another. The specific contents of these judgments, of course, vary widely and often conflict with one another. But despite these variations and conflicts, they have in common the context of the human actions that they variously prescribe or prohibit and hence view as right or wrong. It is thus this context which constitutes the general subject matter of all morality.

How does the consideration of human action serve to ground or justify the ascription and content of human rights? To answer this question, let us return to the connection indicated above between rights and claims. Rights may be had even when they are not claimed, and claims are also not in general sufficient to establish or justify that their objects are rights. As against such an assertoric approach to the connection between claims and rights, I shall follow a dialectically necessary approach. Even if persons' having rights cannot be logically inferred in general from the fact that they make certain claims, it is possible and indeed logically necessary to infer, from the fact that certain objects are the proximate necessary conditions of human action, that all rational agents logically must hold or claim, at least implicitly, that they have rights to such objects. Although what is thus directly inferred is a statement not about persons' rights but about their claiming to have them, this provides a sufficient criterion for the existence of human rights, because the claim must be made or accepted by every rational human agent on his own behalf, so that it holds universally within the context of action, which is the context within which all moral rights ultimately have application. The argument is dialectically necessary in that it proceeds from what all agents logically must claim or accept, on pain of contradiction. To see how this is so, we must briefly consider certain central aspects of action. Since I have presented the argument in some detail elsewhere,[7] I shall here confine myself to outlining the main points.

As we have seen, all moral precepts, regardless of their varying specific contents, are concerned directly or indirectly with how persons ought to act. This is also true of most if not all other practical precepts. Insofar as actions are the possible objects of any such precepts, they are performed by purposive agents. Now, every agent regards his purposes as good according to whatever criteria (not necessarily moral ones) are involved in his acting to fulfill them. This is shown, for example, by the endeavor or at least intention with which each agent approaches the achieving of his purposes. Hence, *a fortiori*, he also, as rational, regards as necessary goods the proximate general necessary conditions of his acting to achieve his purposes. For without these conditions he either would not be able to act for any purposes or goods at all or at least would not be able to act with any chance of succeeding in his purposes. These necessary conditions of his action and successful action are freedom and well-being, where freedom consists in controlling one's behavior by one's unforced choice while having knowledge of relevant circumstances, and well-being consists in having the other general abilities and conditions required for agency. The components of such well-being fall into a hierarchy of three kinds of goods: basic, nonsubtractive, and additive. These will be analyzed more fully below.

In saying that every rational agent regards his freedom and well-being as necessary goods, I am primarily making not a phenomenological descriptive point about the conscious thought processes of agents but rather a dialectically necessary point about what is logically involved in the structure of action. Since agents act for purposes they regard as worth pursuing — for otherwise they would not control their behavior by their unforced choice with a view to achieving their purposes — they must, insofar as they are rational, also regard the necessary conditions of such pursuit as necessary goods. Just as the basic goods are generically the same for all agents, so too are the nonsubtractive and additive goods. I shall call freedom and well-being the *generic features* of action, since they characterize all action or at least all successful action in the respect in which action has been delimited above.

It is from the consideration of freedom and well-being as the necessary goods of action that the ascription and contents of human rights follow. The main point is that with certain qualifications to be indicated below, there is a logical connection between necessary goods and rights. Just as we saw before that from "X is an interest of some person A" it cannot be logically inferred that "A has a right to X," so too this cannot be logically inferred from "X is a good of A" or from "X seems good to A." In all these cases the antecedent is too contingent and variable to ground an ascription of rights. The reason for this is that rights involve *normative necessity*. One way to see this is through the correlativity of rights and strict "oughts" or duties. The judgment "A has a right to X" both entails and is entailed by,

"All other persons ought at least to refrain from interfering with A's
having (or doing) X," where this "ought" includes the idea of something due or owed to A. Under certain circumstances, including
those where the subject or right-holder A is unable to have X by his
own efforts, the rights-judgment also entails and is entailed by,
"Other persons ought to assist A to have X," where again the "ought"
includes the idea of something due or owed to A. Now, these strict
"oughts" involve normative necessity; they state what, as of right,
other persons *must* do. Such necessity is also involved in the frequently
noted use of "due" and "entitlement" as synonyms or at least as components of the substantive use of "right." A person's rights are what
belong to him as his due, what he is entitled to, hence what he can
rightly demand of others. In all these expressions the idea of normative necessity is central.

This necessity is an essential component in the ascription of rights,
but it is not sufficient to logically ground this ascription. Let us recur
to freedom and well-being as the necessary goods of action. From "X
is a necessary good for A" does it logically follow that "A has a right
to X"? To understand this question correctly, we must keep in mind
that "necessary good" is here used in a rational and invariant sense.
It does not refer to the possibly idiosyncratic and unfounded desires
of different protagonists, as when someone asserts, "I must have a
Florida vacation (or a ten-speed bicycle); it is a necessary good for
me." Rather, a "necessary good" is here confined to the truly
grounded requirements of agency; hence, it correctly characterizes
the indispensable conditions that all agents must accept as needed
for their actions.

Now, it might be argued that when "necessary good" is understood
in this universal and rational way, from "X is a necessary good for A"
it does follow that "A has a right to X." For since the idea of a right
involves normative necessity, "A has a right to X" is entailed by "It is
normatively necessary that A have X," and this seems equivalent to
"X is a necessary good for A." There are three interrelated considerations, however, that show that "X is a necessary good for A" is not
sufficient to provide the logical ground for "A has a right to X" as a
matter of logical necessity. First, as we have seen, "A has a right to
X" entails that other persons, B, C, and so forth, have correlative duties toward A. But how can these duties of other persons be logically
derived from "X is a necessary good for A," which refers only to A,
not to other persons?

Second, it must be kept in mind that rights involve not only
"oughts" or normative necessity but also the idea of entitlement, of

something due to the right-holder. There is logical correlativity between "A has a right to X," on the one hand, and "Other persons ought to refrain from interfering with A's having X and ought also, under certain circumstances, to assist A to have X," on the other, only when these "oughts" are viewed as indicating what A is entitled to or ought to have as his due. But in "X is a necessary good for A" this idea of A's entitlement to X, of its being due or owed to him, is not found. Hence, it cannot serve to generate logically the conclusion, "A has a right to X."

A third consideration that shows this is that, as we saw above, a rights-judgment is prescriptive: it advocates or endorses that the subject or right-holder A have the X that is the object of the right. But such advocacy need not be present in "X is a necessary good for A." For this statement, as such, does not necessarily carry with it any advocacy or endorsement on A's behalf by the person who makes the statement, even while he recognizes its truth. Hence, again, "X is a necessary good for A" is not sufficient to logically generate or entail "A has a right to X."

What these considerations indicate is that for the concept of necessary goods logically to generate the concept of rights, both concepts must figure in judgments made by the agent or right-holder himself in accordance with the dialectically necessary method. It will be recalled that this method begins from statements or judgments that are necessarily made or accepted by protagonists or agents, and the method then traces what these statements or judgments logically imply. Thus, in the present context of action, the method requires that the judgments about necessary goods and rights be viewed as being made by the agent himself from within his own internal, conative standpoint in purposive agency.

When this internal, conative view is taken, the logical gaps indicated above between judgments about necessary goods and ascriptions of rights are closed. The agent is now envisaged as saying, "My freedom and well-being are necessary goods." From this there does logically follow his further judgment, "I have rights to freedom and well-being." For the assertion about necessary goods is now not a mere factual means-end statement; on the contrary, because it is made by the agent himself from within his own conative standpoint in purposive agency, it carries his advocacy or endorsement. In effect, he is saying, "I must have freedom and well-being in order to pursue by my actions any of the purposes I want and intend to pursue." Thus his statement is prescriptive.

By the same token, his statement carries the idea of something that is his due, to which he is entitled. It must be kept in mind that these concepts do not have only moral or legal criteria; they may be used with many different kinds of criteria, including intellectual, aesthetic, and prudential ones. In the present context the agent's criterion is prudential: the entitlement he claims to freedom and well-being is grounded in his own needs as an agent who wants to pursue his purposes. He is saying that he has rights to freedom and well-being because these goods are due to him from within his own standpoint as a prospective purposive agent, since he needs these goods in order to act either at all or with the general possibility of success.

This consideration also shows how, from the agent's judgment "My freedom and well-being are necessary goods," there also logically follows a claim on his part against other persons. For he is saying that because he must have freedom and well-being in order to act, he must have whatever further conditions are required for his fulfilling these needs; and these further conditions include especially that other persons at least refrain from interfering with his having freedom and well-being. Thus, the agent's assertion of his necessary needs of agency entails a claim on his part to the noninterference of other persons and also, in certain circumstances, to their help.

There may be further objections against the derivation of the agent's right-claims from his judgment about necessary goods; I have dealt with these elsewhere.[8] What I have tried to show is that every agent must claim or accept, at least implicitly, that he has rights to freedom and well-being, because of the logical connection between rights and necessary goods as involving normative necessity, prescriptiveness, and entitlements when these are viewed from the internal, conative standpoint of the agent himself who makes or accepts the respective judgments. The argument may be summed up by saying that if any agent denies that he has rights to freedom and well-being, he can be shown to contradict himself. For, as we have seen, he must accept (1) "My freedom and well-being are necessary goods." Hence, the agent must also accept (2) "I, as an actual or prospective agent, must have freedom and well-being," and hence also (3) "All other persons must at least refrain from removing or interfering with my freedom and well-being." For if other persons remove or interfere with these, then he will not have what he has said he must have. Now suppose the agent denies (4) "I have rights to freedom and well-being." Then he must also deny (5) "All other persons ought at least to refrain from removing or interfering with my freedom and well-being." By denying (5) he must accept (6) "It is not the case that all other persons ought at least to refrain from removing or interfering with my freedom and well-being," and hence he must also accept (7) "Other persons may (are permitted to) remove or interfere with my freedom and well-being." But (7) contradicts (3). Since, as we have seen, every agent must accept (3), he cannot consistently accept (7). Since (7) is entailed by the denial of (4), "I have rights to freedom and well-being," it follows that any agent who denies that he has rights to freedom and well-being contradicts himself.

III

Thus far I have shown that rights and right-claims are necessarily connected with action, in that every agent, on pain of self-contradiction, must hold or accept that he has rights to the necessary conditions of action. I shall henceforth call these *generic rights,* since freedom and well-being are the generic features of action. As so far presented, however, they are only prudential rights but not yet moral ones, since their criterion, as we have seen, is the agent's own pursuit of his purposes. In order to establish that they are also moral and human rights, we must show that each agent must admit that all other humans also have these rights. For in this way the agent will be committed to take favorable account of the purposes or interests of other persons besides himself. Let us see why he must take this further step.

This involves the question of the ground or sufficient reason or sufficient condition on the basis of which any agent must hold that he has the generic rights. Now, this ground is not subject to his optional or variable decisions. There is one, and only one, ground that every agent logically must accept as the sufficient justifying condition for his having the generic rights, namely, that he is a prospective agent who has purposes he wants to fulfill. Suppose some agent A were to hold that he has these rights only for some more restrictive necessary and sufficient reason R. This would entail that in lacking R he would lack the generic rights. But if A were to accept this conclusion, that he may not have the generic rights, he would contradict himself. For we saw above that it is necessarily true of every agent that he must hold or accept at least implicitly that he has rights to freedom and well-being. Hence, A would be in the position of both affirming and denying that he has the generic rights: affirming it because he is an agent, denying it because he lacks R. To avoid this contradiction, every agent must hold that being a prospective purposive agent is a sufficient reason or condition for having the generic rights.

Because of this sufficient reason, every agent, on pain of self-contradiction, must also accept the generalization that all prospective purposive agents have the generic rights. This generalization is an application of the logical principle of universalizability: if some predicate P belongs to some subject S because S has the quality Q (where the 'because' is that of sufficient reason or condition), then it logically follows that every subject that has Q has P. If any agent A were to deny or refuse to accept this generalization in the case of any other prospective purposive agent, A would contradict himself. For he would be in the position of saying that being a prospective purposive agent both is and is not a sufficient justifying condition for having the generic rights. Hence, on pain of self-contradiction, every agent must accept the generalization that all prospective purposive agents have the generic rights.

Thus, we have now arrived at the basis of human rights. For the generic rights to freedom and well-being are moral rights, since they require of every agent that he take favorable account of the most important interests of all other prospective agents, namely, the interests grounded in their needs for the necessary conditions of agency. And these generic rights are also human rights, since every human being is an actual, prospective, or potential agent. I shall discuss the distribution of these rights among humans more fully below. But first I must also establish that the generic rights are human rights in the further respect indicated above, namely, that they are grounded in or justified by a valid moral criterion or principle.

The above argument for the generic rights as moral rights has already provided the full basis for deriving a supreme moral principle. We have seen that every agent, on pain of self-contradiction, must accept the generalization that all prospective purposive agents have the generic rights to freedom and well-being. From this generalization, because of the correlativity of rights and strict "oughts," it logically follows that every person ought to refrain from interfering with the freedom and well-being of all other persons insofar as they are prospective purposive agents. It also follows that under certain circumstances every person ought to assist other persons to have freedom and well-being, when they cannot have these by their own efforts and he can give them such assistance without comparable cost to himself, although more usually such assistance must operate through appropriate institutions. Since to refrain and to assist in these ways is to act in such a way that one's actions are in accord with the generic rights of one's recipients, every agent is logically committed, on pain of self-contradiction, to accept the following precept: *Act in accord with the generic rights of your recipients as well as of yourself.* I shall call this the *Principle of Generic Consistency*

(PGC), since it combines the formal consideration of consistency with the material consideration of the generic features and rights of agency. To act in accord with someone's right to freedom is, in part, to refrain from coercing him; to act in accord with someone's right to well-being is, in part, to refrain from harming him by adversely affecting his basic, nonsubtractive, or additive goods. In addition, to act in accord with these rights may also require positive assistance. These rights, as thus upheld, are now moral ones because they are concerned to further the interests or goods of persons other than or in addition to the agent. The *PGC*'s central moral requirement is the *equality of generic rights,* since it requires of every agent that he accord to his recipients the same rights to freedom and well-being that he necessarily claims for himself.

The above argument has provided the outline of a rational justification of the Principle of Generic Consistency as the supreme principle of morality, both for the formal reason that if any agent denies or violates the principle he contradicts himself and for the material reason that its content, the generic features of action, necessarily imposes itself on every agent. For it is necessarily true of every agent that he at least implicitly attributes to himself the generic rights and that he acts in accord with his own generic rights; hence, he cannot rationally evade the extension of these rights to his recipients. This material necessity stands in contrast to principles centered in the purposes, inclinations, or ideals for which some agent may contingently act and whose requirements he may hence evade by shifting his desires or opinions. The *PGC* is the supreme principle of morality because its interpersonal requirements, derived from the generic features of action, cannot rationally be evaded by any agent. (It must be kept in mind that action is the universal context of morality.) The main point may be put succinctly as follows: What for any agent are necessarily goods of action, namely, freedom and well-being, are equally necessary goods for his recipients, and he logically must admit that they have as much right to these goods as he does, since the ground or reason for which he rationally claims them for himself also pertains to his recipients.

We have now seen that every agent must hold, on pain of self-contradiction, that all other persons as well as himself have moral rights grounded in the *PGC* as the principle of morality. It follows from the argument to the *PGC* that the primary criterion for having moral rights is that all persons have certain needs relative to their being actual or prospective agents, namely, needs for freedom and well-being as the necessary conditions of action. Simply by virtue of being actual or prospective agents who have certain needs of agency, persons have moral rights to freedom and well-being. Since all humans are such agents having such needs, the generic moral rights to freedom and well-being are human rights.

This argument for human rights has avoided the problem of how rights can be logically derived from facts. For, in proceeding by the dialectically necessary method, it has remained throughout within the facts of agents' necessary judgments about goods and rights. The argument has established not that persons have rights *tout court* but rather that all agents logically must claim or at least accept that they have certain rights. This relativity to agents and their claims does not, however, remove the absoluteness of rights or the categoricalness of the *PGC*. For since agency is the proximate general context of all morality and indeed of all practice, whatever is necessarily justified within the context of agency is also necessary for morality, and what logically must be accepted by every agent is necessarily justified within the context of agency. Thus, the argument has established that since every agent logically must accept that he has rights to freedom and well-being, the having of these rights is morally necessary. Hence, the requirement indicated above is fulfilled: the rights to freedom and well-being exist as human rights because there is a valid moral criterion, the *PGC*, which justifies that all humans have these rights.

Questions may be raised about the extent to which the generic rights as I have defined them are indeed human rights. To be human rights they must be had by every human being simply as such. The generic rights, however, are rights to the necessary conditions of agency. But may not some humans lack these rights because they are incapable of agency in one degree or another? Examples of such humans include children, mentally deficient persons, paraplegics, persons with brain damage, fetuses, and so forth. From these examples it might seem to follow that the generic rights to the necessary conditions of action are not truly human rights in the sense in which such rights were initially defined.

This question rests in part on a variant of the dictum that "ought" implies "can," for it assumes that for some person A to have a right to something X, A must be capable of having or doing X. Now this assumption is correct, but only if the capability in question is correctly interpreted. All normal adult humans are fully capable of action as this has been interpreted here, as voluntary and purposive behavior, for all such persons have the proximate ability to control their behavior by their unforced choice with a view to attaining their goals while having knowledge of relevant circumstances. This description applies even to paraplegics, despite the lesser range of the control of which they are proximately capable, for they can think, choose (although within narrower limits), and plan.

In the other cases mentioned, the capabilities for action are less, and hence their rights too are proportionately less. Children are potential agents in that, with normal maturation, they will develop the full abilities of agency. In their case, as well as in that of mentally deficient persons and persons with brain damage, their possession of the generic rights must be proportional to the degree to which they have the abilities of agency, and this must be with a view to taking on the fullest degree of the generic rights of which they are capable so long as this does not result in harm to themselves or others. All other adult humans have the generic rights in full. In the case of the human fetus, this raises problems of the justification of abortion because of possible conflicts with the rights of the mother; I have considered this elsewhere.[9]

The equation of the generic rights with human rights thus does not derogate from the universality of the latter. It enables us to understand the varying degrees to which the rights are had by certain humans, as well as the connection of human rights with action and practice. The derivation of these rights from the argument for the *PGC* also enables us to understand the traditional view that human rights are grounded in reason so that they have a normative necessity or categorical obligatoriness that goes beyond the variable contents of social customs or positive laws.

IV

There remain two broad questions about human rights as so far delineated. First, the rights to freedom and well-being are very general. What more specific contents do they have, and how are these contents related to one another? Second, human rights are often thought of in terms of political effectuation and legal enforcement. How does this relation operate in the case of the generic rights? Should all of them be legally enforced or only some, and how is this to be determined?

To answer the first question we must analyze the components of well-being and of freedom. It was noted above that well-being, viewed as the abilities and conditions required for agency, comprises three kinds of goods: basic, nonsubtractive, and additive. Basic goods are the essential preconditions of action, such as life, physical integrity, and mental equilibrium. Thus, a person's basic rights—his rights to basic goods—are violated when he is killed, starved, physically incapacitated, terrorized, or subjected to mentally deranging drugs. The basic rights are also violated in such cases as where a person is drowning or starving and another person who, at no comparable cost to himself, could rescue him or give him food knowingly fails to do so.

Nonsubtractive goods are the abilities and conditions required for maintaining undiminished one's level of purpose-fulfillment and one's capabilities for particular actions. A person's nonsubtractive rights are violated when he is adversely affected in his abilities to plan for the future, to have knowledge of facts relevant to his projected actions, to utilize his resources to fulfill his wants, and so forth. Ways of undergoing such adversities include being lied to, cheated, stolen from, or defamed; suffering broken promises; or being subjected to dangerous, degrading, or excessively debilitating conditions of physical labor or housing or other strategic situations of life when resources are available for improvement.

Additive goods are the abilities and conditions required for increasing one's level of purpose-fulfillment and one's capabilities for particular actions. A person's additive rights are violated when his self-esteem is attacked, when he is denied education to the limits of his capacities, or when he is discriminated against on grounds of race, religion, or nationality. This right is also violated when a person's development of the self-regarding virtues of courage, temperance, and prudence is hindered by actions that promote a climate of fear and oppression, or that encourage the spread of physically or mentally harmful practices such as excessive use of drugs, or that contribute to misinformation, ignorance, and superstition, especially as these bear on persons' ability to act effectively in pursuit of their purposes. When a person's right to basic well-being is violated, I shall say that he undergoes basic harm; when his rights to nonsubtractive or additive well-being are violated, I shall say that he undergoes specific harm.

Besides these three components of the right to well-being, the human rights also include the right to freedom. This consists in a person's controlling his actions and his participation in transactions by his own unforced choice or consent and with knowledge of relevant circumstances, so that his behavior is neither compelled nor prevented by the actions of other persons. Hence, a person's right to freedom is violated if he is subjected to violence, coercion, deception, or any other procedures that attack or remove his informed control of his behavior by his own unforced choice. This right includes having a sphere of personal autonomy and privacy whereby one is let alone by others unless and until he unforcedly consents to undergo their action.

In general, whenever a person violates any of these rights to well-being or freedom, his action is morally wrong and he contradicts himself. For he is in the position of saying or holding that a right he necessarily claims for himself insofar as he is a prospective purposive agent is not had by some other person, even though the latter, too, is a prospective purposive agent. Hence, all such morally wrong actions are rationally unjustifiable.

It must also be noted, however, that these rights to freedom and well-being may conflict with one another. For example, the right to freedom of one person A may conflict with the right to well-being of another person B when A uses his freedom to kill, rob, or insult B. Here the duty of other persons to refrain from interfering with A's control of his behavior by his unforced choice may conflict with their duty to prevent B from suffering basic or specific harm when they can do so at no comparable cost to themselves. In addition, different persons' rights to well-being may conflict with one another, as when C must lie to D in order to prevent E from being murdered, or when F must break his promise to G in order to save H from drowning. Moreover, a person's right to freedom may conflict with his own right to well-being, as when he commits suicide or ingests harmful drugs. Here the duty of other persons not to interfere with his control of his behavior by his unforced choice may conflict with their duty to prevent his losing basic goods when they can do so at no comparable cost to themselves.

These conflicts show that human rights are only *prima facie*, not absolute, in that under certain circumstances they may justifiably be overridden. Nothing is gained by saying that what is justifiably overridden is not the right but only its exercise. For since a person's having some right has a justificatory basis, when this basis is removed he no longer has the right. In such a case it is his right itself and not only its exercise that is justifiably removed or overridden.

Another argument for the absoluteness of human rights is that their alleged *prima facie* character stems from their being incompletely described. Thus, it is held that the right to life or the right not to be killed, for example, must be specified more fully as the right not to be killed unless one has committed a murder, or as the right of innocent persons not to be killed. Such devices, however, either include in the description of the right the very overriding conditions that are in question, or else they restrict the distribution of the right so that it is not a right of all humans.

But although human rights may be overridden, this still leaves the Principle of Generic Consistency as an absolute or categorically obligatory moral principle. For the *PGC* sets the criteria for the justifiable overriding of one moral right by another and hence for the resolution of conflicts among rights. The basis of these criteria is that the *PGC* is both a formal and a material principle concerned with transactional consistency regarding the possession and use of the necessary conditions of action. The criteria stem from the *PGC*'s central requirement that there must be mutual respect for freedom and well-being among all prospective purposive agents. Departures from this mutual respect are justified only where they are required either to prevent or rectify antecedent departures, or to avoid greater departures, or to comply with social rules that themselves reflect such respect in the ways indicated in the procedural and instrumental applications of the *PGC*. Thus the criteria for resolving conflicts of rights or duties fall under three headings of progressively lesser importance.

The first criterion for resolving the conflicts of rights is the prevention or removal of transactional inconsistency. If one person or group violates or is about to violate the generic rights of another and thereby incurs transactional inconsistency, action to prevent or remove the inconsistency may be justified. Whether the action should always be undertaken depends on such circumstances as the feasibility and importance for subsequent action of removing the inconsistency: this may be very slight in the case of some lies and very great in the case of basic harms. Thus, although the *PGC* in general prohibits coercion and basic harm, it authorizes and even requires these as punishment and for prevention and correction of antecedent basic harm.

This criterion of the prevention of transactional inconsistency sets a limitation on the right to freedom. This right is overridden when a person intends to use his freedom in order to infringe the freedom or well-being of other persons. Such overriding stems from the *PGC*'s general requirement that each person must act in accord with the generic rights of his recipients, since this requirement sets limits on each person's freedom of action. The prohibition against coercion or harm is itself overridden, however, by two considerations, each of which also stems from the *PGC*. First, one person A may coerce or harm another person B in order to prevent B from coercing or harming either A himself or some other person C. Thus if B physically assaults A or C, A may physically assault B in order to resist or prevent the assault. Second, coercion or harm may be justified if it is inflicted in accordance with social rules or institutions that are themselves justified by the *PGC*. I shall discuss this latter justification below.

A second criterion for resolving conflicts of rights is the degree of their necessity for action. Since every person has rights to the necessary conditions of action, one right takes precedence over another if the good that is the object of the former right is more necessary for the possibility of action, and if that right cannot be protected without violating the latter right. For example, A's right not to be lied to is overridden by B's right not to be murdered or enslaved, where B or C has to lie to A in order to prevent him from committing these crimes against B. A person's right to freedom is also overridden in such ways. It will have been noted that whereas the first criterion for resolving conflicts among rights deals mainly with rights to goods of the same degree of importance, the second criterion deals with goods of different degrees, but within the same general context of preventing transactional inconsistency.

This criterion of degrees of necessity for action also applies to such limiting cases as where a person intends to use his freedom in order to attack his own well-being. As we have seen, there are levels of well-being, such that basic well-being is more necessary for action than nonsubtractive well-being, while the latter in turn is usually more necessary for action than additive well-being. Hence, in general, force may be used at least temporarily to prevent a person from killing or maiming himself, especially so long as there is doubt whether he fulfills the emotional and cognitive conditions of freedom or voluntariness. But such interference with someone's freedom is not justified to prevent him from diminishing his nonsubtractive or additive well-being, because his freedom is itself more necessary for his actions than are these levels of his well-being. The remaining complexities of this issue cannot be dealt with here.[10]

V

The conflicts among rights require further criteria besides the two given so far. To deal with these, we must move from the individual, transactional applications of the *PGC* so far considered to its institutional applications. The latter applications will also bring us to the second general question presented above, concerning the legal enforcement and political effectuation of human rights.

Although this legal, institutional context is perhaps the most familiar area of discussion of human rights, it must be emphasized that these rights also figure centrally in individual interpersonal transactions. A person's human rights to freedom and well-being are violated just as surely, although perhaps less powerfully and irrevocably, if he is kidnapped and held for ransom as if he is subjected to unjust imprisonment; and torture by a private person is just as much an infringement of one's human rights as torture by an agent of the state. So, too, although in lesser degrees, a person's human rights are violated when he is lied to, discriminated against, or made to work for starvation wages when better conditions could be made available. Moreover, a large part, although not the whole, of the human rights that should be legally enforced consist in the legal protection of individuals from suffering violations of their most important human rights to just treatment on the part of individuals or groups other than those representing the state.

To deal with the legal context of the protection of human rights, we must turn to another kind of application of the *PGC* besides the one so far considered. The *PGC* has two different kinds of applications: direct and indirect. In the direct applications, the *PGC*'s requirements are imposed on the actions of individual agents; the actions are morally right and the agents fulfill their moral duties when they act in accord with the generic rights of their recipients as well as of themselves. In the indirect applications, on the other hand, the *PGC*'s requirements are imposed in the first instance on social rules and institutions. These are morally right, and persons acting in accordance with them fulfill their moral duties, when the rules and institutions express or serve to protect or foster the equal freedom and well-being of the persons subject to them. Thus, by the indirect applications recipients may even be coerced or harmed, yet this does not violate their human rights to freedom and well-being, because the rules or institutions that require such coercion or harm are themselves justified by the *PGC*. For example, when the umpire in a baseball game calls three strikes, the batter is out and must leave the batter's box even if he does not consent to this. This calling him out operates to coerce the batter so that he is forced to leave the batter's box. Nevertheless, the umpire's action is morally justified and the batter's right to freedom is not violated insofar as he has freely accepted the rules of the game. Or again, a judge who sentences a criminal to prison operates to coerce and harm him, yet this is morally justified and the criminal's rights to freedom and well-being are not violated insofar as the rules of the criminal law serve to protect and restore the mutuality of occurrent nonharm prescribed by the *PGC*.

As these examples may suggest, the indirect, institutional applica-

tions of the *PGC* are of two kinds. The *procedural* applications derive from the *PGC*'s freedom component: they provide that social
rules and institutions are morally right insofar as the persons subject
to them have freely consented to accept them or have certain consensual procedures freely available to them. The *instrumental* applications derive from the *PGC*'s well-being component: they provide that
social rules and institutions are morally right insofar as they operate
to protect and support the well-being of all persons.

Each of these applications, in turn, is of two sorts. The procedural
applications may be either *optional* or *necessary*. They are optional
according as persons consent to form or to participate in voluntary
associations. The procedural applications are necessary according as
the consent they require operates as a general decision procedure using the civil liberties to provide the authoritative basis, through elections and other consensual methods, of specific laws or governmental
officials.

The *PGC*'s instrumental applications may be either *static* or *dynamic*. The static applications, embodied in the minimal state with
its criminal law, serve to protect persons from occurrent violations of
their rights to basic and other important goods and to punish such
violations. The dynamic applications, embodied in the supportive
state, serve to provide longer-range protections of basic and other
rights where these cannot be obtained by persons through their own
efforts.

In the remainder of this chapter I want to indicate how these distinctions of the *PGC*'s indirect applications help to clarify the question of the legal enforcement of human rights. As we have noted, the
institutions of law and government are instrumentally justified by the
PGC as means for enforcing its most important requirements. Not all
the human rights upheld by the *PGC* should receive legal enforcement. The specific harms done by violations of a person's nonsubtractive rights, such as when he is lied to or when a promise made to
him is broken, are ordinarily less important in their impact on their
recipient's well-being than are the harms done by violations of basic
rights, and hence do not justify the state's coercive legal resources to
combat or correct them.

The human rights that should receive legal enforcement are those
comprised in the last three of the indirect applications of the *PGC*
distinguished above. Each of these applications reflects a certain justification of social rules that set requirements for persons and for the
state. First, there is what I have called the static-instrumental justification of social rules, consisting in the criminal law. This serves to

protect basic and other important rights from occurrent attack by
other persons, including the rights to life, physical integrity, and reputation. But the *PGC* also sets standards or limits as to how this protection is to operate: only persons who have violated these rights of
others are to be punished; all persons must be equal before the law;
trials must be fair; *habeas corpus* must be guaranteed; punishment
must not be cruel, vindictive, or inhuman.

Second, there is the dynamic-instrumental justification of social
rules. This recognizes that persons are dispositionally unequal in
their actual ability to attain and protect their generic rights, especially their rights to basic well-being, and it provides for social rules
that serve to remove this inequality. Thus, where the static phase (the
criminal law) tries to restore an occurrent antecedent status quo of
mutual nonharm, the dynamic phase tries to move toward a new situation in which a previously nonexistent dispositional equality is attained or more closely approximated. Social rules supporting the various components of well-being, but especially basic well-being, are
justified in this dynamic way.

These supportive rules must have several kinds of contents. First,
they must provide for supplying basic goods, such as food and housing, to those persons who cannot obtain them by their own efforts.
Second, they must try to rectify inequalities of additive well-being by
improving the capabilities for productive work of persons who are deficient in this respect. Education is a prime means of such improvement, but also important is whatever strengthens family life and enables parents to give constructive, intelligent, loving nurture to their
children. The wider diffusion of such means is a prime component of
increasing equality of opportunity. Third, the rules must provide for
various public goods that, while helping all the members of the society, serve to increase the opportunities for productive employment.
Fourth, the rules must regulate certain important conditions of well-
being by removing dangerous or degrading conditions of work and
housing.

A third area of legal enforcement of human rights is found in what
I have called the necessary-procedural justification of social rules.
This justification is an application of the *PGC*'s freedom component
to the constitutional structure of the state. It provides that laws and
state officials must be designated by procedures that use the *method
of consent*. This method consists in the availability and use of the
civil liberties in the political process. The objects of these liberties include the actions of speaking, publishing, and associating with
others, so that, as a matter of constitutional requirement, each per-

son is able, if he chooses, to discuss, criticize, and vote for or against the government and to work actively with other persons or groups of various sizes to further his political objectives, including the redress of his socially based grievances. In this way each person has the right to participate actively in the political process.

The civil liberties also extend to contexts of individual and social activity other than the political process. The *PGC*'s protection of the right to freedom requires each person be left free to engage in any action or transaction according to his unforced choice so long as he does not coerce or harm other persons. This requirement sets an important limit on the legitimate powers of the state: it must not interfere with the freedom of the individual except to prevent his coercing or harming others in ways that adversely affect their basic or other important well-being. The criteria of this importance are found in what affects persons' having the abilities and conditions required for purposive action. Thus, an immense array of kinds of action must be exempted from governmental control, while at the same time the freedom to perform these actions must be protected by the state.

These freedoms are hence called "civil liberties" for three interconnected reasons, bearing on three different relations the freedoms must have to the state. First, they are passive and negative in that they must not be restricted or interfered with by the state. Second, they are passive and positive in that they must be protected by the state as rights of persons. Third, they are active in that the actions that are their objects function in the political process to help determine who shall govern in the state. In all relations, the *PGC* requires that the civil liberties pertain equally to each prospective purposive agent (except criminals): each person has an equal right to use his freedom noncoercively and nonharmfully (according to the criteria of harm specified above), to participate freely and actively in the political process, and to be protected by the state in that participation and in his other actions using his freedom in the way just indicated. Insofar as there are diverse states, this equal right pertains to each citizen, and each person has a right to be a citizen of a state having the civil liberties.

We have now seen that the *PGC*'s indirect applications require that three kinds of rights receive legal enforcement and protection: the personal-security rights protected by the criminal law, the social and economic rights protected by the supportive state, and the political and civil rights and liberties protected by the Constitution with its method of consent.

The second of these kinds comprises important phases of the right to well-being, the third encompasses a large part of the right to freedom. I wish to conclude by considering two opposite extreme views about how the social and economic rights figure in the legal enforcement and protection of human rights.

One view is that these rights, including the right to be given food and the other goods needed for alleviating severe economic handicaps and insecurities, cannot be "human" rights because they do not meet two tests: universality and practicability.[11] According to the test of universality, for a moral right to be a human one it must be a right of all persons against all persons: all persons must have the strict duty of acting in accord with the right, and all persons must have the strict right to be treated in the appropriate way. Thus, all persons must be both the agents and the recipients of the modes of action required by the right. This test is passed by the rights to life and to freedom of movement: everyone has the duty to refrain from killing other persons and from interfering with their movements, and everyone has the right to have his life and his freedom of movement respected by other persons. But in the case of the right to be relieved from starvation or severe economic deprivation, it is objected that only some persons have the right: those who are threatened by starvation or deprivation; and only some persons have the duty: those who are able to prevent or relieve this starvation by giving aid.

The answer to this objection need not concede that this right, like other economic and social rights, is universal only in a "weaker" sense in that whereas all persons have the right to be rescued from starvation or deprivation, only some persons have the correlative duty. Within the limits of practicability, all persons have the right and all have the duty. For all persons come under the protection and the requirements of the *PGC* insofar as they are prospective purposive agents. Hence, all the generic rights upheld by the *PGC* have the universality required for being human rights.

It is, indeed, logically impossible that each person be at the same time both the rescuer and the rescued, both the affluent provider and the deprived pauper. Nevertheless, the fact that some prospective purposive agent may not at some time need to be rescued from deprivation or be able to rescue others from deprivation does not remove the facts that he has the right to be rescued when he has the need and that he has the duty to rescue when he has the ability and when other relevant conditions are met. This duty stems, in the way indicated earlier, from the claim he necessarily makes or accepts that he has the generic rights by virtue of being a prospective purposive agent. The universality of a right is not a matter of everyone's actually having the related need, nor is it a matter of everyone's actually fulfilling the correlative duty, let alone of his doing so at all times. Nor is it even a matter of everyone's always being able to fulfill the duty. It is rather a matter of everyone's always having, as a matter of principle, the right to be treated in the appropriate way when he has the need, and the duty to act in accord with the right when the circumstances arise that require such action and when he then has the ability to do so, this ability including consideration of cost to himself.

When it is said that the right to be relieved from economic deprivation and the correlative duty pertain to all persons insofar as they are prospective purposive agents, this does not violate the condition that for human rights to be had one must only be human, as against fulfilling some more restrictive description. As was indicated earlier, all normal humans are prospective purposive agents; the point of introducing this description is only to call attention to the aspect of being human that most directly generates the rights to freedom and well-being. In this regard, the right in question differs from rights that pertain to persons not simply by virtue of being prospective purposive agents but only in some more restricted capacity, such as being teachers as against students, umpires as against batters, or judges as against defendants. The universality of human rights derives from their direct connection with the necessary conditions of action, as against the more restrictive objects with which nongeneric rights are connected. And since both the affluent and the economically deprived are prospective purposive agents, the latter's right to be helped by the former is a human right.

These considerations also apply to the contention that the social and economic rights are not human rights because they do not pass the test of practicability, in that many nations lack the economic means to fulfill these rights. Now, it is indeed the case that whereas the political and civil rights may require nonaction or noninterference rather than positive action on the part of governments, the economic rights require the positive use of economic resources for their effective implementation. This does not, however, militate against governments' taking steps to provide support, to the extent of their available resources, to persons who cannot attain basic economic goods by their own efforts. There is a considerable distance between the position that the same high levels of economic well-being are not attainable in all countries and the position that a more equitable distribution of goods and of means of producing goods is not feasible for countries at the lower end of the scale.

This point is also relevant to a view that stands at the opposite extreme from the one just considered: that for most persons in many parts of the world the social and economic rights are the only human rights that should be legally implemented. According to this view, the political and civil rights, by contrast, are of little importance for persons in the Third World with its predominant illiteracy, traditionalism, poverty, nonindividualist ethos, and lack of regard for the rule of law. This position is epitomized in the dictum, "Food first, freedom later," where the "freedom" in question consists especially in the political and civil liberties. The contention is that until the economic rights to subsistence, housing, and employment are effectively implemented, persons who lack these have little interest or opportunity or need for the political and civil rights and that fulfillment of the former rights is a necessary prerequisite for fulfilling the latter.

A distinction may be drawn between such personal-security rights as *habeas corpus* and noninfliction of torture or cruel punishment, and the political rights of the method of consent with its civil liberties of speech, press, and association. Nevertheless, the latter provide important safeguards for the former. Both these kinds of rights, in turn, are far from being antithetical to, or needless for, the economic and social rights. Indeed, the order of priority may be the reverse of that upheld in the view under consideration. The effective distribution of the civil liberties, far from being a passive effect of the proper distribution of food, housing, and health care, can strongly facilitate the latter distribution. When governments are not subject to the political process of the method of consent, there is to that extent less assurance that the authorities will be responsive to the material needs of all their citizens. As is shown by sad experience in many of the underdeveloped countries, the lack of effective political participation by the masses of the poor permits a drastic unconcern with their needs for food even when it is locally available. [12]

What I have tried to show in this essay is that all the human rights have a rational foundation in the necessary conditions or needs of human action, so that no human agent can deny or violate them except on pain of self-contradiction. Thus, the demands the human rights make on persons are justified by the *PGC* as the supreme principle of morality. It is also through the moral requirements set by this principle that the political and legal order receives its central justification as providing for the protection of human rights. In addition to this instrumental function, possession of the civil liberties together with the effective capacity for participating in the method of consent is required for the dignity and rational autonomy of every prospective purposive agent. Thus, the rationally grounded requirements of human action provide the basis and content of all human rights, both those that apply in individual transactions and those that must be protected by social rules and institutions.

NOTES

1. See W. N. Hohfeld, *Fundamental Legal Conceptions* (New Haven: Yale University Press, 1919); John Salmond, *Jurisprudence,* 10th ed. (London: Sweet and Maxwell, 1947), pp. 229 ff.
2. Robert Nozick, *Anarchy, State and Utopia* (New York: Basic Books, 1974), p. ix.
3. See H. L. A. Hart, "Are There Any Natural Rights?" *Philosophical Review,* 64 (1955): 175 ff.
4. See H. J. McCloskey, "Rights," *Philosophical Quarterly,* 15 (1965): 124. Elsewhere, McCloskey holds that persons have a *prima facie* right to the satisfaction of needs: "Human Needs, Rights and Political Values," *American Philosophical Quarterly,* 13 (1976): 9-10.
5. See Jacques Maritain, *The Rights of Man and Natural Law* (London: Geoffrey Bles, 1944).
6. John Rawls, *A Theory of Justice* (Cambridge, Mass.: Harvard University Press, 1971), chaps. 2, 3.
7. See Alan Gewirth, *Reason and Morality* (Chicago: The University of Chicago Press, 1978), chap. 2.
8. Ibid., pp. 82-103.
9. Ibid., pp. 142-144.
10. See ibid., pp. 259-267.
11. See Maurice Cranston, *What Are Human Rights?* (London: Bodley Head, 1963), pp. 66 ff. See also his contribution to D. D. Raphael, ed., *Political Theory and the Rights of Man* (London: Macmillan, 1967), pp. 96 ff. For the "weaker" sense of the universality of rights referred to below, see Raphael in *Political Theory and the Rights of Man,* pp. 65 ff., 112.
12. See Thomas T. Poleman, "World Food: A Perspective," *Science,* 188 (1975): 515; Pierre R. Crosson, "Institutional Obstacles to World Food Production," ibid., pp. 522, 523; Harry Walters, "Difficult Issues Underlying Food Problems," ibid., p. 530; Gunnar Myrdal, *Asian Drama: An Inquiry in the Poverty of Nations* (New York: Twentieth Century Fund, 1969), vol. II, pp. 895-899; S. Reutlinger and M. Selowsky, *Malnutrition and Poverty* (Baltimore: The Johns Hopkins University Press, 1976).

ADDENDUM:
REPLIES TO SOME CRITICISMS

The foregoing essay was published originally in *Nomos XXIII: Human Rights,* where it was followed by three sets of comments, by Richard B. Friedman, Martin P. Golding, and Arval A. Morris.[1] Because the issues raised by these comments are of considerable importance, I have thought it worthwhile to present the following response.

In my essay and more fully in *Reason and Morality,* I have argued that every actual or prospective agent must hold, on pain of contradiction, that he has rights to freedom and well-being because these are the necessary conditions of his action and of his successful action in general. The rights are, so far, prudential, not moral, in that the justifying ground on the basis of which the agent claims them for himself consists in his own agency-needs as required for his pursuit of his own purposes. Only through a subsequent step do the rights become moral, where a "moral" judgment or claim is defined as one whose maker is concerned to uphold not only his own interests but those of other persons as well. This further step is accomplished by showing, through the principle of universalizability, that the agent must admit that all other prospective agents have the rights he claims for himself.

For convenience of reference, I shall here present a brief restatement of my main argument for the thesis that every agent must hold that he has prudential rights to freedom and well-being.[2] As an agent, he regards the purposes for which he acts as good on whatever criteria (not necessarily moral ones) are involved in his purposes. Hence, he must regard his freedom and well-being, the necessary conditions of his acting for purposes, as necessary goods, so that he implicitly accepts (1) "I must have freedom and well-being" (where this "must" is practical-prescriptive and not merely a dispassionate means-end locution). Now suppose the agent were to deny or reject for himself the statement (2) "I have rights to freedom and well-being." Then, because of the correlativity of rights and strict "oughts," he would also have to deny (3) "All other persons ought at least to refrain from removing or interfering with my freedom and well-being." By virtue of denying (3), the agent would have to accept (4) "It is not the case that all other persons ought at least to refrain from removing or interfering with my freedom and well-being." Hence he would also have to accept (5) "Other persons may (i.e., It is permissible that other persons) remove or interfere with my freedom and well-being." And by virtue of accepting (5), the agent would have to accept (6) "I may not (i.e., It is permissible that I not) have freedom and well-being." But (6) contradicts (1). Since every agent must accept (1), he must reject (6). And since (6) is entailed by the denial of (2), it follows that every agent must reject that denial; so that he must accept (2) "I have rights to freedom and well-being."

Professor Golding presents two main objections to this argument. First, he holds that the very idea of a prudential right does not make sense; he says, "I must confess I haven't grasped" what the term means (p. 169). Now I find this somewhat surprising. At least since Kant (if not Hobbes and Plato) the idea of a prudential "ought" has been familiar in philosophy. It signifies the requirements a person must fulfill (or thinks he must fulfill) with a view to furthering his own self-interest or achieving his own purposes. Such an "ought" is prudential because its justificatory basis or criterion is prudential, consisting in the person's self-interest or in his achieving his own purposes. Why, then, shouldn't this also be the case with the term "a right" (used in the substantive rather than the adjectival sense)? A prudential right, then, is, or is set forth as, a justified claim or entitlement whose justificatory basis or criterion is likewise prudential, in that it is based on a person's furthering his own self-interest or the conditions of his fulfilling his own purposes. It is in this sense that I have held that every agent must hold that he has prudential rights, i.e., rights to have the necessary conditions of agency. He bases this claim on his own agency-needs, not on the needs or purposes of other persons, including the persons to whom he addresses his right-claim.

It is indeed the case that right-claims imply demands or requirements on other persons that they at least not interfere with the claimant's having the objects to which he claims a right. But this is also true of prudential "oughts"; in fact, because these *are* requirements that are based on the speaker's own self-interest or his pursuit of his own purposes, they also imply demands on his part that other persons at least not interfere. In this regard, prudential "oughts" uttered by some person on his own behalf are at least partially correlative with prudential right-claims.

That this concept of a prudential right makes perfectly good sense can be seen in several other related ways. It is well known that there are legal rights as well as moral ones, the initial difference between these being that they are grounded, respectively, in legal and moral justificatory bases or criteria. And as I have shown in some detail, there are also intellectual or logical rights grounded in intellectual or logical justificatory bases or criteria (*Reason and Morality,* pp. 69–71). Hence, since prudence—the agent's self-interest or pursuit of his own purposes as such—is a quite distinct basis of normative discourse and valuation, it also provides a distinct justificatory basis of rights and right-claims. This is not to say that all such rights are conclusively valid or definitive, any more than legal rights are. But there are at least prudential right-*claims,* in that prospective agents hold that they are entitled at least to noninterference with the necessary conditions of their agency. In all these different contexts, moreover, the expression "a right" is not equivocal, any more than the word "good" is equivocal when it is applied with different criteria to different kinds of objects. In each case the rights in question are, in Hohfeld's classification, claim-rights in that they are, or are set forth as, justified claims or entitlements entailing correlative duties to forbear or assist.

A further reason why the concept of a prudential right should not provoke in Golding the shock of nonrecognition is that many of the traditional objections to rights-talk (and hence to the concept of a right) have been based on the view that rights as standardly asserted or claimed are egoistic or self-centered. Thus Marx wrote:

> the so-called rights of man . . . are simply the rights of a member of civil society, that is, of egoistic man, of man separated from other men and from the community . . . . None of the supposed rights of man, therefore, go beyond the egoistic man, man as he is, as a member of civil society; that is, an individual separated from the community, withdrawn into himself, wholly preoccupied with his private interest and acting in accord with his private caprice.[3]

While there is much in this criticism that I do not accept, it shows that at least the *concept* of prudential rights, of rights as being founded on self-interest or the agent's pursuit of his own purposes, is far from novel.

A very large part of Golding's failure to understand the concept of a prudential right stems from his apparent belief that all rights are moral ones. He correctly notes that the starting point of my argument is morally neutral, so that it applies to all agents, including, as he puts it, "the prudent, self-interested agent who is a rational amoralist" (p. 167). From this Golding concludes that the prudent amoralist "does not use" such terms as "rights": "the term 'a right' does not occur in his basic language. The amoralist, so to speak, does not play in the moral ballpark" (pp. 167–68). The error Golding makes here is that of thinking that the concept of rights occurs only "in the moral ballpark." Strictly interpreted, this would rule out not only legal rights (which differ in important respects from moral ones) but also intellectual and prudential rights. He does not see that prudence also supplies, at least for each prudent agent (including the amoralist), a justificatory (although not moral) basis or criterion on which the agent may set forth various right-claims.

Golding says that, "before the prudent amoralist can begin to speak the language of rights at all," a certain addition is required: an appeal to "mutual cooperation and mutual undertakings" (p. 169). He gives as an example a case where "a group of prudent amoralists want to accomplish a task that requires their mutual cooperation" (p. 168) and, therefore, "agree" on certain rules on the basis of which they claim "rights." But Golding is simply mistaken if he thinks that explicit or even tacit agreement on rules or other normative considerations is a necessary condition for the assertion of rights. As I have shown in some detail in *Reason and Morality* (pp. 74–75), right-claims may be addressed to persons with whom one has, or has made, no such agreements. Familiar examples are the claims of rights made by slaves against their masters, the claims made by South African blacks against the exponents of apartheid, and so forth. The whole modern and contemporary drive for human rights in countries whose rulers disavow or violate them is proof that "mutual cooperation and mutual undertakings" are far from being necessary conditions of the intelligibility of right-claims.

In my discussion of the argument presented above (beginning with the agent's regarding his freedom and well-being as necessary goods and ending with his holding that he has rights to them), I gave three reasons why the argument is valid only when it proceeds by the dialectically necessary method, whereby the agent uses first-person discourse from within his own conative standpoint in purposive action. Golding maintains that none of these three reasons succeeds in establishing that the prudential amoral agent must use rights-language or claim rights for himself. But here, too, Golding is mistaken, largely from the same cause as before: that he confines all rights to moral ones.

I shall take up each of the three points in turn. First, when the agent says, "My freedom and well-being are necessary goods," this statement of his is prescriptive in that "it carries *his* advocacy or endorsement" (p. 49; emphasis added); that is, he is advocating that *he* have freedom and well-being. On this point, Golding says that he does not see how this statement "prescribes anything *for someone else*. Does the agent have a 'moral gun' in his recipient's back?" (p. 170; emphasis added). Here, Golding makes two false assumptions: that all prescriptive language must be "moral" and that it must always prescribe "*for* someone else" besides the speaker. In the first instance, the agent is advocating for himself. He is also prescribing *to* other persons. But there is this difference between prescribing *to* and prescribing *for* other persons: the latter, unlike the former, suggests that the other persons recognize or accept the prescription, or rules on which the prescription is based, or at least the authority of the prescriber. This is indicated by Golding's example of the patron in a restaurant telling the waiter he wants a cup of coffee (p. 170). But when the agent advocates his having freedom and well-being and hence prescribes *to* other persons that they at least not interfere with his having these necessary goods, he is not necessarily assuming that the other persons will accept his demand or the normative rules on which it is based, any more than slaves who claim the right to freedom necessarily assume that their masters will recognize their authority to make the claim. All the agent can strictly assume is that the other persons also accept the criteria of deductive and inductive reasoning and that, as prospective agents, they have the same general conative motivations as characterize all agents. Hence, they are capable of understanding and respecting his prudential right-claim; but there is, so far, no assurance that they will in fact comply with it (see *Reason and Morality*, pp. 74–75). Further steps are needed for this purpose.

Second, when I say that the agent's statement about the necessary goods must imply a claim on his part against other persons, Golding objects that this would constitute "an abandonment of moral neutrality by the amoralist," so that his demand that other persons not interfere with his freedom and well-being "is not a claim being made as a matter of right" (p. 171). This objection is incorrect, because the right-claim the agent makes against other persons is not yet a *moral* one, so that, in making it, he does not abandon moral neutrality.

The third point at issue here concerns my contention that the agent, by virtue of holding that freedom and well-being are necessary goods for him, must hold that these goods are due to him, so that he is entitled to them from within his own conative standpoint in purposive agency. Since Golding recognizes no standpoint for right-claims other than a moral one, he says: "I frankly am at a loss to understand what 'due to' could possibly mean here. I cannot see how any entitlement enters into the picture, even on—and perhaps especially on—a prudential criterion" (p. 171). Golding is unaware that prudential criteria as well as moral criteria may serve to ground right-claims. The agent's prudential standpoint in purposive action provides for him a ground of entitlement such that, from within this standpoint, he regards as his due whatever is required for his being an agent (see *Reason and Morality*, pp. 68–73). It is simply arbitrary to reject such a prudential basis as a ground for right-claims and to hold that they are confined to moral criteria, just as it would be obviously false to hold this in the case of "oughts."

I turn now to Golding's second main objection to my argument. This objection is made in two parts. First, in my argument as spelled out above, he holds that "it is far from certain" that step (6) ("I may not have freedom and well-being") "really does contradict" step (1) ("I must have freedom and well-being").[4] His reason for doubting that I have established a genuine contradiction, as my argument requires, is that the "must" in (1) is "a nonnormative 'must,'" while the "may" in (6) is "the normative 'may' of moral license" (p. 172). But here Golding is wrong on both counts. The "must" in (1) is normative: it sets forth a practical requirement which the agent endorses because of his conative attachment to the generic features of his action (see *Reason and Morality*, p. 79). It is irrelevant to say, as Golding does, that this "must" "is hardly prescriptive *for* some other person"; rather, it is prescriptive *to* other persons, in that it sets forth a requirement at least of other persons' noninterference with the agent's freedom and well-being. And the "may not" in (6) is also normative, but it is not the "may" of "*moral* license"; rather it sets forth as permissible the precise negation of what (1) sets forth as normatively necessary or mandatory. Its criterion is prudential, not moral. Indeed, as is required if (1) and (6) are to contradict each other, the criteria of the "must" and the "may" are the same, consisting in the agent's own requirements for agency (see *Reason and Morality,* p. 81).

In the other part of his second main objection, Professor Golding makes a very acute point. He distinguishes between strong and weak denials of a right-claim, where a weak denial does not entail "that some other rights-claim or normative claim is true" (p. 172). He then says that when the agent denies (2) "I have rights to freedom and well-being" and hence also denies (3) "All other persons ought at least to refrain from removing or interfering with my freedom and well-being," he is not thereby logically required to accept (4) "It is not the case that all other persons ought at least to refrain from removing or interfering with my freedom and well-being." For, Golding holds, the prudent amoralist agent should be construed as at most making a weak denial of (2), so that he is not logically committed to accept (4). Indeed, "the prudent amoralist neither asserts nor denies any rights-claim ... because the terminology of 'rights' is not part of his vocabulary" (p. 173).

The first thing I want to say about this objection is that it is precisely the same one I presented against myself in *Reason and Morality* (p. 89):

> This objection is that the agent need make no right-claim or "ought"-judgment at all, either positive or negative. He need not accept either statement (3) given above or its negation (4), for he might be an amoralist who disavows for himself all uses of moral or deontic concepts. Thus, in refusing to assert such a judgment as (2) "I have rights to freedom and well-being" and hence also (3) "All other persons ought at least to refrain from interfering with my freedom and well-being," the amoralist agent would not thereby have to accept (4) "It is not the case that all other persons ought at least to refrain from interfering with my freedom and well-being" .... For, as an amoralist, he would deny that concepts like "ought" and "right" have any valid application, at least in his own case .... [Hence, any statement he might make] would not involve him in the contradictions elicited above, for these all depended on the agent's having to accept the negative "ought"-judgment (4).

This objection raises the following very important question: Can a prudent amoralist agent logically dispense with, or reject for himself, all normative concepts, including deontic ones like "ought" and "rights"? It is Golding's affirmative answer to this question that underlies most of his criticisms of my whole argument. His objection, and my own just given, would be conclusive if the answer to this question were indeed affirmative. But, in fact, the answer is negative. I have shown this in some detail in *Reason and Morality* (pp. 89–95),[5] and the reader is invited to consult the extensive argument I have presented there. (Indeed, the whole section entitled "Generic Rights and Right-Claims" [pp. 63–103] deals in detail with the issues discussed in this Addendum.)

I have space here to present only the barest summary of the argument. First, if something Z threatens the prudent amoralist's basic well-being (for example, his life) and he believes both that the necessary and sufficient condition of his avoiding Z is his doing X and that he can do X, then he will accept for himself such a prudential and prescriptive "ought"-judgment as (7) "I ought to do X." He must accept this "ought" for himself because it signifies the practical requirement he must acknowledge because of his commitment to maintaining his basic well-being and hence the necessary condition of his being an agent. He could reject this "ought" only if he were not even minimally rational or conatively normal, but this would contradict the idea that he is a prudent agent. Hence, every agent, even an amoralist, must accept for himself the use of a deontic concept setting forth a practical requirement for his action based on his own prudential purpose.

Now by virtue of his accepting (7), the agent must also accept (8) "I ought to be free to do X." For without at least the negative freedom of absence of interference, he cannot carry out the requirement he has accepted in (7), that he do X. And, because of the meaning of "free," (8) in turn entails (9) "All other persons ought at least to refrain from interfering with my doing X." Hence, the rational amoralist agent must also accept (9). Since, moreover, the sole reason for which he accepts the requirement that he do X is that this is the necessary and sufficient condition of preserving his basic well-being, (9) entails (10) "All other persons ought at least to refrain from interfering with my basic well-being." Here, as before, the "ought"-judgments (9) and (10) are prudential ones because they are concerned to further the interests or purposes not of the subjects of the judgments but rather of the agent who addresses the judgments to those subjects.

In this way, then, I have argued that every agent, including the prudent amoralist, must accept for himself the use of the deontic concept "ought," not only a self-directed one, as in (7), but also other-directed ones, as in (9) and (10). From these, in turn, it follows that he must accept for himself the concept of a right. For in (10) he holds that noninterference with his basic well-being is a requirement whose fulfillment is owed to him by all other persons because such noninterference is necessary to his continuing to be at least a prospective agent capable of achieving his purposes. Although not all "ought"-judgments entail or are correlative with rights-judgments, the correlativity holds when the person making the "ought"-judgment regards it as setting for other persons duties that they owe to him. For when duties are owed to him, he has a right to their performance or to compliance with them. Now this is the way the agent regards the "ought"-judgment that other persons ought at least to refrain from interfering with his basic well-being. For he does not view the judgment as stating merely an obligation that has some general ground not related to himself; rather, the "ought" in question prescribes the fulfillment of what is necessary to his being a purposive agent.

To see how this point logically involves the concepts of "due" and "owed," we must first recall that these concepts are not confined to specific transactions or relationships; they also apply to the sphere of general rights, such as those of freedom and well-being. Also, these concepts, as well as "rights," are not antithetical to the purview even of the prudent amoralist, because their criterion is here prudential, not moral. We must next note that there is a more general reason, deriving from the nature of rights, as to why he must use such deontic concepts. Every claim-right is based on a justifying ground which establishes that the subject's having a certain object is required or mandatory and that, for this reason, other persons have correlative duties which they owe to the subject. Whenever there is such a justifying ground, the concept of a claim-right is logically called for. Now for any agent as such, including the prudent amoralist, there is a justifying ground which consists in the conditions needed for his being an agent, these conditions including, especially, his basic well-being. As long as he is an agent and intends to continue to be one, the necessary conditions of his being an agent constitute for him the justifying ground for requirements whose fulfillment by other persons he must regard as owed to him, because these conditions are constitutive of the very standpoint from which he proceeds as an agent. Hence, every prospective agent must hold or accept that he has a right to these conditions.

It will not do to say that the prudent amoralist agent accepts no justifying grounds. For, as we have seen, he must accept the idea of requirements both on his own actions and on those of other persons so long as he is even minimally rational and conatively normal. And the idea of a requirement logically involves the idea of a justifying ground as the basis of the requirement.

What follows from this point is that there is a strict "ought," in the sense of what is due or owed, in the prudent amoralist's statement (10) "All other persons ought at least to refrain from interfering with my basic well-being." Hence, (10) entails (11) "I have a right to basic well-being."

This is, of course, an essential part of (2) "I have rights to freedom and well-being." That the prudent amoralist logically must accept the remainder of (2) can be shown by the same sorts of arguments as led to his having to accept (11). Thus even an amoralist must accept that he has prudential rights to freedom and well-being.

What I have tried to establish by this argument, then, is that the prudent amoralist logically cannot dispense with, or reject for himself, all normative concepts, and, more specifically, he cannot dispense with deontic concepts like "ought" and "rights," because he must use these concepts to express the requirements—justified from his prudential standpoint—that must be satisfied if he is to fulfill his own needs of purposive agency. In all this he remains, so far, within his own prudential context; he can use these concepts without having to accept moral criteria. This disposes of the remainder of Golding's objection.

Both Richard Friedman and Arval Morris raise questions about the equal distribution of human rights according to my theory and its Principle of Generic Consistency. Friedman contends that I have not shown why a rational prudent agent "*must* stake his claim to rights to freedom and well-being on the ground of their necessity" as against "a wide variety of possible and indeed well-known grounds for rights," including "individual merit or desert" (pp. 152–53)—grounds that would logically support an unequal rather than equal distribution of rights. And Morris similarly asserts that I am "committed to an elitist conception of human rights," first, because my theory assigns rights not simply to all "humans" as such but rather to "persons" who are agents, and, second, because it holds "that the degree of human agency present in a human being at any given time determines the number and character of human rights that the human being has at that time" (pp. 160, 161).

I have dealt with this question in considerable detail in *Reason and Morality,* in the whole section entitled "The Criterion of Relevant Similarities" (pp. 104–28), and, much more briefly, in "The Basis and Content of Human Rights" (above, pp. 51–52, 54–55). Friedman is mistaken when he says that I have not shown why a rational agent must base his claim to the generic rights "on the ground of their necessity." Although he does not explain the meaning of this phrase, I assume he is referring to characteristics that necessarily belong to all agents equally, as against more specific, unequally distributed characteristics that are not necessarily had by all agents. In "The Basis and Content of Human Rights" (above, p. 51), I wrote: "There is one, and only one, ground that every agent logically must accept as the sufficient justifying condition for having the generic rights, namely, that he is a prospective agent who has purposes he wants to fulfill." The reason for this is that if the agent were to hold the position that he has these rights only for some more restrictive reason R (such as merit, race, or profession), then he would contradict himself. For, according to this position, if the agent were to lack R, he would have to accept for himself, ''I do not have the generic rights''; but it has previously been shown that every agent *must* accept for himself, ''I have the generic rights.'' Since this latter statement logically must be accepted for himself by every agent, he can avoid contradicting himself only by giving up the position that his rights are grounded on some criterion R that is more restrictive than his simply being a prospective purposive agent. And since this latter characteristic belongs equally to all agents, the distribution of the generic rights that follows from it is likewise an equal one.

Although it is true, as Morris points out, that humans differ in their abilities of agency, this does not entail an unequal distribution of the generic rights. For the ground on which each agent claims the generic rights for himself is not simply that he has the abilities of agency but, rather, that he is a prospective agent who has purposes he wants to fulfill; and this ''is an absolute quality, not varying in degree'' (*Reason and Morality*, p. 123).

> It is not the generic features or abilities of action as a whole that directly lead an agent to hold that he has rights to freedom and well-being; it is rather that aspect of the features or abilities whereby he pursues purposes he regards as good . . . . In relation to the justification for having the generic rights, then, being an agent is an absolute or noncomparative condition. Wherever there is an agent—a person who controls or can control his behavior by his unforced choice with knowledge of relevant circumstances in pursuit of purposes he regards as good—there is an implicit claim to have the generic rights. This claim on the part of the agent is not affected by degrees of practical ability or agency. [Ibid., p. 124]

While tragically afflicted persons like Karen Anne Quinlan do indeed have a marked decrease in the generic rights because of their total lack of the abilities of agency, and there is a similar proportionality for mentally deficient persons, who do not have the abilities of agency to the extent indicated in my above definition of an agent, such proportionality or degrees of having the generic rights do not pertain to persons who fulfill the above definition. The definition, and hence the characteristic of being an actual or prospective agent, applies to all normal humans, i.e., persons who can control their behavior in the ways indicated. (See also *Reason and Morality*, pp. 140–45.)

Morris also has another objection to my theory, but it is based on the mistaken view that, according to my argument, given above, the agent holds that his claim to the generic rights is "morally justified" (p. 164). As I have emphasized in my reply to Golding, however, the agent adduces only prudential, not moral, grounds for his right-claim. The moral justification for human rights occurs only in the subsequent step, when the agent recognizes that the ground on which he claims the rights for himself also applies to all other prospective agents. I have discussed this sequence in *Reason and Morality,* pages 145–47.

Notes

1. *Nomos: XXIII: Human Rights,* ed. J. Roland Pennock and John W. Chapman (New York: New York University Press, 1981). Page references in the text, unless otherwise indicated, are to the following essays in this *Nomos* volume: Richard B. Friedman, "The Basis of Human Rights: A Criticism of Gewirth's Theory" (pp. 148–57); Arval A. Morris, "A Differential Theory of Human Rights" (pp. 158–64); Martin P. Golding, "From Prudence to Rights: A Critique" (pp. 165–74).

2. This restatement differs slightly from the argument as presented in "The Basis and Content of Human Rights" (above, p. 50), but the changes make no substantive difference.

3. Karl Marx, "On the Jewish Question," in *The Marx-Engels Reader,* ed. Robert C. Tucker, 2d ed. (New York: W. W. Norton, 1978), pp. 42, 43.

4. In his restatement of my argument Golding uses letters instead of numbers. To bring his restatement into line with my own presentation of the argument, given above, I have changed his letters to the corresponding numbers for the various steps. In the quotation given below, from *Reason and Morality,* page 89, I have also changed the numbers to make the various steps uniform with the version given here.

5. I have also discussed this question in detail elsewhere: "Must One Play the Moral Language Game?" *American Philosophical Quarterly* 7 (1970): 107–18, reprinted here as Essay 2.

2
Must One Play
the Moral Language Game?

The title of this paper may be criticized on the ground (with which I sympathize) that morality is a highly serious matter and hence not a game. Let me point out, then, that the question I am asking may also be put in such ways as these: Must one use (and not merely mention) moral concepts? Must one make any moral judgments at all? Must one act morally, or accept moral obligations, or be moral? To play the moral language game is to use moral concepts in all sincerity and seriousness, and such use involves an acknowledgment by the user that moral concepts apply and ought to apply to his own conduct as well as to that of others. Hence, while it will be advantageous to retain the linguistic emphasis marked by the title, there is no conflict between referring to the "moral language game" and recognizing the seriousness of morality.

I. Analysis of the Question

Three negative views on morality must be distinguished. The *nihilist* holds (whether on extreme positivist or other grounds) that such words as "ought" and "right," at least in moral contexts, are not meaningful at all. The *amoralist*, while granting that such words are meaningful, holds that they have no application, at least in his own case; he denies that there is any valid reason for him to use moral language or to act in accordance with the requirements of any morality. The *moral sceptic*, while admitting that there may well be reasons, even conclusive ones, for using moral language in general and hence for having some morality or other, holds that there is no way to justify any one specific morality as against any other. The amoralist is hence more radical than the moral sceptic, but less so than the nihilist.

While nihilism is an obviously indefensible position, the case is otherwise with the amoralist, and it is to him that my question refers. I am asking whether amoralism can be refuted, that is, whether reasons can be

given which conclusively justify an individual's playing the moral language game and which hence show that it is irrational for him to refrain
from making moral judgments or acting in accordance with any morality
at all. Many contemporary philosophers have given a negative answer to
this question. The following statements are typical:

> There can be no complete non-personal, objective justification for
> acting morally rather than non-morally.[1]
> [A man] may refuse to make any moral judgment at all, even one of
> indifference.... Now it will be obvious that in [this] case there is
> nothing that we can do.... Such a person is not entering the arena of
> moral dispute, and therefore it is impossible to contest with him.[2]
> A man who does not care what happens to other people has no
> reason ... for adopting *any* moral rules.[3]
> For a thoroughly amoral intelligence, nothing in principle can serve
> as a reason for *inducing* him to accept any moral responsibilities.
> Metaphysical elaborations, logical arguments, empirical generaliza-
> tions and data, and, finally, all moral discourse with its lavish,
> complex and ingenious devices of persuasion are wholly inadequate.
> No reasons are possible.[4]
> Put succinctly, using moral language commits me to a moral point
> of view, but nothing commits me to using moral language.... "Is it
> absurd, or self-contradictory, to refuse to consider any issues as what
> they call 'moral issues'?".... When the skeptic's doubts are raised in
> this form, I do not see how they can be quieted.... It follows that
> there is not necessarily any way in which we can *reason* a man into
> thinking morally, or rather into a commitment to *act* morally.[5]

It will have been noted that these statements refer to an *individual's*
using moral language and accepting moral obligations. This is also reflected in the "one" of the title. My question is not whether a society or
group of men must have a morality, but whether an individual must have
or accept any morality, that of his society or any other. Many philosophers, while upholding the Hobbesian answer to the social question, have
confused the issue by assuming that this answer also fits the individual
question. An individual may, however, recognize and even rejoice that his
society has a morality while refusing to accept it or any other for himself.
Such an amoralist need not be refuted by Hobbes's argument that it is
irrational (in the sense of imprudent and appealing to the empirically
improbable) to count on being able to deceive one's fellows. As has been
pointed out by elitists from Callicles to the present (not sharing Hobbes's
de facto egalitarianism), the man of superior strength and cunning may
flout with impunity the rules he upholds for others. Nor can he be convicted of inconsistency on this account; for, so far as has hitherto been

shown, he need not be saying or thinking that other men *ought* to abide by these rules but only, at most, that he *wants* them to do so because it suits his own purposes. There is no contradiction between X's wanting other men to do y because it suits his own purposes and his not wanting to do y himself because this likewise suits his own purposes.

To say that such a person is immoral is, of course, to beg the question, which is whether there is any rational ground for holding that he must himself use such moral concepts with respect to himself. Another line of attack, however, is that the man who has no morality is mentally ill and hence must be put away or given medical treatment rather than be taken seriously as a protagonist of an arguable position. Now it is true that "psychopaths" are sometimes defined in terms of "amoral" behavior.[6] An amoralist need not, however, be a psychopath: he need not be "impulsive" or unable to control his acts in the light of consequences, and in fact he may act both prudently and benevolently. He is similar to the psychopath in not feeling shame, remorse, anxiety, or guilt, but this is not because he is unable to feel these but rather because he regards them as inappropriate or unnecessary.

It may be objected that if the amoralist can decide whether or not to have guilt feelings, then he must be a superman. A similar idea, however, is found in Freud's view of psychoanalytic therapy as aiming to release men from the tyranny of the superego with its guilt feelings introjected from childhood experiences: the mature adult can control these feelings instead of being at their mercy. Indeed, the general point goes back at least to Aristotle's conception of the "self-indulgent" man as one who *chooses* to pursue excessive pleasures and feels no remorse at having done so; and similarly with the "shameless" man (*Nicomachean Ethics,* IV, 9; VII, 7,8). To be sure, there is a difference between occurrent and dispositional choices and controls, between controlling guilt feelings at the very time they might have occurred and the more long-range control over the factors that might lead one to have guilt feelings. Both kinds of control, however, may be attributed to the amoralist. He does not have guilt feelings because he holds that there are no sound reasons for having them.

It is this last feature that gives point to arguing with the amoralist, and it bears on the "must" of my question. The amoralist as I here conceive him (and as is also suggested by the references to "reason" in the last three quotations given above) professes to be guided by reason in that he is prepared to do that for which (logically) good justifying reasons can be given. He accepts the reasons of deductive and inductive logic, including the evidence of empirical facts. But he denies that these reasons justify or require that he make any moral judgments or accept moral obligations;

and he also denies that there is any other "rationality" (including a distinctively moral one) which would rationally justify these things. My question, then, is whether, given the deductive and inductive reasons which the amoralist accepts, he also rationally must, in virtue of accepting these reasons, accept for himself the use of moral language and the corresponding moral obligations. This question is hence not open to the usual charge brought against questions of the "Why should I be moral?" type, that they are circular because their use of "should" already involves accepting moral reasons and hence being moral. The "must" of my question is a logical (deductive and inductive) justificatory "must," not a moral one (nor, of course, a physical one involving force or coercion).

Nor is my question open to the Humean charge that it asks for a (logically impossible) derivation of a "practical" (moral) commitment from the purely "theoretic" reasons of deductive and inductive logic. For the amoralist's commitment to these reasons is practical as well as theoretic: he is already disposed to accept and act upon that to which the weight of deductive and inductive reasons leads; and he is also conatively "normal" in that he has the self-interested motivations common to most men, and is willing to expend the effort needed to fulfill them. (It will be in this morally neutral sense that I use the phrase "rational and normal person" in this paper.) The question, then, is whether, given this rational and conative equipment alone, he must necessarily, despite even an obdurate initial rejection of morality, play the moral language game and accept moral obligations.

But what is meant by "moral" in expressions like "the moral language game"? It must be emphasized that I am using "moral" in the general sense in which it is opposed to "non-moral," not to "immoral." In asking, then, whether the amoralist must play any moral language game at all, we must have some elucidation of the general concept of a morality, a notoriously difficult task. W. K. Frankena has provided a convenient summary of recent attempts at such elucidation. According to this, an individual *X*'s "action-guide" is a moral one or constitutes a morality if and only if it satisfies such criteria as the following:

(A) *X* takes it as prescriptive.
(B) *X* universalizes it.
(C) *X* regards it as definitive, final, over-riding, or supremely authoritative.
(D) It includes or consists of judgments (rules, principles, ideals, etc.) that pronounce actions and agents to be right, wrong, good, bad, etc., simply because of the effect they have on the feelings, interests, ideals, etc., of *other* persons. . . . Here "other" may mean "some other" or "all other."[7]

This list may be criticized on various grounds. Some philosophers have emphasized one or another of these criteria as basic; and it is by no means certain that the five writers quoted above had in mind precisely these criteria of "moral." Since, however, my argument will be less open to charges of undue simplification if it recognizes more rather than fewer requirements as having to be satisfied, I shall adopt the whole list as jointly constituting the criteria of someone's having a morality and using moral language.

II. From "is" to Non-Moral "ought"

The heading of this section must be understood in a second-order rather than a first-order sense. I am not claiming that an "ought"-statement is to be derived from an "is"-statement, but rather that a proposition which says that someone makes an "ought"-statement (or has an "ought"-belief) is entailed by "is"-statements which set forth certain facts about his desires and his other beliefs. Specifically, I shall argue that, given the facts (1) that a rational and normal amoralist X wants to have something y, (2) that he believes that his doing z is a necessary and sufficient means to his having y, (3) that he believes that doing z involves a choice between alternatives and carries a "price" in the sense of some effort and constraint on his part, (4) that he believes that doing z is in his power, and (5) that he does not believe there is any superior counter-consideration to his having y or doing z, it logically follows (6) that he believes that he ought to do z. Note that I say that (6) "logically follows"; I am not merely making a contingent prediction about X's psychology. (6) logically follows from (1)–(5) because the use of an "ought"-statement (or the having of an "ought"-belief) just is the way in which a rational and normal person shows his awareness of the constraints or requirements involved in what he believes he must do to attain something he wants. I am not saying that all "ought"-statements or "ought"-beliefs are of this instrumental sort, but that at least some are.

Let us designate by 'O' statements of the form "I ought to do z." What is it for X to use or say O? Relevant here are two of the previously listed criteria for someone's having a "moral action-guide." First, "X takes it as prescriptive" [criterion (A)]; that is, if X uses O, then he gives an at least *prima facie* endorsement to his doing z and hence regards doing z as a requirement for or constraint on his conduct. Second, X believes that this requirement or constraint is legitimate or valid—in other words, he regards what O expresses as authoritative—in that he believes that there are good or justifying reasons for his doing z. (These need not be *morally* good or justifying reasons.) This latter point is obviously related to criterion (C) above, save that criterion (C) referred to "supremely authoritative." I shall deal with this distinction subsequently.

It is because these features of perscriptiveness and authoritativeness are involved in X's desires and beliefs (1)–(5) listed above that the latter entail his having the "ought"-belief or making the "ought"-statement listed at (6). For since X believes that his doing z is necessary to his having y, which he wants, and he does not believe that there is any superior counter-consideration, he to that extent endorses his doing z, regarding it as a requirement for his conduct justified by reason of his wanting y. For him to regard in this way his doing z is for him to believe that he ought to do z.

This thesis and its accompanying argument may be clarified if we consider some of the objections that may be brought against them.

(a) I seem to be saying that the statement "X believes he ought to do z" is exhaustively derivable from factual statements about X's desires and his other beliefs. But this commits the naturalistic fallacy in one of its familiar forms. Moreover, since the concept of "ought" signifies what goes counter to our inclinations, how can it, or a belief about it, be derived from those very inclinations (or desires)?

(b) Since there is a difference between what one wants and what one ought to want, it is illegitimate to base an "ought"-conclusion on one's wants *per se* and on the means and constraints necessary for their satisfaction. Both the wants themselves and the means to their satisfaction must first be scrutinized to see that they do not conflict with any more pressing obligations.[8]

(c) It is therefore incorrect to say that the factual statements (1)–(5) listed at the beginning of this section entail the statement (6) that "X believes that he *ought* to do z." What they entail is much more modest: either (i) simply that X's doing z is a necessary or sufficient condition of his having y, or (ii) that X wants to do z as a means to his having y, or (iii) that X accepts some such singular imperative as "Let me do z," or (iv) that X says, "So I'll do z," or (v) that X says, "If I'm smart I'll do z."

My answer to *(a)* is that while the concept of "ought" cannot be defined in terms of desires alone, its authoritative and prescriptive features, so far as they enter into a person's "ought"-beliefs, are derivable from the combination of the person's desiring something, his believing that that desire provides a reason or justification for action, and his being aware of the requirements or constraints which the satisfaction of that desire imposes on his other desires and acts. Since the derivation is in part from beliefs about "normative" factors like justificatory reasons and requirements, there is a sense in which it is not naturalistic. In any case, it is false to say that beliefs about the satisfaction of desires or inclinations cannot refer to restraints on or control of other desires. The belief that one ought to go to the dentist is an obvious counter-example.

In answer to *(b)*, it must be recalled that what I am claiming to derive from factual premises about X's wants is not an "ought"-conclusion *tout court* but rather a conclusion that X must have a certain "ought"-belief, given his wants and certain other beliefs of his. It is one thing to say that he must have this "ought"-belief; it is another thing to say that the "ought"-belief is itself justified, all things considered. For the latter statement to be correct, it would be necessary to consider the nature of X's wants and their relation to the wants of other persons. This, however, is not part of my present concern, nor is it necessary to my present argument. It must also be recalled that my derivation of X's "ought"-belief included the statement that "he does not believe there is any superior counter-consideration to his having y or doing z."[9] I used the vague expression "superior counter-consideration" to refer to any factor that might weigh more heavily with X, including any of his other desires or beliefs. Such weighting of factors is, of course, a basic feature of calculative reasoning. Now so far as concerns an amoralist's explicit awareness, these counter-considerations do not include any moral obligations. But it would be incorrect to conclude from this that it is logically illegitimate for him to use the concept of "ought" at all. This concept is neutral as between conflicting practical frameworks; as I shall argue below, it has a common core of meaning both for deontologists and non-deontologists, as well as within moral and nonmoral value systems. In its first-person use "ought" means that the user acknowledges a requirement for or constraint on his conduct, justified by reasons.

This meaning, entailed by statements (1)–(5) listed above, is not conveyed by the proposed substitutes for the "ought"-belief listed under objection *(c)*. Hence those substitutes fail to do justice to the full scope of the statements. (i) The statements present not merely a means-end relationship but reasons for pursuing the means, given that one wants the end. (ii) Nor do the statements imply merely that X wants the means in order to attain the end, as against recognizing that he ought to pursue the means. He may not want the means at all; and even if he does, this is not the same as recognizing the requiredness and constraint involved in there being reasons that justify the sacrifice of his immediate desires. This point also applies to (iii) the singular imperative and (iv) the declaration of a decision. As to (v), when X says, "If I'm smart I'll do z," this cannot be interpreted as a mere conditional prediction such as might be uttered by someone who "plays it cool," as if it concomitantly also implied: "If I'm not smart I won't do z." Such indifference fails to catch the full force of someone's genuinely wanting something and recognizing and accepting the constraints needed to get it. Rather, the phrase, "If I'm smart," must be interpreted to mean: "If I have the intelligence I ought to have...."

Hence, "smart" reintroduces the normativeness or requiredness for which the intended alternative was to be a substitute.

What I have tried to establish thus far, then, is that even an amoralist, so long as he is rational and normal in the senses indicated above, must use the concept of "ought." A person who did not use this concept would not be aware that any requirements or constraints were ever set for his conduct for any reason whatever, including his own self-interested desires. Even if the latter were his only desires, he would not be able to distinguish what he ought and ought not do with a view to satisfying them. So soon as any person begins to deliberate between alternative courses of action to achieve any purpose of his, and thereby rules out some alternatives and accepts others, he necessarily uses the concept of "ought."

III. From Non-Moral "Ought" to Moral "Ought"

According to Prichard, there is "a total difference of meaning" between the moral and the nonmoral "ought," because the latter is exhaustively translatable into the idea of what is necessary to realize an agent's purpose whereas the moral "ought" has no reference to the agent's purpose.[10] For the difference in meaning to be "total," however, a necessary condition would seem to be that the non-moral and moral "oughts" have no meaning in common save perhaps at an extremely general level, just as, for example, "race" meaning a biological classification and "race" meaning an athletic contest have nothing in common save as somehow pertaining (although in different ways) to living phenomena. But Prichard does not think that the moral and non-moral "oughts" are so extremely distant in meaning. For he admits that both "oughts" are imperatives. Now within the general realm of language, "imperative" signifies a much more specific characteristic or function than the two "races" signify in common. If we add to imperativeness (or prescriptiveness) the feature of authoritativeness, it seems more plausible to hold that the moral and the non-moral "oughts" share a central core of meaning, and that the moral "ought" adds to this the other features listed above: universalization, social concern, and supreme authoritativeness. Our task, then, is to show that at least some of the amoralist's uses of "ought" must exhibit these additional features.

The phrase "X universalizes his 'ought'-statements" may be misleading if it suggests that the universalizability of an "ought"-statement is at the option of the speaker. For a singular "ought"-statement necessarily implies a universal statement, regardless of whether the speaker admits this; and insofar as he is rational he necessarily admits it: the implication is so direct that it requires no extensive calculation. Specifically, X's statement, "I ought to do z because I want to have y," is enthymematic; it entails the suppressed major: "All persons who want to have y ought to do z." The basis of this entailment is that, as we have seen, X's "ought"-statement rests on the reason given in the "because"-clause; and it is a logical feature of all reasons that they are implicitly general, referring to a general rule or principle that serves to ground the connection asserted in the particular case.[11] Such a connection must hence obtain in all other cases to which the same rule or reason applies. In X's full statement as given above, he is saying that his possessing the predicate O ("ought to do z") is justified by, has its reason in, his possessing the predicate H ("want to have y"). X is therefore logically committed to accepting the universal proposition that whoever possesses H possesses O.

Problems arise about the scope of this universalization. Since the speaker himself provides the reason justifying his "ought"-statement, what is to prevent him from so individualizing that reason as to restrict its application to himself alone? When X says, "I ought to do z because I want to have y," he may ward off its implication that "all persons who want to have y ought to do z" by adding further qualifications in the "because"-clause: for example, "because I am over six feet tall, born January 1, 1945, on Harper Avenue, Chicago, and named X." The only universalization to which X would be logically committed would hence be: "All persons who want to have y and who were born on Harper Avenue and are named X . . . ought to do z."

The natural reaction to this piling up of "reasons" is: "What on earth does your being born on Harper Avenue or your being named X have to do with whether you ought to do z?" (I shall call this question 'Q'.) The implication of Q is that a justifying reason for an act must not include conditions which are irrelevant in the sense of unnecessary to the connection between the reason and the act for which it is a reason. X might reply, however, that his only reason for the act is that it is he, X, who wants to have y; and there is a necessary connection between (i) the act: someone named X does z; and (ii) the reason: that same person named X has or gets y, which he wants. Nevertheless, the point of Q still remains if we reformulate it as follows (Q_1): "What if your name weren't X? Wouldn't it still be the case that you ought to do z in order to have y?" As Q_1 indicates, X's having the name he has is irrelevant to the necessary connection between (i) and (ii), for the connection would still obtain even if the words "named X" were omitted. To put it formally: when reasons R justify an action A by stating that A is a necessary condition for achieving some end E, R may not include any facts which are such that, on their elimination, the necessary connection between A and E would remain unchanged.

It may still be objected, however, that X's reason for doing the act is so irreducibly egocentric that it cannot be expressed without explicit personal reference to him; hence it cannot be generalized so as to be the "same reason" as any other persons may have for performing their respective acts. "*My* reason for doing z is simply that I want that I have y, and *this* reason is different from any other persons' wanting that *they* have y. I don't care about anyone else's wants but only about my own; and nobody else has *my* wants." What is here claimed is that there is no way, by logic alone, to eliminate indexical expressions like "my" or 'I' from the reason X has given for his doing z. If X's reason can be universalized at all, it must be in a way that retains the individualizing reference to his own personal wants: "All persons who have my want that I have y ought to do z."

The solution of this difficulty requires a closer look at the concept of wanting. Three elements must be distinguished: the person who wants something, his wanting, and what he wants. "Want" as a noun may refer to either of the last two. Now just as one person is numerically different from another, so are their respective wantings; in this sense the "wants" of one person are never numerically the same as those of another. They may, however, be generically or qualitatively the same insofar as the persons may want something in the same (or similar) way, as indicated, for example, by the kinds of effort they put forth to obtain whatever objects they want. If we look next at their wants in the sense of what they want, these too may be the same. Here, however, two alternatives must be distinguished. When we talk of what someone wants, this "what" may be expressed either as the object itself which is wanted or as the combination of the object and the person who wants it. In the first way, we say "X wants (or wants to have) y"; in the second way, "X wants that he have y." Now in the first way it is clear that X and someone else (call him "W") may want the same thing, so that their "wants" are the same. This point holds regardless of such further complexities as that X and W may want either the numerically same lounge chair or a lounge chair; in the latter case they still want the generically same thing, so that "wanting to have a lounge chair" serves as the common or same reason for the acts they perform to obtain one. But in the second way, when it is said that X wants that X have y and W wants that W have y, it may be thought obvious that what X and W want are not the same. And indeed they are not numerically the same. But they may still be generically or proportionally the same, in that X's having y is to X as W's having y is to W. In each case y is the object of X's and W's similar desiderative attitudes, which serve as the same or common reason for their respective efforts to obtain y . To put it in other terms: X's statement, "I want that I have y," is a token of a type which can be truly and relevantly uttered by W and other persons as well. While each of these tokens has a different reference so far as concerns the 'I', they all have a common meaning in that they express the qualitatively same desiderative attitude toward the (numerically or generically) same object. Hence, those other persons' reasons for doing z are the same as X's reason. To deny this would be like holding that one man's reason for doing something can never be the same as another man's because the thoughts in the heads of the two men are numerically different. But such a difference is irrelevant to the concept of the "same reason."

I have now considered and rejected two kinds of individualizing restrictions (deriving from proper names and first-person indexical expressions) on the universalization of X's reason for believing that he ought to do z. More generally, as I have argued elsewhere,[12] even if X's reason signifies a unique property which belongs only to him, still that property is similar or proportional to the properties of other persons, so that X's reason for doing z must apply in a similar or proportional way to those other persons. I shall henceforth use 'S' and 'U' to refer, respectively, to singular and universal "ought"-statements of the form "I ought to do z because I want to have y" and "All persons who want to have y ought to do z," where the latter are derived by universalizing the former in the way discussed above.

Thus far, I have tried to show that X necessarily accepts U, because as a rational and normal person he necessarily makes judgments of form S and necessarily accepts the universalizations which S entails. The claim I now want to make is that statements of form U are moral judgments. To establish this, I must show that U fulfills the four criteria listed above. We have already seen that it fulfills criterion (B), in that X derives it by universalizing S. (I assume that the universalization requirement may be fulfilled either by a singular judgment which one universalizes or by the resulting universal judgment.) Let us now turn to criterion *(D)*, according to which a judgment to be a moral one must "pronounce actions . . . to be right [or] wrong . . . simply because of the effect they have on the feelings, interests, ideals, etc., of *other* persons." In view of the importance of this criterion for our question, we must try to elucidate it properly.

In the first place, criterion (D) refers to moral judgments as pronouncing actions to be "right [or] wrong," whereas my above argument has been in terms of "ought." This, however, raises no difficulty, for in any practical or prescriptive context where "ought" is used, "right" or "wrong" may also, *a fortiori*, be used: "ought" and "right" are related as subalternant and subalternate, so that "X ought to do z" entails "it is right that X do z," although not conversely. This entailment would be broken only if specifications of different contexts or reasons were introduced for the two concepts: if, for example, "ought" were used in connection with prudential or technical reasons and "right" in connection with legal reasons. Such differences of context, however, do not figure in my argument.

Secondly, when criterion (D) says that a moral judgment must "pronounce actions . . . to be right [or] wrong . . . simply because of the effect they have on the feelings, interests, ideals, etc., of *other* persons," the "effect" in question is obviously intended in such a way that an action is pronounced right if it promotes other persons' interests and wrong if it frustrates them, rather than the reverse. The aim of criterion (D) is to emphasize the socially-considerate or social-beneficial requirement of morality, just as when philosophers have raised the question, "Why should one be moral?" they have usually meant, "Why should one support, or act so as to promote, the interests of persons other than oneself?"

Third, although criterion (D) refers directly not to actions but to "judgments" which "pronounce" on actions, the criterion also requires for its fulfillment that one act in appropriate ways in accordance with one's judgments. This is especially clear from the fact that criterion (D) is sequential on criterion (A), according to which "X takes [his action-guide] as prescriptive." The familiar problems of *akrasia* which arise in connection with prescriptivist theories of the relation between moral concepts and action need no special attention here. As was indicated above in my discussion of "ought," when X says, "All persons who want to have y ought to do z," this involves, insofar as his "ought" is prescriptive, that he endorses other persons' doing z, he urges them to do z, he commits himself to act in support of his endorsement, and so forth.

With these elucidations out of the way, I now wish to argue that U fulfills criterion (D). It will be recalled that statements of form U were necessarily accepted by X because, as a rational person, he recognized that they were entailed by his singular statements of form S ("I ought to do z because I want to have y"). Now in accepting statements of form U, "All persons who want to have y ought to do z," X holds that these persons' doing z is right because it will enable them to further or satisfy their respective interests in having y. To be sure, he is not saying that this is right "simply" for this reason, for his accepting the subordinate clause in U is consequent upon his accepting the "because"-clause in S. Since, however, the derivation of U from S is logically necessary, X is ineluctably committed to endorsing other persons' pursuit of their respective interests on the same basis as he endorses his pursuit of his own; he commits himself to accepting on the part of others the same kinds of interest-furthering acts that he upholds for himself. This generalized acceptance also means that X must look at his own proposed act in the light of the possible general performance of similar acts, since by U he declares such general performance to be justified.

Against my claim that U fulfills criterion (D) and is to that extent a moral judgment, it may be objected that there are important differences between the meaning of "ought" in U and the moral meaning of either "ought" or "right." Just as someone who is concerned with other persons' interests only because this causally advances his own interests is held to make prudential rather than moral judgments, so someone whose "ought"-statements (as in U) are concerned with other persons' interests only as a logical consequence of his own self-interested "ought"-statements may be held to be making not a moral judgment but a "derivatively-prudential" one. How can logic alone accomplish the transition from a self-interested "ought" (as in S) to a socially-concerned "ought"? There is, moreover, a difference between the way ends are viewed in U and in a moral judgment [in the sense of criterion (D)]. If someone makes a moral judgment that certain acts are right because they advance the interests of persons other than himself, he implicitly endorses the interests or ends themselves: the acts or means are right because the advancement of those interests is right. But when X says (in U) that all persons who want to have y ought to do z, he is not endorsing their having y or holding that it is right that they have y; he is not committing himself about their ends at all, but is saying only that if they want to have y, the right way to get it is by doing z, where "right" means merely technically efficient. Hence, U is only a technical judgment, not a moral one in the sense of criterion (D).

In answer to these objections, it is important to keep in mind that the question of U's fulfillment of criterion (D) involves what X must accept as justified on the basis of the logical canons to which we have assumed him to be committed. The "transition" accomplished by these canons is simply from an "ought"-predication justified by a certain reason in X's own case to its being justified in all the other cases to which that same reason applies. Such a transition from the individual to the social or universal is no more mysterious in the sphere of practical judgment than it is in the inference from a "mortality"-predication justified in the case of Socrates by reason of his being human to the same predication's being justified in the case of all other humans. It must also be remembered that the meaning of U (including its use of "ought") is to be understood not in isolation but in the light of U's logical derivation from S. This point must be emphasized here and throughout our consideration of U: U is not merely a means-end statement toward which X may be neutral or indifferent; it is rather a personal-prescriptive statement by X. For since U is entailed by S, "ought" must have the same meaning in both statements; hence, since the "ought" in S is prescriptive, so too is the "ought" in U [thus fulfilling criterion (A)]. Moreover, in saying that all persons who want to have y ought to do z, X is endorsing their doing z for the same reason that he endorses (in S) his own doing z. Now since in S he accepts his wanting to have y as a sufficient reason or justification for his doing z, in U he must likewise accept other persons' wanting to have y as sufficient justification for their doing z. The point remains essentially the same if X bases his singular "ought"-statement on further reasons than simply his wanting to have y. In this case he would still regard his wanting to have y, combined with the other reasons, as justifying his doing z; hence he would be logically required to regard other persons' wanting to have y, combined with the other reasons, as similarly justifying their doing z. In either case, X is logically required to regard other persons' wants not with indifference but as legitimating reasons or justifications for their respective actions; he endorses not only the means but also the ends.

A further question may be asked about U's relation to criterion (D): do any interests whatsoever count as fulfilling the criterion? Consider, at one extreme, a statement like: "All persons who want their cars to run smoothly ought to change oil every thousand miles" (U_1); and at the other extreme: "All persons who want to kill other persons without being detected ought to feed them arsenic" (U_2). Neither of these, it may be held, is a moral judgment even if derived from the corresponding singular judgment: not U_1, because the interests of the persons referred to are not sufficiently far-reaching or important; not U_2, because the would-be poisoners consider only their own interests and threaten grave harm to other persons. The objection to U_1, however, really bears on criterion (D). We could say either that *any* interests of persons will count as fulfilling criterion (D) when someone else says that acts are right because they advance those interests; or that even if only "important" interests count, still each individual is the judge of what is important to him; or, finally, that criterion (D) is to be amended so that only what are generally agreed to be important interests are to count, such as those bearing on physical or mental well-being. On either of the first two alternatives U_1 would satisfy criterion (D); on the third alternative it might not, but then it would be easy to find other examples of S where X believes he ought to do something because it is necessary to his basic health or happiness, and these when universalized would satisfy criterion (D) as amended.

As for the objection against U_2, it must be remembered that the salient consideration in determining whether U_2 fulfills criterion (D) is not whether the poisoners' interests are harmful to others but rather whether

X in making or accepting the judgment is holding that certain acts are right because they further the interests of persons other than himself—in this case, the interests of the poisoners. That these interests, and hence also X's judgment endorsing them, are immoral may itself be a sign that the judgment is a moral and not a non-moral one; for one might argue that only what is moral (as opposed to non-moral) can be immoral. But even apart from such an argument, it must be recognized that there are many moralities other than universalist or equalitarian ones; as Frankena points out, "criterion (D) allows for nationalistic and class moralities, for Nazism, for inequalitarianism."[13] I take it that the position upheld by U_2 would fit among such moralities. In general, all the U-statements which X is logically committed to accepting involve the mutuality of his endorsing other men's pursuits of their respective interests on the same basis as he endorses his pursuit of his own.

Another consideration showing that U, regardless of its specific content, fulfills criterion (D) can be found in the connection of both U and S with the idea of mutual freedom. X's statement "I ought to do z" entails "I ought to be free to do z," where "to be free" means not to be interfered with by other persons in doing z. For if it is right that other persons interfere with X's doing z or prevent him from doing z, then it is false that he ought to do z. Similarly, "all persons who want to have y ought to do z" entails "all persons who want to have y ought to be free to do z." But anyone who accepts such universal statements as personal-prescriptive ones endorsing the end as well as the means, as we have seen that X must accept them, must also accept the singular statement, "I ought to refrain from interfering with other persons' doing z if they want to have y." Hence, on the basis of his own self-interested acts and judgments, X must uphold a system of mutual rights and duties in which his "ought"-judgments in support of his own freedom of action entail further "ought"-judgments in which he accords similar freedom to others.

In the argument just given, it must be emphasized that no moral claim on other persons is directly involved in X's statement, "I ought to be free to do z," or in its equivalent statement "other persons ought not to interfere with my doing z." These "oughts," like that in "I ought to do z," derive only from X's egocentric wanting to have y; and this is also true of the "right" in "it is not right that other persons interfere with my doing z." The moral claim [using "moral" in the sense of criterion (D)] comes in subsequently when X universalizes his singular judgment so that it becomes: "All persons who want to have y ought to be free to do z." This universal judgment fulfills criterion (D) in at least two respects. First, it declares other men's unimpeded pursuit of their interests to be right because of its positive effect on *their* respective interests. Secondly, it commits X himself to not interfering with or preventing these other men's doing z, for if X accepts that other men ought to be free to do z, then, by the definition of "free," he admits that he ought not to prevent their doing z. But this moral claim in the universal case involves no ambiguity in the case of X's singular judgment "I ought to be free to do z," for this latter is focused only on X's own interests; hence it does not itself make a moral claim.

It may be objected that "I ought to do z" does not entail "I ought to be free to do z." For "do z" is ambiguous as between attempt and achievement. In competitive situations where both X and W want to have y and each believes he ought to do z in order to get y, it might well be the case that they cannot both do z (for example, marry the boss's daughter). Hence, since "ought" presupposes "can," X would believe only that he ought to *try* to do z. But this belief does not entail that X ought to be free to succeed in doing z so that W or other persons ought not to interfere with X's succeeding in doing z. What it entails is rather that X ought to be free from interference in trying to do z.

Even if we grant this objection, it still involves an acceptance by X of the need for mutual freedom of action in the sense of attempt. That is, X must accept the judgment that other persons ought to be free to pursue (even if not to achieve or attain) their interests or objectives, on the same grounds as he endorses this freedom for himself. And this judgment fulfills criterion (D).

In addition to the negative responsibility of noninterference, it can be shown in a parallel way that X's initial "ought"-statement also logically commits him to accepting the positive responsibility of helping other persons. For suppose X's doing z is impossible without other men's providing various kinds of essential conditions or services, which I shall call p. Hence, when X says "I ought to do z," he must also accept the statement, "Other men ought to do p." For since "ought" presupposes "can," if it is right that other men not do p, without which X cannot do z, then it is false that X ought to do z. To put it otherwise, if one endorses some end, then one must also endorse the necessary means to that end, at least *prima facie* or in the absence of superior counter-considerations. In addition, as we have seen, X must accept the general statement, "All persons who want to have y ought to do z." And insofar as such men's doing z is impossible without other men's doing p, X must also accept that the latter men ought to do p. Now if X is included in this latter group, then he must concede that he too ought to do p. But obviously X is included in this group at least insofar as the "essential conditions" in question involve the maintenance in certain interpersonal relations of a certain modicum of honesty and trustworthiness. Hence, X must do his part toward maintaining such helpful conditions. This consideration also suggests that there are limitations as to the kinds of acts and wants that X may himself justifiably pursue, at least toward some persons.

The fact that X may be able to shirk these responsibilities, and in general to flout rules which he upholds for others, is here irrelevant. For once his initial statement that he ought to do z is given on the basis of his wanting to have y, the basis of the subsequent "ought"-statements to which he is committed is not prudential but logical. The reason why X must endorse other men's pursuit of their interests and accord them the needed freedom and aid is not the prudential or contingent one that if he interferes with or fails to aid other men's acts then he may probably expect them to interfere with or fail to aid his, but rather the logically necessary one that if a reason is held to justify an act because it is of a certain kind, then that reason must, on pain of contradiction, be held to justify all acts of that kind. There is, of course, much room for contingency in moral reasoning. What is at stake, however, in my insistence on the logical rather than prudential basis of X's subsequent "ought"-statements is that if their basis were only prudential, then their validity or requiredness would merely be contingent on the degree to which X could not satisfy his interests or desires without endorsing and helping other men's pursuits of their interests. Hence there would be many kinds of circumstances in which X would simply have no moral obligations of the kinds described. Since, however, the basis of these obligations is logical, their validity is necessary independently of such contingent circumstances.

It must also be noted, however, that the rules which result from such obligations need not be, as with Hobbes, completely egalitarian and universalist: they still might, for example, provide for the hegemony of the physically or mentally stronger over the weaker. But the rules would at least set up a social-moral framework in which X would recognize that, on pain of self-contradiction, his acts in pursuit of his objectives must be affirmatively related to certain common standards bearing on the acts of other persons as well as his own.

Let us, finally, consider whether U fulfills criterion (C) (that X regards his action-guide as "definitive, final, over-riding, or supremely authoritative"). I have said above that X regards his "ought"-statements as authoritative in that he holds that the requirements they impose on his conduct are justified by reasons deriving from his wants. But I also said that one of the factors entering into his statement or belief that he ought to do z because he wants to have y is that "he does not believe there is any superior counter-consideration to his having y or doing z." For if he did believe there was such a superior counter-consideration, he would regard it as removing the requiredness of his doing z. Does this mean that all "ought"-beliefs are regarded by the persons having them as supremely

authoritative? Only in a relative sense, that is, as pertaining to the particular choice-situation in question. The phrase "supremely authoritative," however, is generic: it refers to a general range or kind of reasons
as outweighing other kinds of reasons in respect to validity or legitimacy.
Now it is quite conceivable that X might not even implicitly uphold such a
hierarchy of reasons: he might regard first one kind of end or desire as
most important, then a quite different and even conflicting one, and so
forth. Clearly, however, such a policy (or rather lack of policy) would be
irrational, for it could lead to frustration of the desires which, as a conative being, he is trying to satisfy. To avoid this, he must arrange his ends in
an order of at least relative priority; which is to say that he must regard
some of the reasons for his actions as supremely authoritative at least
within a certain broad range of calculation.

It may be objected, however, that even if X regards some of his action-
guides as supremely authoritative, he does not regard U in this way:
hence his action-guides are not moral ones because those (like U) that
fulfill criterion (D) do not fulfill criterion (C), and conversely. That X does
not regard U as supremely authoritative emerges, first, from the point
traditionally made by deontologists against teleological doctrines: since
the "oughts" both in S and in U derive their authoritativeness for X from
indicating the means to the ends that he wants to achieve, it must be these
ends rather than the "oughts" that he regards as supremely authoritative.
Since, moreover, X accepts U only insofar as it is a logical consequence of
S, he must regard S as superior to U in authoritativeness.

The answer to these objections is that they prove too much. For if what
is derivative can in no way be regarded as supremely authoritative, if a
morality as supremely authoritative consists only in the moral principle but
not in the moral system which is justified by the principle, then no judgments, whether singular or general, could ever be moral ones so long as
they were justified by a superior principle or reason. It seems more
plausible, therefore, to hold that a morality consists not only in some
general range of reasons contained in one or a few supremely authoritative principles but also in the system which is justified by those reasons or
principles. It must also be kept in mind that authoritativeness is basically
a matter of reasons or justifications, not only of motivations. Hence, the
fact that X's practical motivations, at least initially, may be exclusively
self-interested rather than social does not preclude social concerns from
figuring in what he regards as supremely authoritative.

I conclude, then, that U fulfills criterion (C) as well as the other three
criteria of a moral judgment. The above arguments, if sound, have thus
shown that any person, so long as he accepts the reasons of deductive and
inductive logic and is conatively normal, must play the moral language
game and have a morality. This result means, among other things, not

only that amoralism is irrational (in a sense of "irrational" accepted by the amoralist himself as defined above) but also that to prove this there is no need to appeal to any peculiarly moral rationality, if there be any such.

Although I have interpreted the four criteria of "moral" listed above in such a way as to avoid any specifically "emotional" features, including conscience and sympathy (in criteria (C) and (D), respectively), X may well come to have such feelings as contingent consequences of his sincerely holding practical beliefs which fulfill the criteria. Despite the great importance I myself attach to conscience and sympathy, I have not explicitly included them as essential to every morality, for a man may acknowledge obligations which he accepts as prescriptive, generalized, supremely authoritative, and concerned with other persons' interests, out of what he believes to be considered convictions about what is justified or right, even though he feels no sympathy for the other persons and regards conscience as at best unreliable and in any case as dispensable. It must also be remembered that what I have tried to show here is that X, the quondam amoralist, must have *a* morality, must play *some* moral language game. A further argument, using additional materials, is needed to differentiate, among the various possible moralities, the one which can itself be shown to be morally justified. Elsewhere[14] I have tried to sketch such a further argument.

In conclusion, the whole project of this paper may be challenged. Why should we bother with the amoralist at all? Why shouldn't we be content to take the social point of view according to which a morality is required for the very existence of a society; why, in addition, should we take seriously the point of view of some deviant individual who would reject all moral language and hence his moral obligations to any society? I have two answers to such questions. One is that the deviant views of individuals deserve a hearing on their own merits. The other is that it is important to have shown that morality rests on a rational structure which can be used in a non-circular way to refute any attempt at a reasoned rejection of morality.[15]

Notes

1. Kai Nielsen, "Why Should I Be Moral?", *Methodos*, vol. 15 (1963), pp. 297–298.

2. R. M. Hare, *Freedom and Reason* (Oxford, 1963), pp. 100–101.

3. C. H. Whiteley, "Universalisability," *Analysis*, vol. 27 (1966–67), p. 49 (italics in original).

4. A. I. Melden, "Why Be Moral?", *The Journal of Philosophy*, vol. 45 (1948), p. 455 (italics in original).

5. Anthony Ralls, "The Game of Life," *The Philosophical Quarterly*, vol. 16 (1966), pp. 27, 32 (italics in original). For similar statements, see H. D. Aiken, *Reason and Conduct* (New York, 1962), p. 86; A. P. Griffiths, "Justifying Moral Principles," *Proceedings of the*

Aristotelian Society, vol. 58 (1957–58), pp. 104–105, 109; J. C. Thornton, "Can the Moral Point of View Be Justified?", *Australasian Journal of Philosophy*, vol. 42 (1964), p. 32; D. P. Gauthier, "Morality and Advantage," *The Philosophical Review*, vol. 76 (1967), p. 470; G. P. Henderson, "Moral Nihilism," in *Studies in Moral Philosophy*, *American Philosophical Quarterly* Monograph No. 1 (1968), pp. 47ff.

6. See the "Psychiatric Glossary" published by the Committee on Public Information of the American Psychiatric Association, which defines a psychopath as: "A person whose behavior is predominantly amoral or anti-social and characterized by impulsive, irresponsible actions satisfying only immediate and narcissistic interests without concern for obvious and implicit social consequences, accompanied by minimal outward evidence of anxiety or guilt" (quoted in R. L. Jenkins, "The Psychopathic or Antisocial Personality," *Journal of Nervous and Mental Disease*, vol. 131 [1960], p. 318). See also Henry Cleckley, *The Mask of Sanity* (St. Louis, 1950, 2nd ed.), p. 545; Ian Gregory, *Psychiatry, Biological and Social* (Philadelphia, 1961), p. 452; F. J. Braceland and Michael Stock, *Modern Psychiatry* (New York, 1963), p. 334; A. A. Terruwe, *Psychopathic Personality and Neurosis* (New York, 1958), pp. 51–54. Also relevant here are the 19th century expressions used to define the psychopath as a "moral imbecile" and "moral defective," as well as current characterizations of him as showing "absence of ethical and moral appreciation," "loss of all ethical sense," and "affectional irresponsibility." See, e.g., E. A. Strecker, *Basic Psychiatry* (New York, 1952), p. 298; Gregory, *op. cit.*, p. 452; Norman Cameron and Ann Magaret, *Behavior Pathology* (Boston, 1951), p. 205.

7. W. K. Frankena, "The Concept of Morality," *The Journal of Philosophy*, vol. 63 (1966), pp. 688, 689 (italics in original). Frankena has also discussed this subject in two other valuable papers: "Recent Conceptions of Morality" in H. N. Castaneda and George Nakhnikian (eds.), *Morality and the Language of Conduct* (Detroit, 1963), pp. 1–24, and "The Concept of Morality," *University of Colorado Studies, Series in Philosophy*, No. 3 (1967), pp. 1–22. While these two papers are more detailed on several points, they present no important differences of doctrine from that of *The Journal of Philosophy* paper.

8. See the criticisms directed against Max Black, "The Gap Between 'Is' and 'Should'," *The Philosophical Review*, vol. 73 (1964), pp. 165–181, by M. F. Cohen, "'Is' and 'Should': An Unbridged Gap," *ibid.*, vol. 74 (1965), p. 224, and T. Y. Henderson, "The Gap Between Good Strategy and Right Action," *Philosophy*, vol. 41 (1966), pp. 260–267. As is indicated both at the beginning of this section and in my reply to *(b)*, below, my project does not, like Black's or Searle's (see next note), involve deriving an "ought"-statement from an "is"-statement.

9. This statement is similar to but not identical with the *ceteris paribus* clause in J. R. Searle, "How to Derive 'Ought' from 'Is'," *The Philosophical Review*, vol. 73 (1964), pp. 46ff. As his critics pointed out, for this clause to serve its purpose in his attempt to derive the obligation of promise-keeping from factual premises, the clause must itself be evaluative (James and Judith Thomson, "How Not to Derive 'Ought' from 'Is'," *ibid.*, vol. 73 [1964], pp. 512ff.). This criticism does not apply to my above argument, however, because the "superior counter-considerations" are only those which the amoralist already accepts, so that they do not represent a covert "moral" assumption opposed to his own premises.

10. H. A. Prichard, *Moral Obligation* (Oxford, 1949), pp. 90–91.

11. It may be objected that in fields like history and law the giving of reasons for actions, or the use of "because" in causal explanations, may make no reference to any generalizations. (See William Dray, *Laws and Explanation in History* [Oxford, 1957] and H. L. A. Hart and A. M. Honoré, *Causation in the Law* [Oxford, 1959].) It is important, however, not to confuse the logical question of whether a generalization is implied by a "because"-statement with such pragmatic questions as whether historians or lawyers always use these

implications in their work or whether they are able fully to ascertain which one of many different implied generalizations states the sufficient condition of a specific event. Negative answers to the pragmatic questions do not necessitate a negative answer to the logical question. Implicit admissions of this distinction can be found in Hart and Honoré, *ibid.*, pp. 14–15, 20–21.

12. I have discussed the "individualizability objection" to the universalizability thesis more fully elsewhere. See A. Gewirth, "The Non-Trivializability of Universalizability," *Australiasian Journal of Philosophy,* vol. 47 (1969), pp. 123ff. I have also discussed the "criterion of relevant similarities" in "The Generalization Principle," *The Philosophical Review,* vol. 73 (1964), pp. 237ff.

13. "The Concept of Morality," *The Journal of Philosophy,* vol. 63 (1966), p. 692.

14. See A. Gewirth, "Categorial Consistency in Ethics," *The Philosophical Quarterly,* vol. 17 (1967), pp. 289–299.

15. For their comments on an earlier version of this paper I am indebted to various of my colleagues and students, and especially to Dr. Richard Parker.

3
The "Is-Ought" Problem Resolved

When I told one of my philosophical friends the title of this paper, he suggested that I make a slight addition, so that the title would read: "The 'Is-Ought' Problem Resolved — Again?!" Indeed, I agree with his implied conviction that on certain interpretations of it the 'Is-Ought' Problem has already been resolved several times; and I wish to emphasize that these resolutions and the polemical exchanges generated by them have done much to sharpen the issues. Nevertheless, I also maintain that the real 'Is-Ought' Problem has not yet been resolved. I therefore want to do three main things in this paper. First, I shall present what I take to be the real 'Is-Ought' Problem and shall indicate why it is the real one. Second, I shall review the main recent attempts to resolve the Problem and shall show that none of these has succeeded so far as the real 'Is-Ought' Problem is concerned. Third, I shall give my resolution of this real Problem.

I

First, then, what is the real 'Is-Ought' Problem? It will come as no surprise that the Problem is concerned with moral 'oughts'. After all, it was in the context of a discussion of the basis of "moral distinctions" that Hume wrote his famous passage about the need for explaining and justifying the transition from 'is' to 'ought' as copulas of propositions.[1] And in the introduction to a recent anthology devoted to the subject, the editor writes that the 'Is-Ought' Problem is "the central problem in moral philosophy."[2]

---

[1] *Treatise of Human Nature*, III. i. 1 (ed. Selby-Bigge, pp. 469-470).

[2] W.D. Hudson, ed., *The Is-Ought Question* (London: Macmillan and Co., 1969), p. 11.

Now the word 'moral' is used in several different senses. While taking account of these differences, I shall focus on certain paradigm cases of what are undeniably moral 'ought'-judgments which persons have sought to derive from 'is'-statements. These judgments are of two main kinds. One kind sets forth negative moral duties to refrain from inflicting serious harm on other persons. Their paradigm uses have been of this form: "A intends to do X to B in order to gratify A's inclinations although he knows this will bring only great suffering to B; therefore, A ought not to do X to B." The other kind sets forth positive duties to perform certain actions for the benefit of other persons, especially where the latter would otherwise suffer serious harm. Their paradigm uses have been of this sort: "B is drowning and A by throwing him a rope can rescue him; therefore A ought to throw the rope to B;" or "B is starving while A has plenty of food; therefore A ought to give some food to B;" and so forth. In addition to such individual moral duties, persons have also sought to derive more specifically sociopolitical moral 'oughts' from 'is'-statements; for example, "That society is characterized by great inequalities of wealth and power; therefore it ought to be changed;" or "This state respects civil liberties; therefore we ought to that extent to support it;" and so forth.

The 'oughts' presented in these judgments have five important formal and material characteristics, which will constitute five interrelated conditions or tests that must be satisfied by any solution of the real 'Is-Ought' Problem. First, the 'oughts' are moral ones in the sense that they take positive account of the interests of other persons as well as the agent or speaker, especially as regards the distribution of what is considered to be basic well-being. It is this well-being, indicated in the antecedent 'is'-statements, that provides the reasons for the actions urged in the 'ought'-judgments.

Second, these 'oughts' are prescriptive in that their users advocate or seek to guide or influence actions, which they set forth as required by the facts presented in the antecedents. Although not all uses of 'ought' are prescriptive, such advocacy marks the unconditional use of 'ought' as in the above cases, where the antecedent empirical statements serve not to qualify or restrict the 'oughts' but rather to indicate the facts or reasons which make them mandatory.

Third, the 'oughts' are egalitarian in that they require that at least basic well-being be distributed equally as between the agent addressed and his potential recipients, or as among the members of a society. Although such egalitarianism is sometimes made part of the definition of 'moral', and I shall myself sometimes use 'moral' to include both this and the prescriptiveness just mentioned, it seems best to distinguish these considerations, since there may, after all, be non-egalitarian moralities.

A fourth important characteristic of these 'oughts' is that they are determinate. By this I mean that the actions they prescribe have definite contents such that the opposite contents cannot be obtained by the same mode of derivation. Thus, in my above examples, the 'oughts' require, respectively, rescuing, feeding, not harming; at the same time they are opposite-excluding in that one cannot, by the mode of derivation in question, obtain as conclusions 'oughts' which permit or require not rescuing, not feeding, or harming.

A fifth characteristic of these 'oughts', which to some extent encompasses some of the other characteristics, is that they are categorical, not merely hypothetical. By this characteristic, which applies more directly to the individual 'ought'-judgments, I mean that the requirements set forth therein are normatively overriding and ineluctable or necessary, in that their bindingness cannot be removed by, and hence is not contingent on or determined by, variable, escapable features either of the persons addressed or of their social relations. These escapable, non-determining features include the self-interested desires of the persons addressed, their variable choices, opinions, and attitudes, and institutional rules whose obligatoriness may itself be doubtful or variable.

Now it is with 'ought'-judgments having these five characteristics of being moral, prescriptive, egalitarian, determinate, and categorical that the real 'Is-Ought' Problem is concerned. The Problem is this: how can 'ought'-judgments having these five characteristics be logically derived from, or be justified on the basis of, premisses which state empirical facts? As this question suggests, a sixth condition which must be satisfied by any solution of the real 'Is-Ought' Problem is that of non-circularity, especially in the respect that the premisses from which the 'ought'-conclusions are derived must not themselves be moral or prescriptive. The resolution of the Problem calls not only for presenting a derivation which satisfies these six conditions but also for a theory which adequately explains why this derivation is successful and why previous attempts at derivation have been unsuccessful. There may indeed be problems about deriving from empirical statements 'ought'-judgments which lack one or more of these five characteristics; but they are not the real 'Is-Ought' Problem, not only because, having fewer conditions to satisfy, they are easier to resolve, but also because they necessarily fail to cope with the issue of justifying categorical moral 'ought'-judgments, judgments which bear on the most basic requirements of how persons ought to live in relation to one another.

It is the decisive importance of this issue of justification that makes the real 'Is-Ought' Problem at once so central and so difficult for moral philosophy. There is a familiar sequence of considerations at this point. The moral 'ought'-judgments of the sort I mentioned above are not self-evident; hence if they are to be justified at all they must be derived in some way from other statements. These other, justifying statements must themselves be either moral or non-moral (where 'moral' here includes also the characteristics of prescriptiveness and categoricalness). If the justifying statements are moral ones, then there recurs the question of how *they* are to be justified, since they too are not self-evident, and the question continues to recur as we mount through more general moral rules and principles. If, on the other hand, the statements from which the moral 'ought'-judgments are to be derived are non-moral ones, such as the empirical statements that figured in my paradigm cases, then there is the difficulty that the 'ought'-judgments are not derivable from those statements either inductively or deductively, unless we define 'ought' in empirical terms; and such a definition raises many questions of adequacy, including how the 'ought'-judgments can pass the tests of prescriptiveness and categoricalness. But it seems clear that if the moral 'ought'-judgments cannot in any way be justified on the basis of empirical and logical considerations, i.e. by logical derivation from 'is'-statements, then they cannot be definitively justified at all. Hence the crucial importance of the real 'Is-Ought' Problem.

I shall use the expressions *external model* and *internal model* to distinguish the two chief positions on this issue. The external model holds that 'ought' is external to 'is' in that there is a basic logical gap between them: 'ought' cannot be correctly defined in terms of empirical and logical considerations alone, nor can these considerations constitute determinate criteria of 'ought' because any facts adduced as such criteria must ultimately reflect personal and hence variable decisions; consequently, 'ought' cannot be logically derived from 'is'. The internal model upholds the opposite position. The external model asserts also that 'ought'-judgments are not self-evident, so it concludes that they are not capable of any definitive justification at all; they reflect decisions or attitudes to which, at least at an ultimate level, questions of justification are inapplicable. Although logical gaps of some sort have also been held to underlie various other philosophical Problems — for example, in the Problem of Induction there is the logical gap between particular observation-statements and general laws, and in the Mind-Body Problem there is the logical gap between statements about bodily movements and statements about intentional human actions — the 'is-ought' gap is declared by the external model to be much wider than any of these others, for while both sides of the other gaps fall within the 'is', the 'is-ought' gap involves a difference between 'is' and something belonging to an entirely separate category.

The current status of the debate between the external and internal models is as follows. Some of the main arguments for the external model's categorial separation of 'is' from 'ought' have been refuted, but the refutations have not gone far enough to resolve the real 'Is-Ought' Problem. I now want to show this briefly in two phases: first, by considering three of the most familiar arguments for the external model's logical gap, and second by reviewing seven recent attempts to derive 'ought' from 'is'.

II

One argument for the gap is that there is a basic difference in function between empirical statements and moral 'ought'-judgments, in that while the former only describe something, the latter, being prescriptive, take a stand for or against something by advocating or guiding action, so that they cannot be derived from what is non-prescriptive. To this it has been replied that empirical statements may also be used to guide or influence actions. This reply, however, makes the serious concession that such guidance occurs only when the person uttering or hearing the empirical statement has a want or desire to which the fact presented in the statement bears some means-end or other causal relation, as, for example, in the statement "There is a cobra curled up right behind you." This point hence does not satisfy the condition of categoricalness; for, as we saw above, categorical moral 'oughts' present requirements for action which are normatively binding even when the person addressed has no such related self-interested want or desire.

A second familiar argument for the gap is that moral 'ought'-judgments, unlike empirical statements, have no truth-value and hence cannot follow logically from statements having truth-value. In addition to the noncognitivist position that moral 'oughts' express feelings or commands but not beliefs, an important basis of this argument goes back to the classical doctrine of modern philosophy and science according to which the 'is', the world of fact, consists only in material particles moving according to physical laws, so that it contains no moral 'oughts' and hence nothing to which categorical moral 'ought'-judgments can correspond or by reference to which they can be proved or disproved. This classical doctrine superseded the teleological conceptions of ancient and medieval thinkers, which were repeated in other terms in the theories of Hegel, Marx, and Spencer that human history or the whole evolutionary process progressively fulfills moral criteria.

Recent replies to the truth-value gap argument have renewed this teleological emphasis on a more restricted scale by pointing out that there are institutional facts, means-end relations, and eudaemonist conditions which serve to provide correspondence-correlates for 'ought'-judgments. Other replies have contended, first, that sentences need not have truth-values in order to figure in logical relations; second, that the truth-value argument takes a too narrow view of truth since, for example, negative and hypothetical statements are admittedly capable of being true or false without there being facts in the world to which they correspond; and third, that moral 'ought'-judgments have many characteristics regularly taken as conditions of being propositions having truth-value — for example, they are expressed in the indicative mood, they are asserted, denied, believed, disbelieved, questioned, and argued for and against; and such arguments often appeal to empirical facts which are held to provide reasons for believing or disbelieving the judgments.[3]

These replies to the truth-value argument, while sound, do not go far enough to satisfy the conditions of the real 'Is-Ought'

---

[3]For an important recent statement of a teleological approach to moral judgments which utilizes ontological doctrines of Aristotle and Aquinas, see Henry B. Veatch, *For an Ontology of Morals* (Evanston, Ill.: Northwestern University Press, 1971). Other recent arguments for the truth-value of moral judgments can be found in A.C. Ewing, *Sec-*

Problem. Insofar as the replies construe categorical moral 'ought'-judgments as having truth-value by virtue of correspondence, they have not shown to what the judgments must correspond in order to be true. Both institutional facts and means-end relations fail in this respect, for, as I shall indicate more fully below, they do not satisfy the conditions of categoricalness and determinacy. And if instead of a correspondence requirement for the truth of statements we adopt an epistemological requirement, such as that there must at least in principle be ways of confirming or disconfirming the statements, then it has not yet been shown how categorical moral 'ought'-judgments, or at least the most basic ones, are to be confirmed or disconfirmed. Hence, there is as yet no definitive warrant for holding that they are susceptible of truth or falsity.

A third familiar argument for the external model declares that 'ought' cannot be logically derived from 'is' because whatever is in the conclusion must be in the premises and there is no 'ought' in the premises. This argument is easily refutable by a consideration of non-syllogistic modes of inference. But, as I shall go on to show, this refutation does little to resolve the real 'Is-Ought' Problem, for the derivations it authorizes do not satisfy the condition of determinacy.

I shall now briefly review seven recent attempts to derive 'ought' from 'is'. The derivations fall into two groups, formal and material, in that the first four, unlike the last three, do not depend on the specific contents assigned to the 'oughts'.

The four formal derivations clearly fail the test of determinacy, and hence are of little or no help in resolving the real 'Is-Ought' Problem. First, the *truth-functional* derivation applies such rules as that a false proposition materially implies any proposition, and any proposition materially implies the disjunction of itself with any other proposition. Thus, the false proposition "There is no one in this room" materially implies both "We

---

and Thoughts in Moral Philosophy (London: Routledge and Kegan Paul, 1959), ch. 2; Robert J. Fogelin, *Evidence and Meaning* (London: Routledge and Kegan Paul, 1967), p. 135; Jonathan Harrison, *Our Knowledge of Right and Wrong* (London: George Allen and Unwin, 1971), pp. 251 ff.; Alan B. White, *Truth* (London: Macmillan Press, 1970), pp. 57-65; Kurt Baier, *The Moral Point of View* (Ithaca, N.Y.: Cornell University Press, 1958), pp. 173-186; Kai Nielsen, "On Moral Truth," *American Philosophical Quarterly*, Monograph Series No. 1 (1968), pp. 9-25.

ought to rescue drowning persons" and "We ought not to rescue drowning persons."

Second, the *immediate inference by added determinant* derives an 'ought'-conclusion from a subject-predicate 'is'-statement by adding some deontic qualification to both the subject and the predicate.[4] Thus on the one hand we have: "Jones is a millionaire; therefore, if all millionaires ought to help the weak, Jones ought to help the weak." But by the same mode of derivation we also have: "Jones is a millionaire; therefore, if all millionaires ought to refrain from helping the weak, Jones ought to refrain from helping the weak."

Third, there is the *'ought'-'can'* derivation, which, assuming the familiar principle that 'ought' implies 'can', argues by contraposition that if some person cannot perform some action, then it is not the case that he ought to perform it.[5] Since this mode of derivation puts no restrictions on the 'ought'-judgments with which one begins other than the ability of the agent, it also fails the test of determinacy.

Fourth, there is the *ideal procedural* derivation, which begins from facts or purported facts about mental procedures having certain ideal intellectual or emotional characteristics, and then argues that moral 'oughts' are derived either from the procedures themselves or from the results of applying them. The mental procedures in question are characterized as emerging from an 'ideal observer' or some similar source, and the characteristics embodied in these procedures include being fully informed, free, imaginative, calm, willing to universalize, reflecting as fully as possible upon all the relevant facts, and so forth.[6]

Now all these modes of derivation suffer from indeterminacy. For there is no assurance that two persons, reflecting as fully as possible upon all the same facts or otherwise using these mental

[4]For the first two derivations, see A.N. Prior, "The Autonomy of Ethics," *Australasian Journal of Philosophy*, vol. 18 (1960), pp. 199 ff.; George I. Mavrodes, "On Deriving the Normative from the Non-Normative," *Papers of the Michigan Academy of Science, Arts, and Letters*, vol. 53 (1968), pp. 353 ff.

[5]See David Rynin, "The Autonomy of Morals," *Mind*, vol. 66 (1957), p. 313; George I. Mavrodes, "'Is' and 'Ought'," *Analysis*, vol. 28 (1964), pp. 42 ff.; K.E. Tranoy, "'Ought' Implies 'Can': A Bridge from Fact to Norm," *Ratio*, vol. 14 (1972).

[6]See Roderick Firth, "Ethical Absolutism and the Ideal Observer," *Philosophy and Phenomenological Research*, vol. 12 (1951), pp. 317 ff.; Richard B. Brandt, *Ethical Theory* (Englewood Cliffs, N.J.: Prentice-Hall, 1959), ch. 10; Paul W. Taylor, *Normative Discourse* (Englewood Cliffs, N.J.: Prentice-Hall, 1961), ch. 6.

procedures, will arrive at the same moral 'ought'-judgments. And if, to ward off this indeterminacy, we include among the ideal procedural traits such egalitarian moral features as impartiality and sympathy, then the condition of non-circularity is violated.

I turn now to the material 'is-ought' derivations. Each of these rests on a version of the internal model whereby 'ought' is internal to 'is', in that either 'ought' is defined in terms of empirical and logical properties or such properties constitute purportedly determinate criteria of 'ought'. More specifically, 'ought' here means: necessitated or required by reasons stemming from some structured context. A context is structured when it is constituted by laws or rules which determine certain existential or practical necessities. The context in question need not be a practical or even a human one; it may, for example, be the context of physical nature. Thus in such an inference as, "It is lightning, therefore it ought to thunder," the 'ought' means that, given the occurrence of lightning, it is required or necessary that thunder also occur, this necessity stemming from the law-governed context of physical nature. The descriptive causal laws of this context furnish directly or indirectly the major premisses for this derivation of 'ought' from 'is'.[7]

In the practical sphere, similarly, there are various structured contexts which contain requirements for action. These requirements, however, consist not in existential necessities expressible in descriptive predictions of what must occur regardless of human action; they consist rather in directive rules as to what actions must be performed if certain values or purposes are to be achieved, the fulfillment of the rules being contingent on human decision. The contexts constituted by these rules, nevertheless, are factual ones in that they consist in ordered relations whose existence can be ascertained empirically. Three such contexts have figured especially prominently in recent 'is-ought' derivations: the contexts of means-end connections, of institutional rules, and of eudaemonist conditions, i.e. the conditions of human well-being. In each of these contexts, a statement of the form "A ought to do X" means that there is a requirement that A

---

[7] For similar views of the 'univocity' of 'ought' in theoretical and practical contexts, see especially Roger Wertheimer, *The Significance of Sense* (Ithaca, N.Y.: Cornell University Press, 1972), ch. 3. See also Joseph Margolis, *Values and Conduct* (Oxford: Clarendon Press, 1971), ch. 3; Glen O. Allen, "The Is-Ought Question Reformulated and Answered," *Ethics*, vol. 82 (1972), pp. 184 ff.

do X stemming from the structure of that context, i.e. from what must be done by A if one of his ends is to be fulfilled or if he is to participate in some institution with its rules or if he is to promote his or others' well-being. And in each case the derivation of 'ought' from 'is' goes through because the general structure of the respective contexts is presupposed as supplying the relevant major premisses.

From this brief characterization we can see three sharp limitations of these material 'is-ought' derivations, which prevent them from resolving the real 'Is-Ought' Problem. First, the derived 'oughts' are only hypothetical, not categorical. For the derivations are of the form: *If* the respective practical contexts with their requirements are accepted, *then* such and such actions ought to be done. Hence, the requirements represented by the derived 'oughts' are only intra-contextual; their obligatoriness is contingent on persons' variable choices or decisions to accept the context in question, or on some independent justification of the context itself as setting forth valid requirements for action. Second, by the same token, 'ought' as it figures in the internal model as so far explicated is not necessarily prescriptive. For to say that 'ought' means what is required by some structured context is not to say that the speaker who uses such an 'ought' necessarily accepts this requirement as binding either on himself or on his hearers; for he may not accept or commit himself to the context. Third, there arises, as a consequence, what I shall call the *dilemma of commitment.* The person who is deriving 'ought' from 'is' within one of these practical contexts either does or does not choose to accept or commit himself to the context with its requirements. If he does choose to commit himself, then the 'ought' he will derive will indeed be prescriptive, i.e. it will carry his endorsement or advocacy; but the derivation will be circular in that he will simply be resuming in the conclusion a commitment or advocacy which he had already chosen to make in the premiss. The derivation will hence be not from 'is' to 'ought' but rather from prescriptive 'ought' to prescriptive 'ought'. If, on the other hand, the person making the derivation does not choose to commit himself to the context with its requirements, then his derivation will not be circular; but then the 'ought' he derives will not be prescriptive, for it will not carry his advocacy or endorsement of the requirement he derives from the context. None of the three main recent material 'is-ought' derivations is able to resolve this dilemma, so I shall not refer to it again in discussing them; nor shall I repeat the other limitations just mentioned.

I wish, however, briefly to look further at each of these derivations in order to note some other difficulties, especially in connection with determinacy. The fifth derivation, that of *means-
end,* proceeds from the two 'is'-premises that a person wants to
achieve some end or purpose and that his performing a certain
action is the only means to his achieving this end; from these it
infers the conclusion that the person ought to perform the action.[8] This derivation, as indicated above, goes through because
there is assumed from the context some such major premiss as,
"One ought to do that which is the necessary and sufficient means
to achieving one's end." But the derivation does not satisfy the
condition of categoricalness, not only for the general reason
already given but also because it makes the requiredness of the
specific 'ought' to be contingent on the variable wants or desires
of the person addressed, so that he can evade its requirement by
shifting his wants or ends. Also, the derivation does not satisfy
the condition of determinacy, for by this mode of argument one
could infer either that one ought or that one ought not to feed
starving persons or rescue drowning persons, depending upon
one's own selfish wants in the matter.

The sixth mode of derivation, which I shall call the *institutional,* begins from 'is'-statements describing institutional facts
about ways in which persons participate in institutions having
certain requirements or rules, and it concludes with 'ought'-
judgments that the persons in question have certain obligations
by virtue of this participation. The most famous examples of this
institutional derivation in the recent literature have been concerned with the institutions of promising and of buying and
selling. The argument has been that if one participates in these
institutions by making a promise or a purchase, then, by virtue of
the rules of the respective institutions, one is obligated to keep
the promise or to pay for what one buys, and so forth.[9] Again,
certain relevant major premisses are assumed from the context.

This derivation also fails the test of determinacy. One could,

---

[8]See Max Black, "The Gap between 'Is' and 'Should'," *Philosophical Review,* vol. 73
(1964), pp. 165 ff.; also G.H. von Wright, "Practical Inference," *ibid.,* vol. 72 (1963),
pp. 159 ff.

[9]See John Searle, "How to Derive 'Ought' from 'Is'," *Philosophical Review,* vol. 73
(1964), pp. 43 ff.; Searle, *Speech Acts* (Cambridge: University Press, 1969), pp. 132-136
and ch. 8; G.E.M. Anscombe, "On Brute Facts," *Analysis,* vol. 18 (1958), pp. 69 ff.

by the same mode of derivation, infer diametrically opposed 'oughts'. For example, if one participates in the institution of constitutional democracy then one ought to support civil liberties, but if one participates in the institution of dictatorship then one ought to oppose such liberties, and if one participates in the institution of slavery then one ought to regard some humans as other humans' property, and so forth.[10] If, to ward off this indeterminacy, one stipulates that only those arrangements are to be considered institutions which are voluntarily accepted or agreed upon by all their participants, then this would not only restrict unduly the concept of an institution, but it would also violate the condition of non-circularity. For now the derivation would not begin from a morally neutral 'is'-statement, since the initial presumption would be that the institution in question fulfills the moral requirement of not being coercively imposed on its participants. Similarly, if we try further to avoid the indeterminacy of the institutional derivation by beginning from the institution of morality itself, or from "the moral point of view," and building into it such egalitarian moral requirements as that the good of everyone alike is to be promoted or that the ends of all persons are to be harmonized so far as possible, this would again violate the condition of non-circularity, since its starting-point would not be morally neutral.

The seventh and last mode of derivation to be considered I shall call the *eudaemonist,* from the Greek word for well-being. This assumes that the meaning or criterion of the moral 'ought' is to be found in the context of human well-being, so that "A morally ought to do X" means that doing X is required for the attainment of human well-being or for the avoidance of ill-being. With this definition, one can argue deductively from the factual premiss that certain actions are necessary for human well-being to the conclusion that those actions morally ought to be performed.[11]

This mode of derivation is, however, circular because its premisses about what constitutes human well-being or harm, far from being straightforwardly factual or descriptive, represent moral commitments about what is worth striving for or what interests of persons other than the agent are worth promoting. Consider,

---

[10]See my "Obligation: Political, Legal, Moral," *Nomos,* vol. XII (1970), pp. 55 ff.

[11]See Philippa Foot, "Moral Arguments," *Mind,* vol. 67 (1958), pp. 502 ff.; "Moral Beliefs," *Proceedings of the Aristotelian Society,* vol. 59 (1958-59), pp. 83 ff.

for example, the moral disagreements between religionists and secularists, between pacifists and militarists, between romantics and practical-minded persons, and so forth; and in addition there is the dispute between teleologists and deontologists over whether moral 'oughts' are tied to any considerations of well-being at all. Because of such disputes, the eudaemonist derivation does not yield determinate 'oughts'. Nor are the 'oughts' categorical, since their content depends on persons' variable opinions about what constitutes well-being and morality. Moreover, the eudaemonist derivation fails to cope with the crucial moral problem of distribution, of *whose* well-being ought to be promoted and whose harm avoided.[12]

I conclude, then, that while these recent 'is-ought' derivations have made valuable contributions, none has succeeded in resolving the real 'Is-Ought' Problem.

III

In this final section I want to show how 'ought'-judgments which are categorical, determinate, prescriptive, egalitarian, and moral can be logically and non-circularly derived from 'is'-statements which describe empirical facts about the world. I shall do this by presenting a certain version of what I have called the internal model. But my version differs in important respects from those considered above. The main bases of these differences comprise two interrelated points, one about the context, the other about method.

The factual context within which my argument will proceed is that of the generic features of action. This context is both logically prior to and more invariable and inescapable than the other contexts appealed to in the attempted material 'is-ought' derivations considered above. In those derivations, as we have seen, there were two sorts of variabilities, each of which made the 'ought'-conclusions hypothetical rather than categorical. The arguments went as follows: Given a certain structured context, certain actions are necessary or required by that context. The necessities here were hence hypothetical in that, while one had

[12]For some of these objections, see D.Z. Phillips, "On Morality's Having a Point," in Hudson, *op. cit.*, pp. 228 ff. These difficulties, as well as the dilemma of commitment presented above, are not taken account of by Peter Singer, "The Triviality of the Debate over 'Is-Ought' and the Definition of 'Moral'," *American Philosophical Quarterly*, vol. 10 (1973), pp. 51 ff.

first to accept the respective contexts as normatively binding, as justifiably setting forth requirements for action, this acceptance was not itself necessary, but was rather a matter of one's choice. I shall call this the acceptance-variability of the respective contexts. In addition, the specific contents of each context could vary; that is, even if one accepted the context in general, one might adopt different ends, participate in different institutions, have different conceptions of well-being, and these diversities generated quite different and even opposed 'ought'-conclusions. I shall call this the content-variability of the respective contexts. So there was a double hypotheticalness in these arguments, and this accounted for their failure to satisfy the conditions of categoricalness and determinacy.

In the context of the generic features of action, on the other hand, neither of these variabilities is found. There is no acceptance-variability, for it is not open to any person intentionally to evade or reject the context of action. To be sure, one might try to carry out such rejection by intentionally committing suicide, ingesting sleep-inducing drugs, selling oneself into slavery, and so forth. But not only would this intentional removal of oneself from the context of action obviously carry a crushing price, but moreover the very acts of taking these evading steps would themselves be actions, and hence the necessary conditions of actions, their generic features, would be fulfilled in the very process of removing oneself from further involvement in the context of action. Similarly, if one views actions in terms of their generic features there is no content-variability in the context of actions; for although actions may, of course, be of many different sorts, they all have certain generic features in common, features which are necessarily exhibited by any instance of action, and these necessary features logically generate certain requirements or 'oughts' regardless of the specific differences of kinds of action. Because of this lack of acceptance-variability and content-variability, the 'oughts' derived from the context of the generic features of action have a necessity which enables them to satisfy the conditions of categoricalness and determinacy. I shall, in fact, try to show that the relation of the theory of action to moral philosophy is much closer and more substantive than has hitherto been thought.

It is to be noted that I am here using the word 'action' in a quite strict sense. In this sense, human movements or behaviors are not actions if they occur from one or more of the following kinds of cause: (a) direct compulsion by someone or something external to the person; (b) causes internal to the person, such as reflexes, ignorance, or disease, which decisively contribute, in ways beyond his control, to the occurrence of the behavior; (c) indirect compulsion whereby the person's choice to emit some behavior is forced by someone else's coercion. In contrast to such behaviors, actions in the strict sense have the generic features of being voluntary and purposive. By 'voluntary' I mean that the agent occurrently or dispositionally controls his behavior by his unforced choice, knowing the various proximate circumstances of his action. By 'purposive' I mean that the agent intends to do what he does, envisaging some purpose or goal which may consist either in the performance of the action itself or in some outcome of that performance; in either case, insofar as it is the purpose of his action the agent regards it as some sort of good. These generic features also mean that actions are characterized by freedom and relative well-being on the part of the agent: by freedom in virtue of their uncoerced character and the agent's control over them; by well-being in the relative sense that the agent's purpose is to do or obtain something he regards as good, although not necessarily good in terms either of morality or even of his own self-interest.

The direct relevance of action in the strict sense to the 'Is-Ought' Problem can be seen from the fact that 'ought'-judgments are primarily concerned with action in this sense. When it is said, not only in moral or political precepts but also in prudential, technical, institutional, and other practical precepts, that some person ought to do something, the assumption of the speaker, at least prospectively, is that the person addressed is an actual or potential agent who can control his behavior with a view to achieving the objective set forth in the precept, and that the agent will set some sort of preferred priority either on this objective or on the ones for which he would otherwise act. As this last point indicates, actions in the strict sense include behaviors whereby agents may violate as well as fulfill moral, political, and other practical precepts, and they also include behaviors which are indifferent in relation to such precepts.

In addition to this consideration, the direct rational justification for focusing on the generic features of action is that, being invariable, they impose themselves on every agent, as against the particular contents of his actions which vary with his different and possibly arbitrary inclinations, and also that, being necessary to all action, they take priority for the agent over the particular purposes for which he may contingently act.

Before proceeding to the derivation, I must say something about the method I shall follow. Philosophers have, of course, dealt with and disagreed over the nature of their operations and results; in this regard they have used such phrases as 'rational reconstruction', 'conceptual analysis', 'criteriological connection', 'phenomenological description', 'inductive generalization', and so forth. I cannot, of course, deal with this issue here. But in order to facilitate understanding of what I shall try to do, I should point out that I shall use what I call a dialectically necessary method. My method is dialectical in a sense closely related to that referred to in the Socratic dialogues and in Aristotle: that is, it begins from assumptions, statements, or claims made by protagonists — in this case, the agent — and it examines what these logically imply. The method is dialectically necessary, however, in that the assumptions or claims in question are necessarily made by agents; they reflect not some protagonist's variable opinions, interests, or ideals but rather the necessary structure of purposive action as viewed by the agent. One aspect of this necessity has already been suggested in my statements about the invariability of the context of the generic features of action. On the basis of these necessary contents, I shall show that every agent is logically committed to making or at least accepting certain determinate, categorical moral 'ought'-judgments. Although I shall characterize the steps leading to this logical commitment as entailments, my argument will not be materially affected if the connections in question are interpreted in some less stringent way, so long as their necessary connection with the context of the generic features of action is kept in view.

It will constitute no objection to my use of this method that agents do not necessarily perform speech acts or make linguistic utterances. For on the basis of their actions certain thought-contents can be attributed to them in either direct or indirect discourse. If we see someone running very hard in order to catch a bus, we can safely infer, without stopping him and asking him, that he thinks it is worth his effort to try to catch that bus, just as if we see someone reading a book with avid interest we don't have to see whether he is moving his lips in order to attribute to him such a judgment as, "It is worth my attention reading this book," according to whatever criterion of worth is involved in his purpose of reading. Moreover, although there is in general a difference between entailment-relations among propositions and relations of belief of those propositions — if p entails q, this does not entail that someone's believing that p entails his believing that q — nevertheless I shall here attribute to the agent belief in or acceptance of certain propositions on the basis of their being entailed by other propositions he accepts. The justification for this is that the entailments in question are so direct that awareness of them can safely be attributed to any person who is sufficiently rational to be able to control his behavior by his unforced choice with a view to achieving his purposes.

Enough of preliminaries. I shall now undertake to show how 'ought'-judgments having the five required characteristics are logically derivable from 'is'-statements which describe the occurrence of actions in the strict sense defined above. Although the argument will involve various complexities, some of which I have treated in detail elsewhere, I can indicate enough of the main lines in what follows.

To begin with, that purposive actions occur or that some person performs an action is an empirical fact which can be stated in descriptive, empirical propositions regardless of whether the statements are made by the agent himself or by other persons. As made by the agent himself, the statement may be put formally as, "I do X for purpose E." Although there has been an abortive attempt to argue that assertions of the performance or occurrence of actions are ascriptive rather than descriptive in that they make moral or legal judgments about the agent's responsibility, this attempt has, by general agreement, been definitively refuted.[13] And although some utterances of this form are performatory in Austin's sense, most are not. In a somewhat different direction we can also disregard here Cartesian doubts about the possibility of empirically ascertaining that the choices and purposes involved in action are in fact occurrently or dispositionally present. This disregard is especially warranted because, in accordance with my dialectical method, I shall be considering actions as they are viewed and referred to by the agent himself.

From this empirical premiss, the agent's statement that he performs an action, the derivation will now proceed in four main steps. The first step involves the point that action as viewed by

---

[13]See H.L.A. Hart, "The Ascription of Rights and Responsibilities," *Proceedings of the Aristotelian Society*, vol. 49 (1948-49); P.T. Geach, "Ascriptivism," *Philosophical Review*, vol. 69 (1960), pp. 221 ff.; Hart, *Punishment and Responsibility* (Oxford: Clarendon Press, 1968), Preface.

the agent has, in virtue of its purposiveness, a certain evaluative element. To see this, we must note that action is not a mere physical occurrence in which the entities concerned make no choices and guide themselves for the sake of no purposes. Nor is the agent's attitude toward his action merely a passive or contemplative one; the action is not something that happens to him from causes beyond his control. On the contrary, the agent's relation to the action he brings about is conative and evaluative, for he acts for some purpose which seems to him to be good. In acting, the agent envisages more or less clearly some preferred outcome, some objective or goal which he wants to achieve, where such wanting may be either intentional or inclinational. This goal is regarded by the agent as worth aiming at or pursuing; for if he did not so regard it he would not unforcedly choose to move from quiescence or non-action to action with a view to achieving the goal. This conception of worth constitutes a valuing on the part of the agent; he regards the object of his action as having at least sufficient value to merit his acting to attain it, according to whatever criteria are involved in his action. These criteria of value need not be moral nor even hedonic; they run the full range of the purposes for which the agent acts. Now 'value' in this broad sense is synonymous with 'good' in a similarly broad sense encompassing a wide range of nonmoral as well as moral criteria. Hence, since the agent values, at least instrumentally, the purposes or objects for which he acts, it can also be said that he regards these objects as at least instrumentally good according to whatever criteria lead him to try to achieve his purpose. He may, of course, also regard his purpose as bad on other criteria, and he may regret the narrow range of alternatives open to him among which he chooses. Still, so long as his choice is not forced, by the very fact that he chooses to act he shows that he regards his action as worth performing and hence as good at least relatively to his not acting at all or to his acting for other purposes which are open to him. The presence of choice and purpose in action thus gives it a structure such that, from the standpoint of the agent, "I do X for purpose E" entails "X and E are good." Since the latter statement is a value-judgment, or at least the function of such a judgment, to this extent from the standpoint of the agent the 'fact-value' gap, even if not the 'is-ought' gap, is already bridged in action.

The agent's positive evaluative judgment extends not only to his particular action and purpose but also to the generic features which characterize all his actions. Since his action is a means to attaining something he regards as good, even if this is only the performance of the action itself, he regards as good the voluntariness or freedom which is an essential feature of his action, for without this he would not be able to act for any purpose at all. He also regards as good those basic aspects of his well-being which are the necessary conditions both of the existence and of the success of all his actions, and which hence are not relative to his particular purposes and not subject to the disagreements that we saw earlier attach to different interpretations of well-being as a whole. This basic well-being comprises certain physical and psychological dispositions ranging from life and physical integrity to a feeling of confidence as to the general possibility of attaining one's goals.

In connection with this point, it should be noted that whereas the eudaemonist derivation considered above, like other naturalistic doctrines, left itself open to the objection that what it regards as well-being is not really good or is not considered good by some persons, my present argument does not incur this objection. For, being dialectical, the argument proceeds from within the standpoint of the agent himself and his own purposes and conceptions of well-being, whatever they may be. But as against the means-end derivation considered above, my argument, being dialectically *necessary*, does not depend for its direct content upon the contingent and variable purposes which different persons may have and the means required for these; it depends rather upon the necessary means which are required for any purposive actions, and which any agent must therefore regard as good. Thus, because freedom and basic well-being are at least instrumentally necessary to all the agent's actions for purposes, from the agent's standpoint his statement, "I do X for purpose E" entails not only "X and E are good" but also "My freedom and basic well-being are good as the necessary conditions of all my actions."

From this first main step there follows a second, bearing on justifications and right-claims. In virtue of his positive evaluations the agent regards himself as justified in performing his actions and in having the freedom and basic well-being which generically figure in all his actions, and he implicitly makes a corresponding right-claim. To regard something as justified on some criterion is to hold that its rightness is or can be established according to that criterion, and to have toward it a corresponding attitude of endorsement. Now an important, even if not the only, basis of an action's being right from the standpoint of its agent is that he regards it as having a good purpose. The agent therefore regards his action as justified by this goodness. But, *a fortiori*, he especially regards himself as justified in having freedom and basic well-being, since these are the necessary conditions of all his actions and hence of any purposes or goals he may attain or pursue through action.

This justificatory attitude takes the logical form of a claim on the part of the agent that he has a right to perform his actions and to have freedom and basic well-being. Even if there is not in every case a correct inference from an agent's regarding X as good to his claiming a right to X, the inference does hold from within the agent's standpoint insofar as X consists in freedom and basic well-being, because of the strategic relation of these goods to all his purposive actions. In the case of every claim to have a right to X, a necessary condition is that X seem directly or indirectly good to the claimant, and a sufficient condition is that he regard X as a basic good such as is required for his pursuit of any other goods. For it is central to the concept of a right, at least where it is advanced as a claim by individuals, that its primary, even if not its only, application is to the proximate prerequisites of any purposive actions, since without the direct capacity for such action the claimant, beyond making the claim itself, would not be able to move toward anything he regards as good. It is this elemental aspect of right-claims that seems to me to underlie Jefferson's asserting as self-evident that all men have inalienable rights to life, liberty, and the pursuit of happiness. Put in the dialectically necessary terms I am using here, this says that since every agent regards as basic goods the freedom and basic well-being which are the proximate necessary conditions of his acting for the achievement of any of his purposes, and since the criterion of claiming justifications and rights, so far as the agent is concerned, consists in the first instance in such proximate necessary conditions, it follows that any agent must claim, at least implicitly, that he has a right to freedom and basic well-being. And this right-claim is prescriptive: it carries the agent's advocacy or endorsement.

According to this second main step, then, action as viewed by the agent has a normative as well as an evaluative structure, in that it involves right-claims as well as judgments of good. From the agent's standpoint, his judgment "My freedom and basic well-being are good as the necessary conditions of all my actions"

entails "I have a right to freedom and basic well-being."[14] This
second step is, of course, crucial for the 'is-ought' derivation,
since the normative concept of having a right either already is, or
is directly translatable into, a deontic concept. Nevertheless, in
order to show how all five conditions of the real 'Is-Ought' Problem are to be satisfied, I must go through two further steps.

The third main step involves the consideration that, given the
agent's claim that he has a right to freedom and basic well-being,
he is logically committed to a generalization of this right-claim to
all prospective agents and hence to all persons. To see this, we
must note that every right-claim is made on behalf of some person or group with an at least implicit recognition of the description or sufficient reason which is held to ground the right. This
description or sufficient reason may be quite general or quite
particular, but in any case the person who claims some right must
admit, on pain of contradiction, that this right also belongs to
any other persons to whom that description or reason applies.
This necessity is an exemplification of the logical principle of
universalizability: if some predicate P belongs to some subject S
because S has the property Q (where the 'because' is that of sufficient reason or condition), then P must also belong to all other
subjects S_1, S_2, . . . S_n which have Q. If one denies this implication in the case of some individual, such as S_1, which has Q,
then one contradicts oneself, for in saying that P belongs to S
because S has Q one implies that all Q is P, but in denying this in
the case of S_1, which has Q, one says that some Q is not P.

The crucial question in the present context concerns the description or sufficient reason which the agent adduces as decisively relevant in claiming that he has a right to freedom and
basic well-being. Many philosophers have held that there is no
logical limit in this respect, that any agent can choose whatever
description or sufficient reason he likes without committing any
logical error. He may claim that he has the rights in question
because and only because, for example, he is white or male or
American or a philosopher or an atheist, or for that matter because he is named Wordsworth Donisthorpe or because he was
born on such and such a date at such and such a place, and so
forth. And, of course, depending on the property he adduces as a

---

[14]For more detailed arguments for the above two steps, see my "The Normative Structure of Action," *Review of Metaphysics*, vol. 25 (1971), pp. 238 ff.

sufficient reason for his right-claim, he will be logically required to grant only that these rights belong to all other persons who have this property, including, at the extreme, the class consisting only of one member, himself.

In opposition to this view, I hold that the agent logically must adduce only a certain description or sufficient reason as the ground of his claim that he has a right to freedom and basic well-being. This description or sufficient reason is that he is a prospective agent who has purposes he wants to fulfill. If the agent adduces anything less general than this as his exclusive justifying description, then, by the preceding argument, he can be shown to contradict himself. Let us designate by the letter R such a more restrictive description. Examples of R would include, "My name is Wordsworth Donisthorpe" and the other descriptions just mentioned. Now let us ask the agent whether, while being an agent, he would still claim to have the rights of freedom and basic well-being even if he were not R. If he answers yes, then he contradicts his assertion that he has these rights only insofar as he is R. He would hence have to admit that he is mistaken in restricting his justificatory description to R. But if he answers no, i.e. if he says that while being an agent he would not claim these rights if he were not R, then he can be shown to contradict himself with regard to the generic features of action. For, as we have seen, it is necessarily true of every agent both that he requires freedom and basic well-being in order to act and that he hence implicitly claims the right to have freedom and basic well-being. For an agent not to claim these rights would mean that he does not act for purposes he regards as good at all and that he does not regard his actions, with their necessary conditions of freedom and basic well-being, as justified by the goodness of his purpose. But this in turn would mean that he is not an agent, which contradicts the initial assumption. Thus, to avoid contradicting himself, the agent must admit that he would claim to have the rights of freedom and basic well-being even if he were not R, and hence that the description or sufficient reason for which he claims these rights is not anything less general than that he is a prospective agent who has purposes he wants to fulfill.[15]

---

[15] I have presented this and related arguments more fully in "The Justification of Egalitarian Justice," *American Philosophical Quarterly*, vol. 8 (1971), pp. 331 ff., and in *Moral Rationality*, The Lindley Lecture for 1972 (University of Kansas, 1972).

It is also this generality that explains why, in the necessary description or sufficient reason of his having these rights, I have referred to a '*prospective* agent who has purposes he wants to fulfill.' For the agent claims these rights not only in his present action with its particular purpose but in all his actions. To restrict to his present purpose his reason for claiming the rights of freedom and basic well-being would be to overlook the fact that he regards these as goods in respect of all his actions and purposes, not only his present one.

Since, then, the agent, in order to avoid contradicting himself, must claim that he has the rights of freedom and basic well-being for the sufficient reason that he is a prospective agent who has purposes he wants to fulfill, he logically must accept the generalization that all prospective agents who have purposes they want to fulfill, and hence all persons, have the rights of freedom and basic well-being. This generalization is a direct application of the principle of universalizability; and if the agent denies the generalization, then, as we have seen, he contradicts himself. For on the one hand in holding, as he logically must, that he has the rights of freedom and basic well-being because he is a prospective purposive agent, he implies that all prospective purposive agents have these rights; but on the other hand he holds that some prospective purposive agent does not have these rights.

I shall henceforth refer to the agent who avoids such contradictions, and who hence accepts the opposed logically necessary statements, as a 'rational agent.' It will be noted that this is the minimal and most basic sense of 'rational' as applied to persons and that its criterion is a purely logical one, involving consistency or the avoidance of self-contradiction. Thus we have seen that, by virtue of accepting the statement "I have a right to freedom and basic well-being," the rational agent must also accept "I have these rights for the sufficient reason that I am a prospective purposive agent," and hence that "All prospective purposive agents have a right to freedom and basic well-being." The rational agent must therefore advocate or endorse these rights for all other persons on the same ground as he advocates them for himself.

The fourth and final main step moves directly from this generalized right-claim to a correlative 'ought'-judgment. For all rights are logically correlative with at least negative duties or 'oughts', in that for any person A to have a right to have or do something X entails that all other persons ought to refrain from interfering either with A's having or doing X or at least with A's trying to have or do X. Hence, since the agent logically had to admit that "All prospective purposive agents have a right to freedom and basic well-being," he must also logically accept the 'ought'-judgment, "I ought to refrain from interfering with the freedom and basic well-being of all prospective purposive agents," and hence of all persons. Interference with their freedom would constitute coercion; interference with their basic well-being would constitute basic harm. Thus we have seen that from the initial empirical premiss, "I do X for purpose E," there logically follows the 'ought'-judgment, "I ought to refrain from coercing other persons or inflicting basic harm on them." The agent is logically compelled to admit these 'oughts', on pain of contradiction.

The general principle of these 'oughts' or duties may be expressed as the following precept addressed to every agent: *Apply to your recipient the same generic features of action that you apply to yourself.* I shall call this the *Principle of Generic Consistency (PGC)*, since it combines the formal consideration of consistency, as found in the above universalization argument, with the material consideration of the generic features of action, including the right-claims which the agent necessarily makes. The *PGC* is an egalitarian universalist moral principle since it requires an equal distribution of the most basic rights of action. It says to every agent that just as, in acting, he necessarily applies to himself and claims as rights for himself the generic features of action, voluntariness or freedom and purposiveness at least in the sense of basic well-being, so he ought to apply these same generic features to all the recipients of his actions by allowing them also to have freedom and basic well-being and hence by refraining from coercing them or inflicting basic harm on them. This means that the agent ought to be impartial as between himself and other persons when the latter's freedom and basic well-being are at stake, so that he ought to respect other persons' freedom and basic well-being as well as his own. And as we have seen, if the agent denies or violates this principle, then he contradicts himself.

The *PGC* has as direct or indirect logical consequences egalitarian moral 'ought'-judgments of the paradigmatic sort that I presented at the outset. Given the *PGC*, there directly follows the negative duty not to inflict serious gratuitous harm on other persons. There also directly follows the positive duty to perform such actions as rescuing drowning persons or feeding starving persons, especially when this can be done at relatively little cost to oneself. For the *PGC* prohibits inflicting basic harms on other persons; but to refrain from performing such actions as rescuing and feeding in the circumstances described would be to inflict basic harms on the persons in need and would hence violate the impartiality required by the *PGC*. It would mean that while the agent participates in the situation voluntarily and with basic well-being, not to mention his other purposes, he prevents his recipients from doing so. Although there is indeed a distinction between causing a basic harm to occur and merely permitting it to occur by one's inaction, such intentional inaction in the described circumstances is itself an action that interferes with the basic well-being of the persons in need. For it prevents, by means under the agent's control and with his knowledge, the occurrence of transactions which would remove the basic harms in question.

The *PGC* also has as its indirect consequences sociopolitical moral 'ought'-judgments requiring actions in support of civil liberties and in opposition to great inequalities of wealth and power. While I do not have the time now to go into such institutional applications, the general point is that since the *PGC* requires an equal distribution of the most basic rights of action, freedom and basic well-being, it also requires legal, political, and economic institutions which foster such libertarian and egalitarian rights, and it hence requires actions which support such institutions. Unlike the direct institutional derivations considered earlier, if the obligations grounded in various institutions are to be justified, then the institutions themselves must first be justifiable through the *PGC*.[16] And it is by rules based on such justified institutions that conflicts arising from agents' use of their freedom are to be resolved.

This, then, concludes my argument. So far as concerns the particular paradigmatic moral 'ought'-judgments which I presented at the outset, I have not derived them directly from their antecedent 'is'-statements about B's starving and so forth; rather I have treated these combinations as enthymemes having such specific 'ought'-premises as: "Whenever some person is starving and someone else can relieve him at no comparable cost to himself, he ought to do so." These 'ought'-premises, however, follow from the *PGC*, and the *PGC* in turn follows, through the steps I

---

[16] For fuller discussion of how institutional obligations are derived from the *PGC*, see my "Obligation: Political, Legal, Moral," *op. cit.*, (above, n. 10). See also my "Categorial Consistency in Ethics," *Philosophical Quarterly*, vol. 17 (1967), pp. 289 ff.

have indicated, from the 'is'-statement made by the agent that he performs actions for purposes. Hence, the particular moral 'ought'-judgments have been derived, through several intermediate steps, from an empirical 'is'-statement.

I have here presented, then, a complex version of what I have called the internal model of the relation between 'ought' and 'is'. I have not directly defined 'ought' in terms of 'is'; rather, I have held that the application of 'ought' is entailed by the correlative concept of having a right. The agent's application of this concept, in turn, has been derived from the concept of goods which are the necessary conditions of all his actions, since he necessarily claims that he has a right to at least these goods. And the agent's application of the concept of good, finally, has been derived from his acting for purposes. Since the agent's assertion that he acts for purposes is an empirical, descriptive statement, I have in this indirect way derived 'ought' from 'is'. Whether the derivation is at each point definitional or is rather of some other non-arbitrary sort does not materially affect my argument, so long as its necessary relation to the context of action is recognized.

If this derivation has been successful, if it constitutes a resolution of the real 'Is-Ought' Problem, then the 'ought'-judgments which I have derived have the five characteristics indicated in my first section. Let us examine whether this is so. We have already seen that the *PGC* and the more specific 'ought'-judgments that follow from it are moral and egalitarian. They are also prescriptive, since they follow logically from the agent's prescriptive claim that he has a right to freedom and basic well-being. And they are determinate, for they rule out the coercion and basic harm which we saw were permitted by other 'is-ought' derivations.

It may be questioned, however, whether the condition of categoricalness has been satisfied. The objection would be that there is a conflict between the categorical and the dialectical. Since my argument has been dialectical in that it proceeds from within the standpoint of the agent, including the evaluations and right-claims he makes, the *PGC* and the ensuing ought-judgments I have derived are valid, so holds the objection, only relatively to the agent's standpoint, but not absolutely. Even if the agent is logically compelled to uphold certain 'ought'-judgments, given his initial statement that he performs actions for purposes, this does not establish that those judgments are really correct or binding. Hence, their 'oughts' are not categorical.

My reply to this objection is that the dialectically *necessary* aspect of my method gives the 'ought'-conclusions a more than contingent or hypothetical status. Since moral 'oughts' apply only or primarily to the context of action and hence to agents, to have shown that certain 'ought'-judgments logically must be granted by all agents, on pain of contradiction, is to give the judgments an absolute status since their validity is logically ineluctable within the whole context of their possible application. It will be recalled that in my original specification I said that for 'ought'-judgments to be categorical the normative bindingness of the requirements they set forth cannot be removed or evaded by variable, escapable features of the persons addressed, including their self-interested desires or their contingent choices, opinions, and attitudes. This condition of categoricalness is fulfilled by the *PGC*'s 'ought'-judgment.

This necessity also explicates the respect in which moral judgments have truth-value. The *PGC* and the moral judgments that follow from it are true in that they correspond to the concept of a rational agent, for they indicate what logically must be admitted by such an agent. As I noted above, the criterion of 'rational' here is a purely logical one.

Finally, what of the condition of non-circularity? Although my argument began from the agent's empirical statements that he performs actions, I then pointed out that actions as viewed by him have certain ineluctable evaluative and normative elements. Doesn't this mean that I have reached a normative or at least a prescriptive 'ought'-conclusion only by putting normativeness or prescriptiveness into my premiss about action? It was this question that figured in the 'dilemma of commitment' that I presented above. Now an assumption of this dilemma was that for any person who undertakes to derive 'ought' from 'is' within some context, it is open to him to choose or to refrain from choosing to commit himself to that context with its requirements. As we have seen, however, it is impossible intentionally to refrain from committing oneself to the context of the generic features of action, for any such refraining would itself exhibit those features. Hence, the 'ought' which is derived within that context is prescriptive; but nevertheless the derivation is not circular, because the derived 'ought' reflects not a dispensable choice or commitment but rather a necessity which is not subject to any choice or decision on the part of the agent. The objector hence cannot say, "You've reached a commitment or prescription in the conclusion only because you've already chosen to put the commitment or pre-scription into your premiss;" for the latter commitment in the premiss is not one that the deriver has *chosen* or has *put into* the premiss. Rather, the commitment is there in the nature of the case, and all he is doing is recognize it; but he cannot evade it. In any event, as already noted, the initial premiss of the derivation is the agent's empirical statement that he performs actions for pur-poses; and the prescriptiveness of the moral 'ought'-conclusion is accounted for more specifically by the advocacy embodied in his right-claim together with its logical generalization.

What I have tried to show here, then, is that the 'is' of the per-formance of actions having the generic features logically gen-erates the 'ought' of categorical moral judgments; or, in other words, that the fact of being a purposive agent logically requires, on pain of self-contradiction, an acknowledgment that one ought to act in certain basic moral ways. To summarize: Because ac-tions are conative and value-pursuing, they commit the agent to advocate or endorse for himself the rights of freedom and basic well-being which are the proximate necessary prerequisites of all his acting; hence, he makes judgments which fulfill the condition of prescriptiveness. Because the agent must advocate these rights for general reasons stemming from his simply being a prospective purposive agent, his advocacy must logically be extended to all other persons; hence, his judgments fulfill the conditions of being moral and egalitarian. And because this extension is based on the generic and hence inescapable features of action, it logically can-not be evaded or reversed regardless of any variable desires, choices, or attitudes on the part of the agent; hence, his judg-ments fulfill the conditions of determinacy and categoricalness. In this way, then, by an analysis of the generic features of action and their normative implications, I have argued that the real 'Is-Ought' Problem is resolved.

4
The Golden Rule Rationalized

THE Golden Rule is the common moral denominator of all the world's major religions.[1] In one of its most famous formulations it says, "Do unto others as you would have them do unto you." The Rule's imperative ("Do . . .") may be interpreted as an "ought," as prescribing how persons morally ought to act toward others or at least how it is morally right for them to act toward others. Thus the Golden Rule sets forth a criterion of the moral rightness of interpersonal actions, or transactions. This criterion consists in the agent's desires or wishes for himself *qua* recipient: what determines the moral rightness of a transaction initiated or controlled by some person is whether he would himself want to undergo such a transaction at the hands of other persons.

I

There are at least two traditional criticisms of the Golden Rule as a moral criterion or principle. First, the agent's wishes for himself *qua* recipient may not be in accord with his recipient's own wishes as to how he is to be treated. As Bernard Shaw put it in a famous quip, "Do not do unto others as you would that they should do unto you. Their tastes may not be the same."[2] Thus, if the agent A treats his recipient B as A himself would want to be treated, this may inflict gratuitous suffering on B, for B may not want to be treated in this way. For example, a person who likes others to quarrel or intrigue with him would be authorized by the Golden Rule to quarrel with others or involve them in networks of intrigue regardless of their own wishes in the matter; a *roué* who would want some young woman to climb into his bed at night would be justified in climbing into her bed at night; a fanatical believer in the sanctity of contracts who would want others to imprison him for defaulting on his debts would be allowed to imprison persons who default on their debts to him, and so forth.

A second criticism of the Golden Rule is that the agent's wishes for himself *qua* recipient may go counter to many justified social rules, legal, economic, and other. Even if the agent's wishes for himself are not opposed to those of his recipient, both sets of wishes may be immoral. As Sidgwick put it, "one might wish for another's cooperation in sin, and be willing to reciprocate it."[3] For example, a law-violator A who bribes a corrupt policeman B may be treating B as A would himself want to be treated.

The point of this criticism can be brought out further if the Golden Rule is given its negative formulation: "Do not do unto others as you would not have them do unto you." On this formulation together with the preceding positive one, accord with the agent's wishes for himself *qua* recipient is both the necessary and the sufficient condition of the moral rightness of transactions. The difficulty of its being a necessary condition is frequently illustrated by the case of a criminal before a judge; as Kant put it, "on the basis (of the Golden Rule), the criminal would be able to dispute with the judges who punish him."[4] For on this interpretation of the Golden Rule the judges would be justified in meting out punishment to the criminal only if they would be willing to receive such treatment themselves, so that the criminal could appeal to their own dislike for being punished as a basis for arguing that their sentencing of him is morally wrong. Not only criminal punishment but the collection of money owed by recalcitrant borrowers, the payment of lesser wages for inferior work, the giving of lower grades to poorer students, and the infliction of many similar sorts of hardships would be prohibited by the Golden Rule whenever it could be shown that the respective agents would not themselves want to undergo such adverse treatment. The Rule does not recognize the existence of justified disparities of merit and reward among agents and their recipients, including those which arise in competitive relations. More generally, in making the agent's wishes for himself *qua* recipient the criterion of right actions, the Rule ignores that various institutions may set requirements which are justified without regard to those wishes.

It is sometimes held that these difficulties of the Golden Rule can be avoided if it is given a "general interpretation" rather than a "particular interpretation."[5] These interpretations differ with regard to just which desires or wishes of the agent *qua* recipient should determine how he ought to act. The particular interpretation makes decisive the agent's particular wishes or preferences as to the particular actions which he would want to receive from others. The general interpretation, on the other hand, makes decisive the more general principles or standards on which the agent would want others to act toward him. As Marcus Singer puts it, according to the particular interpretation, "whatever in particular I would have others do to or for me, I should do to or for them," but according to the general interpretation "I am to treat others . . . on the same principles or standards as I would have them apply in their treatment of me."[6]

This distinction is a plausible one, and it might be thought that the general interpretation is able to surmount at least the first difficulty stemming from the difference between an agent's particular desires for himself *qua* recipient and the particular desires of his recipients. Closer scrutiny, however, shows that this is not the case. For the "general interpretation" turns out to embody two different conceptions, neither of which is able to resolve the difficulties of the Golden Rule.

One conception is that which Singer calls the "Inversion" of the Golden Rule. This says, "Do unto others as *they* would have you do unto them." As Singer correctly notes, this conception is quite unacceptable, for it "is tantamount to: 'Always do what anyone else wants you to do,' which in turn is equivalent to a universal requirement of perfect or absolute altruism, the absurdity of which is so manifest as not to require detailing."[7]

Nevertheless, some of Singer's own formulations of the general interpretation of the Golden Rule embody precisely this Inversion conception. For example, he writes:

> What I have to consider is the general ways in which I would have others behave in their treatment of me. And what I would have them do, in abstraction from any of my particular desires, and all that I am entitled to expect them to do, is to take account of my interests, desires, needs, and wishes — which may be different from theirs — and either satisfy them or at least not willfully frustrate them. If I would have others take account of my interests and wishes in their treatment of me, even though my interests and wishes may differ considerably from their own, then what the Golden Rule in this interpretation requires of me is that I should take account of the interests and wishes of others in my treatment of them.[8]

The phrase "take account of" is vague; a sadist, for example, takes account of his victim's wishes, since such taking account is necessary to his aim of violating those wishes. What Singer means, of course, as the second sentence of the quoted passage shows, is that the agent should either "satisfy" his recipient's wishes or else "not willfully frustrate them." But this then is largely identical with the Inversion conception of the Golden Rule: it requires that the agent always treat his recipient as the latter wishes to be treated, or at least that he not intentionally contravene those wishes. And, as has been emphasized, this is unacceptable as a general principle. It is too permissive for the recipient and too restrictive for the agent.[9]

The other conception of the general interpretation which Singer offers, without explicitly differentiating it from the Inversion conception, is one which I shall call that of Rule-Reciprocity. He presents this in such passages as the following: "I am to treat others *as* I would have them treat me, that is, on the same principle or standard as I would have them apply in their treatment of me." "One should act in relation to others *on the same principles or standards* that one would have them apply in their treatment of oneself."[10] According to this conception, the independent variable determining what the agent ought to do consists in the general principle or standard which the agent would want to have applied to him by others. The result, however, is that the Golden Rule is now too restrictive for the recipient and too permissive for the agent. For on this conception the Rule authorizes an agent to do whatever he wishes to his recipients so long as the general standard or principle on which he acts is one that he would also want or be willing to have applied to himself. But this view incurs the first difficulty of the Golden Rule sketched above. It would allow recipients to be oppressed by the principles or standards upheld by the quarreler, the *roué*, the fanatical believer in the sanctity of contracts, and so forth. The principles of action which such agents would be willing to undergo as recipients may be excessively onerous to other recipients because the latter do not share the agents' preferences or ideals or for other reasons.[11]

We may summarize these difficulties of the "general interpretation" of the Golden Rule as follows. This interpretation seems to admit of two distinct emphases: one which looks at proposed actions from the standpoint of the recipient and one which looks at them from the standpoint of the agent. In the former case the agent is to act toward others as he would want them to act toward him if he had their desires; he must hence treat them as they want to be treated. In the latter case the agent is to act toward others according to the principles on which he would want them to act toward him. Which of these emphases is adopted seems to depend on how the agent's wants for himself *qua* recipient are described. "Do unto others as you would have them do unto you." But I would have others treat me as I wish; therefore, I ought to treat them as they wish. Or, I would have others act toward me according to certain principles which

I accept; therefore, I ought to act according to those principles in relation to them. (If I act toward them according to principles which *they* accept, this is equivalent to the former case, where I treat them as they want to be treated.) Thus, the description of the agent's wants for himself *qua* recipient may say either that he wants others to accede to his own wishes or that he wants others to act toward him according to certain principles. Each description yields different and unacceptable results. The former description supports the Inversion conception, to the possible detriment of the agent's wishes; the latter description supports the Rule-Reciprocity conception, to the possible detriment of the recipient's wishes.

Is there any way, then, of "saving" the Golden Rule and thereby avoiding the contrast between its universal (and universalist) appeal and its crippling difficulties? A frequent reaction to the presentation of these difficulties is that one must look to the "spirit" rather than to the "letter" of the Rule. This is fair enough; but it leaves untouched the question of how, specifically, the Rule is to be interpreted so as to conform to its spirit while avoiding literal difficulties like those just presented.

Let us, however, try to follow up this suggestion. It seems safe to say that the spirit or intention of the Golden Rule, violated by all the interpretations so far considered, is mutualist or egalitarian: the actions it requires must be such as fulfill neither the agent's desires alone at the potential expense of his recipients' desires, nor the recipients' desires alone at the potential expense of the agent's desires. Instead, the actions must be such as make proper provision for fulfilling the desires both of the agent and of the recipient. It might be thought that the formulation which most directly satisfies this requirement is: Act in accord with your recipient's desires as well as your own, including the principles upheld by your recipient as well as by yourself. I shall call this the *Generic* interpretation of the Golden Rule, since it refers to desires as such without restriction to specific descriptions of desires either of the agent or of the recipient. Since this interpretation provides that the agent act in accord with his own desires, it avoids the difficulty of the Inversion conception; and since it provides that the agent act also in accord with his recipient's desires, it avoids the difficulty of the Rule-Reciprocity conception. Its difference from the latter needs some further comment. It is one thing to say that an action or a principle of action is justified if its agent is willing to be the recipient of such an action. It is quite a different thing to say that an action or a principle of action is justified if both its recipient and its agent are willing to accept it. In the former case the *justificans* of the principle consists in the desires of only the agent, although in two different capacities, while in the latter case it consists in the desires of both the agent and the recipient, that is, of all the persons who are involved in transactions according to the principle. This makes a considerable difference. Thus while the Rule-Reciprocity interpretation of the Golden Rule may provide for satisfying the agent's desires at the expense of his recipient's desires, this is prohibited by the Generic interpretation.

This interpretation, however, does not solve all the difficulties of the Golden Rule. For it does not tell the agent what to do when his desires conflict with those of his actual or potential recipients. If the *roué* acts in accord with his own desires, including the principles he upholds, he will climb into the girl's bed; if he acts in accord with her desires, he will not. If the hard-working citizen acts in accord with his own desires, he will refuse to give money to the drunken beggar, but if he acts in accord with the latter's desires, he will give him money to spend on further liquor. The Generic interpretation does indeed pose a challenge to the agent to act so as to accommodate his own wants or desires, including the general principles he upholds, to those of his recipient while not frustrating either set of wants or desires. But the interpretation provides no guidance concerning how this accommodation or compromise is to proceed in cases of conflict.

In addition, the second difficulty mentioned earlier must still be met: even if, following the Generic interpretation, the agent acts in accord with his recipient's desires as well as his own, his action may go counter to justified social rules. Thus the previous example of the law-violator who bribes the corrupt policeman applies also against the Generic interpretation. It may be held that in such a case the law-violator is offending against the desires of the many law-abiding citizens who would be affronted or wronged by his bribery, so that he is not acting in accord with their desires as well as his own. This, however, raises the question of just which persons are to count as the "others" toward whom one acts. If the wishes or desires of even those persons who are affected only remotely or by way of principled disapproval are to be included among such "others," then the possibility of conflicting desires becomes even more acute.

The trouble with all the interpretations so far considered is that, amid the mutualist form of the Golden Rule, they take as their contents contingent wants or desires, whether of the agent or of his recipients or both, and whether particular or general. The interpretations make such wants or desires the independent bases for determining the rightness of actions. Now wants may be of various kinds: There are differences between what one actively wants, what one idly wishes for, and what one would merely be willing to accept, perhaps with various degrees of enthusiasm or reluctance; there are also differences between self-interested wants, including hedonic inclinations, and disinterested wants, including those which seek to achieve some general principle or ideal; in addition, there are differences between long-range wants and immediate wants, between wants based on adequate information and wants based on ignorance, between conscious and unconscious wants, and so forth. The Golden Rule would have to be interpreted differently insofar as "want" is interpreted in these different ways. In its standard formulations, however, the Golden Rule does not explicitly provide any clue for differentiating among these sorts of wants or desires. Thus in the New Testament the Greek word translated as "would have" or "would want" is Θέλητε (thelēte, Latin vultis),[12] which has a quite general desiderative sense.

When wants or desires are taken indiscriminately as the independent bases for determining the rightness of actions, including the desires of the agent *qua* recipient or of the recipient himself, the result is either the potential oppressiveness and one-sidedness of the Rule-Reciprocity and Inversion conceptions or the potential unresolved conflicts of the Generic interpretation. The reason why the basis in wants or desires may have these results is that the wants in question include contingent predilections which may vary from one person to another, so that the desires of the agent and of his recipient may conflict both with one another and with justified social rules. The Golden Rule is most plausible when it focuses on certain standard desires which all persons are normally thought to have for themselves, such as protection against physical violence and other harms. But the Rule is not, of course, limited to such desires, nor are they held so universally that some persons may not be willing to surrender them for the sake of various ideals or interests. If the Golden Rule is to be saved, then, its criterion of rightness must be separated from the contingency and potential arbitrariness which attach to desires taken without qualification.

II

I now want to suggest that these difficulties of the Golden Rule are to be resolved not by completely surrendering the Rule's substantive basis in the desires of the agent for himself *qua* recipient, but rather by adding the requirement that the desires in question must be *rational*. Thus the Golden Rule should be amended to read: Do unto others as you would rationally want them to do unto you. I shall call this the *Rational Golden Rule*, and I shall say that the Golden Rule is "rationalized" when its form and content are made to include this reference to rationality. Similarly, the Generic interpretation of the Rule should be amended to read: Act in accord with your recipient's rational desires as well as your own. The difficulties of the Golden Rule noted above have been elicited by noting that its applications may conflict with intuitions most of us have about the morally right ways to act toward other persons. To rationalize the Rule by grounding it in rational desires serves not only to save these intuitions but also to show how they and all other correct moral judgments have a rational basis.

It is obviously of crucial importance how "rational" is interpreted in this context. Although the word has been used with many different meanings which have given rise to a sizeable literature, for present purposes we may distinguish just two possibilities. Either "rational" is used in a normatively moral sense or in a morally neutral sense. By a normatively moral sense I mean one where its user takes sides on normative moral issues by directly identifying "rational" with one or another preferred way of treating other persons. Such identification sometimes occurs by giving a certain egalitarian moral content to the concept of a "moral reason," as when it is said that a moral reason for rules of action requires that the rules must be for the good of everyone alike or that they must serve to harmonize the interests of all the persons affected.[13]

This normative moral interpretation of "rational" incurs serious problems. It does not, of itself, show why the opposed contents or ways of treating other persons may not be rational; it seems to settle substantive moral issues by linguistic fiat; it does not indicate how this use of "rational" is related to other standard uses of the word and to more general criteria of rationality. In the present context, moreover, such an interpretation of "rational" would make the Golden Rule superfluous. For the Rule purports to set forth the criterion of moral rightness. But if the word "rational" already comprises such a criterion, then there is no need to tell the agent that he should act toward others as he would rationally desire *that they act toward him*. It would be sufficient to tell the agent to act rationally, for "rational" would already mean or include the criterion of moral rightness. Hence, the Golden Rule's emphasis on mutuality or reciprocity of desires would be redundant.

A parallel difficulty is incurred by Samuel Clarke's principle of "equity," which Sidgwick said is "the 'Golden Rule' precisely stated." According to Clarke's principle, "Whatever I judge reasonable or unreasonable for another to do for me, that, by the same judgment, I declare reasonable or unreasonable that I in the like case should do for him."[14] If criteria of reasonableness vary from one person to another, then the problem of divergent "tastes" is not resolved; while if "reasonable" is interpreted as having some definite normative moral sense, then the mutuality of the Golden Rule becomes superfluous since one must already know what is morally right. In any case, we are still left with the problem of determining what it is reasonable for other persons to do to oneself.

A similar point applies to the move made by St. Augustine and Thomas Aquinas when, having distinguished between "rational will" (*voluntas*) and "appetite" (*cupiditas*), they insisted that only the former figures in the Golden Rule,[15] which is thus to be interpreted as saying: Do unto others as you would rationally will that they do unto you. The distinction between *voluntas* and *cupiditas* is said to be that the objects of the former are goods (*bona*) while the objects of the latter are evils (*mala*). The question now turns on the nature of the "goods" which are held to be uniquely the objects of *voluntas* as against *cupiditas*. They cannot include non-moral goods like sexual pleasure or wealth, since these are also the objects of *cupiditas*. If, on the other hand, the goods in question are intended to be moral ones, as seems likely, then the Golden Rule would now say that an agent ought to do to others only those morally good things which he would want others to do to him. This would mean, however, that the Rule would no longer be a first moral principle determining what are moral goods and evils. For on this interpretation, in order to apply the Rule one would already have to know, independently of the Rule, what are the moral goods and evils. Moreover, on this interpretation there would again be little or no point in the Rule's referring to the agent's rational wants for himself *qua* recipient as determining what he ought to do. For insofar as what one ought to do is what is morally good, the latter, if we know what it consists in, provides of itself a sufficient criterion of right action; there is no need to add that the agent must want that other persons do these morally good things to him.

If, however, a normative moral interpretation of "rational" incurs these failings, is anything better forthcoming from a morally neutral interpretation, which directly takes no sides on the moral issue of how persons ought to treat one another? From a morally neutral meaning of "rational" whereby the agent is to act toward his recipients as he would rationally want them to act toward him, how can an acceptable normatively moral content be derived for the Golden Rule? The answer is given by the consideration that when certain morally neutral rational requirements are imposed on the agent's desires, there logically emerges a normative moral content which resolves the traditional difficulties of the Rule.

The morally neutral rational requirements in question are the canons of deductive and inductive logic, including among the latter its beginning-points in sense-experience. Deductive logic is here viewed as including the conceptual analysis by which the components of a complex concept are found to pertain to the concept with logical necessity, so that it is contradictory to affirm that the complex concept applies and to deny that its component concepts apply. When conceptual analysis is brought to bear on the concepts of action and wanting, a principle is derived which replaces the contingent desires of the traditional interpretations of the Golden Rule by a certain necessary content. This content is one of *rights* to the generic features of action. In this new formulation, the Golden Rule will read as follows: Do unto others as you have a right that they do unto you. Or, to put it in its Generic formulation: Act in accord with the generic rights of your recipients as well as of yourself.

Since I have presented the argument for this in various other places,[16] I shall merely summarize the main points here. We begin from the agent who wants to attain various of his purposes. Such wants are necessarily attributable to every agent, for what it means to be an agent is that one controls one's behavior with a view to achieving ends which constitute one's reasons for acting, and which one hence intends to achieve. Since the agent regards his purposes as good according to whatever criteria (not necessarily moral ones) are involved in his reasons for acting, he must hold *a fortiori* that the generic features which characterize all his actions, and which are the proximate necessary conditions of his acting for purposes, are necessary goods. These generic features consist in the freedom or voluntariness whereby he controls or initiates his behavior by his unforced choice, and in the purposiveness or well-being whereby he sets goals for himself and has the abilities required for achieving them. Because freedom and well-being are necessary goods to the agent, he must hold at least implicitly that he has rights to them, in that all other persons ought to refrain from interfering with his having freedom and well-being. I shall call these *generic rights*, since they are rights to the generic features of action. If some agent were to deny that he has these rights, he would contradict himself. For he would then judge both that freedom and well-being are necessary goods which he upholds for himself as the conditions of his acting for any other goods, and also that it is permissible for other persons to interfere with his having these necessary goods.

Every agent must hold that he has the generic rights on the ground or for the sufficient reason that he is a prospective agent who has purposes he wants to fulfill. Suppose some agent were to maintain that he has these rights only for some more restrictive reason R. Since this would entail that in lacking R he would lack the generic rights, A would thereby contradict himself. For since, as we have seen, it is necessarily true of every agent that he holds implicitly that he has the generic rights, A would be in the position of holding both that he has the generic rights and that, as lacking R, he does not have these rights. Thus, on pain of self-contradiction, every agent must accept the generalization that all prospective purposive agents have the generic rights because, as we have seen, he must hold that being a prospective purposive agent is a sufficient condition or reason for having the generic rights. This generalization entails that the agent ought to refrain from interfering with the freedom and well-being of all other persons insofar as they are prospective purposive agents; this is the same as to say that he must refrain from coercing and harming them. Since to refrain from such interferences is to act in such a way that one's actions are in accord with the generic rights of all other persons, every agent is logically committed, on pain of inconsistency, to accept the following precept: *Act in accord with the generic rights of your recipients as well as yourself.* I call this the *Principle of Generic Consistency (PGC)*, since it combines the formal consideration of consistency with the material consideration of the generic features and rights of action.

It will be noted that the *PGC* is the same as the Generic interpretation of the Golden Rule, except that the "desires" of the latter are replaced by "generic rights." The *PGC* also retains the mutualist, egalitarian form of the spirit of the Golden Rule, but again with the substantive difference that the agent is to act toward others not according to his wishes or desires for himself *qua* recipient but rather according to his generic rights as well as those of his recipients. By the above analysis, however, the agent rationally desires to act in this way. He rationally desires to act in accord with his own generic rights because, if his freedom and well-being are interfered with by other persons, he will not be able to act, either at all or at least successfully. The force of "rational" is here in part a matter of means-end calculation and hence of inductive inference, but it is mainly a matter of conceptual analysis whereby the agent becomes aware of the necessary conditions of his action and applies this awareness to his conative concern with achievement of his purposes. Since it is necessarily true of the agent that he wants to achieve his purposes and since his having the generic rights is logically necessary to such achievement, the rational agent, being aware of this logical necessity, wants to have and act in accord with his generic rights.

The agent also rationally desires to act in accord with the generic rights of his recipients. As we have seen, if he violates or denies the *PGC* he contradicts himself. To incur or accept self-contradiction is to violate the most basic logical canon of rationality. Thus when the requirement of rationality is imposed on the wants or desires of an agent who intends to achieve his purposes, there logically emerges a certain normative moral principle consisting in equality or mutuality of rights to freedom and well-being. Every rational agent, in the sense of "rational" just indicated, necessarily accepts this principle.

When it is said that every agent rationally desires to act in accord with the generic rights of his recipients as well as of himself, the force of "rationally" is not that every agent always has or acts from rational desires. It is rather that, insofar as his desires are rational, they have such action as their object. If the agent heeds the canons of deductive logic as these are applied to the analysis of what it is to be an agent who wants to achieve his purposes, he will recognize that in order to avoid self-contradiction he must act in accord with the generic rights of his recipients as well as of himself, and he will also recognize that he must control his effective desires accordingly. Thus the canons of deductive rationality when applied to the concept of agency entail a normative moral conclusion. Since these canons, consisting ultimately in the principle of contradiction, are the most basic conditions of any justificatory argument, the agent logically must accept the *PGC* on pain of losing all justification for his actions. But since the desires from which the agent acts may not in fact be rational ones, the *PGC*'s prescriptive force is not redundant: what the *PGC* tells the agent to do is not something which he inevitably does.

We must now consider how the *PGC* is logically equivalent to the Rational Golden Rule which tells the agent that he should do unto others as he would rationally want them to do unto him. There seems to be a difference here. For in the Rational Golden Rule the object of the agent's rational desires is the actions of *other persons* toward himself — do unto others as you rationally want *them* to do unto you. But in the *PGC* as just explicated, the object of the agent's rational desires is rather *his own* actions toward other persons — do unto others as *you* rationally want to do unto them — since the agent rationally wants that *he* act in accord with his recipients' generic rights as well as his own. In view of this difference, the following question arises. The agent's rightful actions are to be determined by his rational desires; but are these to be his rational desires as to how *others* are to act toward himself, or are they to be his rational desires as to how *he* is to act toward others, that is, in accord with their generic rights as well as his own? It might seem that these two alternatives would yield different results.

The most direct answer to this question is that, according to both the Rational Golden Rule and the *PGC*, all persons should act toward one another according to their rational desires for such interpersonal action. The objects of these rational desires, as shown by the argument given above, are the generic rights of the respective recipients as well as of the respective agents. Since there are these same objects in each case, there is no difference between what one rationally wants others to do to oneself and what one rationally wants oneself to do to others. Thus the Rational Golden Rule's precept — Do unto others as you rationally want them to do unto you — is logically equivalent to the *PGC*, which may now be put as follows: Do unto others as you rationally want to do unto them, namely, to act in accord with their generic rights as well as your own.

Let us examine somewhat more fully how it is that the agent's rational desires for the actions of other persons toward himself have the same general contents or objects as are had by his rational desires for his own actions toward other persons. He rationally wants other persons to act toward himself in accord with his own generic rights, since the objects of these rights are the necessary conditions of his own actions. Hence, by the Rational Golden Rule, he also ought to act toward other persons in accord with their generic rights. Since this logical consequence of the Rational Golden Rule is rationally derived from the Rule, the agent whose desires are governed by it has rational desires as determined by the Rule. But these desires of his, by this logical consequence of the Rational Golden Rule, now have as their objects his own actions toward other persons: he ought to act in accord with his recipients' generic rights. Thus the Rational Golden Rule, like the *PGC*, sets for the agent's conduct requirements based on his rational desires as to how he is to act toward other persons, namely, in accord with their generic rights.

This result can also be established in another way. The requirement that one act in accord with the generic rights of one's recipients is not only a logical consequence of the Rational Golden Rule; it also logically follows, independently of this Rule, from the agent's rational desire for himself *qua* recipient. For in rationally wanting that other persons act toward himself in accord with his generic rights, he holds (because of the correlativity of rights and "oughts") that other persons ought to refrain from interfering with his freedom and well-being, and he holds this for the sufficient reason that he is a prospective purposive agent. Hence, he must also hold, on pain of self-contradiction, that there ought to be such refraining from interference in the case of all prospective purposive agents: their freedom and well-being too ought to be respected and not interfered with. From this it follows that the agent himself ought to refrain from interfering with the freedom and well-being of other persons insofar as they are prospective purposive agents, so that he ought to act toward them in accord with their generic rights. Moreover, he rationally desires to act in this way, since it logically follows from his rational desire for himself *qua* recipient. But this rational desire of his now has as its object his own actions toward other persons: he rationally wants that he act toward other persons in accord with their generic rights. Since this rational desire is identical in its object with what is required by the Rational Golden Rule, it follows that this Rule, like the *PGC*, requires that the agent act toward others as he rationally wants himself to act toward them, namely, in accord with their generic rights.

In the above arguments I have assumed what may be called rational-desire-transfers: if A rationally desires that *p*, and *p* entails *q*, then A rationally desires that *q*. Now desire-transfers do not obtain universally, any more than do belief-transfers. But rational-desire-transfers do obtain. For insofar as one's desires are rational in the sense of conforming to the canons of deductive logic, one must rationally desire, or at least be predisposed to desire, whatever is entailed by what one rationally desires in the first place. If one rejects the logical consequent, then, so far as one becomes aware of this, one will also reject, and in this sense not rationally desire, the antecedent.

There still remains a question about the limits of the agent's rational desires for himself *qua* recipient. Why should he confine his demands on other persons, his rational desires concerning how they should treat him, to the generic rights? Since the basis of his right-claim is prudential, why shouldn't he rationally want that they fulfill *all* his desires? If this were indeed what he rationally wanted, then the Rational Golden Rule would unacceptably entail the Inversion of the Golden Rule: Do unto others whatever they desire that you do unto them.

The main answer to this question is that the Rational Golden Rule, including its criterion of rationality, must be interpreted in the light of the *PGC* with its own fuller development of rationality. This development proceeds in terms of the agent's right-claim to the necessary conditions of action. For the *PGC* is derived from the conceptual analysis of action, including what every agent must claim on the basis of the necessary conditions of his agency, which conditions are themselves ascertained by conceptual analysis. Thus the argument to the *PGC* abstracts from the divergent and possibly idiosyncratic desires which may characterize different agents. The argument for every agent's having to make an implicit right-claim holds only insofar as the object of the right-claim is the necessary goods of action, namely, freedom and well-being. The agent is in the position of saying that because these goods are necessary for his action, it is necessary that other persons not interfere with his having them; and this latter necessity, viewed in terms of the agent's conative pursuit of his purposes, is equivalent to his "ought"-judgment that other persons ought to refrain from interfering with his freedom and well-being. Since the agent regards this as a duty owed to himself which he is entitled to have fulfilled, his "ought"-judgment is logically equivalent to a right-claim. Thus it is only to the necessary goods of action that the agent is logically justified in making a right-claim. As we have seen, if he were to deny that he has rights to these goods, he would contradict himself. But he would not contradict himself if he were to deny that he does not have rights to other goods.

If the agent were to claim rights to whatever he might want, including all the objects of his particular contingent desires, then not only would there be a tremendous prolif-eration of right-claims, but the agent would also be aware that he would be subject to an unmanageable barrage of right-claims from other persons. For the agent, as rational, knows that if he makes a claim on other persons for a certain sufficient reason, then he logically must accept that other persons too have such claims on him insofar as they too fulfill that sufficient reason. Since, as we have seen, the only sufficient reason on which the agent is logically entitled to base his right-claim is that he is a prospective purpo-sive agent, he must accept that all other prospective purposive agents also have the rights he claims for himself. Hence, to avoid burdening himself with such an unfulfill-able plethora of claims from other persons, the agent must limit his claims to the necessary conditions of action, the generic rights.

It has now been shown how the Rational Golden Rule is logically equivalent to the *PGC*. For the sake of convenience the following respective parallel formulations of them may be given: (1) Do unto others as you rationally want them to do unto you. (2) Do unto others in accord with their generic rights as well as your own. Still another formulation was also given above: (3) Do unto others as you have a right that they do unto you. The equivalence of (3) to (2) obtains once it is recognized that (3), like (1), must be interpreted in the light of (2). For what the agent has a right that other persons do to him is that they act in accord with his generic rights, that is, that they respect his freedom and well-being. Thus, he ought to respect the freedom and well-being of his recipients. Such respect is also what the agent rationally wants that other persons exhibit toward himself, as the *PGC* requires.

III

As we have seen, the generic rights are rights to freedom and well-being. The *PGC* and the Rational Golden Rule tell every agent that he should preserve a rationally grounded mutuality or equality between his generic rights and those of his recipients. The specific applications of the *PGC* are of two kinds, direct and indirect. In the direct applications, the *PGC*'s requirements are imposed on particular transactions, while in the indirect applications the requirements are imposed in the first instance on social rules and institutions, so that particular transactions are right or justified when they conform to social rules which are themselves justified through the *PGC*. Since the nature of man is associative and interactive, wherever there is a conflict between the direct and the indirect applications, the latter have priority.

The *PGC*'s direct applications require that the agent act in accord with his recipi-ents' rights to freedom as well as his own. Since it is necessarily true of the agent that he participates freely or voluntarily in transactions he initiates or controls, he must also allow his recipients to participate freely or voluntarily. This means that he must refrain from coercing his recipients, so that their participation in transactions must be subject to their own unforced choice or consent.

Similarly, the agent must act in accord with his recipients' rights to well-being as well as his own. Most generally, well-being consists in having the various abilities and conditions which every agent must regard as goods because they are needed for successful action. These fall into a hierarchy determined by the degree of their necessity for action. Basic goods, such as life and physical integrity, are the necessary preconditions of action. Non-subtractive goods are the abilities and conditions needed for maintaining undiminished one's level of purpose-fulfillment, and additive goods are the abilities and conditions needed for raising that level. Thus the *PGC*, in its well-being component, prohibits interferences with basic goods through killing and physical assault (except in self-defense); it also prohibits lying, stealing, and promise-breaking, which interfere with non-subtractive goods; and it requires the parental care and the social arrangements which contribute to additive goods. The *PGC* also requires positive actions in circumstances where voluntary inaction would cause or permit the occurrence of basic harms.

The *PGC* and the Rational Golden Rule overcome the difficulties of the Golden Rule indicated above. The general reason for this is that whereas the traditional Golden Rule allows the rightness of actions to be determined by the agent's even arbitrary or contingent desires for himself *qua* recipient, the *PGC* and the Rational Golden Rule require that the agent's desires for himself *qua* recipient be subjected to rational requirements. As we have seen, these requirements serve both to limit the scope of the agent's determining desires for himself *qua* recipient and to assure that his own recipients are entitled to the same generic emoluments of action as he claims for himself. Thus the mutualist and beneficent intentions of the traditional Golden Rule are fulfilled and its crippling difficulties avoided.

Where the traditional Golden Rule allows the agent to oppress his recipients when his own desires for himself *qua* recipient go counter to his recipient's desires, the *PGC* prohibits such oppression. For the rightness of a transaction is now determined by the agent's rational desires for himself *qua* recipient, and such rational desires require that he act in accord with his recipients' generic rights as well as his own. Thus the actions of the quarreler, of the *roué*, and of the imprisoner of debtors are prohibited by the Rational Golden Rule, since such actions violate their recipients' rights to freedom or well-being or both. The requirement that the agent's desires for himself *qua* recipient be rational also obviates the difficulty of the Inversion conception of the traditional Golden Rule, whereby the agent must fulfill his recipients' arbitrary desires regardless of the cost to himself. For the Rational Golden Rule and the *PGC* require that the agent act in accord with his own generic rights as well as those of his recipient.

We saw above that in the Generic interpretation of the traditional Golden Rule, which tells the agent to act in accord with his recipients' desires as well as his own, no provision was made for situations where the agent's desires conflict with the desires of his recipients. The case is otherwise, however, when the desires in question must be rational. For this involves that desires are ruled out from consideration when they require actions which violate the generic rights of their recipients; similarly, the recipients' desires must not intend violation of other persons' generic rights.

There may still be conflicts between the generic rights of the agent and of his recipients. For example, the agent's right to freedom may conflict with his recipients' right to well-being, and indeed the agent's right to freedom may also conflict with his own right to well-being. But in the first place, such conflicts are far fewer than the conflicts among desires taken indiscriminately. And in the second place, the fact that the generic rights are derived from the necessary conditions of agency provides a rational basis for resolving conflicts among specific rights. For, other things being equal, one right takes precedence over another to the degree to which the former is more necessary for action than is the latter. For example, A's right not to be killed takes precedence over B's right to be told the truth when the two are in conflict, and C's right to be saved from drowning takes precedence over D's right to be free from any encumbrances on his leisure.

Where the traditional Golden Rule permits actions which go counter to justified social rules, this is not the case with the Rational Golden Rule or the *PGC*. For the *PGC* provides the ultimate basis for the justification of social rules. All such rules, to be justified, must be derivable from the *PGC* either procedurally or instrumentally, that is, either as deriving from voluntary agreement and hence from the right to freedom, or as deriving from the requirements of well-being. The rules of voluntary associations such as baseball teams are justified in the former way; the rules of the minimum state with its criminal law are justified in the latter way. It is hence not open to any person who participates in such justified groupings to try to evade the requirements of their rules on the ground that he would not want to be treated as the rules require. The arbitrary or contingent desires of the participants, including the law-violator and the corrupt policeman, must here give way to the rational desires which are in conformity with the respective social rules.

Although the *PGC* as the basis of the Rational Golden Rule deals primarily with the generic rights and hence prescribes strict "oughts" to agents, it can also deal with the myriad moral situations which involve other rights, as well as those which bear on supererogatory rather than strict duties, whether they concern simple amenities or heroic and saintly actions. On the one hand, all other rights, in order to be justified, must derive directly or indirectly from the generic rights. On the other hand, so far as concerns supererogatory actions, their recipients, by definition, do not have rights to them, such that severe censure or even coercion is justified if the conduct in question is not forthcoming. Nevertheless, every person insofar as he is rational must desire that he be the recipient of such supererogatory actions in relevant circumstances; hence, according to the Rational Golden Rule, it is right or fitting that he perform such actions toward others. For although the actions in question are not matters of rights or strict duties, they go in the same direction as do the generic rights, serving to advance the freedom or well-being of their recipients either directly or by promoting a social context in which these necessary goods are furthered. Because of these connections with the generic rights, every rational person must want that he be the recipient of such supererogatory actions in relevant circumstances. Hence, the Rational Golden Rule provides for the rightness of such actions. The Rational Golden Rule and the *PGC*, like the traditional Golden Rule, require that an agent treat his recipients according to the same rules or principles as the agent wants for his own treatment. But whereas the traditional Golden Rule leaves completely open and indeterminate the contents of the agent's wants for himself and hence of the rules or principles, the *PGC* focuses on what the agent necessarily wants or values insofar as he is rational, namely that he be acted on in accord with his generic rights. Applications of the *PGC* and the Rational Golden Rule, unlike those of the traditional Golden Rule, cannot be immoral because they cannot be tailored, in their antecedents, to the agent's variable inclinations or ideals without regard to the generic rights of their recipients. The Rational Golden Rule and the *PGC* hence provide in their applications an indefeasible guarantee of reciprocal fairness to both agents and recipients.

This normative moral point also has a deeper logical corollary. The traditional Golden Rule leaves open the question of why any person ought to act in accordance with it. Even if the Rule is assimilated to or derived from a principle of universalizability, that what is right for one person must be right for any relevantly similar person in similar circumstances, the criterion of relevant similarity is still left subject to all the variabilities which we saw to attach to the contingent desires or predilections of agents. The Rational Golden Rule, on the other hand, contains within itself both a formal and a material necessity which determines quite conclusively why every person ought to obey it. Formally, the Rational Golden Rule, like the *PGC*, is necessary in that to deny or violate it is to contradict oneself. Materially, this self-contradiction is inescapable because, unlike the traditional Golden Rule, the Rational Golden Rule and the *PGC* are derived from the necessities of purposive agency. It is not the contingent desires of agents but rather aspects of agency which cannot rationally be varied or evaded by any agent that determine the content of the Rational Golden Rule and the *PGC*. Thus, when the Golden Rule is rationalized it has a conclusive rational justification which the traditional Golden Rule lacks. Nevertheless, such rationality may be said to be implicit in the traditional Golden Rule because it serves to preserve and elucidate the Rule's mutualist intentions in a logically necessary way.

FOOTNOTES

[1] See, *The Eleven Religions and Their Proverbial Lore*, ed. S. G. Champion (London, 1944), pp. xvi–xviii, 18, 44, 84, 90, 104, 129, 153, 160, 161, 194, 215, 218, 265, 302; R. E. Hume, *The World's Living Religions* (New York, 1949), pp. 265–266.

[2] George Bernard Shaw, *Man and Superman*, app., "Maxims for Revolutionists" in *Collected Works of Bernard Shaw* X (New York, 1930):217.

[3] Henry Sidgwick, *The Methods of Ethics*, 7th ed. (London, 1907), p. 380.

[4] *Foundations of the Metaphysics of Morals* VI (Akademie ed.): 430 n.; trans., H. J. Paton, *The Moral Law* (London, 1947), p. 97 n. See John Selden, "Equity" in *Table Talk*, xxxvii, s.v., ed. S. H. Reynolds (Oxford, 1892), pp. 61–62.

[5] See Marcus G. Singer, "The Golden Rule," *Philosophy* 38 (1963):293–314; W. T. Blackstone, "The Golden Rule: A Defense," *Southern Journal of Philosophy* 3 (1965):172–177. Despite the criticisms of Singer's interpretation which I present below, his article helped to clarify the Golden Rule's import. For another statement of the "general interpretation," see R. M. Hare, *Freedom and Reason* (Oxford, 1963), p. 113.

[6] Singer, "The Golden Rule," pp. 299–300.

[7] *Ibid.*, pp. 294–296.

[8] *Ibid.*, p. 300.

[9] The Inversion conception is also upheld by G. H. von Wright, *The Varieties of Goodness* (London, 1963), p. 201: "If the Golden Rule is formulated in a way which is independent of the presupposition of similar wants, it would run as follows: Do to others what they want you to do to them, and don't do to others what they do not want you to do to them." Subsequently (p. 202), von Wright recognizes that the "positive part" of this rule requires "some 'check' on the demands which men have on their neighbour's good services."

[10] Singer, "The Golden Rule," pp. 300, 301; emphases in original.

[11] This criticism also applies to what Kurt Baier calls "the condition of 'reversibility,' that is, that the behavior in question must be acceptable to a person whether he is at the 'giving' or 'receiving' end of it" (*The Moral Point of View* (Ithaca, N.Y., 1958), p. 202). Such behavior, while acceptable to its agent in his capacity both as agent and as recipient, may still not be acceptable to its recipient.

[12] Matthew 7:12; Luke 6:31.

[13] See Baier, *The Moral Point of View*, pp. 200–201; Stephen E. Toulmin, *An Examination of the Place of Reason in Ethics* (Cambridge, 1950), p. 145.

[14] Samuel Clarke, *Discourse upon Natural Religion*, in *British Moralists*, ed. L. A. Selby-Bigge II (Oxford, 1897):24; or in *British Moralists, 1650–1800*, ed. D. D. Raphael I (Oxford, 1969): 208. See also Sidgwick, *The Methods of Ethics*, p. 385.

[15] St. Augustine, *De Sermone Domini in Monte*, II. 74, in *Augustini Opera Omnia*, vol. III, Pars Altera, col. 1587 (Paris, 1837). Thomas Aquinas, *Catena Aurea Super Matthaei Evangelium*, cap. vii, 6, in *Sancti Thomae Aquinatis Opera Omnia* XI (New York, 1949):99.

[16] See my "Categorial Consistency in Ethics," *Philosophical Quarterly* 17 (1967):289–299; "Obligation: Political, Legal, Moral," *Nomos XII: Political and Legal Obligation* (1970), pp. 55–88; "The Normative Structure of Action," *Review of Metaphysics* 25 (1971):238–261; "The Justification of Egalitarian Justice," *American Philosophical Quarterly* 8 (1971):331–341; "Moral Rationality," Lindley Lecture, University of Kansas (1972), "The 'Is-Ought' Problem Resolved," *Proceedings and Addresses of the American Philosophical Association* 47 (1974): 34–61. In my forthcoming book, *Reason and Morality,* I present the whole argument more extensively.

5
Can Utilitarianism
Justify Any Moral Rights?

The difficulties of providing an adequate answer to the question "Can utilitarianism justify any moral rights?" stem at least in part from the complexity of its main terms. It is well known that there are many varieties of utilitarianism, and this multiplicity is further complicated when we try to place historical utilitarian thinkers under one or another of these varieties. In addition, there are different senses in which utilitarianism, in any of its varieties, may be held to "justify" certain actions or policies. Also, there are many different kinds of rights, including moral rights, and there are familiar problems about the nature of rights and how their "existence" can be proved or justified. And, besides all these difficulties, there is the problem of just how rights differ from utilitarian norms. For if the difference between them cannot be clearly established, then it is also difficult to accept the question's apparent implication: that "utilitarianism" is one kind of thing and "moral rights" another.

While I cannot hope to deal with all these difficulties here, I shall try to make at least a dent in them by examining a paper by David Lyons.[1] I shall use his essay as a way of bringing out and resolving some of the chief problems about the justificatory relation of utilitarianism to rights. One of my main points will be that progress on this question requires a fuller awareness of the distinction between the two relata than is displayed in Lyons' paper.

To provide an initial, neutral focus for the discussion, let us begin with the following formula for the general structure of a right (in its basic form of a claim-right): "A has a right to X against B by virtue of Y." There are five main elements or variables here: first, the Subject or the right-holder (A); second, the Nature of the right; third, the Object (X) of the right, what it is a right to; fourth, the Respondent (B) of the right, the person or persons who have the correlative duty to act or to forbear as the right requires; fifth, the Ground (Y) or justificatory basis of the right. (I capitalize each of these variables in order to make more explicit their roles in the following discussion.)

While the Nature of a right involves many complexities, for initial purposes we may characterize it as a justified claim or entitlement to some Object. Correlative duties are incumbent on Respondents to act or to forbear in ways required for the fulfillment of the justified claim.

I. The Utility-Rights Dilemma

Like other antiutilitarian theorists of rights, Lyons is confronted by what I shall call the *Utility-Rights Dilemma*. The Objects of rights either are or are not components of human goods or welfare. If they are such components, then the appeal to rights is really an appeal to utility, so that the rights theorist may be a utilitarian after all. For, on this view, since the Objects of rights are goods or welfare components, they can be weighed against, and possibly be outweighed by, other components of human goods or welfare. Consequently, the obligatoriness of fulfilling any right will be contingent on a calculus whereby that action is obligatory which produces the most good, even if this involves infringing the right. If, on the other hand, the Objects of rights are not components of human goods or welfare, then the question arises of why rights are important and wherein lies the obligatoriness of fulfilling them. If the Objects of rights are of no value, contribute nothing to human welfare, then what good are rights? I shall refer to these alternatives, respectively, as the welfare horn and the nonwelfare horn.

Lyons' position seems to fall now on one side of this dilemma, now on the other. On the one hand, he seems to uphold the nonwelfare horn. For he defines utilitarianism as "the theory that the only sound, fundamental basis for normative (or moral) appraisal is the promotion of human welfare." Since he holds that rights provide a basis for moral appraisal different from the one utilitarianism provides, his definition suggests that rights are not concerned with "the promotion of human welfare." A similar conclusion is suggested by his assertion that "rights . . . have a normative life of their own, with implications that are neither reducible to nor traceable by direct considerations of utility." In keeping with this assertion, he says, in referring to his right to life, that, in acting so as to save it, "I need not show that my life is valuable or useful."

On the other hand, Lyons also seems to uphold the welfare horn of the dilemma. Thus, referring to his example of Mary's rights to the use of a private driveway and garage that she has rented, he says that "Mary's rights, to be defensible, must have some foundation in human interests or welfare and are limited in turn by similar considerations." Hence, he goes on to admit that "*very substantial* utilities or disutilities outweigh the moral force of Mary's rights," even though it is not the case that "*minimal increments* of utility are sufficient to outweigh" these rights. (Here and in all other quotations from Lyons, the emphases are in the original.)

Apart from his seeming to straddle both sides of the Utility-Rights Dilemma, there are several difficulties with Lyons' position. If morally defensible rights "must have some foundation in human interests or welfare," then how are they different from utilitarian norms, which are concerned with "the promotion of human welfare"? Lyons' answer is quite unsatisfactory. As we have seen, he says that the moral force of rights, in a case like Mary's use of the driveway, is outweighed only by "very substantial utilities or disutilities," not by "minimal increments of utility." A utilitarian, however, could completely accept this distinction. He would say that Mary's rights, like any others, consist in, or at least have as their Objects, certain components of welfare, and that their moral force, the obligatoriness of actually fulfilling them, is contingent on their relation to other components of welfare with which they may conflict. The rights must be fulfilled only when these other components (Lyons' "minimal increments of utility") do not outweigh the welfare components of the rights. But when the other components consist in "very substantial utilities or disutilities," or in what Lyons also calls "pressing needs," the rights must give way to these. Hence, so far as he has been able to show, he fully accepts the welfare horn of the Utility-Rights Dilemma, so that, on his position, moral rights are not in principle distinct from utilitarian norms in general. Thus, he is really a utilitarian after all.

Lyons strenuously tries to avoid this upshot. He denies that "utilitarian reasoning *generally* determines how Mary and others may justifiably act." He insists that, once morally defensible rights are established, utilitarian "modes of reasoning are illicit." But he fails to show that or how this is so. He correctly denies that all rights are necessarily absolute (although he does not consider the possibility that there may be *some* absolute rights); and, so far as he has shown, this denial entails that rights may be overridden by certain utilities.

At one point Lyons explicitly tries to differentiate his position on moral rights from utilitarianism. He says:

> Why should we suppose that arguments based on moral rights diverge from welfare considerations? The answer has to do with the normative character of rights. If I have a right to something, this provides *an argumentative threshold* against objections to my doing it, as well as a presumption against others' interference. Considerations that might otherwise be sufficient objection to my so acting, in the absence

of my having the right, or that might justify others' interference, are ineffective in its presence. . . . I call this argumentative threshold character the *normative force* of moral rights.

So far, however, Lyons has not shown either that moral rights are different from welfare considerations or what aspect of rights gives them the "normative force" he ascribes to them. The example he provides, of the right to life, is of little help; indeed, it confuses the issue. He says that his right to life "entails that I may act to save it and that others may not interfere, even if these acts or the results would otherwise be subject to sound criticism. I need not show that my life is valuable or useful, and the fact that my defending it would have bad overall consequences or is otherwise objectionable does not show that my defending it is wrong, or that others' interference is not wrong."

One trouble with this statement is that it obscures what Lyons later admits, that moral rights "must have some foundation in human interests or welfare and are limited in turn by similar considerations." It is irrelevant to say that he "need not show that my life is valuable or useful." Of course he doesn't have to show this, for it is obvious that his life has enormous value for him. But isn't it equally obvious that his right to life has at least some of its "foundation" in this value? Moreover, when he says that he may act to save his life even if "my defending it would have bad overall consequences or is otherwise objectionable," how does this square with his subsequent admission that "very substantial utilities or disutilities outweigh the moral force of" certain rights? Suppose that the person whose life is involved has gone on a murderous rampage and can be stopped only by being killed. In this case, does he still have the right to life, and is it still morally permissible for him to act to save it even if his defending it would have such obviously "bad overall consequences"?

A related way in which Lyons tries to differentiate moral rights from utilitarian norms is through the contrast between a general maximizing criterion and the specific "difference" that rights make. He says that, according to utilitarianism, "Mary is fully justified in exercising her legal rights only when and in a manner in which she can promote human welfare to the maximum degree possible." But this pattern of reasoning "seems to clash with the idea that Mary's rights are morally defensible and thus have moral force. For it assumes that Mary's rights *make no difference* to what she and others may justifiably do. . . . She need not act so as to maximize utility when she exercises her rights."

Now this reference to "maximizing" is indeed important in differentiating rights from utilitarianism. But as Lyons uses it and related notions, it does not succeed in making the desired differentiation. For one thing, much of the point of his story about Mary consists in the great utility of her having a private garage and driveway, so that the normative "difference" made by her having the right to use these is, in his story, justified by its impact on her needs or welfare. One wonders whether he would claim the same justification and hence the same normative "difference" if the person who had rented the garage and driveway, and hence had the "right" in question, were a member of a criminal gang or a millionaire who used his car for driving to assignations. For another thing, as we have seen, Lyons does not hold that Mary's rights are "absolute"; on the contrary, "very substantial utilities or disutilities outweigh the moral force of Mary's rights," while "minimal increments of utility" do not. This disjunction seems to invoke the very criterion of maximizing utility that Lyons officially wishes to reject or at least to differentiate from reasoning about rights.

These difficulties in Lyons' position are more basic than the one he ascribes to the utilitarian view of rights, for they bear on the very possibility of distinguishing reasoning about rights from utilitarian calculation. He holds that a utilitarian official must always be prepared to violate any legal right if his doing so will "promote human welfare," so that he "cannot regard Mary's rights as making that difference to the evaluation of conduct that we supposed those rights do." But how distinct is this from Lyons' own position? To be sure, he may be interpreted as holding that the utilitarian official is prepared to violate Mary's rights even if "minimal increments of utility" will thereby result, whereas Lyons holds that only "very substantial utilities or disutilities outweigh the moral force of Mary's rights." But Lyons has given us no way of measuring utilities so as to distinguish between "minimal" and "substantial" increments. Moreover, the utilitarian may well hold that in his own measurement of utilities he must give an important place to the regularized expectations authorized by Mary's legal rights as well as by the "pressing needs" subserved by her having these rights. Consequently, his utilitarian calculus will allow infringing her rights only when the utilities gained by the infringement are greater than what she derives from fulfillment of her needs and expectations. How different is this from Lyons' position?

One of the main sources of Lyons' difficulties is that he is quite hazy about two of the elements of moral rights distinguished above: their Nature and their Ground. He does not make clear what constitutes moral rights and what there is about them that gives them their normative force or obligatoriness. Thus he does almost nothing to counterbalance his utilitarian-sounding admission that moral rights "must have some foundation in human interests or welfare" by indicating any further Ground that would differentiate moral rights from utilitarian norms. The definition he provides for "moral rights" is merely negative: they "exist independently of social recognition and enforcement"; they "simply do not depend on social recognition or enforcement." Well, then, what do they depend on? What is their Ground or justifying basis? Apart from his utilitarian-sounding admission, just cited (which is quite unhelpful to his antiutilitarian thesis), Lyons provides no answer to this question.

II. The Differences between Utilities and Moral Rights

So far as Lyons has been able to show, then, moral rights (and morally defensible legal rights) are not appreciably different from utilitarian norms. I now want to establish that there are, indeed, important differences. Some of the distinctions I shall use for this purpose are quite familiar. But, as Lyons' difficulties attest, the distinctions must be put into a more general theoretical framework if they are to do the required job. Since I have elsewhere developed the relevant considerations in some detail, I shall present the main points here in summary and somewhat dogmatic form, while referring the reader to other writings of mine for fuller arguments, as well as for the necessary qualifications and elucidations.[2]

It must be kept in mind that the points to be presented here are not only conceptual but also normative, in that they involve requirements for individual action and social policy. These requirements, in turn, derive from a rationally justified moral principle, which I have called the Principle of Generic Consistency (PGC). The PGC is addressed to every actual or prospective agent; its main precept is: "Act in accord with the generic rights of your recipients as well as of yourself." (I shall explain the meaning of "generic rights" below.) It is this principle that provides the ultimate Ground or justifying basis of moral rights and that shows why the most important of these rights must belong equally to all prospective agents as their Subjects.

The difficulties we found in Lyons' position were focused primarily on the Objects of rights, where he was confronted by the Utility-Rights Dilemma. The PGC shows how this dilemma is to be avoided. The Objects of moral rights are indeed components of human goods or welfare, so that to this extent the welfare horn of the dilemma must be accepted.[3] But from this it does not follow that we are committed to a utilitarian weighing of the Objects of rights against other goods or interests. The main reasons for this, stemming from the Ground of moral rights, are, first, that the Objects in question are much more determinate and, second, that the Subjects of moral rights must be viewed distributively, not collectively or aggregatively.

The PGC establishes that all prospective purposive agents have equal rights to the necessary conditions of human action and of successful action in general. These conditions are necessary goods in that they are what any person must have if he is to be able to act either at all or with some chances of success in achieving the purposes of his actions. Because they are such necessary goods, the conditions in question are the generic features of all action and of successful action in general, and the rights to them are, correspondingly, *generic rights*. There are two main kinds of these necessary goods: freedom and well-being, where freedom consists in controlling one's behavior by one's unforced choice while having knowledge of relevant circumstances, and well-being comprises the substantive general abilities and conditions needed for fulfilling one's purposes. The components of such well-being fall into a hierarchy of three kinds of goods: *basic, nonsubtractive,* and *additive*.

Basic goods are the essential preconditions of action, such as life, physical integrity, and mental equilibrium. Nonsubtractive goods are the abilities and conditions required for maintaining undiminished one's level of purpose-fulfillment and one's capabilities for particular actions. Additive goods are the abilities and conditions required for increasing one's level of purpose-fulfillment and one's capabilities for particular actions. Examples of nonsubtractive goods are not being lied to or stolen from; examples of additive goods are self-esteem and education. I have elsewhere shown that the rights to these necessary goods of action—that is, basic, nonsubtractive, and additive rights—underlie or constitute all of the more general moral rights, especially those now called "human rights," and that all prospective agents have these rights equally.[4]

It is because the *PGC* establishes that the Objects of moral rights are the necessary goods of action and that their Subjects are all prospective agents equally that it avoids the difficulties raised by the Utility-Rights Dilemma. We saw that, according to Lyons, moral rights (and morally defensible legal rights), because they "must have some foundation in human interests or welfare," may be outweighed by "very substantial utilities"; and, so far as he was able to show, this subjected moral rights to a utilitarian calculus. The problem arose because, lacking an adequate conception of the Ground of moral rights, Lyons was unable to defend some familiar contrasts between utilitarianism and moral rights. His paper indicates that he is indeed aware of these contrasts. But what is at issue is not simply his intentions but his ability to fulfill them in the light of problems like the Utility-Rights Dilemma.

Let us briefly recall some of the contrasts between moral rights and utilitarianism in order to see how the *PGC* is able to explicate and defend them. These contrasts bear on all five of the elements of a right distinguished above. In the formula "A has a right to X against B by virtue of Y," the *PGC* shows that the Nature of a moral right involves not only that it is a justified claim or entitlement had by A but also that it is his own moral property,[5] something that belongs individually to him, so that he can justifiably control his having its Object and can justifiably demand of other persons, the Respondents, that by appropriate actions or forbearances they respect his having its Object. The reason why the right is his moral property is given by the Ground or justifying basis of moral rights, and this in turn refers also to the Objects of the rights in the way indicated above. The primary Objects of moral rights consist in the necessary goods of action, namely, freedom and well-being; and the *PGC* and the arguments leading to it show that all prospective agents equally have rights to these goods because they need them in order to act either at all or with any chance of success in achieving their purposes. The primary Subjects of moral rights, then, are not simply persons, let alone sentient beings; they are prospective agents, persons who have the ability to control their behavior by their unforced choice, with knowledge of relevant circumstances, in order to achieve their purposes. (By a Principle of Proportionality, other beings, such as children, fetuses, mentally deficient persons, and animals, can be shown to have moral rights in lesser degrees.)[6] The *PGC* shows that moral rights belong equally to all prospective agents.

On all these points, utilitarianism differs sharply. The Ground or justifying basis on which it ascribes goods to persons is not their own individual needs or requirements for agency, so that these goods belong to persons as their own moral property. Rather, the criterion of the utilitarian ascription of goods is primarily aggregative rather than distributive: what it requires is the maximizing of utility—the allocation of goods that will promote the greatest total or average utility. Bentham's egalitarian dictum, "Everybody to count for one, nobody for more than one,"[7] provides not for equal distribution of goods among persons but only for impartial consideration of persons as loci of goods in adding up the total amount of goods. Nor is the utilitarian calculus advanced appreciably toward equality by its traditional emphasis, found at least beginning with Hume, on the diminishing marginal utility of money and other goods. For the utilitarians go on to recognize that the need for incentives sharply limits the degree to which equal distribution may serve to maximize utility.[8] The primary emphasis is still aggregative, not distributive.

There is a similar contrast with regard to the Subjects or possessors of rights. Although utilitarianism agrees with the doctrine of moral rights—in opposition to organicist theories—that the possessors of goods or utilities are individual persons, utilitarianism does not specify them as prospective agents; on the contrary, it makes the ultimate possessors or Subjects of rights to be the collective whole of all humans or even of all sentient beings. For it is the requirements of maximizing utility, and hence of what it diffusely calls the "general welfare," that are the primary Ground and Subject of utilitarian judgments. In its results, consequently, utilitarianism may coincide with organicist theories much more closely than with theories of moral rights. For what is required in order to maximize utility overall may infringe the individual's own entitlements or rights to the goods he needs for his own possibilities of action or of successful agency.

These considerations also involve a contrast with regard to Objects. Whereas the Objects of moral rights consist primarily in the necessary goods required for agency, the goods or values dealt with in utilitarianism are much more diffuse and eclectic. Into the utilitarian calculus, all utilities, even all preferences, enter indiscriminately, at least in the first instance, and there is hence the possibility that large amounts of some small good will outweigh a basic good of one distinct individual.

On the basis of these contrasts, we can see how Lyons' difficulties with the Utility-Rights Dilemma are to be avoided. Although the Objects of moral rights are components of human goods or welfare, this does not entail that they enter into a utilitarian calculus. For the Objects in question are not goods or utilities indiscriminately but are rather the necessary goods of action; and what the *PGC* requires is not that these be maximized, regardless of the particular Subjects to whom they may belong, but rather that they be had by each of the individual prospective agents whose moral property they are.

It is indeed the case that while some individual moral rights are absolute,[9] most are not. But it is important to emphasize that the criteria for the overriding of rights derive not from a utilitarian calculus but rather from the same distributive moral principle or Ground that justifies the having of moral rights in the first place. Each prospective agent has a right to the basic and other necessary goods of action, and this right cannot be overridden or outweighed by considerations about the aggregation or maximizing of goods. Hence, even if the removal of basic goods from one person A would result in many other persons' having many more goods and, thus, in a larger sum total of goods, this removal is prohibited by the *PGC*. Each person's right to the basic goods must first be fulfilled; the distributive criterion is primary. This primacy, moreover, is not a matter of arbitrary preference; it has deep theoretical justification in the rational basis of morality itself.[10]

When the *PGC* justifies the overriding of some right, the overriding must be only by another right, not merely by considerations of goods, values, or interests as such. It is because all prospective agents have equal moral rights that a right of one person may override the right of another person. The overriding considerations or Grounds consist in the moral rights of *other* prospective agents, and the point of the overriding is to help to equalize or at least to protect certain basic rights—rights to basic goods—when some persons lack them or are threatened with losing them. For the *PGC* establishes that what is rationally justified and required is the equality of generic rights, not the maximization of their Objects without regard to which persons are entitled to them.

A primary criterion set by the *PGC* for the overriding of some rights by others consists in the degrees of necessity of various goods for action. Since the primary Objects and Grounds of moral rights comprise the necessary goods of action, one right R overrides another right S if the good that is the Object of R is more necessary for action than is the good that is the Object of S. For example, A's nonsubtractive right not to be lied to is overridden by B's basic right not to be murdered when these rights conflict so that both cannot be fulfilled. Here it is not a utilitarian calculus about overall utility but rather the comparative bearing of rights on the individuals' needs of action that justifies the overriding of one personal right by another. A similar point applies to more complex social issues of taxation, when some persons' additive rights to wealth and income are overridden by other persons' basic rights to subsistence and other basic needs. In such cases the application of the criterion of degrees of necessity for action requires a context of institutional rules.

This way of distinguishing between moral rights in terms of their Objects' degrees of necessity for action may bear some resemblance to Lyons' distinction between "very substantial utilities" and "minimal increments" of utility. But the distinctions are different from each other because of all the contrasts that, as I have indicated above, exist between the *PGC* and utilitarianism with respect to the Objects, Subjects, and Grounds of moral rights. Simply by calling the Objects in question "utilities," Lyons obscures the difference between the objects of utilitarian norms and the Objects of moral rights. And, by his failure to provide a Ground for moral rights and to indicate their specific Subjects, he is unable, contrary to his intentions, to ward off the absorption of his "utilities" into a utilitarian calculus. The upshot is that the *PGC*'s distinctions, unlike Lyons', do not lend themselves to the utilitarian aggregative weighing that the Utility-Rights Dilemma held to be entailed by its welfare horn.

It must also be noted that when the *PGC* authorizes the possible overriding of some persons' less necessary rights by other persons' more necessary rights, this does not contradict the idea that the overridden rights are the moral property of the individuals who have them. There would be a contradiction only if the moral property in question were held to be absolute or if the relation of rights to the varyingly necessary goods of action were overlooked.[11] What the *PGC* requires, however, is that the generic rights (but not necessarily all the results of exercising them) be equalized among all prospective agents. The Ground or justifying basis of these moral rights, then, is found not only in the necessary goodness of their Objects but also in the rational egalitarian principle of distribution that affects their Subjects. For utilitarianism, on the other hand, the justifying basis of actions and policies is found in the maximization of goods taken indiscriminately.

From these considerations there emerges a related shortcoming of Lyons' analysis. His central contention turns on the familiar distinction between act- and rule-utilitarianism. He holds *(a)* that rule-utilitarianism may "accommodate" moral rights (or morally defensible legal rights), while act-utilitarianism cannot, and *(b)* that, to be consistent, a utilitarian official in his individual actions or conduct would have to follow the requirements of act-utilitarianism rather than those of rule-utilitarianism. Thus Lyons says: "It does seem plausible that institutions conforming to utilitarian requirements or to the dictates of economic efficiency would incorporate rights." He twice adds: "I know of no general argument that could deny this possibility."

What Lyons fails to see here is that the difficulties he correctly attributes to the act-utilitarian view of rights also infect rule-utilitarianism. Even if the rules of utilitarian institutions confer rights, the rules in question cannot take adequate account of the rights because of the oppositions between moral rights and utilitarianism with regard to the various elements indicated above. Utilitarian rules would confer rights, not because of each person's own needs of agency, but for utilitarian Grounds or reasons, focused on the requirements of maximizing utility. Hence, the rules' ascription of rights is derivative and calculative in a way in which the *PGC*'s ascription is not. Since the primary aim of utilitarian rules is to maximize utility overall, the way in which rights get distributed is always worked out with a view not simply to the individual person's needs of agency but rather to the production of the greatest total or average amount of goods. Thus there is always the possibility that *rules* as well as *actions* justified by the utilitarian calculus may require removing rather than protecting goods that belong to individuals as a matter of their moral rights when such removal serves to maximize utility overall. The calculus may require using some persons only as means for others, without regard for the former's own rights.

III. Essential and Accidental Justifications

It follows from this that only in a certain limited sense can utilitarianism be held to justify any moral rights. A distinction must be drawn between *essential* and *accidental* justification. To justify something X is to show or establish that it is correct, valid, or required. When X receives an essential justification, its correctness is established from Grounds or premises that are directly appropriate to X. But when X receives an accidental justification, the Grounds or premises from which its correctness is established are not directly appropriate to X but consist rather in considerations that are conceptually or causally external to X. For example, the assertion that there are 5,000 persons at a certain public gathering is accidentally justified if it is based only on the assurance given by an entrepreneur who has a personal stake in its being believed that so many persons are present; the assertion that there is a fire nearby is accidentally justified if it is based only on the sight and sound of a fire truck racing down the street. Even if each of these assertions turns out to be correct or true, the Grounds on which they are made or accepted are not adequate bases of justification. In contrast, an essential justification of the first assertion would be based on some such method as a direct count; of the second assertion, on the actual seeing of flames or smelling of smoke.

Utilitarian justifications of moral rights are only accidental, not essential, because the aggregative Grounds on which they are based are not directly appropriate to the distributive allocation of the necessary goods of agency to each individual prospective agent. As a consequence, even if the utilitarian calculation comes out in such a way as to justify rules or institutions that require that each prospective agent be given control over these goods for himself, this is an accidental result. Unlike the requirements of the *PGC*, it is not based directly on what each individual must have in order to fulfill his needs of agency.

Moral rights when based on utilitarian justifications or Grounds are hence precarious; for the utilitarian calculus, being aggregative rather than distributive in its Ground or criterion, may, *whether it is applied to acts or to rules,* come out against certain individuals' having the relevant goods. The case is otherwise, however, when moral rights are justified by the *PGC*. This is so for several reasons. First, as indicated above, the *PGC*'s justifications are essential, not accidental, so that they do not admit the influence, for the allocation of moral rights, of considerations that may be antithetical to each individual's needs of agency. Second, the *PGC* allows rights to be overridden only by other rights, not by considerations of general utility whose contents may not include the necessary goods of action. In cases of such overriding, the criterion of degrees of necessity for action assures that basic rights, whose Objects are the essential preconditions of action, will not be infringed for the sake of other goods or utilities even when the aggregate of these latter, summed for a larger number of persons, can be somehow shown to add up to more overall utility than do the basic goods of a few or even one prospective agent. The *PGC* does not permit, for example, the actual or highly probable infliction of cancer on a few persons, such as certain industrial workers, even if a "cost-benefit analysis" may show that the "costs" of preventing the infliction outweigh its "benefits."[12] There are other problems about the overriding of some rights by others, including conditions of disaster or catastrophe. I have tried to deal with some of these issues elsewhere.[13]

The overriding of some rights by others may also require reference to an institutional context of legal rules. Such a context provides the proximate Ground of what Lyons calls "morally defensible legal rights" in contrast to moral rights per se. It must be noted, however, that the legal order itself must be justified by the *PGC* in ways that involve what I have called the "indirect applications" of the principle.[14] In general, a legal order is justified when it serves to protect the generic rights that derive from the direct applications of the *PGC*. Legal rights that derive from a morally justified legal framework—such as, in Lyons' example, Mary's right to the exclusive use of her garage and driveway—are justified in a related way. Although a fuller discussion would have to deal with such rights specifically, the criteria in question are provided by the *PGC* in the ways already indicated above.

IV. Alternative Structures of Rights-Duties Relations

The contrasts drawn above between the *PGC* and utilitarianism may be further elucidated by comparing two different structures of normative argument in their bearing on the status of rights and their relation to duties. The structure of the *PGC* contains three main elements, in the following order:

1. Necessary goods or action-needs of individuals.
2. Rights as individuals' moral property in the fulfillment of these needs.
3. Duties of other individuals or of government to act or to forbear with a view to securing these rights.

The structure of utilitarian rights also contains three main elements, in the following order:

1. Utilities or goods in general, or general utility.
2. Duties of individuals or of government to maximize these utilities.
3. Possible rights of individuals consequential on or productive of this maximization.

From these two sequences it can be seen that, while rights provide the basis of duties for the *PGC*, the relation is the reverse for utilitarianism.

Rights are justified by utilitarianism only insofar as they may be instrumental to fulfilling the duties incumbent on all individuals and on
government to promote or maximize general utility. Thus, while the *PGC*
makes primary the rights needed to provide for each individual the necessary goods of action within an egalitarian-universalist system in which
these rights are equally guaranteed for all, utilitarianism gives rights a role
subordinate to the maximizing of overall utility. We have already noted
the implications of this contrast.

In attributing the above sequence to utilitarianism, I am referring to its
overall conceptual structure, not to more restricted contexts involving
only legal rights and duties. It is in such a more restricted context that
Bentham says that the law that confers a right on one party imposes a duty
or an obligation on some other party.[15] He is here dealing directly only
with legal rights and duties, not with moral ones. In contrast, he uses what
seems to be the moral "ought" in passages where the requirements of the
principle of utility are directly presented, such as the following: "Of an
action that is conformable to the principle of utility, one may always say
either that it is one that ought to be done, or at least that it is not one that
ought not to be done."[16] "It has been shown that the happiness of the
individuals of whom a community is composed, that is, their pleasures
and their security, is the end and the sole end which the legislator ought to
have in view."[17] In such passages the moral "ought" has the status
assigned to it in the second step of the utilitarian sequence listed above.

It should also be noted that the utilities or goods listed in the first step of
the utilitarian sequence are not viewed, at least initially, as the moral
property of determinate individual persons. The locus of these goods is
initially more diffuse; they pertain to, or consist in, the "general happiness" or "general utility." The word "general," like the word "common" in "common good," is ambiguous as between aggregative and distributive meanings. In the former meaning, "general utility" and "common good" signify the sum total of utilities or goods in some group or
community, without any implication about how these goods are to be
distributed among the individuals composing the group. In the distributive
meaning, "common good" signifies that the good in question is equally
common to, equally had by, all the members of the group. For Bentham,
the primary meaning is aggregative; thus he says that "the interest of the
community" consists in "the sum of the interests of the several members
who compose it."[18] This aggregative meaning entails that the rights of
individuals are given the subordinate status noted above.

In certain respects, John Stuart Mill's sequence of argument may seem
closer to that of the *PGC* than to utilitarianism. He declares that the
primary Object of moral rights is security, "the most vital of all inter-

ests," "the most indispensable of all necessaries, after physical nutriment," "the very groundwork of our existence."[19] He here suggests the kind of qualitative differentiation among various Objects of rights that the *PGC* recognizes in distinguishing between basic, nonsubtractive, and additive rights. Mill's statements about security also suggest that persons have moral rights simply in virtue of their basic needs, hence independently of the requirements of social utility or the general welfare, especially where these are viewed as aggregative maximizing conditions.

Nevertheless, despite his emphasis on the connection between rights and the basic needs of individuals, Mill retains the utilitarian derivation of rights from general utility. Thus he says: "To have a right, then, is, I conceive, to have something which society ought to defend me in the posssession of. If the objector goes on to ask, why it ought? I can give him no other reason than general utility."[20]

Why did Mill give this answer? Why didn't he say simply that society ought to defend me in the possession of my rights because their Objects are "the very groundwork of [my] existence"? It might be thought that the following two questions must be distinguished: first, Why (or with what justification) does an individual have any rights?; second, Why should society defend these rights? Nevertheless, if the second question is given Mill's utilitarian answer, this seems to suggest a possible opposition or at least difference between "general utility" and the basic needs of individuals. Mill's general utilitarian position admits this contrast. And by his utilitarian answer to the justificatory question of why society should defend an individual's possession of his rights, Mill falls into the utilitarian position of subordinating individual rights to general utility.

A similar contrast is found in Mill's theory of liberty. Just as he said that the Objects of rights are basic needs of individuals, so he held that the Ground or justifying basis of individual liberty is "the permanent interests of a man as a progressive being." And he connected this with "individuality as one of the elements of well-being."[21] On the other hand, when he came to the question whether individual liberty may be interfered with, the justification he offered consisted not in the interests of individuals but rather in "the general interests of mankind," "whether the general welfare will or will not be promoted."[22] Thus, in the final analysis Mill, too, follows the utilitarian sequence rather than that of the *PGC*.

The utilitarian sequence has a significant implication for the status of moral rights in their relation to duties, for whereas, in the *PGC*'s sequence, duties are derivative from rights, in the utilitarian sequence rights are derivative from duties. It is important to see the basis of each of these derivations. Since the rights dealt with in the *PGC*'s sequence are claim-rights, to which duties are *correlative,* in what sense can it be that duties are *derivative* from rights in that sequence? The answer is that duties are correlative with rights precisely because they are derivative from rights. That is, the ground of one person B's having a duty toward another person A is that A has a right that B act or refrain from acting toward A in the way that is required if A is to have the Object of the right. For example, it is because A has a basic right to life that B has a duty to refrain from killing him; it is because A has a nonsubtractive right that promises made to him be kept that B has a duty to keep his promise to A. The relation of "because" here is both conceptual and teleological. The duty exists for the sake of the right, not conversely. It is not the case that the Ground of A's having a right against B is that B has a duty to A. The right generates the duty, not conversely.

The existence of the right can indeed be inferred from the existence of the duty, as correlativity requires. But two qualifications must be noted. First, just as it is only claim-rights, but not "liberties" or "privileges" (in Hohfeld's sense), that entail correlative duties, [23] so it is only strict duties, but not looser duties of generosity or charity, that entail correlative rights. Second, the validity of inferring claim-rights from strict duties is not antithetical to the unique grounding of the latter in the former. The relation is analogous to that of parents and children: each is logically correlative with the other, so that the (past or present) existence of parents can be inferred from the existence of children; yet, in the causal sequence, the latter are derivative from the former, but not conversely.

In the utilitarian sequence, on the other hand, rights are derivative from duties. Rights have no prior independent status or Ground in the action-needs of individual persons. On the contrary, what is primary is the good of maximum utility. Duties derive from the moral requirement of contributing as effectively as possible to this maximization. Rights arise, if at all, as ways of helping to fulfill these duties or as results of the fulfillment. The right is for the sake of the duty and its utility-maximizing purpose, not conversely. Hence, if any right proves antithetical to such fulfillment, the right must be overridden.

It is worth noting that this derivative, subordinate role of rights is also found in the organicist idealist tradition. The structure of argument presented by Bosanquet, for example, contains four main elements, in the following order:

1. The common good.
2. Social positions or functions as instrumental to the common good.
3. Duties to fulfill the requirements of positions.
4. Rights as powers instrumental to the performance of duties.

According to Bosanquet's sequence, the common good is the ideal fulfillment of every "real self" as a member of a community that promotes the good life. Individuals have "positions" or "functions" insofar as they can make unique contributions to such a life. The conditions of these positions constitute duties or obligations that are incumbent on individuals for the sake of the positions. This is especially the case insofar as the conditions of the positions require enforcement. Rights, finally, are powers instrumental to the performance of duties, so that rights arise in virtue of social positions.

> All rights, then, are powers instrumental to making the best of human capacities, and can only be recognized or exercised upon this ground. In this sense, the duty is the purpose with a view to which the right is secured, and not merely a corresponding obligation equally derived from a common ground; and the right and duty are not distinguished as something claimed by self and something owed to others, but the duty as an imperative purpose, and the right as a power secured because instrumental to it.[24]

There are, of course, many differences between the utilitarians' "general utility" and the idealists' "common good," although Bosanquet also uses a kind of aggregative language when he refers to that "which would promote the best life of the whole" as the "maximization of our being."[25] But the utilitarians and idealists have in common that, in contrast to the *PGC*, they assign a subordinate role to the rights of persons, making them derivative from, because instrumental to, duties toward the social whole. This contrast has many further implications for the status of human rights as well as for the whole question of the proper relation of rights to social duties and responsibilities.

It is also important to note, however, that insistence on the subordination of certain rights to social ends may in fact be a way of protecting other important rights. R. H. Tawney, for example, presents a doctrine that is verbally close to Bosanquet's:

> All rights, in short, are conditional and derivative, because all power should be conditional and derivative. They are derived from the end or purpose of the society in which they exist. They are conditional on being used to contribute to the attainment of that end, not to thwart it. And this means in practice that, if society is to be healthy, men must regard themselves not as the owners of rights, but as trustees for the discharge of functions and the instruments of a social purpose.[26]

Here, Tawney proceeds in a sequence parallel to Bosanquet's, from "social end or purpose" to "functions" for contributing to that end and, from these, to rights as instrumental to the discharge of functions. But the rights Tawney has mainly in view are property rights, or "rights to pecuniary gain";[27] what he opposes is "the doctrine that every person and organization have an unlimited right to exploit their economic opportunities as fully as they please.''[28] And the duties, services, or functions to which these rights must be subordinated consist in contributing to a certain "social end": the fulfillment of persons' basic needs, including the "need for security," which is "fundamental."[29] These needs, however, are the Objects of certain basic rights of individual persons, as these rights have been defined in this essay. To this extent, Tawney's doctrine, despite its explicit antiindividualist emphasis, may be construed on the pattern of the criterion of degrees of necessity referred to above, whereby certain rights of persons are to be subordinated to other more important rights in cases of conflict. Such a staunch defender of property rights as John Locke also made them subordinate to the rights of the poor to the fulfillment of "pressing wants."[30] It is less clear whether Bosanquet's definition of the "common good" as the ideal fulfillment of every "real self" makes similar provision for the fulfillment of individuals' basic needs.

Tawney's doctrine, however, still leaves unresolved many crucial problems about the normative status of the "needs" he says are "fundamental." Why is fulfillment of these needs basic to the "social purpose"? Should all persons' basic needs be fulfilled equally? If a person does not have a *right* to this fulfillment, then what sort of claim, if any, does he have? What guarantee is there, or should there be, that the needs will be fulfilled, and what sort of control does or should each person have over this fulfillment? By seeming to make all rights subordinate to "a social purpose," Tawney leaves in a normatively unstable and unclear position the very need-fulfillment he says is "fundamental."

It remains, then, that when rights are assigned a normatively subordinate status, as in the utilitarian, idealist, and socialist doctrines, this renders normatively doubtful the individual's possession of the Objects to which rights-principles like the *PGC* hold he is entitled. Even if utilitarianism and other aggregative or collectivist theories also ascribe such Objects to him (whether or not in terms of rights), his possession of these Objects is rendered much less direct and normatively less sure because it is derivative from and contingent on broader social goals that do not, as such, comprise rights of individual persons. It is the derivative position of rights in relation to the aggregated sum of utilities that differentiates utilitarianism from principles like the *PGC* that directly base rights on the action-needs of individuals. And it is because of this difference that utilitarianism can provide only accidental justifications for moral rights.

Notes

1. A shorter version of this essay was presented at the annual meeting of the American Society for Political and Legal Philosophy held January 3–4, 1980, in Phoenix, Arizona. It was written as an invited commentary on David Lyons' paper "Utility and Rights," an expanded version of which has been published in *Nomos XXIV: Ethics, Economics, and the Law*, ed. J. Roland Pennock and John W. Chapman (New York: New York University Press, 1982). All quotations from Lyons are from this paper.

2. See my *Reason and Morality* (Chicago: University of Chicago Press, 1978), and Essays 1, 7, 8, and 9 of the present book.

3. It is sometimes argued that the Objects of rights need not be goods or interests of the Subjects of the rights. For example, S. I. Benn says: "I may have rights that are not to my advantage. A right to drink myself to death without interference would not be logically absurd" ("Rights," *Encyclopedia of Philosophy*, ed. Paul Edwards [New York: Collier-Macmillan, 1967], vol. 7, p. 196). For similar arguments, see George P. Fletcher, "The Right to Life," *Georgia Law Review* 13 (1979): 1372–75.

These arguments can be answered in at least two ways: assertorically and dialectically. Assertorically, a distinction must be drawn between particular and general Objects of rights. For example, freedom is a general Object and a good, but some particular uses of freedom may not be good. The controverted proposition would then say that the Objects of moral rights are general goods (see my reference below to "generic rights"). Dialectically, the controverted proposition would say that when any person *claims* that he has a right to X, it must be the case that he *thinks* X is a good, at least for himself.

The relation of rights to goods also raises more general questions about deontological theories which hold, for example, that the duty to respect the rights of persons has nothing to do with whether anyone stands to benefit thereby. For a version of such a theory, see H. L. A. Hart, "Are There Any Natural Rights?" *Philosophical Review* 64 (1955): 175–91, at pp. 180–82; and Hart, "Bentham on Legal Rights," in *Oxford Essays in Jurisprudence*, 2d ser., ed. A. W. B. Simpson (Oxford: Clarendon Press, 1973), pp. 171–201. I have briefly discussed this issue in *Reason and Morality*, pp. 75–77. For a more general discussion of deontological moral theories, see A. Gewirth, "Ethics," *Encyclopaedia Britannica*, 15th ed. (1974), vol. 6, pp. 976–98, at pp. 990–94.

4. See Gewirth, *Reason and Morality*, chaps 3–4, and "The Basis and Content of Human Rights" (Essay 1, above).

5. I borrow this expression from H. L. A. Hart, "Are There Any Natural Rights?" *Philosophical Review* 64 (1955): 182.

6. See Gewirth, *Reason and Morality*, pp. 121–25, 141–45.

7. See J. S. Mill, *Utilitarianism*, chap. 5 (Everyman's edition, p. 58).

8. See Hume, *Enquiry Concerning the Principles of Morals*, Section III, Part ii (ed. Selby-Bigge, pp. 193 ff.); J. Bentham, *Theory of Legislation*, ed. C. K. Ogden (London: Routledge & Kegan Paul, 1928), p. 104; H. Sidgwick, *Principles of Political Economy* (London: Macmillan, 1901), pp. 519 ff.; Sidgwick, *Elements of Politics* (London: Macmillan, 1919), pp. 160 ff.

9. I have argued for this in "AreThere Any Absolute Rights?" and "Human Rights and the Prevention of Cancer" (Essays 9 and 7, below).

10. See *Reason and Morality*, esp. pp. 135, 145–50, 164–69, 183–87, 200–206.

11. Examples of these positions can be found in Robert Nozick, *Anarchy, State, and Utopia* (New York: Basic Books, 1974), pp. 28–33, 170, 173, 238, and in Judith Jarvis Thomson, "Some Ruminations on Rights," *Arizona Law Review* 19 (1977): 49 ff.

12. See my "Human Rights and the Prevention of Cancer" (Essay 7).

13. See "Are There Any Absolute Rights?" (Essay 9).

14. *Reason and Morality*, pp. 200–201, 272 ff.

15. Bentham, *Introduction to the Principles of Morals and Legislation* (New York: Hafner Publishing Co., 1948), chap. XVI, sec. xxv (pp. 224–25 n.).

16. Ibid., chap. I, sec. x (p. 4).

17. Ibid., chap. III, sec. i (p. 24).

18. Ibid., chap. I, sec. iv (p. 3). Cf. ibid., chap. IV, sec. v (pp. 30–31).

19. J. S. Mill, *Utilitarianism*, chap. 5 (Everyman's ed., p. 50).

20. Ibid. (p. 50).

21. J. S. Mill, *On Liberty*, chaps. 1, 3 (Everyman's ed., pp. 74, 114).

22. Ibid., chaps. 4, 5 (pp. 132, 150).

23. See W. N. Hohfeld, *Fundamental Legal Conceptions* (New Haven: Yale University Press, 1964), pp. 36 ff.

24. Bernard Bosanquet, *The Philosophical Theory of the State*, 4th ed. (London: Macmillan, 1951), pp. 187–201. The quotation is from page 195. For a somewhat similar doctrine, see T. H. Green, *Lectures on the Principles of Political Obligation* (London: Longmans, Green, 1941), pp. 41–48, 142–59.

25. Bosanquet, p. 174. See also p. 170.

26. R. H. Tawney, *The Acquisitive Society* (London: G. Bell & Sons, 1921), p. 54.

27. Ibid., p. 108.

28. Ibid., p. 44.

29. Ibid., p. 83.

30. John Locke, *First Treatise of Government*, sec. 42 (in Locke, *Two Treatises of Government*, ed. Peter Laslett [Cambridge, Eng.: At the University Press, 1960], p. 188): "God the Lord and Father of all has given no one of his children such a property, in his peculiar portion of the things of this world, but that he has given his needy brother a right to the surplusage of his goods; so that it cannot justly be denied him, when his pressing wants call for it."

6
The Future of Ethics:
The Moral Powers of Reason

The assigned topic for this symposium, stated in the main title of my paper, is ambiguous in several ways. The word "ethics" may signify descriptive ethics, normative ethics, meta-ethics, and others. The ambiguity of the words "the future of" is perhaps more subtle. In talking of the future of X, one may be referring to what will happen to X regardless of one's own exertions or, if one includes the effect of one's own exertions, what one hopes will happen to X or what one thinks ought to happen.

Despite the views of certain extreme Marxists and others, I shall assume that the future of ethics is under the collective control of philosophers and other thinkers, although it will and should be influenced by external events. I shall also assume that this collective control will continue to be distributive in that it is and should be constituted by the contributions of many distinct individuals having different points of view and upholding different theses. This does not mean that I think all ethical positions are equally sound or correct. But the freedom to think, experiment, and communicate is indispensable to the possibility of moving toward sounder or more correct positions. Hence, the pluralism in question is intellectually as well as morally superior to the rival monisms in which such free communication is inhibited or prevented.

I

It is often remarked nowadays that philosophical ethics is in a much healthier state than it was two decades ago. The ground of this judgment is that whereas philoshical ethicists had previously engaged in sterile disputes over meta-ethics, they have for some years now been pursuing fruitful, relevant inquiries in normative ethics, inquiries into first-order substantive moral issues. These issues run a vast gamut: a list of familiar examples would include abortion, euthanasia, legal punishment, civil disobedience, human rights, animal rights, civil liberties, political freedom, environmental protection, social justice, international distributive justice, world hunger, war, poverty, racism, sexism, and many more. Many of these problems, such as nuclear war, redound reflexively on the future of ethics itself, for it is an analytic truth that if mankind has no future, then neither has ethics. The contention is that now at last moral philosophers are doing what they should have been doing all along: trying to clarify and if possible to resolve, or at least to provide rational guidance on, the pressing moral issues of their time.

I agree with this judgment, but only in part. There is a danger that present and future work in ethics will return to the one-sided emphasis on normative ethics which was superseded in the post-World War II period by an equally one-sided concentration on meta-ethics. There was an important reason for the latter concentration, a reason as old as Plato. Philosophers were propounding, and disagreeing over, extensive normative ethical doctrines; but they were doing little on the logical and epistemological questions of how their disagreements might be resolved or how, in any fundamental way, their doctrines could be supported or justified. In particular, they dealt very little with the nature and possibilities of moral justification. Consequently, critical philosophers, especially the logical positivists, rightly pointed out that the area of moral and political philosophy was one of claims and counter-claims among rival theories or "ideologies," with no intellectual means being provided for settling the disputes. Thus the stage was set for the emotivist and other non-cognitivist meta-ethics.

There were, however, serious shortcomings in this meta-ethical "revolution." First, it concentrated far too much on very general questions about the "meaning" of moral terms. Whereas Plato, for example, discussed the meaning of specific moral terms, such as "justice," "courage," "temperance," recent meta-ethicists focused on the most general terms, "good" and "ought." But this focus, unlike the earlier one, while it may have made some contribution to the philosophy of language, was valuable at best only as a brief prelude to normative ethics, not as the main show that it in fact became. For it did little or nothing to give any normative moral guidance. Hence, its ethical relevance was slight.

Insofar as the focus on the most general ethical terms was sound, it was because what the meta-ethicists were really concerned about was questions of the justification of moral judgments. In asking whether the primary meaning of "good" is "descriptive," "emotive," or "non-natural," and so forth, the meta-ethicists were trying to ascertain whether or not moral judgments using "good" can be confirmed or justified by empirical methods, or only by intuition, or by no cognitive methods at all. An explicit concern with justification would have removed much waste motion and sterile scholasticism.

A second shortcoming of recent meta-ethics is that, when it did deal explicitly with questions of justification, it did so in a normative moral vacuum. It was as if philosophers of science dealing with the nature of scientific proof were to proceed as if they had no knowledge of any actual, valid scientific proofs or arguments but were asking, within a scientific vacuum, whether and how any scientific proof at all is possible. Similarly the meta-ethicists, trying to maintain complete moral neutrality and generality, refused to admit, *qua* philosophers, that they already had, even tentatively, any moral justificatory arguments that were sound or valid and that served to establish moral judgments that were themselves sound or valid. Nor did they even try to ascertain or set forth such judgments; instead, they declared, with ill-concealed contempt, that this was a job for "preachers," editorialists, and other presumed non-thinkers. The trouble with this stance, apart from its anti-intellectualist view of normative ethics, was that, accepting no specific moral arguments or even beliefs as a valid basis from which to proceed, the meta-ethicists could come up only with very general, hypothetical, abstract results. These did little or nothing to clarify the justificatory problems of actual moral argument, with its assumptions of correctness or validity.

In contrast to such abstractness and vacuity, meta-ethical justificatory inquiry should go hand in hand with normative ethical inquiry. This kind of combination is as old as Plato; their separation is a recent aberration. It is here that I find a serious shortcoming in the work of many contemporary moral philosophers. (There are, however, some important exceptions.) While enthusiastically dealing with contemporary moral problems, these philosophers have neglected the complementary meta-ethical justificatory side of their enterprise. They have been trying to tell us what is morally good or right on these problems, but they have not engaged in inquiries about how, if at all, they know that what they are telling us is morally good or right. To be sure, they have often given specific arguments for their positions; they have not, for the most part, set forth peremptory pronouncements with no attempt at reasoning or proof. Moreover, some division of labor is permissible. as is some plunging *in medias res*. But the philosophers in question have engaged far too little in groundwork investigations into the nature of the reasonings or proofs involved in their judgments. In particular, they have not done enough to make explicit the principles on which their arguments rest, and how these principles are justified as against their rivals. As a consequence. contemporary

moral philosophers have returned ethics to the relatively uncritical,
quasi-intuitionist condition that characterized it prior to the emotivist
meta-ethical critiques of the 1940's.

This condition often takes the form of merging normative ethics
with descriptive ethics. By the latter I mean a factual rendition of the
moral views actually upheld in a given society. Many contemporary
moral philosophers, influenced in part by the later Wittgenstein. assert
that "our" moral views are in order just as they are, so that they need no
separate justification or examination, especially at the level of basic
principles. Now it is indeed the case that, partly because of the struggle
against Nazism in World War II, there has emerged a greater consensus against certain especially abominable forms of racism and for
certain minimal sorts of equality. But it is important to be aware that
even this consensus has its limits and that to ignore the extensive areas
of moral dissensus, exhibited in deeds even more than in words, is to
fall into an unrealistic parochialism poorly suited to philosophers.

Closely related both to descriptive ethics and to meta-ethics are
such fields as moral psychology and moral sociology. Important as they
are, they do not and should not take the place of normative ethics.
Hence, while I agree with Elizabeth Anscombe that it is highly desirable
to have a sound philosophy of psychology, I do not think that until it is
developed normative ethics should be "banished totally from our
minds." ([1]: p. 15, see also pp. 4-5.)

What I am saying. then, is that an excessive, one-sided, undiscern-
ing emphasis on meta-ethics in the recent past has been succeeded by
an excessive, one-sided, uncritical emphasis on normative ethics in the
present. What is needed for the future is an organically unified combination of the two, whereby the moral philospher both inquires into
what is morally good or right on more or less specific moral issues as
well as on basic moral principles and inquires also, in a self-critical way,
into the methods of justifying his conclusions on these issues. Meta-
ethics without normative ethics is empty; normative ethics without
meta-ethics is blind.

II

In the remainder of this paper I shall discuss a unificatory tendency
that I consider especially promising. After the copious development of
emotivist and other non-cognitivist meta-ethics which contributed extensively to the separation from normative ethics that I have decried,
there has arisen a rationalist position that does justice to the former's
insights but also goes far beyond them—in the first instance because it

regards the making and supporting of moral judgments as a rational enterprise. This position is not entirely antithetical to non-cognitivism because it recognizes, for example, that imperatives and other non-propositional forms of discourse may figure in logical relations. But the rationalists have engaged both in the meta-ethical task of examining how moral principles and judgments can be justified and in the normative ethical task of actually presenting and developing on a rational basis what they regard as justified moral principles and arguments. I wish here to take a critical look at some of these rationalist developments to see how adequate they are to their ethical tasks. This will be to inquire into the moral power of reason.

It is important, to begin with, to consider what is meant by "rational" when it is said, for example, that morality or the making of moral judgments is a rational enterprise. In this regard we may distinguish two main different rationalist positions, which I shall call *substantive* and *procedural*. This distinction is parallel to two different uses of the word "reason." In one use, we talk of "a reason" in the sense of a ground, including a principle or proposition that is presented to explain or justify actions. In the other use, as in the verb "to reason," we refer to procedures or operations of reasoning or inference. These two uses are distinct in at least the following respect: what serves as a reason or ground in some argument or action may not itself have been ascertained by reasoning. While there are many different varieties of both substantive and procedural rationalism in ethics, I shall here briefly examine only a few especially prominent examples.

One recent substantive rationalist position holds that certain principles are by definition morally right in that they state what constitutes "good reasons" in ethics or what is the very meaning of a "moral reason." Such philosophers say, for example, "the reason" for a moral judgment consists in "the fact that it is used to harmonize people's actions," ([10]: p. 145) or that moral reasons "must be for the good of everyone alike." ([2]: p. 100) The objection to this position is similar to the objection against ethical intuitionism. Just as the latter tried to settle substantive moral issues by an appeal to dogmatic pronouncements which it called "intuitions," so the "moral reasons" approach tries to settle such issues by linguistic fiat. This approach ignores the existence of rival moral principles and "reasons," and it offers no argument in support of its own principles. In particular, it does not even try to show how its "moral reasons" have themselves been ascertained by reason, i.e. by reasoning. Hence, as Russell said in another connection, the substantive rationalist position merely exhibits the advantages of theft over honest toil.

The procedural rationalist position is more promising. Unlike the substantive approach just considered, it uses "reason" in a morally neutral way; it does not incorporate its own morally favored principles into the very meaning of "(a) moral reason." It tries to show how morally right principles and judgments can be ascertained or established by reasoning; hence it is directly concerned with moral justificatory argument. We may distinguish two main varieties of procedural rationalism, according to the kinds of reasoning they invoke for this justificatory task. One kind is *probabilistic*, the other *apodictic*. The distinction between these is roughly parallel to the distinction between inductive and deductive logic. The probabilistic rationalists put their main emphasis on the empirical methods of the natural and social sciences and on the empirical facts that figure in and are discovered by such sciences. The apodictic rationalists, on the other hand, put their main emphasis on considerations of consistency or avoidance of contradiction and on logically necessary connections. Hence the probabilistic rationalist claims to establish only probabilities, while the apodictic rationalist claims to establish necessary truths.

Within the present limits of space I cannot hope to deal exhaustively with the disagreements between these two positions over what can be accomplished in ethics by each of the kinds of reason they espouse. The future of ethics is, I believe, bound up to a large extent with the issue they pose as to the moral powers of reason. It is all very well to say that we need to use both inductive and deductive reasoning in ethics, both empirical facts and logically necessary connections, and so forth. But at certain crucial points a choice must be made between these, for their claims, when fully developed, are incompatible with one another.

My own view, to put it directly, is that probabilistic rationalism is incapable of fulfilling the justificatory task it sets for itself, i.e. the task of showing how the use of inductive reasoning and empirical facts can serve to establish or justify morally right principles and hence to show how the morally right is to be distinguished from the morally wrong. Fortunately, a well-developed example of probabilistic rationalism is available in the recent book by my co-symposiast, Richard Brandt ([3]), and I shall now examine its performance on the justificatory question. (In my [8], p. 17-21, I have examined other attempts at an inductive justification of moral principles.)

III

Brandt says that he uses "the term 'rational' to refer to actions, desires, or moral systems which survive maximal criticism and correction by facts and logic" ([3]: p. 10). He holds that the justification of a moral code to some person consists in showing that the person would favor or support that code if he were fully rational ([3]: pp. 185-88, 244). A person is fully rational if he is fully informed and uses this information to criticize his actions and desires; he is "a person in whom the mechanisms underlying desire, pleasure, and action have been fully suffused by relevant available information" ([3]: p. 88). This suffusion operates in part by "cognitive psychotherapy," which is the "whole process of confronting desires with relevant information, by repeatedly representing it, in an ideally vivid way, and at an appropriate time" ([3]: p. 113). "By 'ideally vivid way' I mean that the person gets the information at the focus of attention, with maximal vividness and detail, and with no hesitation or doubt about its truth" ([3]: pp. 111-12). He must use "all available information," which consists in "propositions accepted by the science of the agent's day, plus factual propositions justified by publicly available evidence (including testimony of others about themselves) and the principles of logic" ([3]: p. 13).

There is much that is commendable in Brandt's emphasis on the use of empirical knowledge for the criticism of persons' actual desires. While the invocation of something like his "cognitive psychotherapy" is not entirely new even in recent moral philosophy (see [4], esp. Ch. 6; [5]. I have reviewed [5] in [6].), he makes excellent use of it as a general critical device. But in its specific application to the justification of moral judgments and principles, it has very serious limitations.

What Brandt is saying is that probabilistic rationality, the recourse to cognitive considerations consisting in empirical facts and scientific knowledge, provides the justificatory basis for ascertaining what moral code or system is morally right and hence the criterion for distinguishing the morally right from the morally wrong. For he holds that a justified moral code is one that would be chosen by a "fully rational person," defined as one who relies as fully as possible on such cognitive considerations. And Brandt also holds that the code that would probably be chosen by such a person is some form of utilitarianism, a system "the currency of which would maximize the expectable happiness or welfare of some large group, the size of the group depending on the benevolence of the chooser" ([3]: p. 208).

In putting such heavy stress on cognitive considerations, Brandt does not ignore the influence of non-cognitive factors like desires and aversions (which he also calls "valences"). On the contrary, he emphasizes that it is the influence of different valences that leads even "fully rational persons" to disagree over moral issues ([3]: p. 202). But he also holds that when such persons take account of certain "simplifying facts," the range of their disagreements is greatly narrowed and they will be led to opt for some form of utilitarianism. Such taking account is itself a function of what Brandt calls "rationality."

The simplifying facts in question are of two sorts: "the irrationality of many desires" and the "viability" or causal feasibility of a moral system. Brandt's contention, then, is that when a rational person, in choosing a moral system, rejects irrational desires and confines himself to what is viable, the moral system he thereby chooses is justified or morally right. Or, to put it otherwise, Brandt is saying that choices based only on rational desires and on viability are sufficient justificatory conditions or criteria for the rightness of moral rules and principles. I shall refer to the restrictions to rational desires and to viability as his *sub-criteria* of moral rightness, since they are subordinate to and derivative from his general criterion of rational choice: of what a fully rational person would choose as a moral code of his society. I shall now show that these sub-criteria, and hence the general criterion of probabilistic rationality from which they derive, are inadequate for the justificatory task Brandt assigns to them.

Consider first the sub-criterion of the restriction to rational desires. Brandt says that in choosing a moral system a fully rational person will not be influenced by irrational desires or aversions. He lists and analyzes four types of such desires: those "based on false beliefs, those produced artificially in the process of culture transmission (and which could not have developed by experience with their objects), those based on generalization from untypical examples, and those deriving from early deprivations" ([3]: p. 209).

Now this sub-criterion does indeed serve to remove or disjustify many rules, principles, and systems that Brandt as well as many other persons would regard as morally wrong. For example, racist, sexist, and nationalist moral codes, and the desires that would enter into choosing them as one's preferred morality, may be based on false beliefs about the intellectual or other superiority of some race, sex, or nation over others. Similarly, Brandt shows how the aversions of some philosophers to various sexual and other practices are produced by "desire-arousal in culture transmission" without their having any direct familiarity with these practices ([3]: pp. 209-11).

The sub-criterion of the restriction to rational desires is not, however, able to remove or disjustify other principles or systems that Brandt as well as I would regard as morally wrong. Consider, for example, certain strongly elitist principles or codes that assign maximal rights of freedom and well-being to certain groups of persons and minimal rights to other groups. Slavery is an extreme version of such a system. Suppose, following Aristotle or Nietzsche, such a drastically inegalitarian system is defended on the ground that there are certain intellectual or aesthetic values that are the highest intrinsic goods and that persons should have rights only in proportion to their ability to achieve or contribute to these values. Thus at the one extreme there would be "masters" or rulers, and at the other extreme "helots" or slaves.

It would be difficult to show that the desire for such a moral system incurs any of the deficiencies that Brandt lists as "irrational." The desire need not be based on false beliefs if, for example, it is indeed the case that persons differ markedly in their ability to achieve or contribute to the values in question. It must be emphasized that to believe there are such differences is quite distinct from believing that specific groups of persons classified according to color, sex, religion, or nationality all fall into just one or another range of these differences. The belief that such specific groups can be correlated with different degrees of attainment of the respective values can probably be shown to be false. But the falsity of such empirical correlations does not prove that the differentiations themselves do not exist at all.

Nor need the desire for such an elitist moral system be such as is "produced artificially in the process of culture transmission." The fact that Aristotle and Nietzsche, living in two very different cultures, upheld similarly inegalitarian systems at least suggests a quite different genesis for their respective desires. Brandt seems to hold that either false belief or artificial "desire-arousal in cultural transmission" underlies all cases where certain "behavioral consequences" are "desired intrinsically," such as, in my example, the exaltation of certain intellectual or aesthetic values. Such an ascribed etiology, however, fails to do justice to the autonomous reflection of philosophers and other thinkers. Brandt himself says that desires for intrinsic values may be "rational, provided they could have been acquired by reflection on facts and from reactions which will not dissipate in cognitive psychotherapy" ([3]: p. 212). He would have a hard time showing that the desires for the intrinsic values on which many philosophers and other thinkers have based their espousal of markedly inegalitarian moral systems do not fulfill this criterion of rationality.

What, now, of the other sub-criterion, that of viability? By the "viability" of a moral sytem Brandt means its "causal feasibility," the probability of its actually existing or coming about. His point is that rational persons, in making choices, will be influenced by the degree of likelihood that their choices will be effective in bringing about what they want. Now since slavery and other drastically inegalitarian moral systems or codes have actually existed throughout human history, it might be thought that they readily meet this condition of viability. Brandt, however, thinks otherwise. His reason for so thinking, however, is not entirely clear. He writes:

> An effective moral system must strike a responsive chord in other people; others must see how they have a stake in it. Once people come to view a provision of a moral code as burdensome, with no benefits to themselves or those they care about, their attachment to it is undermined. It is at least close to the truth that a moral code is not viable unless its provisions can be wanted by most persons in the society ([3]: pp. 213-14).

This passage seems to assume a certain kind of democratic or majoritarian character for the morality that actually obtains or is current in a society: that it must be freely accepted by most of the members. Even if this condition is met, it would still permit enslavement of a disliked minority. But the condition itself is antithetical to Brandt's claim that his purely "formal" conception of a moral code "is not intended to win any normative battles" ([3]: pp. 170, 176). For it takes sides on the normative issue of the conflict between particularist (including elitist) and universalist moral codes. Having defined individual moral codes in the "formal" terms of an individual's intrinsic motivations toward certain kinds of actions, his guilt feelings for failures to act in these ways, and similar considerations ([3]: pp. 165-170), Brandt then defines the "moral code of a given society" in terms of the frequency with which the same enjoined or prohibited behaviors are found among the individual moral codes. "We can then pick out those items that are virtually universal among adults, and entitle them the 'social moral code'" ([3]: p. 172).

While this frequentist definition seems innocent enough, it has the serious consequence that every "social moral code" must have at least majority acquiescence or acceptance. Hence, Brandt's central question, "What kind of social moral code would a fully rational person tend to support?" is skewed in such a way as to rule out the elitist who, on what he regards as entirely rational grounds, supports for his society a moral code which he does not believe or expect most of its members to accept freely. I think it is indeed part of the concept of a moral precept or code that the persons addressed by it are assumed to be able to control their behavior by their unforced choice with a view to achieving what the precept enjoins. But this does not entail that such persons must agree with, let alone welcome, the content of the precept or code. Hence, an elitist may regard as viable even a social moral code which the bulk of a society's members initially reject if he believes the code can be imposed on them by force or fraud or both. It will therefore be the code by which the whole society will live and which even its subordinated and oppressed members will accept, although at first not freely. Such a moral code will be "social" in the sense that it applies to and imposes requirements or constraints, although very differential ones, on all or most members of a society, even though it will not be "social" in the further sense of being freely accepted, let alone welcomed, by all the members. In keying his definition of a "social moral code" to the latter as well as the former meaning of "social," Brandt introduces, contrary to his professed morally neutral intention, a normative, democratic moral element into his definition.

Despite considerable ambivalence on this matter, Brandt does present considerations that leave open the possibility both of an elitist social moral code and of different degrees of acceptance of actual social moral codes. For example, he acknowledges that a rational person may aim at supporting varying degrees of "currency" of a moral code in some society ([3]: p. 192). He also says that there may be features of a social moral code that are not "publicly known" ([3]: pp. 173-174). And he admits that a quite inegalitarian social moral code may in fact exist and be chosen by a "fully rational person." Thus he writes:

> A selfish chooser among moral systems need not suppose that others are as rational and selfish as himself. . . the selfish person may not feel any necessity to support a system convincing to others in the long run. . . If he has an advantage in an existing economic system, why should he support moral principles critical of it, just because those principles will hardly command the allegiance of rational people in the long-term future? ([3]: pp. 220-21).

Here the possibility is admitted that a social moral code may not be welcomed or freely accepted by all the persons who will live under it.

Brandt does not explicitly note, however, that his underlying principle of probabilistic rationality commits him to the possibility of a far more restrictive, particularist, elitist moral code than the rather moderate rule-utilitarianism that he holds to be actually justified by his principle. He says that "all rational persons would agree on some core features" of a moral system, "say, *prima facie* prohibition of unprovoked assault, slander, theft of property, rape, breach of promise" ([3]: p. 243). But his principle cannot rule out enslavement, and with it at least some degree of the adverse actions just listed, unless, by his conception of a "social moral code," he makes it a matter of definition that the code must have universal or at least some general acceptance in a given society. And if he does this, then, contrary to his intention, his justifica-

tion of utilitarianism will result not from the empirical consideration of
what a rational person will choose but rather from his definition.

I shall not here go into the familiar problems confronting utilitarianism as a moral system. Brandt tries to deal with the problem of
distributive justice in Ch. 16. One of his main points, long upheld by
utilitarians at least as far back as Hume, is that, because of the diminishing marginal utility of money, equality of wealth tends to maximize
welfare. With the other utilitarians, however, Brandt also notes that the
need for incentives requires a departure from equal distribution ([3]:
pp. 319 ff.). He does not notice that utilitariansim might also justify
slavery as a way of getting unpleasant or dangerous work done. I have
discussed some of these issues in [7].

I conclude that Brandt's criterion of probabilistic rationality, with
its two sub-criteria of rational desires and viability, is inadequate for
distinguishing between the morally right and the morally wrong in the
way he intends. The basis of this inadequacy is that the content of the
criterion is too contingent to be able to rule out the moral alternatives
he disfavors. It is not rationality in Brandt's probabilistic sense that is
violated by elitists and other would-be oppressors of the sorts
epitomized in my above example. The "cognitive psychotherapy"
whereby he eliminates desires based on false beliefs and on other
cognitive inadequacies still leaves available to the "rational chooser"
many valences—desires and aversions—that would favor such drastically inegalitarian systems as slavery.

This result is closely connected with certain more basic features
and shortcomings of Brandt's probabilistic rationalism. To begin with,
his conception of justification is relativistic in two respects. It is not a
question of justifying a moral system *tout court* but rather of justifying a
moral system for or to some person. And what is justified for one even
fully rational person may not be justified for another, because they may
have divergent residual desires and aversions.

> The possibility has been left open that the social moral code which would
> be supported by one person if he were fully rational is not exactly the
> same as the one which would be supported by another person if her were
> fully rational. If so, then the moral system that is justified for one person
> is not necessarily the same as the one that is justified for another ([3]: p.
> 188).

In keeping with this relativism, Brandt distinguishes between the
moral systems that would be supported by rational persons who are
"perfectly benevolent," "perfectly selfish," and intermediate cases. He
admits that "Conceivably some fully rational people will have no be-

nevolent desires at all" ([3]: p. 206). But one wonders: if he is going to cater to "perfectly selfish" rational persons, then why not also to "perfectly sadistic" ones, or at least to those who are "perfectly elitist," "perfectly imperialist," and so forth? His conception of rationality does not rule out such types. He says, indeed, that

> We must be satisfied with plausibility rather than certainty ([3]: p. 208).

> It is no failure to be unable to demonstrate what in principle cannot be demonstrated. If we succeed in seeing clearly which moral principles can be justified to whom, and why, we have done as much as is humanly possible ([3]: p. 221).

But this apparently laudable modesty of aspiration not only has the unfortunate relativistic result just noted; it also cuts the ground out from under the very character of morality as a normatively binding set of requirements.

Brandt's probabilistic rationalism is unable to fulfill two basic conditions of morality and moral justification: categoricalness and determinacy. It is unable to do justice to the idea of a morality as imposing categorical obligations on persons, that is, obligations they are required to fulfill regardless of their own contingent desires or predilections, and regardless also of the requirements set by institutions like etiquette or law whose obligatoriness may be doubtful or variable. For Brandt's criterion allows even "fully rational persons" to pick and choose among different moral systems according to their own predilections. Because of this, Brandt's criterion is also lacking in determinacy. The morality it justifies does not have definite contents such that the opposite contents are ruled out or prohibited; rather, for different "fully rational persons" there may be different moral requirements, depending on what they may be led to support by their varying degress of selfishness or benevolence (and perhaps also other variable dispositions). These are very serious shortcomings in any conception of morality.

What we want to know when we ask about moral justification is what actions, policies, and institutions are morally right. where "morally" includes at least in part the idea of categorical obligatoriness and supreme authoritativeness. This question is distinct from the question of what "fully rational" persons in Brandt's sense will choose, where the idea of "fully rational" leaves available the influence of many variable, contingent predilections that may affect in different, very serious ways the most important interests of other persons. Moral obligation must operate to control such predilections rather than being controlled by them. This is why the moral power of probabilistic rationalism is very deficient.

IV

I have little space left to deal with the other main variety of procedural rationalism, which I have called "apodictic." Fortunately, books are available that embody full-length treatments of this variety, so I can be brief in discussing it.

It will be recalled that apodictic rationalism puts the main emphasis of its use of reasoning on the establishment of logically necessary connections and hence on the avoidance of inconsistency. There are two main versions of such rationalism: *partial* and *full*. The distinction between these depends on the fact that in all apodictic rationalisms a logically necessary form is imposed on certain contents. Now in partial apodictic rationalism these contents are contingent, while in full apodictic rationalism the contents are themselves also logically necessary.

Hare ([9]) provides an example of the partial variety. He allows an interlocutor—call him Bates—to make any particular reasoned moral judgment he likes, such as:

Ames ought to be jailed because he is a defaulting debtor.

Hare then points out that by the principle of universalizability Bates is logically committed to the generalization,

All defaulting debtors ought to be jailed.

Here the logically necessary form of universalizability has been imposed on the contingent content of Bates' initial moral judgment. Hare then points out that Bates may or may not be willing to accept the resulting generalization, especially in its possible application to himself. If he is a "normal" person, he will not accept it; if he is a "fanatic" about the sanctity of contracts, he will. (The example of the defaulting debtor is from [9], Ch. 6.)

The partial version of apodictic rationalism has many of the same defects as we saw in Brandt's probabilistic rationalism. Because its content consists in contingent judgments, it allows the persons addressed by general moral judgments to evade the effects of the judgments whenever they dislike those effects because of their variable inclinations or ideals. This version of apodictic rationalism hence cannot definitively rule out even genocide, and it provides no basis for categorical and determinate moral obligations.

There remains full apodictic rationalism, a version of which I have presented in [8]. In such rationalism, not only the form but also the contents of moral principles and judgments are logically necessary. The contents in question consist in the generic features of action, those features that necessarily pertain to all action and successful action in general. These features are ascertained by the conceptual analysis of action, and it is shown that they entail certain right-claims on the part of all agents. The supreme principle of morality is derived by applying to these right-claims the logical form of consistency. For it follows from this application that every agent, on pain of self-contradiction, must admit that all other agents as well as himself have rights to the generic features of action, namely, freedom and well-being. This generalization entails the Principle of Generic Consistency (*PGC*), which is addressed to every agent:

Act in accord with the generic rights of your recipients as well as of yourself.

The *PGC* says that every agent ought to act with respect for his recipients' freedom and well-being as well as his own.

By virtue of its having a necessary content as well as a necessary form, the *PGC* achieves the categoricalness and determinacy that we saw were lacking in the other versions of ethical rationalism considered above. For the generic features of action, whose contents enter into the principle and its derivation, necessarily pertain to every agent. Hence they, and the principle derived from them, impose themselves with normative necessity on every agent, so that the moral requirements set forth in the *PGC* cannot be rejected or denied by any agent, on pain of self-contradiction. This normative necessity removes the possibility, permitted by the other varieties of ethical rationalism, that either the justified contents or the justified acceptance of moral principles may be influenced or varied by persons' contingent desires or predilections. In combination with these considerations of categoricalness and determinacy, the content of the *PGC* provides abiding protection for equal rights to the most indispensable needs of action on the part of all actual or prospective agents.

In conclusion, may I express the cautious hope that, because of the characteristics I have briefly sketched (but which are developed in detail in *Reason and Morality*), the future of ethics lies with full apodictic rationalism. I have tried to indicate why it is this version of rationalism, despite its forbidding name, that best brings out the moral powers of reason. In making this large claim, I of course welcome the free, pluralistic communication and criticism to which I referred at the beginning of the paper.

REFERENCES

[1]   G. E. M. Anscombe, "Modern Moral Philosophy," Philosophy 33(1958).
[2]   Kurt Baier, *The Moral Point of View* (Ithaca, NY: Cornell University Press, 1958).
[3]   Richard B. Brandt, *A Theory of the Good and Right* (Oxford: Clarendon Press, 1979).
[4]   Abraham Edel, *Ethical Judgment: The Use of Science in Ethics* (Glencoe, IL: The Free Press, 1955).
[5]   Lewis S. Feuer, *Psychoanalysis and Ethics* (Springfield, IL: Charles C. Thomas, 1955).
[6]   Alan Gewirth, *Review of Lewis S. Feuer's Psychoanalysis and Ethics*, Ethics 66(1956), pp. 139-42.
[7]   _____, "Can Utilitarianism Justify Any Moral Rights?" In J. Roland Pennock and John W. Chapman, eds., Nomos XXIV: *Ethics, Economics, and the Law, (forthcoming)*.
[8]   _____, *Reason and Morality* (Chicago: University of Chicago Press, 1978).
[9]   R. M. Hare. *Freedom and Reason* (Oxford: Clarendon Press, 1963).
[10] Stephen E. Toulmin, *An Examination of the Place of Reason in Ethics* (Cambridge: Cambridge University Press, 1950).

Part II
Essays on Applications

7
Human Rights
and the Prevention of Cancer

Every person has a basic human right not to have cancer inflicted on him by the action of other persons. I shall call this right the RNIC (the Right to the Non-Infliction of Cancer). Since it is a species of the right not to be killed or severely injured, the RNIC is perhaps too obvious to need any justificatory argument. Nevertheless, it raises questions of interpretation that have an important bearing both on the ascription of responsibility and on the requirements of social policy.

Closely related to the RNIC is a further right, which I shall call the right of informed control. Each person has a right to have informed control over the conditions relevant to the possible infliction of cancer on himself. This is also a basic human right not only because of its connection with well-being but also because informed control is a component of freedom, which is a necessary condition of action and of successful action.[1]

I

To understand the RNIC, we must consider what it is to inflict cancer on other persons, who is responsible for this infliction, and how it can be prevented. Although the RNIC requires that all persons refrain from inflicting cancer on others, as a practical matter it is only some persons who are in a position to do such inflicting and to prevent it, so that they must especially be viewed as the respondents having the correlative duty to forbear and to prevent. The above questions about infliction hence come down to the issue of the causal and moral responsibility for other persons' getting cancer.

According to current estimates, 80% to 90% of all cancers are caused by the controllable actions of human beings. In the case of cigarette smoking the victims may be held to inflict the cancer on themselves. But in very many cases, it is other persons who cause the victims to get cancer, and it is to such cases that the RNIC directly applies. So far as our present knowledge goes, this causation occurs from an increasingly familiar variety of interrelated policies and situations, stemming in part from the vast explosion of physicochemical technology since World War II, that expose the recipients or victims to carcinogenic dangers: in industrial occupations, through air, water, and land pollution, by food additives and pesticides, and in many other ways. The victims include workers in factories producing asbestos and vinyl chloride, consumers of sodium nitrite and various chemical emissions, and very many other workers and consumers. Bioassays have shown the cancerous effects of various substances on test animals, and epidemiological studies have shown the relative distribution of cancerous effects or symptoms among persons who are exposed to the substances, as contrasted with persons not so exposed. In this way we have learned which substances are correlated with which symptoms—for example, vinyl chloride with cancer of the liver, asbestos with certain forms of lung cancer, and so forth—and we can thereby come considerably closer to establishing causal connections.[2]

Serious efforts to prevent these cancers must be determined by the specific principles that underlie the RNIC and the right of informed control. First, if we know which substances are causally related to cancer, then exposure to these substances must be prohibited or carefully regulated. Second, every effort must be made to acquire the relevant knowledge and to publicize the results. Hence a major part of the causal and moral responsibility for inflicting various cancers can be attributed to manufacturers, employers, and sellers of various products who control the situations in which the cancers are caused if these persons are made aware of the causal connections and do nothing to stop the actions and policies, in the industrial processes and in marketing, which lead to the cancerous effects. A secondary responsibility can also be attributed to government officials, ranging from legislators to administrators charged with enforcing already existing laws, if, while having knowledge of these carcinogenic dangers, they do not take adequate steps to prevent them.

The basis of this responsibility is similar to that which applies to other forms of killing. The general prohibition against killing innocent humans extends not only to murder but also to manslaughter and other kinds of homicide, including those that stem from advertently negligent and other actions whose likely or foreseeable outcome is the death of their recipients. The general point is that if someone knows or has good reasons to believe that actions or policies under his control operate to cause cancer in other persons, then if he continues these actions or policies, he is in the position of inflicting cancer on these other persons, and he violates a basic human right: he is both causally and morally responsible for the resulting deaths and other serious harms. I shall refer to this as the *informed control criterion* for attributing responsibility.

This criterion is distinct from the criterion of intentionality. To be responsible for inflicting lethal harms, a person need not intend or desire to produce such harms, either as an end or as a means. It is sufficient if the harms come about as an unintended but foreseeable and controllable effect of what he does. For since he knows or has good reasons to believe that actions or policies under his control will lead to the harms in question, he can control whether the harms will occur, so that it is within his power to prevent or at least lessen the probability of their occurrence by ceasing to engage in these actions. Thus, just as all persons have a right to informed control, so far as possible, over the conditions relevant to their incurring cancer and other serious harms, so the causal and moral responsibility for inflicting cancer can be attributed to persons who have informed control over other persons' suffering the lethal harms of cancer.

There is a problem about the informed control criterion for attributing responsibility. Consider, for example, the case of automobile manufacturers. They know, on the basis of statistics accumulated over many years, that a certain percentage of the cars they make and sell will be involved in highway deaths and crippling injuries. Hence, since the actions and policies of making automobiles are under the manufacturers' control, why can't we say that they too are causally and morally responsible for inflicting these deaths and injuries on the victims and hence violate their basic human rights? Or consider the case of the civil disobedients during the 1950's and 1960's who knew or had good reasons to believe that their unauthorized marches, demonstrations, sit-ins, burning of draft cards, and similar activities frequently led or threatened to lead to riots, bloodshed, and other serious harms, including deaths. Since the actions and policies of engaging in such activities were under the control of the civil disobedients, why can't we correctly say that Martin Luther King and the other demonstrators also were causally and morally responsible for inflicting these injuries and deaths on the respective victims and hence violated their human rights?

To answer these questions, I shall refer to a certain principle about the attribution of legal and moral responsibility, which, paraphrasing Hart and Honoré, I shall call the "principle of the intervening action."[3] The point of this principle is that when there is a causal connection between some person A's doing some action X and some other person C's incurring a certain harm Z, this causal connection is "negatived" or removed if, between X and Z, there intervenes some other action Y of some person B who knows the relevant circumstances of his action and who intends to produce Z or who produces Z through recklessness. For example, suppose Ames negligently leaves open an elevator shaft—call this action X—and Carson falls through the shaft and is severely injured—call this harm Z. According to the principle, the causal connection between X and Z is negatived or removed, so far as moral and legal responsibility is concerned, if some other person Bates, who knows the elevator is not there, intentionally or recklessly entices Carson to step into the elevator shaft. Here it is Bates's intervening action Y that is the direct cause of Carson's falling through the elevator shaft and suffering the harm Z, and for purposes of assigning responsibility this action Y removes or "negatives" the causal connection between X and Z, and hence also removes Ames's responsibility for the injuries suffered by Carson. The reason for this removal is that Bates's intervening action Y of enticing Carson to step into the absent elevator is the more direct or proximate cause of his getting hurt, and unlike Ames's negligence, Bates's action is the sufficient condition of the injury as it actually occurred. Even if Bates does not intentionally bring about the injury, he is still culpable according to the informed control criterion, for he knows that the elevator is not there and he controls the sequence of events whereby Carson is injured.

The principle of the intervening action enables us to see the difference between the case of the producers of carcinogens and the cases of the automobile manufacturers and the civil disobedients. In the latter cases, an intervening action Y of other persons occurs between the initial action X and the harms suffered Z. When the automobile manufacturers turn out cars, this does not itself usually cause or explain the suffering of injuries by the drivers and car occupants. There intervenes the reckless car operation of the drivers—their going too fast, not using seat belts, driving while drunk, and so forth, all of which are under the drivers' own direct and informed control. Similarly, when the civil disobedients staged demonstrations and there ensued riots and injuries, it was their vehement, determined opponents whose intervention directly operated as the sufficient conditions of the riots and injuries. These opponents voluntarily and with relevant knowledge engaged in the violent resistance and counteraction, which were hence under their control; and this counteraction negatived or removed the causal connection between the demonstrations and the injuries. Thus it was not the auto manufacturers and the civil disobedients who can correctly be held to have inflicted the respective injuries, but rather the drivers and the counter-demonstrators, so that, on the informed control criterion, the causal and moral responsibility lies with them.

In the case of the producers of most carcinogens, on the other hand (omitting for now the manufacturers of cigarettes), there is no similar intervening action between their production or marketing activities and

the incurring of cancer. The workers, consumers, and other persons affected do not actively and knowingly contribute to their getting cancer in
the ways in which the drivers and the rioting opponents actively and
knowingly contribute to the ensuing injuries. To be sure, the workers
work and the consumers eat and so forth, and these actions are under
their respective control. But such actions are part of the normal course of
everyday life; they do not involve new intervening actions that go outside
the presumed normal cause-effect sequences on the part of persons who
are informed about the carcinogenic properties of the substances they
use; hence their actions do not break or "negative" the causal connection
between the exposure to carcinogens and the getting of cancer. It is for
this reason that the cancers may correctly be said to be other-inflicted, i.e.
inflicted on the victims by other persons, the manufacturers or distributors, who hence are guilty of violating the RNIC, as against the
self-inflicted cancers that result from such actions as cigarette smoking, or
the self-inflicted injuries that result from reckless car-driving.

It may still be contended that part of the causal and moral responsibility
for inflicting cancer on workers and consumers rests with the victims
themselves, in that they have at least a prudential obligation to use due
caution just as motorists do. There is indeed some merit in this contention; but it is important to note its limits. The contention may be viewed as
resting in part on the hoary maxim *caveat emptor*. Since workers and
consumers are buyers or takers of offers made by employers, distributors,
and so forth, the maxim says that it is these buyers who must exercise
proper caution in accepting the offers.

While the maxim has much plausibility as a counsel of prudence, it has
serious limitations when viewed morally. We can especially see this if we
look at a general point about the moral principle which is at the basis of a
civilized society. This is a principle of mutual trust, of mutual respect for
certain basic rights: that persons will not, in the normal course of life,
knowingly inflict physical harm on one another, that they will abstain
from such harms insofar as it is in their power to do so, insofar as they can
informedly control their relevant conduct. The normal course of life, in a
society like ours, includes hiring persons for work and selling substances
for use, including consumption of food and other materials. Hence, when
workers agree to work for others and when consumers agree to buy various products, they have a right to assume, on the basis of this moral
principle, that the work and the products will not be physically harmful to
them in ways beyond their normal ability to control, or at least, if there is
knowledge or good reason to believe that the products are harmful, as in
the case of cigarettes, that full knowledge and publicity will be given to
this fact. Failing this knowledge and publicity, the primary responsibility

for inflicting cancer on workers and buyers, and thereby violating a basic human right, rests with the employers and producers, since it is they who knowingly offer the conditions of work and the products for sale. What is especially serious about this infliction, by contrast with cases to which the principle of the intervening action applies, is that there is not the same opportunity on the part of the victims to control, with relevant knowledge, the causal factors that proximately impose the cancerous harms on them, so that their own right of informed control is violated.

The most direct requirement that the RNIC lays on the responsible agents is simply that they cease and desist from these lethal policies. This requirement must be enforced by the state because of the pervasiveness and seriousness of the harms in question, especially where the actual or potential victims lack the power and the knowledge to enforce the requirement themselves, and because the voluntary cooperation of the agents in stopping such infliction cannot be assumed. Whether this enforcement takes the form of an outright ban on the use of certain substances or the setting of standards that specify the levels at which various potential carcinogens may be used, in either case there must be appropriate sanctions or penalties for the violators. In addition, sufficient information must be made available so that all persons potentially affected may be able to help to control the conditions that affect them so severely. Thus both the state and the various employers, manufacturers, and distributors are the respondents of the RNIC, and their correlative duties have to an eminent degree the moral seriousness and coercibility that go with all basic human rights.

II

I have thus far presented the RNIC as an absolute right not to have cancer inflicted on one by the action of other persons. I now want to look more closely at the respects in which it is indeed absolute.

To say that someone has an absolute right to have or do something X means that his having or doing X cannot justifiably be overridden by any other considerations, so that there is a completely exceptionless prohibition on all other persons against interfering with the right-holder's having or doing X. Now there are familiar difficulties with trying to show that any right is absolute, including not only the First Amendment rights to speech, press, and assembly but even the right to life, including the right of innocent persons not to be killed. Without going into these, we must note the more specific difficulties that arise if we try to construe the RNIC as an absolute right.

The difficulties I have in mind are not those that may stem from certain utilitarian consequentialist ways of overriding the RNIC whereby it might be argued that cancer may justifiably be inflicted on some persons in order to maximize utility, if great goods may be attained or great evils avoided thereby. Such arguments may take either the science fiction form, whereby inflicting cancer on one person would somehow lead to eternal bliss for everyone else, or a somewhat more sober form whereby, for example, injecting cancerous cells into someone's bloodstream would somehow help to provide an experimental basis for finding a cure for certain cancers. While the right even of an innocent person to life may not be absolute, the kinds of crisis situations in which this right might be overridden are not applicable to violating any person's right not to have cancer inflicted on him, no matter how many other persons might be benefited thereby.

It must also be noted that the RNIC deals only with the infliction of cancer on some person without his consent or against his will. Thus it does not directly apply to a case where someone may give his informed, unforced consent to have cancer cells injected in him in the context of experimental research toward finding an effective cure or therapy. In such a case the cancer that may result is to be regarded as self-inflicted rather than other-inflicted. I shall deal below with some other aspects of such presumed consent.

There appear, however, to be ways of overriding the RNIC that appeal neither to the kind of utilitarian consequentialism just mentioned nor to presumed consent. These ways may seem to lead to the conclusion that the prohibition against inflicting cancer on other persons should be *prima facie* and probabilistic rather than absolute and apodictic.

We may distinguish two areas of such probabilism. The first bears on the cause-effect relation between exposure to various substances and the incurring of cancer. It will be recalled that in explicating the RNIC I said that if someone "knows or has good reasons to believe" that actions or policies under his control operate to produce cancer in other persons, then he is in the position of inflicting cancer on these other persons. The question now is: when can someone be said to know or to have good reasons to believe that his actions inflict cancer?

The difficulty here is that the causal relation in question seems to be one of degree. Some substances, such as β-naphthylamine and asbestos, have a very high ability to induce cancer. But with other substances the ability and the correlative risk, as determined on a statistical frequency basis, are much lower. There is a currently unresolved controversy on this question of degrees. One view holds that there is a threshold of dosage of carcinogens, below which they do not induce cancers; the other view holds that there is no such threshold, in that any amount of a carcinogen, no matter how small, may lead to cancerous tumors. This latter view is reflected in the Delaney clause that deals with food additives: "no additive shall be deemed safe if it is found to induce cancer when ingested by man or animal, or if it is found, after tests which are appropriate for the evaluation of the safety of food additives, to induce cancer in man or animal...."[4] Here, then, use of the additives in question is strictly prohibited without regard to the degree of risk to humans at any level of use, and without regard to possible benefits.

The merits of such a blanket prohibition, in the case of other substances as well as food additives, are clear. So long as it is not known which particular workers in the various potentially lethal occupations will get cancer and which not, and similarly which consumers of the various suspect food additives and other substances, the only completely safe course would seem to be a blanket prohibition of the respective exposures. To the objection that such absolutism would entail prohibiting the use of automobiles and of many other modern conveniences, since these too carry the risk of death, the reply is, as before, that automobiles do not usually become harmful apart from the controllable, variable actions of the persons who use them, so that they do not pose the risk of death from external causes, i.e. causes external to their users, in the way that carcinogens do.

On the alternate view of the threshold controversy, it is maintained that just as automobiles may be made safer by a variety of devices that are within the power of their makers and users, so too the risks of getting cancer from various substances may be reduced by lowering the degree of exposure to them. For example, even in the case of vinyl chloride, an exposure standard of one part per million is thought to render it relatively even if not absolutely safe for the workers who are exposed to it, especially by contrast with the previous unregulated concentration of 200 to 5,000 parts per million.

I have two conclusions on this issue, one firm, the other tentative. The firm conclusion is that, in keeping with the right of informed control, it is necessary to try to reduce further the ignorance reflected in the varying probabilities of the cause-effect relations involved in carcinogenesis. For this purpose, intensive research must be pursued, within the limits of safety to humans, to ascertain the more specific causal variables, so that we understand more fully just which substances, at what levels of exposure, carry what risks of cancer to which persons. And the results of this research must be fully disseminated and used both in manufacturing and marketing operations and in appropriate legislation.

My more tentative conclusion is that, in contrast to construing the RNIC as an absolute right against even the slightest risk of cancer, a sliding scale may be introduced. Whether the use of or exposure to some substance should be prohibited should depend on the degree to which it poses the risk of cancer, as shown by bioassays and epidemiological studies. If the risks are very slight, so that, for example, use of the substance increases the chance of getting cancer from 1 in 10,000 to 2 in 10,000, or if the risk can be made very slight by drastically reducing the level of exposure, as in the case just cited of vinyl chloride, and if no substitutes are available, then use of it may be permitted, subject to stringent safeguards.

Does this conclusion entail that the RNIC is not an absolute right? The answer depends on how the word "inflict" is construed. If "inflict" is viewed solely as causal, with no reference to moral responsibility of the agent, then there is a sense in which the tentative conclusion I have reached would remove the absoluteness of the RNIC. For while the conclusion does not say that there may be exceptions to the prohibition against actually inflicting cancer, it does say that certain minimal risks of inducing cancer may be allowed, or that the risk of cancer may be increased so long as the level attained is still very low in the way just indicated.

The case is otherwise, however, if the RNIC's prohibition against inflicting cancer is viewed in the light of the ascription of moral responsibility. Since the RNIC is a strict right, it entails that persons strictly ought to refrain from inflicting cancer on other persons. Now this "ought," like other moral "oughts" addressed to agents, is limited by the possibility of informed control, and hence of knowing the likelihood of one's actions causing such infliction. For insofar as "ought" implies "can," to say that A ought not to do X implies that he can refrain from doing X and also that he can have the knowledge needed for such refraining. Thus, the extent of the RNIC's requirement and of the moral responsibility that stems from violating it is likewise limited by this possibility of knowledge.

In this context of moral responsibility, then, the RNIC is to be construed as entailing: Don't inflict cancer on other persons so far as you can know or have good reason to believe that any of your actions will constitute or produce such infliction, and don't increase the risk of cancer for other persons beyond the minimal level just indicated. On this construal, the RNIC remains an absolute right even where it allows certain minimal risks of persons' getting cancer as a result of the actions of other persons. For the latter are morally responsible only if they can know or can have good reasons for believing that their action will lead to other persons' getting cancer. Where they do not and cannot have such knowledge, the informed control criterion for ascribing responsibility does not apply, nor, usually, does the intentionality criterion. This point is a quite general one. In the case of every moral precept addressed to actual or prospective agents, there is the limitation of their being able to know whether the actions they perform are or are not instances of what the precept prescribes or prohibits. The degree of such knowledge may vary with different circumstances. But especially in cases where the prohibition is as important as in the case of not inflicting cancer, there also remains the requirement that one must try as fully as possible to ascertain whether one's actions will in fact constitute an infliction of cancer, so that the right of informed control is again of central importance.

III

Let us now turn to a second area of probabilism that may be invoked to mitigate the absoluteness of the RNIC's prohibition against inflicting cancer, and that has been implicitly present in my preceding discussion. This area bears not on the varying probabilities of the cause-effect relations themselves in the production of cancer, but rather on a weighing of certain values in reaction to those probabilities. The weighing in question is concerned with the relation between the benefits obtained by prohibiting carcinogenic exposures and the costs of such prohibitions; or alternatively with the relation between the benefits obtained by accepting certain risks of cancer and the costs of accepting those risks. It is here a matter of the cost-benefit analysis dearly beloved of economists, which is simply the contemporary version of the pleasure-pain calculus long pursued by utilitarians.

In view of the extreme importance for human well-being of preventing cancer, and the human right to the non-infliction of cancer, now can the avoidance of such infliction be legitimately subjected to a cost-benefit analysis whereby its benefits are weighed against various costs? The better to understand this question, let us compare the problem of preventing cancer with such a situation as where coal miners are trapped in a mine by an explosion. So long as there is any hope of rescuing the miners, all possible means are used to effect a rescue. Except where other human lives are at stake, questions of cost are deemed irrelevant, and so too is the number of miners; lesser efforts would not be made to rescue one miner than to rescue fifty, except insofar as less equipment might be needed to rescue one. The basis of such unlimited effort to save human lives is that the right of an innocent person to continue to live is normally regarded as absolute, being limited only by the right to life of other persons, and human life is considered to be priceless, in the literal sense of being without price: it is incommensurable with, cannot be measured in terms of, money or any other material goods that might be needed to preserve the life or lives that are endangered.

There are obvious dissimilarities between such a situation and the prevention of cancer. In the former case the lethal danger is actual and immediate, not potential and remote; it is a danger to determinate individuals, not to some general percentage or statistical frequency out of a much larger, less determinate population; and the life-saving operations that are called for are similarly determinate and immediate. Partly because of these differences and partly for other reasons, economists and others have engaged in the cost-benefit analyses mentioned before. There is, after all, time for calculation, and the calculation bears especially on how much, from among the total values both of the individuals directly concerned and of society at large, it is worth spending in order to avoid the risks of cancer and other lethal harms.

To see how such cost-benefit analyses are even minimally plausible in this context, we may note that many kinds of human decisions involve at least implicit views as to the monetary value of human life. Examples are when someone takes out a life insurance policy, when society takes or fails to take measures to improve automobile safety, and when a court awards money damages to a family one of whose members has been killed through someone else's fault. Morally repugnant as it may be, then, putting a specific money evaluation on human life seems to be a feature of at least some segments of individual and social decision-making.

Accepting for the present at least the possibility of such a procedure, we may ask how the money value of a human life is to be estimated. Economists have answered this question in different ways, but the way that is most favored is based on the familiar idea of a Pareto improvement.[5] According to this, one allocation of resources is an improvement over another if it involves at least one person's being made better off while no person is made worse off. The criterion of being made better off consists simply in the preferences of the person concerned, so that if some person prefers allocation X to allocation Y, then he is made better off by X than by Y. And if no person prefers Y to X, then the change from X to Y is a Pareto improvement. Thus if some person A is willing to accept some life-risking situation R on payment to him of a certain sum of money S by another person B who is willing to make this payment, then A's having R and S together is to that extent a Pareto improvement over the situation or allocation where he does not have R and S. On this view, the monetary value of A's life to himself is measured by the minimum sum of money he is willing to accept to compensate for the risk of losing his life in some activity or other.

There is a direct application of this Pareto criterion to the case of cancer, especially as this is incurred by industrial workers in various occupations. According to the criterion, the risk of cancer may be imposed on some worker in some job if he is willing to accept that risk on payment to him of a certain sum of money. Since he prefers a situation where he works at some carcinogenically risky job and hence earns money to a situation where he has no job at all, or since he prefers a carcinogenically riskier job at more pay to a less risky job at less pay, while in each case no one else is made worse off, it follows that the former situation is in each case a Pareto improvement over the latter. Hence, in contrast to the earlier position whereby human life is priceless and the RNIC is an absolute right, according to this new position human life turns out to have a price, and the right to the noninfliction of cancer is now limited not only by unavoidable deficiencies of knowledge but also by the willingness of potential victims to accept financial compensation.

There are, however, serious difficulties with this probabilistic alternative. I shall waive the question of whether the risk of getting cancer can be rationally compensated for by any amount of money or other satisfactions. It might be thought that the RNIC is not affected by such cases, since the risk of cancer is here assumed to be imposed on some person with his consent. But there still remain the questions of whether this consent is informed and unforced. Is each of the persons who chooses among alternatives able to know the degree of risk of the possibly carcinogenic alternative for which compensation is required? In the case of the industrial workers in factories making asbestos, kepone, vinyl chloride, and other lethal substances, they were surely not aware of the risks during the years that elapsed between their initial exposure and the time when some of them came down with cancer. For them, consequently, the Pareto criterion would not apply insofar as it assumes that the persons who express their preferences by their acceptance of compensation for risks are aware of the magnitude of the risks. And even when, as is increasingly the case in recent years, research is pursued into carcinogens and its results are made public, there remains the question of whether complicated statistical calculations can be understood and used by the workers who are most vulnerable to their possibly varying implications. In such circumstances it becomes very difficult to apply the right of informed control.

The Pareto criterion's applicability is also dubious over a wide range of cases because of a difficulty bearing on distributive justice. Since the poorer a person is the greater is the marginal utility for him of a given sum of money, whereas the opposite is true the richer a person is, the poor are willing to accept much greater risks for considerably less money. Thus, in effect, they and their relative poverty are exploited as a way of getting them to do dangerous work far beyond what others will accept. While this is, of course, a very old story, it casts doubt on the economists' model of citizens' sovereignty where workers "voluntarily" accept compensation for risks and thereby show that they consider themselves to be better off than they would be without the risks and the compensation. For many workers are in effect confronted with a forced choice, since the alternative to their taking the risky job with its slightly added compensation is their not having any job at all. Where workers and others do not have the power to ward off such risks by themselves, it is an indispensable function of government to protect such persons from having to make such forced choices, and hence to protect their right both to the non-infliction of cancer and to the non-imposition of serious risks of cancer. This function can be generalized to the more extensive duty of the supportive state to try to provide opportunities and means of knowledge and well-being so as to reduce the vulnerability of poorer persons to such coercive alternatives. In this and other respects, the prevention of other-inflicted cancers merges into more general issues of the distribution of power and wealth in a society.

A quite central difficulty with this application of cost-benefit analysis is that human life or health is not a commodity to be bought, sold, or bid for on the market. Thus the Pareto criterion is mistaken in principle insofar as it assumes that any great risk of death can be compensated for by any amount of money. There are important differences in this regard between engaging in carcinogenic work risks, on the one hand, and buying life insurance, driving cars, or doing aerial acrobatic stunts, on the other. Even though in buying life insurance one implicitly places a certain monetary value on one's life, this is different from undertaking the risk of carcinogenic work for pay. In buying life insurance one recognizes that death is inevitable for everyone sooner or later, and one does not thereby voluntarily incur the serious risk of death. But to undertake the risk of cancer by one's work is not itself inevitable, so that the compensation involves putting a market price on one's life in the context of a controllable, avoidable choice. In addition, the worker in a carcinogenic industry usually does not have the same kind of control over his degree of risk as does the driver of a car or an aerial acrobat. Hence the case for outright prohibition of more than minimal risk in the former case is much stronger than it is with regard to auto driving or aerial acrobatics despite the dangers of death common to these kinds of cases.

A further issue about the economic valuation of human life bears on who does the valuing. It is one thing for a person to put a money value on his own life where he has a relatively unforced choice between alternative ways of life and work. It is another thing for other persons to put this money valuation on his life, as is done when the benefits of making jobs less risky and hence prolonging workers' lives are weighed against alternative uses of public money, such as building new roads or ball parks. In such cases the worker and his life are made economic objects vulnerable to the preferences or choices of other persons rather than of himself. The very possibility of making such choices on such grounds represents a drastic lowering of public morality.

A related criticism must be made of the suggestion that the Pareto criterion should be applied to tax firms or manufacturers so as to encourage them to remove or lower the levels at which their workers are exposed to cancer.[6] For a firm may choose or prefer to pay the tax rather than remove the risk, while passing the tax on to its customers and, under conditions of oligopoly, suffering little or no financial drain. Such payment would be small comfort to the workers who continue to be exposed to lethal dangers. This taxational incentive approach also has the severe difficulty previously noted, that it makes persons' lives and health matters of bargaining or purchase rather than viewing them as basic goods and rights not subject to such cost-benefit calculation.

IV

Thus far I have been dealing with a view of cancer as inflicted on persons against their will by the direct or indirect actions of other persons. It is to these interpersonal transactions that the RNIC directly applies. As against such other-inflicted cancers, let us briefly consider the lung cancer derived from cigarette smoking as a self-inflicted kind of harm. This distinction between other-inflicted and self-inflicted harms may be contested in the case of cigarettes on the ground that the blandishments of advertisers and, for young people, the models set by their peers constitute externally-caused incentives to smoke, so that the resulting lung cancers are here also other-inflicted. There is indeed some truth to this, especially in the case of the cigarette manufacturers. Since the lethal impact of smoking cannot be controlled by individual smokers in anything like the same degree that motorists can control the dangers of auto driving, cigarette manufacturers bear a much heavier responsibility for the resulting deaths than do auto manufacturers. The principle of the intervening action applies in much lesser degree to the former than to the latter because the actions of making cigarettes easily available and attractive have a much closer causal connection to the ensuing lethal harms, despite the intervention of the victims' choices to smoke.

I shall here assume, however, that the final choice to smoke rests with the individual himself, and that he is capable of withstanding the advertisers' blandishments. The fact remains that his smoking may be morally wrong because he may impose serious burdens on others. If he becomes hospitalized, his family suffers and he uses extremely valuable and costly facilities and services for which he may not be able to pay, or even if he can, he still makes extremely stringent demands on others which his knowing, controllable actions might have prevented. He also violates both an important prudential duty to himself and also a moral duty to himself as a rational person who is aware of the moral requirements of not burdening others.[7]

How, then, should the self-inflicted carcinogenesis of cigarette smoking be dealt with? While outright prohibition is a possibility, it would perhaps be too violative of individual freedom and, as with the 18th Amendment, there would be too many possibilities of abuse and evasion. On the other hand, simply to leave the smoker alone would also be unacceptable because, even if we give up all paternalistic concern for his own well-being, there would still remain the problem of externalities, the costs he imposes on others.

The solution I suggest is that the smoker should be made to bear the full cost of his habit, including its external effects. These could be calculated in terms of the excess medical facilities, support of his dependents, and other costs he imposes on others. This would be an application of the Pareto criterion in that the smoker would have to compensate those who would otherwise bear the costs of his habit. If he chooses to pay this compensation, the outcome is a Pareto improvement, since he prefers his smoking together with paying the extra money for it to going without smoking, while, since other persons are compensated, they are not made worse off.

Why is such a compensation permissible in the smoker's case and not in the case of workers in carcinogenic industries? In each case it is the inflicter of cancer who has to pay. There is, however, a difference between a person paying others in order to inflict cancer on himself and his paying his workers in order to inflict cancer on them. The latter, as we have seen, violates the RNIC while the former does not. There is also a difference between the potential cancer victim's paying others, as in the smoking case, and others' paying him, as in the occupational health case. But there is also a more important difference. The industrial worker who is allowed to take money compensation for working in a high-risk industry is told, in effect, that he must choose between losing his job or livelihood and risking his life to cancer. This is an inadmissible choice. The smoker, on the other hand, is confronted with a choice between saving his life from cancer and saving his money, or, alternatively, between continuing his enjoyment of smoking, thereby risking his own life, and paying a larger sum of money. This choice, whatever its psychological hardship for the smoker, is not of the same order of extreme objective adversity as in the case of the high-risk worker. The initial much greater relative economic vulnerability of the unskilled industrial workers makes a crucial difference.

I conclude, then, that the probabilistic issues of the carcinogenic cause-effect relations and cost-benefit analysis do not materially affect the conclusion drawn earlier. So far as the moral responsibility of agents is concerned, the Right to the Non-Infliction of Cancer is an absolute human right, and it requires the most determined efforts both to ascertain when such infliction is likely to occur and to take all possible steps to prevent it, and thereby to make its respondents fulfill their correlative duties.[8]

Notes

1. On the grounding of human rights in freedom and well-being as the necessary conditions of human action, see my *Reason and Morality* (Chicago, 1978), pp. 63–103. In chs. 2 and 4, I also explain the distinction between "basic" and other human rights.

2. Useful recent surveys are Larry Agran, *The Cancer Connection* (Boston, 1977); and *Annals of the New York Academy of Sciences,* vol. 271 (1976): *Occupational Carcinogenesis.* See also the summary of the latter in Phyllis Lehmann, *Cancer and the Worker* (New York, 1977).

3. See H. L. A. Hart and A. M. Honoré, *Causation in the Law* (Oxford, 1959), pp. 128 ff., 195 ff., 292 ff.

4. *U.S. Code* 21, 348 (c) (3). For this reference and for a valuable discussion of related issues I am indebted to Jerome Cornfield, "Carcinogenic Risk Assessment," *Science,* vol 198 (18 November 1977), pp. 693–699.

5. Cf. E. J. Mishan, "Evaluation of Life and Limb: A Theoretical Approach," *Journal of Political Economy,* vol. 79 (1971), pp. 687–705; M. W. Jones-Lee, *The Value of Life: An Economic Analysis* (Chicago, 1976), chs. 1–3.

6. See Albert L. Nichols and Richard Zeckhauser, "Government Comes to the Workplace: An Assessment of OSHA," *The Public Interest,* no. 49 (Fall 1977), 64 ff.

7. I have discussed relevant aspects of duties to oneself and prudential virtues in *Reason and Morality, op. cit.,* pp. 242–244, and 333–338.

8. Versions of this paper were read at the Brown University Conference on Biomedical Ethics, March 10, 1978, and at the annual western meeting of the American Philosophical Association in Cincinnati, Ohio, April 28, 1978. For helpful discussions, I am indebted to my wife Marcella, to Professor Elwood V. Jensen, Director of the Ben May Cancer Laboratory at the University of Chicago, and to Dr. Sidney Cobb, Professor of Community Health and Psychiatry at Brown University.

8
Starvation and Human Rights

Do PERSONS THREATENED WITH STARVATION HAVE A STRICT RIGHT TO BE given food by those who have it in abundance? This question is, of course, far from academic. But its analysis and development can throw light not only on one of the most pressing moral issues of our time but also on the ability of moral philosophy to deal with such issues. The reason why this ability is called into question is that the topic of rights and duties bearing on relief of starvation involves serious conflicts both of interests and of moral criteria. The capacity of a moral philosophy for clarifying and resolving such conflicts provides an important test of its adequacy.

I

Although recent moral philosophers, following on the work of legal thinkers,[1] have done much to clarify the concept of a right, they have devoted considerably less attention to the criteria for having rights when these are moral ones. The conceptual and criterial questions are, of course, related, but still they are distinct. If, for example, we know that for one person A to have a strict right to something X is for A to be entitled to X and also for some other person or persons to have a strict duty to provide X for A as his due or to assist A's having X or at least to refrain from interfering with A's having X, this does not tell us when or why A is entitled to X and when or why the other person or persons have such a strict duty to A. Further conceptual considerations may of course be added to indicate the grounds or reasons for which A has the right or other persons have the correlative duty. But these considerations are then not only conceptual but also ultimately moral because, in addition to telling something about the meaning of a word or concept, they give or suggest justificatory answers to controverted moral problems.

We may distinguish at least two criterial questions about moral rights. First, there is the general question: How, if at all, can it be known that any persons have any such rights? Second, there is the more specific question:

Who has moral rights to what, and how, if at all, can this be known? Both questions ask for the ground or reason for having moral rights. Although moral rights, by definition, have moral grounds or criteria, there still remain the questions of whether moral reasons can justify anyone's having rights at all, what are those reasons, and what rights do they justify as belonging to which persons.

Recent moral philosophers have provided at least four different answers to these criterial questions. The intuitionist answer that humans' possession of certain unalienable rights is self-evident can be found at least from the Declaration of Independence to Nozick's peremptory assertion that "Individuals have rights, and there are things no person or group may do to them (without violating their rights)."[2] Like other intuitionist positions, this one is impotent in the face of conflicting intuitions. The institutionalist answer that rights arise from transactions grounded in formal or informal rules of institutions, such as promising,[3] incurs the difficulty that there may be morally wrong institutions, so an independent justification must still be given for the institutional or transactional rules which are held to ground the rights. A third answer is that persons have rights because they have interests.[4] This, however, indicates at most a necessary condition for having rights, since there would be an enormous and indeed unmanageable proliferation of rights if the having of any interest X were sufficient to generate a right to X. Even if "interests" are restricted to basic or primary interests or needs, the logical question still remains of how a normative conclusion about rights can be derived from factual premises about empirically ascertainable characteristics such as the having of interests. The fourth answer, that persons have rights because they have intrinsic worth or dignity or are ends in themselves or children of God, may be held simply to reduplicate the doctrine to be justified. Such characterizations are directly or ultimately normative, and if one is doubtful about whether persons have rights one will be equally doubtful about the characterizations which were invoked to justify it.

I shall now approach the problem of the criterion for having rights through their familiar connection with claims. Rights may, of course, be had even when they are not claimed, and claims are also not in general sufficient to establish or justify that their objects are rights. As against such an assertoric approach to the relation between claims and rights, I shall follow a dialectically necessary approach. Even if persons' having rights cannot be logically inferred in general from the fact that they make certain claims, it is possible and indeed logically necessary to infer from the fact that certain objects are proximate necessary conditions of human action that all rational agents logically must hold or claim, at least implicitly, that they have rights to such objects. Thus the criterion for having at least certain basic moral rights will be shown to depend on the consideration that all persons have certain needs relative to their being actual or prospective agents, namely, needs for the necessary conditions of action. At the same time, the logical problem of how rights can be inferred from facts will be avoided because the argument proceeds through the conceptual analysis of human action. By this analysis, from the necessary conditions of action a certain fact is inferred about rational agents that they logically must claim or at least accept that they have rights to these necessary conditions. Although what is thus directly inferred is a statement not about persons' rights but about their claiming to have them, this provides a sufficient criterion for rights because the claim must be made or accepted by all rational agents so that it holds universally within the context of action, which is the context within which all rights ultimately have application. The argument is dialectically necessary in that it proceeds from what all agents must claim or accept, on pain of contradiction. To see how this is so, we must briefly consider central aspects of action. Since I have presented the argument in some detail in various other places,[5] I shall here confine myself to outlining the main points.

All moral and other practical precepts, regardless of their varying specific contents, are concerned directly or indirectly with how persons ought to act. Insofar as actions are the possible objects of any such precepts, they are performed by purposive agents. As is shown by the endeavor which each agent contributes to achieving his purposes, he regards his purposes as good according to whatever criteria (not necessarily moral ones) are involved in his acting to fulfill them. Hence, the agent also a fortiori regards as necessary goods the proximate necessary conditions of his acting to achieve his purposes. These conditions, which pertain alike to all actual or prospective agents, are freedom and well-being, where freedom consists in controlling one's behavior by one's unforced choice while having knowledge of relevant circumstances, and well-being consists in having the other general abilities and conditions required for agency. The components of such well-being fall into a hierarchy of goods. Basic goods are the essential preconditions of action, such as life, physical integrity, and mental equilibrium. Nonsubtractive goods are the abilities and conditions required for maintaining undiminished one's level of purpose-fulfillment, while additive goods are the abilities and conditions required for increasing that level. Just as the basic goods are generically the same for all agents, so too are the nonsubtractive and additive goods. I shall call freedom and well-being the *generic features* of action, since they characterize all action, or at least all successful action, in the respect in which "action" has been delimited above.

Every rational agent logically must claim or accept, at least implicitly, that he has rights to freedom and well-being. If any agent were to deny that he has these rights, he would contradict himself. For in holding, as he rationally must, that freedom and well-being are necessary conditions of his agency, he holds that they are necessary goods; and because of his conative attachment to his purposes he holds that it is necessary that he have these goods in that he (prudentially) ought to have them. The meaning of this "ought" includes the idea of necessary restrictions on the interference of other persons with his having freedom and well-being. The agent holds that these restrictions are justified and are owed to him, from the standpoint of his own prudential purposes, because of their necessity for his engaging in action. If he were to deny that he has rights to freedom and well-being, then he would hold that it is permissible for other persons to interfere with his having these goods, so that it is all right that he not have them. This, however, would contradict his conviction that it is necessary that he have them because they are necessary goods without which he cannot be an agent. Hence, every agent must hold or claim, on pain of self-contradiction, that he has rights to freedom and well-being. I shall call them *generic rights,* because they are rights to the generic features of action. They are not yet moral rights but only prudential ones, since their ground is the agent's own pursuit of his purposes, whatever they may be. For the rights to be also moral ones, they must be shown to have a further ground in the agent's favorable consideration of the purposes or interests of other persons besides himself. Let us see why the agent must also take this further step.

Every agent must hold that he has the generic rights on the ground or for the sufficient reason that he is a prospective agent who has purposes he wants to fulfill. Suppose some agent A were to hold that he has these rights only for some more restrictive reason R. Since this would entail that in lacking R he would lack the generic rights, A would thereby contradict himself. For since, as was shown above, it is necessarily true of every agent that he holds implicitly that he has rights to freedom and well-being, A would be in the position of saying both that he has the generic rights and that, as lacking R, he does not have these rights. Thus, on pain of self-contradiction, every agent must accept the generalization that all prospective purposive agents have the generic rights, because, as we have seen, he must hold that being a prospective purposive agent is a sufficient condition or reason for having the generic rights. This generalization entails that the agent ought to refrain from interfering with the freedom and well-being of all other persons insofar as they are prospective purposive agents. Since to refrain from such interference is to act in such a way that one's actions are in accord with the generic rights of all other persons, every agent is logically committed, on pain of inconsistency, to accept the following precept: Act in accord with the generic rights of your recipients as well as of yourself. I shall call this the Principle of Generic Consistency (PGC), since it combines the formal consideration of consistency with the material consideration of the generic features and rights of agency.

To act in accord with someone's right to freedom is to refrain from coercing him; to act in accord with someone's right to well-being is to refrain from harming him. These rights, as thus upheld, are now moral ones because they are concerned to further the interests or goods of persons other than or in addition to the agent.

The above argument has provided the outline of a rational justification of the PGC, both for the formal reason that to deny or violate the principle is to contradict oneself and for the material reason that its content, comprising the generic features of action, necessarily imposes itself on every agent, as against the purposes, interests, inclinations, or ideals for which some agent may contingently act and whose requirements he may hence evade by shifting his desires or opinions. The PGC is the supreme principle of morality because its interpersonal requirements, derived from the generic features of action, cannot rationally be evaded by any agent. The main point, put succinctly, is that what for any agent are necessarily goods of action, namely, freedom and well-being, are equally goods to his recipients, and he logically must admit that they have as much right to these goods as he does, since the ground or reason for which he rationally claims them for himself also pertains to his recipients.

It follows from the argument to the PGC that the primary criterion for someone's having moral rights is that he is an actual or prospective agent having certain necessary needs relative to his agency. The argument has established this conclusion through what I have called a dialectically necessary method, in that it has proceeded from what logically must be upheld or admitted by every agent. Although the conclusion is thus relative to the requirements of agency, this relativity still enables the PGC and its ensuing criterion to be categorical. For since agency is the proximate general context of all morality and indeed of all practice, whatever is necessarily justified within the context of agency is also necessary for morality, and what must logically be accepted by every agent is necessarily justified within the context of agency. What has been established, then, is that simply by virtue of being actual or prospective agents who have certain needs of agency, persons have moral rights to freedom and well-being.

Since all humans are such agents, the generic rights to freedom and well-being are human rights. They are strict rights in that they entail correlative obligations on the part of persons other than the right-holder. But they are also primarily negative rights in that the primary obligation of these other persons is to refrain from interfering with the right-holder's freedom and well-being. There are, however, certain kinds of situations where, if some person A is inactive in the face of serious harm impending to another person B, A interferes with B's basic well-being. In such situations the PGC with its criterion of rights requires action rather than refraining from action because to refrain is to interfere with someone's basic well-being and hence constitutes a violation of his right to well-being.

I shall now apply these considerations of the PGC to the case of starvation. It is obvious that starvation is a basic harm, a deprivation of basic well-being. Since every person has a right to well-being, he has a right that other persons not interfere with his well-being, and other persons have the correlative duty not to interfere. Under what circumstances does this duty require positive action to prevent other persons from starving? I shall deal with this question, first, by considering certain conceptual matters; second, by applying the PGC to the problem of starvation within interpersonal morality; and third, by extending this application to international morality.

II

If some person A lacks a component of basic well-being such as food, this does not of itself entail that he lacks an effective right to food. In general a person lacks an effective right to something X if and only if he has a right to X and this right of his is violated. Thus, although it is indeed a necessary condition of A's lacking an effective right to X that he in fact lacks X (where this lack is either occurrent or dispositional, as the case may be), this is not a sufficient condition, for he may not have a right to X. But even if A has a right to X and he in fact lacks X, it still does not follow that he lacks an effective right to X. As we have seen, that A has a right to X entails that all other persons ought to refrain from interfering with A's having X. Hence, for A to have an effective right to X entails that all other persons do in fact refrain from interfering with A's having X, where A has a right to X. Such interference constitutes a violation of A's right to have X. Consequently, although every prospective purposive agent has a right to basic well-being, if A, who is a prospective purposive agent, lacks some component of basic well-being such as food, this does not of itself entail that A lacks an effective right to food unless his lack of food is caused by the interference of some other person or persons.

Such interference may occur in different ways. Persons may quite involuntarily cause obstacles to be put in the way of A's having food, with the result that he lacks food. For example, from ignorance of methods of scientific farming, from lack of required fertilizer, or through other circumstances beyond their control, persons may bring about a crop failure, with the result that A starves. Such persons do not, however, violate A's right to have food, for this violation would be a failure to fulfill their duty to refrain from interfering with A's having food—the duty which is entailed by A's having a right to food. Insofar as "ought" implies "can," since the persons in question are assumed to be unable to refrain from interfering with A's having food, it follows that they do not have the duty to refrain from such interference. (I here use "duty" in the general sense in which it is equivalent to a practical "ought," not in the more restricted sense in which it signifies a task assigned by social rules to some role or status.) Similarly, if other persons do not have enough food to supply their own minimal needs, then they are unable to provide food for A so that they have no duty to do so. Here again A's right to have food is so far not violated.

It is also possible that A may himself be the cause of his lack of food. He may intentionally starve himself for a variety of reasons, including a desire to lose weight or to go on a hunger strike. Or he may be too lazy to take care of himself or to work and hence to supply his basic needs. In such cases A's lack of food does not show that other persons have interfered with his having food; hence, they have not violated his right to have food.

In order to determine, then, whether A's right to have food has been violated and by whom, we must exclude both the involuntary actions and nonactions of other persons and the voluntary actions of A himself. What remains is the voluntary actions of other persons. For these persons to have the duty of supplying A with food, so that their interfering with his having food constitutes a violation of his right, they must both be aware that he lacks food from causes beyond his control and be able to repair this lack. They must have sufficient resources to have a surplus from their own basic food needs so as to be able to transfer some to A. By virtue of this ability, it is within their control to determine by their own unforced choice whether or not A has food. If, under these circumstances, A lacks food and they withhold food from him, then they voluntarily interfere with his having food and hence inflict basic harm on him. Thereby they violate his right to have food.

The better to understand this argument, which is derived from the PGC, let us apply it to a particular case of interpersonal morality. Suppose Ames, a bachelor, has a very large amount of food while Bates, another bachelor who lives nearby, is starving to death. None of the voluntary factors mentioned above applies to Bates. Ames knows of Bates's plight but doesn't want to give away any of his food, despite Bates's appeals for help. Bates dies of starvation.

In depicting this situation I have intentionally provided only the most meagre details about Bates's involuntary starvation, omitting all reference to any other psychological, historical, or institutional contexts. In the situation as thus depicted, the PGC supplies the sufficient ground for Ames's duty to give food to Bates. The principle prescribes, as a matter of strict duty, that agents refrain from inflicting basic harms on their recipients where such infliction violates the recipients' rights to basic well-being. But since Ames, in failing to give food to Bates, inflicts a basic harm on him, Ames violates

Bates's right to food. Ames thereby violates a strict duty imposed by the PGC. Since to violate the PGC is to incur self-contradiction, Ames's violation is shown to lack the most basic kind of rational justification.

Certain questions must now be considered about this application of the PGC. The principle sets a requirement for every agent, that he act in accord with the generic rights of his recipients. Since, however, Ames is passive and inert in the face of Bates's starving, it may be objected that Ames is here not an agent and hence not subject to the PGC's requirement. In reply, we must note that for someone to be an agent he need not engage in gross physical movement; it is sufficient that he engages in voluntary and purposive behavior. Ames is here an agent because his inaction in the face of Bates's plight is something he unforcedly chooses for purposes of his own while knowing of Bates's urgent need for food. Bates, moreover, is here Ames's recipient, since Ames's intentional knowing inaction crucially affects Bates's effective possession of the right to basic well-being. If Ames had given food to Bates, Bates would not have died; since he did not give food to Bates, Bates died.

It may be further objected that even if Ames's inaction crucially affects Bates's basic well-being, it is not the cause of Bates's death, nor does Ames bear any responsibility for it. For only a "positive" event can cause another event to occur; the mere absence of an event, as in Ames's inaction, cannot be a cause. But since the PGC prohibits that an agent inflict basic harm on his recipient, that is, that he positively act to cause his recipient to suffer basic harm, such as by killing him, it follows that Ames has not violated the PGC.

The answer to this objection is that an event, and a fortiori a harmful event, may be caused by a person's inaction or other omission as well as by his positive action. A train wreck may be caused by a signalman's omitting to move a switch; a man's failure to reach a physician in time may cause him to die of appendicitis. In such cases, what is properly singled out as the cause of the event is the particular antecedent circumstance, an omission, which makes the difference from the normal course of events (where "normal" may have either a statistical or a normative interpretation) and which is such that, if it had not occurred, the event would not have occurred. Ames's omission, his voluntary and purposive failure to give food to Bates, is the cause of the latter's death because Ames is subject to a valid normative rule which he has violated, and which is such that, if he had obeyed it, Bates would not have died.

There is indeed a difference between the cases of the train wreck and of Bates's death from starvation. The signalman's failure to move the switch is not only a violation of a valid prescriptive rule to which he is subject; it is also a deviation from a regular pattern of operations and of accompanying expectations so that it makes the difference from what regularly occurs and is hence the cause of the unusual occurrence of the collision. In the case of Bates's death, on the other hand, there may not be an ongoing rule-regulated system of expectations to which Ames's inaction comes as an exception. Nevertheless, even if Ames and Bates live in a society in which, as a matter of empirical fact, persons are not expected to care for one another, Ames's inaction is still morally wrong and the cause of Bates's death. What makes it such a cause is that Ames, as a rational agent, is aware of and is subject to the moral requirements of the PGC. It is against the background of these requirements that Ames's intentional failure to give food to Bates counts as the cause of his death. This background is a normative moral one and not, as in the case of the signalman, an empirical one. It is indeed the case that Bates would have died even if Ames had not lived nearby or had known nothing of Bates's plight. But, given the actual circumstances of Ames's knowledge, proximity, and easy ability to fulfill the PGC's requirement, the PGC makes it appropriate and indeed mandatory to single out Ames's inaction as the cause of Bates's death. For the PGC, as the supreme principle of morality, provides the primary normative standard, deviation from which is the relevant description or consideration in accounting for such an event.

It may also be objected that there remains another important difference between the cases of the signalman and of Ames. The railroad rules require that the signalman positively do something, so that he is blameable for the omission. But the PGC requires rather that an agent *not* do something: that he refrain from causing basic harm. Since Ames does not do something when he fails to give food to Bates, he has not violated the PGC as the signalman has violated the railroad rules. It must be noted, however, that the PGC does impose on every agent the duty to respect his recipients' rights to well being as well as his own. Such respect includes that he not treat them as mere means to his own purpose-fulfillment with no positive consideration for their own well-being. In ignoring Bates's plight, Ames fails to respect Bates's right to well-being; he permits a process to continue which he knows to be drastically harmful to Bates and which he could have reversed without any comparable cost to himself. In thus failing to respect Bates's right to well-being, Ames violates the PGC's prohibition against inflicting basic harm.

This consideration also bears on the possible objection that if Ames is the cause of Bates's starving to death, then he is also the cause of many other events which he could have prevented, such as a nearby cat's chasing and killing a mouse, or a neighbor boy's lacking a cherished bicycle which Ames could have bought for him. This objection requires that we supply a differentiating ground to distinguish when someone's inaction is and is not a cause of events which he fails to prevent.

Such a ground is given by the PGC. Since the principle requires that each agent act in accord with the generic rights of his recipients insofar as the latter are prospective purposive agents, it does not apply to cats and mice, which lack the capacities of knowledge, reflective choice, and control required for agency. As for the case of the bicycle, the principle does not impose the strict duty of positive beneficence in the sense of providing particular additive goods for other persons. Thus the neighbor's boy does not have a strict right to the bicycle or to Ames's buying it for him. The PGC bears rather on the right to well-being; it requires that each agent respect the well-being of others, where well-being signifies having the abilities and conditions required for agency. Thus the PGC provides what is relevant to the causal description of events characterized by the inaction of prospective agents.

III

This conclusion has an obvious bearing on one of the central sociopolitical problems of our age: the extreme contrast between the great affluence of some nations and the great poverty of others, where millions of persons in Asia and Africa are threatened or actually engulfed by famine. One way to deal with this problem is to note that the PGC, in addition to its direct applications to the actions of individual persons toward their individual recipients, also applies indirectly to such actions through the mediation of social rules or laws. In such indirect applications the PGC requires that laws have certain contents which are instrumental toward persons' treating one another with the mutual respect for rights directly required by the principle. Since the PGC requires the relief of starvation, it also requires that such relief be facilitated, where necessary, by appropriate legal measures to be undertaken by the political authorities.

This indirect application, however, deals with the relation of each state to its individual members, not with the relation of states to one another. How is this latter relation to be treated? Since states are not individual persons, there seems to be a gap between a principle of personal morality concerned with relations among individuals and the kind of morality which should govern international relations. This gap must be bridged if international morality is not to be left completely separated from a general rational moral principle and if the application of moral philosophy to complex social problems is to be given adequate rational guidance.

The relation of states to one another may be assimilated to the relation between individual persons when one nation, through the actions of its government, is able to affect the basic well-being of sizeable numbers of persons in the other nation. It is true that these actions lack certain elements of the voluntariness or freedom and purposiveness which are the generic features of individual actions: In constitutional regimes the behavior of government officials is controlled and directed not by their individual choices and purposes but rather by legal rules. Nevertheless, insofar as these rules result in turn from the advocacy of individuals and groups within the society, the rules and the ensuing actions or inactions may be assimilated to the voluntary and purposive behavior of individual agents. And just as individuals implicitly claim rights to freedom and well-being on the ground of their being prospective purposive agents, a similar implicit claim may be attributed to states insofar as freedom and well-being are required at least for the actions of their corporate representatives as well as for the population at large. The recipient states, in turn, may also be assimilated to the individual recipients of particular actions, for at least two reasons. The states consist of individual persons who are prospective purposive agents, and their basic well-being may be drastically affected by the action or inaction of other states. The actions of states toward one another are not, then, devoid of the personal cognitive and volitional controls which characterize the actions of individuals so that the causal and moral responsibility found among the latter may also be attributed to the conduct of societies and their relevant political officials. Thus the requirements of personal morality may be extended, with due qualifications, to the morality of the relations between states or nations.

From this it follows that, just as Ames had a strict duty to give food to Bates, so Nation A has a strict duty to give food to Nation B where Nation A has an overabundance of food while Nation B lacks sufficient food to feed its population so that sizeable numbers are threatened with starvation. Nation B has a correlative strict right to be given this food, for it is relevantly similar to Nation A in that regard in which the members of the latter implicitly claim for themselves rights to freedom and well-being. The members of Nation B, like those of Nation A, need food for survival and hence for agency, and they necessarily claim a right to food on this ground. To give this food is a moral duty for Nation A quite apart from considerations of self-interest. It may well be the case that underdeveloped nations will promote increasing international tension and unrest unless they are given relief from the pressures of underdevelopment and resulting insecurity, including the danger or actuality of famine. But even if such threatening tendencies can be kept securely in check, the moral duty is no less urgent.

This urgency is also unaffected by historical considerations, although these may affect the specific nature of Nation A's moral obligation to Nation B. If Nation A has had an exploitative relation to Nation B, coercively extracting copious goods from the latter and giving little in return, then Nation A may bear considerable responsibility for Nation B's underdevelopment, including its inability to ward off famine. In such a case, Nation A owes Nation B assistance, including food supplies, as a matter of compensatory justice. But even if the United States as well as other developed countries which are plausible exemplars of Nation A have not had such a relation to many underdeveloped countries (there is disagreement on this question),[6] this does not affect Nation A's strict moral duty to prevent starvation in Nation B, and the latter's strict moral right to be given food where it is unable to help itself.

At least two alternatives to this position may be upheld. One is that Nation B does not have a strict moral right to be given food; such giving by Nation A is only an act of charity or generosity and thus only a "loose" or "imperfect" duty, but not a strict duty of justice. The other alternative is that although Nation B may have a strict moral right to be given food, this is not a human right but only a more special or localized right.

The former alternative must be rejected because, as we have seen, every person, qua prospective purposive agent, must accept that all other persons as well as himself have strict rights to freedom and well-being which are the necessary conditions of agency. Since such a claim is logically ineluctable within the context of agency, no actual or prospective agent can deny or reject it except at the price of self-contradiction. The necessary conditions of agency include having sufficient food at least for subsistence, and persons' rights to such food are violated when it is withheld under circumstances like those discussed above. This applies to Nation A and Nation B viewed as composed of actual or prospective purposive agents.

The latter alternative turns on the precise meaning to be given to "human rights." The point of this consideration is that if the right to be rescued from starvation is not a human right, then to prove that the right exists requires showing something more than that the starving persons are human. One would have to show in addition that some promise has been given, or some contract arranged, or that some other specific transaction or undertaking has occurred which serves to ground the right.

Cranston has offered three tests for a moral right's being a "human" one.[7] The test of paramount importance is obviously met by the right to food for averting starvation. The test of practicability is met at least in the short run: Nation A is assumed to have an adequate surplus of food from which it can supply Nation B's immediate needs, although, as we shall see, problems of capability arise for the longer run.

The main difficulty is in the test of universality. According to Cranston, for a moral right to be a human one it must be a right of all men against all men: all men must have the strict duty of acting in accord with the right, and all men must have the strict right to be treated in the appropriate way. Thus all men must be both the agents and the recipients of the modes of action required by the right. This test is passed by the rights to life and to freedom of movement: Everyone has the duty to refrain from killing other persons and from interfering with their movements, and everyone has the right to have his life and his freedom of movement respected by other persons. But in the case of the right to be prevented from starving, only some persons have the right—those who are threatened by starvation—and only some persons have the duty—those who are able to prevent this starvation by giving food.

The answer to this objection need not concede that this right, like other economic and social rights, is universal, only a "weaker" sense, in that while all men have the right to be rescued from starvation, only some men have the correlative duty.[8] Within the limits of practicability, all men have the right and all have the duty. It is, indeed, logically impossible that each man be at the same time both the rescuer and the rescued, both the affluent provider and the starving pauper. In contrast, it is logically quite possible that each man at the same time both respect the lives of all other men and have his own life respected by all other men. Nevertheless, the right to be rescued from starvation is a strong human right in that both it and the correlative duty pertain to all men insofar as they are prospective purposive agents. That this is so is shown by the PGC, which is addressed to all agents and which requires that each agent respect the well-being of all his recipients as well as of himself. Where such respect requires positive action to rescue other persons from starvation, the requirement can, of course, be fulfilled only by some persons toward some other persons. But this does not alter the fact that all persons come under the protection and the requirements of the PGC both as agents and as recipients. Hence, all the generic rights upheld by the PGC have the universality required for being human rights.

When it is said that the right to be rescued from starvation and the correlative duty pertain to all men insofar as they are prospective purposive agents, this does not violate the condition that for human rights to be had, one need only be human, as against fulfilling some more restrictive description. As was indicated earlier, all normal humans are prospective purposive agents; the point of introducing this description is only to call attention to the aspect of being human which most directly generates the rights to freedom and well-being. The fact that some prospective purposive agent may not at some time be able to rescue others from starvation does not remove the fact that he has a duty to do so when he does have the ability. As we have seen, this duty stems, in the way indicated earlier, from the claim he necessarily makes or accepts that he has the generic rights by virtue of being a prospective purposive agent. The universality of a right, so far as concerns the duty it imposes, is not primarily a matter of everyone's actually fulfilling the duty, let alone his doing so at all times. Nor is it even a matter of everyone's always being able to fulfill the duty. It is rather a matter of everyone's always having the duty to act accordingly when the circumstances arise which require such action and when he then has the ability to do so, this ability including consideration of cost to himself.

Even though the circumstances and the ability are not always present, the duty (and hence the correlative right) is still universal because it pertains in principle to every prospective purposive agent. In this regard it differs from duties which pertain to persons not simply by virtue of being prospective purposive agents but only in some more restricted capacity, such as being teachers as against students, umpires as against batters, or judges as against defendants. The universality of human rights derives from their direct connection with the necessary conditions of action, as against the more restrictive objects with which nongeneric rights are connected. And since Nation A and Nation B are composed of prospective purposive agents, the latter's right to be given food by Nation A is a human right.

IV

Thus far I have argued from a somewhat simplified model of the relation between Nation A and Nation B, where the human right of the latter to be given food by the former stems simply from what the PGC requires by virtue of the relation between impending starvation and abundant means of preventing it. We must now consider some factors which complicate the model and thereby bring it closer to reality. These factors consist in various diversities: between short-run and long-run problems, and between the conditions and values that may exist within both Nation B and Nation A. These diversities give rise to conflicts not only of interests but also of relevant moral criteria.

Although, as indicated above, to talk of "Nation A" and "Nation B" as distinct substantive entities analogous to Ames and Bates is in some respects justified, the analogy breaks down in a crucial respect. It is not nations that are fed but individual persons. Thus when it is said that "Nation B" is starving, this is an abbreviation for the statement that sizeable numbers of individuals in Nation B are starving. The salient point is that who gets food in Nation B is determined not only by the existence or availability of food supplies within Nation B but also by the distribution of wealth and other forms of power, including effective mechanisms for providing food. Thus in many of the underdeveloped nations those who are rich have abundant food while those who are poor have very little. This contrasts at least in degree if not in kind with the relation between rich and poor in developed nations but the difference of degree is often very great.[9]

In this regard, the relation of Nation A to Nation B is different from Ames's relation to Bates. Bates is not internally divided into rich and poor parts of himself (unless he may be described, with doubtful relevance, as being spiritually rich while corporeally poor). Thus the directness of Ames's relation of obligation to Bates is replaced by a more complex relation wherein

Nation A's obligation to Nation B consists not merely in sending food but in seeing to it that the food is effectively distributed to those poor persons who need it. If, however, the social and political structure of distributive justice, or rather injustice, in Nation B is one of the chief causes of the starvation or serious malnutrition of sizeable masses of its inhabitants, then it would seem that Nation A cannot fulfill its moral obligation without interfering with that structure. Such interference raises problems of a political nature; it may involve restrictions on the freedom of the political authorities in Nation B.[10] Thus Nation A may be faced with a conflict of moral obligations: between the obligation to prevent the starvation of masses of persons in Nation B and the obligation to respect the political freedom of individuals and officials in that state.

This conflict is aggravated when the problems of starvation are viewed in long-run terms. There is evidence that when famine is averted in such a state as Nation B, its population tends to increase, especially when concomitant improvements occur in health care. This, however, aggravates the problem of distributing a limited food supply whose growth does not keep pace with the growth in population. Hence, the Malthusian warnings against population growth outstripping food supplies have been newly applied on an international scale in such assertions as that sending food to avert starvation in underdeveloped countries simply encourages further population growth and thereby leads to increased subsequent famines. It might seem, then, that Nation A's moral obligation to send food to the existing people of Nation B is also in conflict with a further moral obligation: to refrain from actions which lead to future famines in Nation B. If, moreover, the people of Nation B will not voluntarily desist from producing more children than can be supported by their available food supply—an assumption for which there is considerable evidence[11]—then it may seem that the conflict of moral obligations just noted inevitably extends to the point where Nation A's moral obligation to send food is in conflict with its moral obligation to refrain from interfering with the procreative freedom of persons in Nation B.

In addition to these conflicts, the moral duty to send food may also be held to clash with certain rights within Nation A itself. The acquisition and dispatching of food supplies will presumably be paid for by taxes levied proportionately on the citizens of Nation A. But it may be objected that to compel someone to contribute to such provision against his will is to violate his rights to freedom and property. It is to use him as a mere means for the benefit of other persons. The uniqueness and separateness of each individual, however, preclude making him a means to some greater social good.[12] Since the PGC requires that the agent act in accord with the generic rights of his recipients as well as of himself, it may seem that the principle itself is involved in internal conflict on this point, for if Nation A must act in accord with Nation B's right to basic well-being, then Nation A cannot also act in accord with its own right to freedom.

All four of the conflicts just indicated bear on the discordant tendencies of the rights to freedom and to well-being, both where these rights belong to the same party and where the agent's right to freedom clashes with his recipient's rights to well-being. Nation A's moral obligation to send food to Nation B stems from the PGC's requirement that the agent act in accord with his recipients' right to well-being, where such action requires at a minimum that the agent refrain from inflicting basic harm on others by letting them undergo a starvation which it is in his proximate capacity to prevent. This moral obligation with regard to Nation B's well-being conflicts with Nation A's moral obligation to act in accord with Nation B's rights to political and procreative freedom as well as with Nation A's own right to freedom. For present purposes, there need not be any separate consideration of Nation A's moral obligation to refrain from actions which may lead to future famines in Nation B. For since the actions in question are here viewed as contributing to unchecked population growth, the problems they raise may be assimilated to the moral obligation to respect the procreative freedom of persons in Nation B.

The first point to be noted about these conflicts of obligations is that the freedoms which form one of their respective poles are of different degrees of moral importance. What determines such degrees is shown by the PGC's derivation from the rights of agency. These rights fall into an order of priority in that one right is morally more mandatory than another insofar as the former is more necessary for agency. We saw above that every prospective agent must regard his freedom as a necessary good in that it is a necessary condition of his acting in pursuit of his purposes. But cases of such freedom may vary in several relevant ways. Most obviously, there is the distinction between long-range or dispositional freedom and short-range or occurrent freedom. If, for example, one is imprisoned, then one loses one's ability to perform a wide variety of actions which would otherwise be subject to one's unforced choice. If, on the other hand, a locked door prevents one's using it to enter a building, one's freedom is only momentarily interfered with if another adjacent unlocked door is available. In addition to this quantitative difference, there is also a qualitative distinction as to the kinds of actions one is free to perform. While many considerations are relevant here, actions may be distinguished according to their bearing on one's ability to perform many further actions, so that the freedom to eat when one is hungry is qualitatively different from the freedom to play some game about which one feels relatively indifferent.

I shall now briefly indicate how the PGC, through the consideration of such distinctions, helps to resolve the conflicts of obligations noted above. Let us begin with the conflict between Nation A's moral obligation to send food to

Nation B and Nation A's own right to freedom. The latter right stops where it serves to inflict serious harm on other persons by failing to prevent the severe loss of well-being entailed by starvation. The reason for this may be put in either of two interrelated ways. Nation A has no right to use its freedom in such fashion as to contribute to serious harm for Nation B. The rights of starving persons to be fed take precedence over the rights of other persons to make free use of all their property because the former rights are obviously more important for agency than the latter.

It may be objected that if individuals' rights to freedom and property may be invaded whenever this is needed to prevent harm to other persons, then there will be no limit to such invasion and hence in effect no rights. This slippery-slope contention fails, however, because in the present argument the harms in question are limited to interferences with basic goods. These are serious enough in their destructive effects on agency to require, as a matter of strict justice, such legally sanctioned intervention.

Persons are not treated as mere means when they are taxed in order to help persons who are starving or are otherwise in dire need of basic goods. As was indicated above in discussing the universality of the right to be saved from starvation, the principle underlying the taxation of the affluent to help the needy is concerned with protecting equally the rights of all persons, including the affluent. The PGC requires that all prospective purposive agents refrain from inflicting basic harm on one another. The fact that only some persons may actually be in a position to perform such infliction at a particular time, and hence do not then need to have their rights protected, does not alter the universality of the protection of rights. Such protection is not only occurrent but also dispositional and a matter of principle; it manifests an impartial concern for any and all persons whose basic rights may need protection. Hence, the PGC's requirement involves treating all persons as ends, not merely as means.

There is a further way of resolving the conflict between the freedom and the moral obligations of individuals within Nation A. The taxation whereby Nation A finances its food exports to Nation B derives from a commonly accepted decision procedure based on an electoral method which is itself an application of the PGC's generic rule of freedom. This application is a necessary-procedural one. Just as in its direct individual applications the PGC requires that each person be allowed to control his behavior by his own unforced choice without coercion by other persons, so in its indirect institutional applications where masses of persons are involved in structured interdependent relations, the PGC requires that there be a decision procedure resting on civil liberties wherein each person can uncoercedly participate in setting forth his views and in voting, with the decision going to some previously agreed majority or plurality. The procedure is itself on a higher level of authority than the decisions reached by its means, so that those decisions cannot rightly extend to abolishing the procedure itself or the freedom and well-being required for its operation. There may indeed be a conflict between the freedom of the procedure and the required outcome of averting starvation. This conflict is strongly mitigated, however, by the fact that the procedure is tied to the other rational components of the PGC, especially the duty to prevent basic harms.

The other conflicts of obligations mentioned above cannot be resolved as readily as can the conflicts within Nation A, for there may be no legal, institutional framework embracing Nations A and B which provides a decision procedure jointly accepted by them. It might be thought, in view of the immense seriousness of the threat to basic well-being, that draconian interventions are required, including compulsory sterilization and coercive replacement of uncooperative regimes. The use of such methods might, indeed, be justified on utilitarian grounds. These grounds are consequentialist: the end of maximizing well-being justifies the means. No special consideration needs to be given to freedom: it must at most take its place among the other "values" which are to be "weighed." Utilitarianism is at the opposite pole from libertarianism, for which freedom is the only value.

As against these extremes, the PGC requires that the freedom of one's recipients be maintained as long as possible, and that every possible effort be made to combine freedom with well-being. The use of coercive methods like those mentioned above would, indeed, be serious violations of the rights to freedom and to basic well-being in Nation B. In addition, it would open the door for other developed nations to impose enslavement and even genocide while proclaiming the same lofty motives. The absence of a commonly accepted civil-libertarian decision procedure makes such a slippery-slope argument more potentially applicable than when it is applied within Nation A. Realistic note must also be taken of further possible immoral abuses of power by Nation A itself.

The civil-libertarian decision procedure must, nevertheless, be used as fully as possible to resolve the other conflicts mentioned previously. It was noted above that there may be a conflict between Nation A's moral obligation to send food in order to prevent starvation in Nation B and Nation A's moral obligation to respect Nation B's political freedom, if the latter's sociopolitical structure is one of the chief obstacles to an equitable distribution of food supplies. The very sending of food, however, with the concomitant expression of deep concern by Nation A, may itself be held to constitute interference with Nation B's internal affairs. Such expression of concern is justified regardless of its impact on the sensitivities of governing officials in Nation B, because the right to basic well-being on the part of its inhabitants takes precedence over the officials' right to be spared embarrassment. Where the nutritional needs of poor persons in Nation B are ignored by its governing officials who derive their power from richer segments of the population, the offer of Nation A to send food must be accompanied by full use of methods to assure that the needy can make their voices heard so that their needs are met. So far as possible, civil-libertarian procedures must be encouraged within Nation B. The justification for this stems both from the intrinsic value of the civil liberties as human rights and from the contribution they can make, when equitably distributed, to the equitable distribution within Nation B of food and other components of basic well-being.

As against military intervention to guarantee that food supplies reach those who need them, the entire set of problems must be exhibited in a rational context which provides a common understanding of causes, rights, and duties. This common understanding must be pursued in ways which lead to mutual practical support of remedial measures. Other kinds of aid, such as fertilizer and money for land-purchase, must also be channeled so as to go to the poor and hence help toward the greater equalization of wealth and power, whose maldistribution causes a large segment of the problem of famine and malnutrition.

A similar approach must be taken to the conflict between Nation A's moral obligations to prevent starvation in Nation B and to respect its procreative freedom. Between the extremes of compulsory sterilization and completely unchecked population growth there are many different alternatives, some of which are more respectful of equal freedom than others. Procreative freedom ranks very high among human freedoms for many obvious reasons. But in countries like Nation B its use is often a response to conditions of extreme poverty, in that the having of many children is viewed as necessary to assure basic well-being and future economic security. It seems, then, that if there is to be any possibility of checking excessive population growth in Nation B by voluntary means, these economic causes must be ameliorated. Ways must be found so that couples' having more than two children is not, and is not viewed by them as, a necessary condition of their avoiding poverty and economic insecurity.

This is in part a bootstrap problem because excessive population growth exacerbates the very poverty which in turn promotes the excess. Nevertheless, measures like those indicated above can be of value. The more equitable distribution of fertilizer and machinery which help to avoid famine can also help to raise living standards. This must be accompanied by information about birth control, provision of contraceptives, and appropriate incentives to use them.

The consideration of the relief of starvation as a human right has suggested that it is closely connected with the civil liberties so highly prized in the Western constitutional democracies as human rights. There may, indeed,

be political dictatorships which promote an equitable distribution of food and
hence secure one human right at the expense of another. But, entirely apart
from the problem of assuring that even in these countries uncontrolled political power will continue to work in this direction, in many underdeveloped
countries dictatorship has the opposite effect, so that both kinds of human
rights are violated. The relief of starvation is a political as well as a technical
problem, and the moral guidance of both sorts of problem requires that the
freedom of the recipients be protected equally with their well-being, and this
for the sake of well-being itself.

NOTES

1. See W. N. Hohfeld, *Fundamental Legal Conceptions* (New Haven: Yale
University Press, 1919); John Salmond, *Jurisprudence,* 10th ed. (London: Sweet and
Maxwell, 1947), pp. 229ff.
2. Robert Nozick, *Anarchy, State, and Utopia* (New York: Basic Books,
1974), p. ix.
3. Cf. H. L. A. Hart, "Are There Any Natural Rights?," *Philosophical Review* 64 (1955): 175ff.
4. Cf. H. J. McCloskey, "Rights," *Philosophical Quarterly* 15 (1965): 124.
Elsewhere, McCloskey holds that persons have a prima facie right to the satisfaction of
needs: "Human Needs, Rights and Political Values," *American Philosophical Quarterly* 13 (1976): 9-10.
5. See my "Categorial Consistency in Ethics," *Philosophical Quarterly* 17
(1967): 289-99; "Obligation: Political, Legal, Moral," in J. R. Pennock and J. W.
Chapman, eds., Nomos no. 12, *Political and Legal Obligation* (New York: Lieber-
Atherton, 1970), pp. 55-88; "The Normative Structure of Action," *Review of
Metaphysics* 25 (1971): 238-61; "The Justification of Egalitarian Justice," *American
Philosophical Quarterly* 8 (1971): 331-41; "Moral Rationality," Lindley Lecture,
University of Kansas, 1972; "The 'Is-Ought' Problem Resolved," *Proceedings and
Addresses of the American Philosophical Association* 47 (1974): 34-61. In my *Reason
and Morality* (Chicago: University of Chicago Press, 1978) I present the whole argument more extensively.
6. See, on the one hand, Paul Baran, *The Political Economy of Growth* (New
York: Monthly Review Press, 1957), esp. ch. 5; and on the other, P. T. Bauer, *Dissent
on Development* (Cambridge, Mass.: Harvard University Press, 1976).
7. Maurice Cranston, *What Are Human Rights?* (London: Bodley Head, 1973),
pp. 66ff. See also his contribution in D. D. Raphael, ed., *Political Theory and the
Rights of Man* (London: Macmillan & Co., 1967), pp. 96ff.
8. Raphael in *Political Theory and the Rights of Man,* pp. 65ff., 112.
9. See Thomas T. Poleman, "World Food: A Perspective," *Science* 188
(1975): 515. (This whole issue of *Science* [9 May 1975] is devoted to important
articles on the world food problem.) Cf. also Gunnar Myrdal, *Asian Drama: An
Inquiry in the Poverty of Nations* (New York: Twentieth Fund, 1969), vol. 2, pp.

895-99, and S. Reutlinger and M. Selowsky, *Malnutrition and Poverty* (Baltimore: Johns Hopkins University Press, 1976).

10. Cf. Pierre R. Crosson, "Institutional Obstacles to Expansion of World Food Production," *Science* 188 (1975): 522, 523, and Harry Walters, "Difficult Issues Underlying Food Problems," ibid., 530.

11. See Kingsley Davis, "Population Policy: Will Current Programs Succeed?," *Science* 158 (1967): 730ff.

12. See Nozick, *Anarchy,* pp. 30-33, 170, 179n., 238.

9
Are There Any Absolute Rights?

It is a widely held opinion that there are no absolute rights. Consider what would be generally regarded as the most plausible candidate: the right to life. This right entails at least the negative duty to refrain from killing any human being. But it is contended that this duty may be overridden, that a person may be justifiably killed if this is the only way to prevent him from killing some other, innocent person, or if he is engaged in combat in the army of an unjust aggressor nation with which one's own country is at war. It is also maintained that even an innocent person may justifiably be killed if failure to do so will lead to the deaths of other such persons. Thus an innocent person's right to life is held to be overridden when a fat man stuck in the mouth of a cave prevents the exit of speleologists who will otherwise drown, or when a child or some other guiltless person is strapped onto the front of an aggressor's tank, or when an explorer's choice to kill one among a group of harmless natives about to be executed is the necessary and sufficient condition of the others' being spared, or when the driver of a runaway trolley can avoid killing five persons on one track only by killing one person on another track.[1] And topping all such tragic examples is the catastrophic situation where a nuclear war or some other unmitigated disaster can be avoided only by infringing some innocent person's right to life.

[1]For the cave example, see Philippa Foot, "The Problem of Abortion and the Doctrine of Double Effect", *Oxford Review*, no. 5 (1967), p. 7. For the "innocent shield" and the tank, see Robert Nozick, *Anarchy, State, and Utopia* (New York, 1974), p. 35, and Judith J. Thomson, *Self-Defense and Rights* (Lindley Lecture, University of Kansas, 1976), p. 11. For the explorer and the natives, see Bernard Williams, "A Critique of Utilitarianism", in J. J. C. Smart and B. Williams, *Utilitarianism For and Against* (Cambridge, 1973), pp. 98-9. For the trolley example, see Foot, *op. cit.*, p. 8, and Judith J. Thomson, "Killing, Letting Die, and the Trolley Problem", *The Monist*, 59 (1976), pp. 206 ff. I have borrowed from Thomson's *Self-Defense and Rights*, p. 10, the terminological distinction used below between "infringing" and "violating" a right.

Despite such cases, I shall argue that certain rights can be shown to be absolute. But first the concept of an absolute right must be clarified.

I

1. I begin with the Hohfeldian point that the rights here in question are claim-rights (as against liberties, powers, and so forth) in that they are justified claims or entitlements to the carrying out of correlative duties, positive or negative. A duty is a requirement that some action be performed or not be performed; in the latter, negative case, the requirement constitutes a prohibition.

A right is *fulfilled* when the correlative duty is carried out, i.e., when the required action is performed or the prohibited action is not performed. A right is *infringed* when the correlative duty is not carried out, i.e., when the required action is not performed or the prohibited action is performed. Thus someone's right to life is infringed when the prohibited action of killing him is performed; someone's right to medical care is infringed when the required action of providing him with medical care is not performed. A right is *violated* when it is unjustifiably infringed, i.e., when the required action is unjustifiably not performed or the prohibited action is unjustifiably performed. And a right is *overridden* when it is justifiably infringed, so that there is sufficient justification for not carrying out the correlative duty, and the required action is justifiably not performed or the prohibited action is justifiably performed.

A right is *absolute* when it cannot be overridden in any circumstances, so that it can never be justifiably infringed and it must be fulfilled without any exceptions.

The idea of an absolute right is thus doubly normative: it includes not only the idea, common to all claim-rights, of a justified claim or entitlement to the performance or non-performance of certain actions, but also the idea of the exceptionless justifiability of performing or not performing those actions as required. These components show that the question whether there are any absolute rights demands for its adequate answer an explicit concern with criteria of justification. I shall here assume what I have elsewhere argued for in some detail: that these criteria, insofar as they are valid, are ultimately based on a certain supreme principle of morality, the Principle of Generic Consistency (*PGC*).[2] This principle requires of every agent that he act in accord with the generic rights of his recipients as well as of himself, i.e., that he fulfil these rights. The generic rights are rights to the necessary conditions of action, freedom and well-being, where the latter is defined in terms of the various substantive abilities and conditions needed for action and for successful action in general. The *PGC* provides the ultimate

[2]Alan Gewirth, *Reason and Morality* (Chicago, 1978), pp. 135 ff., 197-198, 343-44.

justificatory basis for the validity of these rights by showing that they are equally had by all prospective purposive agents, and it also provides in general for the ordering of the rights in cases of conflict. Thus if two moral rights are so related that each can be fulfilled only by infringing the other, that right takes precedence whose fulfilment is more necessary for action. This criterion of degrees of necessity for action explains, for example, why one person's right not to be lied to must give way to another person's right not to be killed when these two rights are in conflict. In some cases the application of this criterion requires a context of institutional rules.

2. The general formula of a right is as follows: "A has a right to X against B by virtue of Y". In addition to the right itself, there are four elements here: the *subject* of the right, the right-holder (A); the *object* of the right (X); the *respondent* of the right, the person who has the correlative duty (B); and the *justificatory basis* or *ground* of the right (Y). I shall refer to these elements jointly as the *contents* of the right. Each of the elements may vary in generality. Various rights may conflict with one another as to one or another of these elements, so that not all rights can be absolute.

One aspect of these conflicts is especially important for understanding the question of absolute rights. Although, as noted above, the *objects* of moral rights are hierarchically ordered (according to the degree of their necessity for action), this is not true of the *subjects* of the rights. If one class or group of persons inherently had superior moral rights over another class or group (as was held to be the case throughout much of human history), any conflict between their respective rights would be readily resolvable: the rights of the former group would always take precedence, they would never be overridden (at least by the rights of members of other groups), and to this extent they would be absolute.[3] It is because (as is shown by the *PGC* as well as by other moral principles) moral rights are equally distributed among all human persons as prospective purposive agents that some of the main conflicts of rights arise. This is most obviously the case where one person's right to life conflicts with another person's, since in the absence of guilt on either side, it is assumed that the two persons have equal rights. Thus the difficulty of supporting the thesis that there are absolute rights derives much of its force from its connection with the principle that all persons are equal in their moral rights.

3. The differentiation of the elements of rights serves to explicate the various levels at which rights may be held to be absolute. We may distinguish three such levels. The first is that of *Principle Absolutism*. According to this, what is absolute, and thus always valid and never overridden, is only some moral principle of a very high degree of generality which, referring to

---

[3]Cf. Friedrich Nietzsche, *The Will to Power*, sec. 872: "The great majority of men have no right to existence, but are a misfortune to higher men" (trans. Walter Kaufmann (New York, 1967), p. 467). See also Nietzsche, *Beyond Good and Evil*, sec. 260 (trans. Kaufmann (New York, 1966), p. 206).

the subjects, the respondents, and especially the objects of rights in a relatively undifferentiated way, presents a general formula for all the diverse duties of all respondents or agents toward all subjects or recipients. The *PGC* is such a principle; so too are the Golden Rule, the law of love, Kant's categorical imperative, and the principle of utility. Principle Absolutism, however, may leave open the question whether any specific rights are always absolute, and what is to be done in cases of conflict. Even act-utilitarianism might be an example of Principle Absolutism, for it may be interpreted as saying that those rights are absolute whose fulfilment would serve to maximize utility overall. These rights, whatever they may be, might of course vary in their specific contents from one situation to another.

At the opposite extreme is *Individual Absolutism*, according to which an individual person has an absolute right to some particular object at a particular time and place when all grounds for overriding the right in the particular case have been overcome. But this still leaves open the question of what are the general grounds or criteria for overriding any right, and what are the other specific relevant contents of such rights.

It is at the intermediate level, that of *Rule Absolutism*, that the question of absolute rights arises most directly. At this level, the rights whose absoluteness is in question are characterized in terms of specific objects with possible specification also of subjects and respondents, so that a specific rule can be stated describing the content of the right and the correlative duty. The description will not use proper names and other individual referring expressions, as in the case of Individual Absolutism, nor will it consist only in a general formula applicable to many specifically different kinds of rights and duties and hence of objects, subjects, and respondents, as in the case of Principle Absolutism. It is at this level that one asks whether the right to life of all persons or of all innocent persons is absolute, whether the rights to freedom of speech and of religion are absolute, and so forth.

The rights whose absoluteness is considered at the level of Rule Absolutism may vary in degree of generality, in that their objects, their subjects, and their respondents may be given with greater or lesser specificity. Thus there is greater specificity as we move along the following scale: the right of all persons to life, the right of all innocent persons to life, the right of all innocent persons to an economically secure life, the right of children to receive an economically secure and emotionally satisfying life from their parents, and so forth.

This variability raises the following problem. For a right to be absolute, it must be conclusively valid without any exceptions. But, as we have seen, rights may vary in generality, and all the resulting specifications of their objects, subjects, or respondents may constitute exceptions to the more general rights in which such specifications are not present. For example, the right of innocent persons to life may incorporate an exception to the right of all persons to life, for the rule embodying the former right may be stated thus: All persons have a right not to be killed except when the persons are not innocent, or except when such killing is directly required in order to prevent them from killing somebody else. Similarly, when it is said that all persons have a right to life, the specification of 'persons' may suggest (although it does not strictly entail) the exception-making rule that all animals (or even all organisms) have a right to life except when they are not persons (or not human). Hence, since an absolute right is one that is valid without any exceptions, it may be concluded either that no rights are absolute because all involve some specification, or that all rights are equally absolute because once their specifications are admitted they are entirely valid without any further exceptions.

The solution to this problem consists in seeing that not all specifications of the subjects, objects, or respondents of moral rights constitute the kinds of exception whose applicability to a right debars it from being absolute. I shall indicate three criteria for permissible specifications. First, when it is asked concerning some moral right whether it is absolute, the kind of specification that may be incorporated in the right can only be such as results in a concept that is recognizable to ordinary practical thinking. This excludes rights that are "overloaded with exceptions" as well as those whose application would require intricate utilitarian calculations.[4]

Second, the specifications must be justifiable through a valid moral principle. Since, as we saw above, the idea of an absolute right is doubly normative, a right with its specification would not even begin to be a candidate for absoluteness unless the specification were morally justified and could hence be admitted as a condition of the justifiability of the moral right. There is, for example, a good moral justification for incorporating the restriction of innocence on the subjects of the right not to be killed; but there is not a similarly good moral justification for incorporating racial, religious, and other such particularist specifications. It must be emphasized, however, that this moral specification guarantees only that the right thus specified is an appropriate candidate for being absolute; it is, of itself, not decisive as to whether the right *is* absolute.

A third criterion is that the permissible specification of a right must exclude any reference to the possibly disastrous consequences of fulfilling the right. Since a chief difficulty posed against absolute rights is that for any right there can be cases in which its fulfilment may have disastrous consequences, to put this reference into the very description of the right would remove one of the main grounds for raising the question of absoluteness.

The relation between rights and disasters is complicated by the fact that the latter, when caused by the actions of persons, are themselves infringe-

---

[4]See R. M. Hare, "Principles", *Proceedings of the Aristotelian Society*, 73 (1972-73), pp. 7 ff. This paper is also relevant to some of the other issues of "exceptions" discussed above. See also Marcus G. Singer, *Generalization in Ethics* (New York, 1961), pp. 100-103, 124-133, and David Lyons, "Mill's Theory of Morality", *Noûs*, 10 (1976), pp. 112-13.

ments of rights. This point casts a new light on the consequentialist's thesis that there are no absolute rights. For when he says that every right may be overridden if this is required in order to avoid certain catastrophes— such as when torture alone will enable the authorities to ascertain where a terrorist has hidden a fused charge of dynamite—the consequentialist is appealing to basic rights. He is saying that in such a case one right—the right not to be tortured—is overridden by another right—the right to life of the many potential victims of the explosion. This raises the following question. Can the process of one right's overriding another continue indefinitely or does the process come to a stop with absolute rights?

In order to deal with this question, two points must be kept in mind. First, even when catastrophes threatening the infringement of basic rights are invoked to override other rights, at least part of the problem created by such conflict depends, as was noted above, on the assumption that all the persons involved have equal moral rights. There would be no serious conflict of rights and no problem about absolute rights if, for example, the rights of the persons threatened by the catastrophe were deemed inferior to those of persons not so threatened.

Second, despite the close connection between rights in general and the rights threatened by disastrous consequences, it is important to distinguish them. For if the appeal to avoidance of disastrous consequences were to be construed simply as an appeal for the fulfilment or protection of certain basic rights, then, on the assumption that certain disasters must always be avoided when they are threatened, the consequentialist would himself be an absolutist. We can escape this untoward result and render more coherent the opposition between absolutism and consequentialism if we recognize a further important assumption of the question whether there are any absolute rights. Amid the various possible specifications of Rule Absolutism, the rights in question are the normative property of *distinct individuals*.[5] In referring to some event as a "disaster" or a "catastrophe", on the other hand, what is often meant is that a large mass of individuals *taken collectively* loses some basic good to which they have a right. It is their *aggregate* loss that constitutes the catastrophe. (This, of course, accounts for the close connection between the appeal to disastrous consequences and utilitarianism.) Thus the question whether there are any absolute rights is to be construed as asking whether distinct individuals, each of whom has equal moral rights (and who are to be characterized, according to the conditions of Rule Absolutism, by specifications that are morally justifiable and recognizable to ordinary practical thinking), have any rights that may never be overridden by any other considerations, including even their catastrophic consequences for collective rights.

[5]Cf. H. L. A. Hart, "Are There Any Natural Rights?", *Philosophical Review*, 64 (1955), p. 182, and Hart, "Bentham on Legal Rights", in *Oxford Essays in Jurisprudence*, 2nd Series, ed. A. W. B. Simpson (Oxford, 1973), p. 193.

II

4. We must now examine the merits of the prime consequentialist argument against the possibility of absolute moral rights: that circumstances can always be imagined in which the consequences of fulfilling the rights would be so disastrous that their requirements would be overridden. The formal structure of the argument is as follows: (1) If R, then D. (2) O ($\sim$D). (3) Therefore, O($\sim$R). For example, (1) if some person's right to life is fulfilled in certain circumstances, then some great disaster may or will occur. But (2) such disaster ought never to (be allowed to) occur. Hence, (3) in such circumstances the right ought not to be fulfilled, so that it is not absolute.

Proponents of this argument have usually failed to notice that a parallel argument can be given in the opposite direction. If exceptions to the fulfilment of any moral right can be justified by imagining the possible disastrous consequences of fulfilling it, why cannot exceptionless moral rights be justified by giving them such contents that their infringement would be unspeakably evil? The argument to this effect may be put formally as follows: (1) If $\sim$R, then E. (2) O($\sim$E). (3) Therefore, O(R). For example, (1) if a mother's right not to be tortured to death by her own son is not fulfilled, then there will be unspeakable evil. But (2) such evil ought never to (be allowed to) occur. Hence, (3) the right ought to be fulfilled without any exceptions, so that it is absolute.

Two preliminary points must be made about these arguments. First, despite their formal parallelism, there is an important difference in the meaning of 'then' in their respective first premises. In the first argument, 'then' signifies a consequential causal connection: if someone's right to life is fulfilled, there may or will ensue as a result the quite distinct phenomenon of a certain great disaster. But in the second argument, 'then' signifies a moral conceptual relation: the unspeakable evil is not a causal *consequence* of a mother's being tortured to death by her own son; it is rather a central moral constituent of it. Thus the second argument is not consequentialist, as the first one is, despite the fact that each of their respective first premises has the logical form of antecedent and consequent.

A related point bears on the second argument's specification of the right in question as a mother's right not to be tortured to death by her own son. This specification does not transgress the third requirement given above for permissible specifications: that reference to disastrous consequences must not be included in the formulation of the right. For the torturing to death is not a disastrous causal consequence of infringing the right; it is directly an infringement of the right itself, just as not being tortured to death by her own son is not a consequence of fulfilling the right but *is* the right. This distinction can perhaps be seen more clearly in such a less extreme case as the right not to be lied to. Being told a lie is not a causal *consequence* of infringing this right; rather, it just is an infringement of the right. In each case, moreover, the first two requirements for permissible specifications of moral rights are also satisfied: their contents are recognizable to ordinary practical thinking and they are justified by a valid moral principle.

5. Let us now consider the right mentioned above: a mother's right not to be tortured to death by her own son. Assume (although these specifications are here quite dispensable) that she is innocent of any crime and has no knowledge of any. What justifiable exception could there be to such a right? I shall construct an example which, though fanciful, has sufficient analogues in past and present thought and action to make it relevant to the status of rights in the real world.[6]

Suppose a clandestine group of political extremists have obtained an arsenal of nuclear weapons; to prove that they have the weapons and know how to use them, they have kidnapped a leading scientist, shown him the weapons, and then released him to make a public corroborative statement. The terrorists have now announced that they will use the weapons against a designated large distant city unless a certain prominent resident of the city, a young politically active lawyer named Abrams, tortures his mother to death, this torturing to be carried out publicly in a certain way at a specified place and time in that city. Since the gang members have already murdered several other prominent residents of the city, their threat is quite credible. Their declared motive is to advance their cause by showing how powerful they are and by unmasking the moralistic pretensions of their political opponents.

Ought Abrams to torture his mother to death in order to prevent the threatened nuclear catastrophe? Might he not merely pretend to torture his mother, so that she could then be safely hidden while the hunt for the gang members continued? Entirely apart from the fact that the gang could easily pierce this deception, the main objection to the very raising of such questions is the moral one that they seem to hold open the possibility of acquiescing and participating in an unspeakably evil project. To inflict such extreme harm on one's mother would be an ultimate act of betrayal; in performing or even contemplating the performance of such an action the son would lose all self-respect and would regard his life as no longer worth living.[7] A mother's right not to be tortured to death by her own son is beyond any compromise. It is absolute.

[6]Cf. Aristotle, *Nicomachean Ethics*, III. 1. 1110a5, 27, and H. V. Dicks, *Licensed Mass Murder: A Socio-Psychological Study of Some S.S. Killers* (London, 1972). For similar extreme examples, see I. M. Crombie, "Moral Principles", in *Christian Ethics and Contemporary Philosophy*, ed. Ian T. Ramsey (New York, 1966), p. 258; Paul Ramsey, "The Case of the Curious Exception", in *Norm and Context in Christian Ethics*, ed. Gene H. Outka and P. Ramsey (New York, 1968), pp. 101, 127 ff.; Donald Evans, "Paul Ramsey on Exceptionless Moral Rules", *American Journal of Jurisprudence*, 16 (1971), pp. 204, 207; John M. Swomley, Jr., in *The Situation Ethics Debate*, ed. Harvey Cox (Philadelphia, 1968), p. 87. I have elsewhere argued for another absolute right: the right to the non-infliction of cancer. See Alan Gewirth, "Human Rights and the Prevention of Cancer", *American Philosophical Quarterly*, 17 (1980), pp. 117-25.

[7]This reference to the minimal moral conditions of a worthwhile life is, of course, an ancient theme; see Aristotle, *Nicomachean Ethics*, III. 1. 1110a 27; IV. 3. 1124b 7; IX. 8. 1169a 20 ff. For an excellent contemporary statement, see Alan Donagan, *The*

This absoluteness may be analysed in several different interrelated dimensions, all stemming from the supreme principle of morality. The principle requires respect for the rights of all persons to the necessary conditions of human action, and this includes respect for the persons themselves as having the rational capacity to reflect on their purposes and to control their behaviour in the light of such reflection. The principle hence prohibits using any person merely as a means to the well-being of other persons. For a son to torture his mother to death even to protect the lives of others would be an extreme violation of this principle and hence of these rights, as would any attempt by others to force such an action. For this reason, the concept appropriate to it is not merely 'wrong' but such others as 'despicable', 'dishonourable', 'base', 'monstrous'. In the scale of moral modalities, such concepts function as the contrary extremes of concepts like the supererogatory. What is supererogatory is not merely good or right but goes beyond these in various ways; it includes saintly and heroic actions whose moral merit surpasses what is strictly required of agents. In parallel fashion, what is base, dishonourable, or despicable is not merely bad or wrong but goes beyond these in moral demerit since it subverts even the minimal worth or dignity both of its agent and of its recipient and hence the basic presuppositions of morality itself. Just as the supererogatory is superlatively good, so the despicable is superlatively evil and diabolic, and its moral wrongness is so rotten that a morally decent person will not even consider doing it. This is but another way of saying that the rights it would violate must remain absolute.

6. There is, however, another side to this story. What of the thousands of innocent persons in the distant city whose lives are imperilled by the threatened nuclear explosion? Don't they too have rights to life which, because of their numbers, are far superior to the mother's right? May they not contend that while it is all very well for Abrams to preserve his moral purity by not killing his mother, he has no right to purchase this at the expense of their lives, thereby treating them as mere means to his ends and violating their own rights? Thus it may be argued that the morally correct description of the alternative confronting Abrams is not simply that it is one of not violating or violating an innocent person's right to life, but rather not violating one innocent person's right to life and thereby violating the right to life of thousands of other innocent persons through being partly responsible for their deaths, or violating one innocent person's right to life and thereby protecting or fulfilling the right to life of thousands of other innocent persons. We have here a tragic conflict of rights and an illustration of the heavy price exacted by moral absolutism. The aggregative consequentialist who holds that that action ought always to be performed which maxi-

Theory of Morality (Chicago, 1977), especially pp. 156-57, 183. For other recent discussions of the relation of the agent's character and intentions to moral absolutism, see John Casey, "Actions and Consequences", in Morality and Moral Reasoning, ed. J. Casey (London, 1971), pp. 155-7, 195 ff.; R. A. Duff, "Absolute Principles and Double Effect", Analysis, 36 (1976), pp. 73 ff.; P. T. Geach, The Virtues (Cambridge, 1977), pp. 113-17.

mizes utility or minimizes disutility would maintain that in such a situation the lives of the thousands must be preferred.

An initial answer may be that terrorists who make such demands and issue such threats cannot be trusted to keep their word not to drop the bombs if the mother is tortured to death; and even if they now do keep their word, acceding in this case would only lead to further escalated demands and threats. It may also be argued that it is irrational to perpetrate a sure evil in order to forestall what is so far only a possible or threatened evil. Philippa Foot has sagely commented on cases of this sort that if it is the son's duty to kill his mother in order to save the lives of the many other innocent residents of the city, then "anyone who wants us to do something we think wrong has only to threaten that otherwise he himself will do something we think worse".[8] Much depends, however, on the nature of the "wrong" and the "worse". If someone threatens to commit suicide or to kill innocent hostages if we do not break our promise to do some relatively unimportant action, breaking the promise would be the obviously right course, by the criterion of degrees of necessity for action. The special difficulty of the present case stems from the fact that the conflicting rights are of the same supreme degree of importance.

It may be contended, however, that this whole answer, focusing on the probable outcome of obeying the terrorists' demands, is a consequentialist argument and, as such, is not available to the absolutist who insists that Abrams must not torture his mother to death whatever the consequences.[9] This contention imputes to the absolutist a kind of indifference or even callousness to the sufferings of others that is not warranted by a correct understanding of his position. He can be concerned about consequences so long as he does not regard them as possibly superseding or diminishing the right and duty he regards as absolute. It is a matter of priorities. So long as the mother's right not to be tortured to death by her son is unqualifiedly respected, the absolutist can seek ways to mitigate the threatened disastrous consequences and possibly to avert them altogether. A parallel case is found in the theory of legal punishment: the retributivist, while asserting that punishment must be meted out only to the persons who deserve it because of the crimes they have committed, may also uphold punishment for its deterrent effect so long as the latter, consequentialist consideration is subordinated to and limited by the conditions of the former, antecedentalist consideration.[10] Thus the absolutist can accommodate at least part of the consequentialist's substantive concerns within the limits of his own principle.

Is any other answer available to the absolutist, one that reflects the core of his position? Various lines of argument may be used to show that in refusing to torture his mother to death Abrams is not violating the rights

[8]"The Problem of Abortion and the Doctrine of Double Effect" (see n. 1), p. 10.
[9]See Jonathan Bennett, "Whatever the Consequences", *Analysis*, 26 (1966), pp. 89-91.
[10]See Gewirth, *Reason and Morality*, pp. 294-9.

of the multitudes of other residents who may die as a result, because he is not morally responsible for their deaths. Thus the absolutist can maintain that even if these others die they still have an absolute right to life because the infringement of their right is not justified by the argument he upholds. At least three different distinctions may be adduced for this purpose. In the unqualified form in which they have hitherto been presented, however, they are not successful in establishing the envisaged conclusion.

One distinction is between direct and oblique intention. When Abrams refrains from torturing his mother to death, he does not directly intend the many ensuing deaths of the other inhabitants either as end or as means. These are only the foreseen but unintended side-effects of his action or, in this case, inaction. Hence, he is not morally responsible for those deaths.

Apart from other difficulties with the doctrine of double effect, this distinction as so far stated does not serve to exculpate Abrams. Consider some parallels. Industrialists who pollute the environment with poisonous chemicals and manufacturers who use carcinogenic food additives do not directly intend the resulting deaths; these are only the unintended but foreseen side-effects of what they do directly intend, namely, to provide profitable demand-fulfilling commodities. The entrepreneurs in question may even maintain that the enormous economic contributions they make to the gross national product outweigh in importance the relatively few deaths that regrettably occur. Still, since they have good reason to believe that deaths will occur from causes under their control, the fact that they do not directly intend the deaths does not remove their causal and moral responsibility for them. Isn't this also true of Abrams's relation to the deaths of the city's residents?

A second distinction drawn by some absolutists is between killing and letting die. This distinction is often merged with others with which it is not entirely identical, such as the distinctions between commission and omission, between harming and not helping, between strict duties and generosity or supererogation. For the present discussion, however, the subtle differences between these may be overlooked. The contention, then, is that in refraining from killing his mother, Abrams does not kill the many innocent persons who will die as a result; he only lets them die. But one does not have the same strict moral duty to help persons or to prevent their dying as one has not to kill them; one is responsible only for what one does, not for what one merely allows to happen. Hence, Abrams is not morally responsible for the deaths he fails to prevent by letting the many innocent persons die, so that he does not violate their rights to life.

The difficulty with this argument is that the duties bearing on the right to life include not only that one not kill innocent persons but also that one not let them die when one can prevent their dying at no comparable cost. If, for example, one can rescue a drowning man by throwing him a rope, one has a moral duty to throw him the rope. Failure to do so is morally culpable. Hence, to this extent the son who lets the many residents die when he can prevent this by means within his power is morally responsible for their deaths.

A third distinction is between respecting other persons and avoiding bad consequences. Respect for persons is an obligation so fundamental that it cannot be overridden even to prevent evil consequences from befalling some persons. If such prevention requires an action whereby respect is withheld from persons, then that action must not be performed, whatever the consequences.

One of the difficulties with this important distinction is that it is unclear. May not respect be withheld from a person by failing to avert from him some evil consequence? How can Abrams be held to respect the thousands of innocent persons or their rights if he lets them die when he could have prevented this? The distinction also fails to provide for degrees of moral urgency. One fails to respect a person if one lies to him or steals from him; but sometimes the only way to prevent the death of one innocent person may be by stealing from or telling a lie to some other innocent person. In such a case, respect for one person may lead to disrespect of a more serious kind for some other innocent person.

7. None of the above distinctions, then, serves its intended purpose of defending the absolutist against the consequentialist. They do not show that the son's refusal to torture his mother to death does not violate the other persons' rights to life and that he is not morally responsible for their deaths. Nevertheless, the distinctions can be supplemented in a way that does serve to establish these conclusions.

The required supplement is provided by the principle of the intervening action. According to this principle, when there is a causal connection between some person A's performing some action (or inaction) X and some other person C's incurring a certain harm Z, A's moral responsibility for Z is removed if, between X and Z, there intervenes some other action Y of some person B who knows the relevant circumstances of his action and who intends to produce Z or who produces Z through recklessness. The reason for this removal is that B's intervening action Y is the more direct or proximate cause of Z and, unlike A's action (or inaction), Y is the sufficient condition of Z as it actually occurs.[11]

An example of this principle may help to show its connection with the absolutist thesis. Martin Luther King Jr. was repeatedly told that because he led demonstrations in support of civil rights, he was morally responsible for the disorders, riots, and deaths that ensued and that were shaking the American Republic to its foundations.[12] By the principle of the intervening

[11]Cf. H. L. A. Hart and A. M. Honoré, *Causation in the Law* (Oxford, 1959), pp. 69 ff., 127 ff., 292 ff. For an application of this principle in a related context, see Gewirth, "Human Rights and the Prevention of Cancer" (n. 6 above), pp. 118-9.

[12]See, e.g., Charles E. Whittaker in Whittaker and William Sloane Coffin Jr., *Law, Order and Civil Disobedience* (Washington, D.C., 1967), pp. 11 ff.

action, however, it was King's opponents who were responsible because their intervention operated as the sufficient conditions of the riots and injuries. King might also have replied that the Republic would not be worth saving if the price that had to be paid was the violation of the civil rights of black Americans. As for the rights of the other Americans to peace and order, the reply would be that these rights cannot justifiably be secured at the price of the rights of blacks.

It follows from the principle of the intervening action that it is not the son but rather the terrorists who are morally as well as causally responsible for the many deaths that do or may ensue on his refusal to torture his mother to death. The important point is not that he lets these persons die rather than kills them, or that he does not harm them but only fails to help them, or that he intends their deaths only obliquely but not directly. The point is rather that it is only through the intervening lethal actions of the terrorists that his refusal eventuates in the many deaths. Since the moral responsibility is not the son's, it does not affect his moral duty not to torture his mother to death, so that her correlative right remains absolute.

This point also serves to answer some related questions about the rights of the many in relation to the mother's right. Since the son's refusal to torture his mother to death is justified, it may seem that the many deaths to which that refusal will lead are also justified, so that the rights to life of these many innocent persons are not absolute. But since they are innocent, why aren't their rights to life as absolute as the mother's? If, on the other hand, their deaths are unjustified, as seems obvious, then isn't the son's refusal to torture his mother to death also unjustified, since it leads to those deaths? But from this it would follow that the mother's right not to be tortured to death by her son is not absolute, for if the son's not infringing her right is unjustified, then his infringing it would presumably be justified.

The solution to this difficulty is that it is a fallacy to infer, from the two premises (1) the son's refusal to kill his mother is justified and (2) many innocent persons die as a result of that refusal, to the conclusion (3) their deaths are justified. For, by the principle of the intervening action, the son's refusal is not causally or morally responsible for the deaths; rather, it is the terrorists who are responsible. Hence, the justification referred to in (1) does not carry through to (2). Since the terrorists' action in ordering the killings is unjustified, the resulting deaths are unjustified. Hence, the rights to life of the many innocent victims remain absolute even if they are killed as a result of the son's justified refusal, and it is not he who violates their rights. He may be said to intend the many deaths obliquely, in that they are a foreseen but unwanted side-effect of his refusal. But he is not responsible for that side-effect because of the terrorists' intervening action.

It would be unjustified to violate the mother's right to life in order to protect the rights to life of the many other residents of the city. For rights cannot be justifiably protected by violating another right which, according to the criterion of degrees of necessity for action, is at least equally important. Hence, the many other residents do not have a right that the mother's right to life be violated for their sakes. To be sure, the mother also does not have a right that their equally important rights be violated in order to protect hers. But here too it must be emphasized that in protecting his mother's right the son does not violate the rights of the others; for by the principle of the intervening action, it is not he who is causally or morally responsible for their deaths. Hence too he is not treating them as mere means to his or his mother's ends.

8. Where, then, does this leave us? From the absoluteness of the mother's right not to be tortured to death by her son, does it follow that in the described circumstances a nuclear explosion should be permitted to occur over the city so that countless thousands of innocent persons may be killed, possibly including Abrams and his mother?

Properly to deal with this question, it is vitally important to distinguish between abstract and concrete absolutism. The abstract absolutist at no point takes account of consequences or of empirical or causal connections that may affect the subsequent outcomes of the two alternatives he considers. He views the alternatives as being both mutually exclusive and exhaustive. His sole concern is for the moral guiltlessness of the agent, as against the effects of the agent's choices for human weal or woe.

In contrast, as I suggested earlier, the concrete absolutist is concerned with consequences and empirical connections, but always within the limits of the right he upholds as absolute. His consequentialism is thus limited rather than unlimited. Because of his concern with empirical connections, he takes account of a broader range of possible alternatives than the simple dualism to which the abstract absolutist confines himself. His primary focus is not on the moral guiltlessness of the agent but rather on the basic rights of persons not to be subjected to unspeakable evils. Within this focus, however, the concrete absolutist is also deeply concerned with the effects of the fulfilment of these rights on the basic well-being of other persons.

The significance of this distinction can be seen by applying it to the case of Abrams. If he is an abstract absolutist, he deals with only two alternatives which he regards as mutually exclusive as well as exhaustive: (1) he tortures his mother to death; (2) the terrorists drop a nuclear bomb killing thousands of innocent persons. For the reasons indicated above, he rejects (1). He is thereby open to the accusation that he chooses (2) or at least that he allows (2) to happen, although the principle of the intervening action exempts him from moral guilt or responsibility.

If, however, Abrams is a concrete absolutist, then he does not regard himself as being confronted only by these two terrible alternatives, nor does he regard them or their negations as mutually exclusive. His thought-processes include the following additional considerations. In accordance with a point suggested above, he recognizes that his doing (1) will not assure the non-occurrence of (2). On the contrary, his doing (1) will probably lead to further threats of the occurrence of (2) unless he or someone else performs further unspeakably evil actions (3), (4), and so forth. (A parallel example may be found in Hitler's demand for Czechoslovakia at Munich after his taking over of Austria, his further demand for Poland after the capitulation regarding Czechoslovakia, and the ensuing tragedies.) Moreover, (2) may occur even if Abrams does (1). For persons who are prepared to threaten that they will do (2) cannot be trusted to keep their word.

On the other hand, Abrams further reasons, his not doing (1) may well not lead to (2). This may be so for several reasons. He or the authorities or both must try to engage the terrorists in a dialogue in which their grievances are publicized and seriously considered. Whatever elements of rationality may exist among the terrorists will thereby be reinforced, so that other alternatives may be presented. At the same time, a vigorous search and preventive action must be pursued so as to avert the threatened bombing and to avoid any recurrences of the threat.

It is such concrete absolutism, taking due account of consequences and of possible alternatives, that constitutes the preferred pattern of ethical reasoning. It serves to protect the rights presupposed in the very possibility of a moral community while at the same time it gives the greatest probability of averting the threatened catastrophe. In the remainder of this paper, I shall assume the background of concrete absolutism.

III

9. I have thus far argued that the right of a mother not to be tortured to death by her son is absolute. But the arguments would also ground an extension of the kind of right here at issue to many other subjects and respondents, including fathers, daughters, wives, husbands, grandparents, cousins, and friends. So there are many absolute rights, on the criterion of plurality supplied by Rule Absolutism.

It is sometimes held that moral obligations are "agent-relative" in that, at least in cases of conflict, one ought to give priority to the welfare of those persons with whom one has special ties of family or affection.[13] Applied to the present question, this view would suggest that the subjects having the absolute right that must be respected by respondents are limited to the kinds of relations listed above. It may also be thought that as we move away from familial and affectional relations, the proposed subjects of rights come to resemble more closely the anonymous masses of other persons who would be killed by a nuclear explosion, so that a quantitative measure of numbers of lives lost would become a more cogent consideration in allocating rights.

These conclusions, however, do not follow. Most of the arguments I have given above for the mother's absolute right not to be tortured to death apply to other possible human subjects without such specifications. My purpose in beginning with such an extreme case as the mother-son relation was to focus the issue as sharply as possible; but, this focus once gained, it may be

---

[13]See Derek Parfit, "Innumerate Ethics", *Philosophy and Public Affairs*, 7 No. 4 (1978), p. 287.

widened in the ways just indicated. Although the mother has indeed a greater right to receive effective concern from her son than from other, unrelated persons, the unjustifiability of violating rights that are on the same level of necessity for action is not affected either by degrees of family relationship or by the numbers of persons affected. Abrams would not be justified in torturing to death some other innocent person in the described circumstances, and in failing to murder he would not be morally responsible for the deaths of other innocent persons who might be murdered by someone else as a consequence.

These considerations also apply to various progressively less extreme objects of rights than the not being tortured to death to which I have so far confined the discussion. The general content of these objects may be stated as follows: All innocent persons have an absolute right not to be made the intended victims of a homicidal project. This right, despite its increase in generality over the object, subject, and respondents of the previous right, still conforms to the requirements of Rule Absolutism. The word 'intended' here refers both to direct and to oblique intention, with the latter being subject to the principle of the intervening action. The word 'project' is meant to indicate a definite, deliberate design; hence, it excludes the kind of unforeseeable immediate crisis where, for example, the unfortunate driver of a trolley whose brakes have failed must choose between killing one person or five. The absolute right imposes a prohibition on any form of active participation in a homicidal project against innocent persons, whether by the original designers or by those who would accept its conditions with a view to warding off what they would regard as worse consequences. The meaning of 'innocent' raises many questions of interpretation into which I have no space to enter here, but some of its main criteria may be gathered from the first paragraph of this paper. As for 'persons', this refers to all prospective purposive agents.

The right not to be made the intended victim of a homicidal project is not the only specific absolute right, but it is surely one of the most important. The general point underlying all absolute rights stems from the moral principle presented earlier. At the level of Principle Absolutism, it may be stated as follows: Agents and institutions are absolutely prohibited from degrading persons, treating them as if they had no rights or dignity. The benefit of this prohibition extends to all persons, innocent or guilty; for the latter, when they are justly punished, are still treated as responsible moral agents who are capable of understanding the principle of morality and acting accordingly, and the punishment must not be cruel or arbitrary. Other specific absolute rights may also be generated from this principle. Since the principle requires of every agent that he act in accord with the generic rights of his recipients as well as of himself, specific rights are absolute insofar as they serve to protect the basic presuppositions of the valid principle of morality in its equal application to all persons.

10
Individual Rights
and Political-Military Obligations

Should any person in a society like ours be subject to military conscription? This question involves many complex issues, ranging from the grounds of political obligation to the present and future conditions of United States–Soviet relations. I cannot, of course, deal with all these issues here. Elsewhere[1] I have discussed some of the chief considerations bearing on political obligation as it derives from the supreme principle of morality, and I shall summarize these in what follows. I shall begin, however, with a brief presentation of certain leading ideas about the justification of military conscription as seen in the light of the considerations just mentioned, and I shall then go on to provide some of the needed elucidations and qualifications.

Military Conscription and Ethical Individualism

One of the main issues of the justifiability of military conscription may be put as follows. The primary justification of the political authority possessed by states and governments is that they secure or protect certain important rights of individual persons. But military service removes or endangers the objects of two of the most basic of these rights: life and liberty. Conscripts may lose their lives in combat, and their freedom is severely restricted when they are subjected to military duty. It would seem to follow, then, that a state cannot be justified in imposing the requirement of military service on any of its citizens, for such requirement removes or endangers the very objects whose protection constitutes the primary justification of the state's authority.

It may be contended that this conclusion does not follow, for there are many areas where the state justifiably limits persons' possession of objects it is designed to protect. For example, one justification of the state's authority is that it protects the right to property; but still it justifiably imposes taxes, which remove from persons some of their property, in order to be able to carry on its necessary functions. Similarly, it may be held that the state can justifiably impose military conscription, even though this removes much liberty and may endanger life, insofar as this is needed to preserve the state and thereby to help it carry on its necessary functions.

This reply is inadequate. For, apart from all other questions about the justifiability of taxation, we must note that the objects removed by taxation are far less important for the fundamental rights of persons than are the objects removed or threatened by military conscription. We may, of course, regard taxation as a "conscripting" of property, or conscription as a "taxing" of life and liberty. But these verbal maneuvers do not affect the main point, which bears on the benefits persons receive from the state's protecting their rights. While it may be rational for a person to give up some of his property if this enables him to keep the rest securely and to acquire more, it is not in any comparable way rational for him to give up or to endanger his life. And it is also the extensiveness of the loss of liberty in military service, the drastic subjection to military orders and regimentation, that distinguishes the conscript's lot from that of the tax-payer.

One premise of the above remarks should be made explicit. I am here, so far, assuming ethical individualism. This is not to be understood, how-ever, in the perhaps more usual sense that the individual's judgment or conscience is to be the decisive source or criterion for determining what is morally right and wrong.[2] By "ethical individualism" I mean to refer to ends or values rather than to epistemic or decisional sources. It is the goods and rights of individuals that constitute the primary criterion or end of moral rightness. Thus the state or society itself is to be viewed as valuationally instrumental, not final: it is a means to protect the rights of individuals rather than an end or good in itself. Hence, the preservation of the state or of the nation is valuable and worthy only insofar as this is of benefit to its individual members. The problem we have been considering is how the state, while being but a means to an end, can justifiably act to remove or endanger the end itself.

Another way to put part of this point is to say that distributive criteria must take priority over aggregative or collective criteria. What is morally right must be assayed primarily by reference to the rights of each several person rather than by reference to the good of the collective whole or the summation or maximization of goods. In this way, the primary moral principle must be a deontological one of distributive justice rather than an aggregative or collectivist principle such as utilitarianism or organicism. Aggregative or collective goods may be justifiably invoked only as means to distributive goods. Hence, again, it seems impossible to justify military conscription, given its drastic subordination of distributive to collective goods.

I shall subsequently present several qualifications of the point just made. But, remaining for now within the ethical individualism so far sketched, we can see the severe difficulty it poses for the question of justifying military conscription. If the state exists to protect the rights of individuals, then how can it be justified in removing or threatening those very rights? It is easy to dispose of many answers. For example, it may be said that military conscription does not remove rights but only the objects of the rights: not, for example, the right to liberty but only liberty itself. But this distinction, while perhaps plausible in some contexts, is here an empty one. Rights, after all, have objects, they are rights to something; and if these objects are removed, then the right, too, is infringed. It is no comfort at all to assure someone who is about to be killed that he still has the *right* to life; all he is about to lose is life itself. Another answer is that the ethical individualism upheld here would make legal punishment impossible. How can the state justifiably send someone to prison and thereby deprive him of his freedom if one of its main justifications is its protection of the right to freedom? The answer is that the criminal's loss of freedom has an entirely different basis from the conscript's. The criminal has violated some other person's right by removing from him certain important goods to which he has a right, and punishment is justified as a way of redressing the balance of mutual nonaggression that the criminal has voluntarily disrupted. No such fault can be attributed to the conscript as such, so that his being deprived of freedom lacks any comparable justification. It will be noted that the ground here adduced for punishment is retributive and distributive rather than utilitarian or aggregative.

Other suggestions for the justification of military conscription run parallel to the problem of the justification of political obligation and incur comparable difficulties. It may be said, for example, that military conscription is justified if it is needed for the common good. But this raises the questions of what is meant by "common good" and whether, in any of its meanings, it can rightly override the rights of individuals. For present purposes, we may distinguish two main meanings. First, "common good" may be interpreted aggregatively or collectively to mean the good either of many individuals summed together or of the community taken as a collective whole having a value distinct from that of its individual members. In either case, to say that the common good so interpreted may override the basic goods of some individuals is to uphold a collectivist sacrifice of a few to the many or the "whole." On this view, it would be justified to enslave the few if this would lead to more overall good. There is no adequate basis for thus preferring the whole to the part or even for attributing value to the aggregate or collective whole as against its individual members.

Second, "common good" may be interpreted distributively or individualistically so that it refers to goods that are common to—equally held by—each of the individual members of some group or community. But now if it is said that military conscription is justified because it promotes the common good taken in this distributive sense, then the question still remains how the goods in question are equally common both to all the nonconscripted members of society and to the individuals who are conscripted and thereby lose some of their most basic goods. The common good taken distributively cannot justify coercively sacrificing the goods of some persons for the sake of others.

Another familiar group of answers to the question of justifying military conscription is that individuals owe services to the state in return for the benefits they receive from it. Under this heading come such familiar concepts as "fair play" and "gratitude." The answers are perhaps equally familiar.[3] First, if individuals have no choice but to receive certain benefits, then it is implausible that they owe any services in return. Second, it may be questioned whether the benefits received are so great as to justify losing liberty and possibly life. Third, there is the problem of drastically unequal benefits. It may be questioned whether any services are owed by those who live impoverished, degraded lives in squalid ghettos.

Finally, an appeal may be made to one or another version of contractualism, either in the ideal form upheld by John Rawls or in the empirical form found in various theories of consent. All these versions have severe difficulties that disqualify them as theories either of morality in general or of social justice or political obligation.[4] And these difficulties apply even more strongly to the problem of military conscription.

The Primacy of Moral Obligation

Where, then, does this leave us? Must we conclude that military conscription cannot be morally justified at all?

Such a conclusion would be premature. The difficulties discussed above have arisen because the problem has not been pushed back far enough. The problem of military conscription requires for its adequate answer a solution of the problem of political obligation: Why are persons morally obligated to obey the laws of some state or government? For military conscription is imposed by the laws of a state; hence, although the solution of the problem of political obligation may not be a sufficient condition of the solution of the problem of justifying military conscription, it is at least a necessary condition. And the solution of the problem of political obligation, in turn, requires an understanding of the basic principles of morality, since the problem is one of the moral justification of persons' political bonds. On these principles, I shall recur to some of the considerations mentioned in my opening paragraph.

To begin with, we must note the primacy of moral obligation. This primacy is suggested by the very concept of a morality, but ultimately it requires detailed justificatory argument. A morality is a set of categorically obligatory requirements for action that are addressed, at least in part, to every actual or prospective agent and that are concerned with furthering the interests, especially the most important interests, of persons or recipients other than, or in addition to, the agent or the speaker. It will be noted that this definition combines two kinds of considerations: formal and material. The *formal* consideration is that moral requirements are categorically obligatory and are addressed at least in part to every agent. The requirements are categorically obligatory in that compliance with them is mandatory on the part of every person addressed by them, regardless of whether he wants to accept them or their results and regardless also of the requirements of any other institutions, such as law or etiquette, whose obligatoriness may itself be doubtful or variable. Ultimately, what is categorically obligatory is the whole system of morality as deriving from its supreme principle, so that, while one moral requirement may be overridden by another, it may not be overridden by any nonmoral requirement, nor can its normative bindingness be escaped simply by shifting one's inclinations, opinions, or ideals.

This formal consideration, taken by itself, still leaves open three main questions, two of which involve the *material* consideration in the above definition of morality. One question is the proof or justification of the claim the formal consideration embodies for the categorical obligatoriness of morality. I call this the *authoritative question* of moral philosophy. One of the most famous ways of expressing it is to ask: Why should one be moral? In particular, why should moral requirements take precedence over all other practical requirements, including political and legal ones? The other two questions bear on the specific contents to which this claim attaches. In the definition of morality just given, these contents or material components were presented in general terms, as being "concerned with furthering the interests, especially the most important interests, of persons or recipients other than, or in addition to, the agent or the speaker." So the second question is: What are the "most important interests" of persons? And the third is: *Which* persons should have their most important interests furthered or favorably considered in action? I call the latter two questions, respectively, the *substantive question* and the *distributive question* of moral philosophy, and both bear on the *material* considerations that are combined with the formal one in the definition of morality presented above.

In *Reason and Morality* I have given detailed arguments for certain answers to each of these three questions. The general basis of the answers consists in a certain supreme principle of morality which prescribes fulfillment of the conditions that are needed by every prospective purposive agent if he is to be able to act either at all or with some chance of success in achieving his purposes. The principle says to every agent that just as, in acting, he acts in accord with his own rights to agency, so too ought he to act in accord with his recipients' rights to agency. This "ought," when fully spelled out, specifies all the moral obligations owed by individuals to one another in their various personal transactions. The principle has a rigorously rational foundation both for the material reason that it is grounded in the necessary conditions of human action and for the formal reason that denial or violation of the principle involves self-contradiction on the part of the agent.

I have elsewhere indicated somewhat more explicitly how these considerations provide answers to each of the three central questions of moral philosophy. The substantive and distributive questions are answered by showing that every agent must act in accord with the rights of his recipients to the necessary goods or conditions of action, consisting in freedom and well-being. The recipients in question comprise other prospective purposive agents, whose specific range may vary in different interpersonal and more broadly institutional contexts. It has been shown that every prospective purposive agent has equally the generic rights, i.e., rights to the generic features of action which constitute the necessary goods of agency, viz., freedom and well-being. Thus the substantive and distributive answers uphold an equality of generic rights among all actual or prospective agents. The authoritative question of moral philosophy is answered in two ways: formally and materially. The formal answer is that the answers just indicated to the substantive and distributive questions are necessarily true, in that any agent who rejects or denies them is caught in a contradiction. Hence, for any agent's position to be rationally justified, he logically must accept the principle that embodies these answers. The appeal to consistency constitutes a culminating structural argument for the normative necessity of accepting this supreme moral principle, for it shows that the indicated substantive and distributive answers are so conclusive that logical inconsistency results from rejecting them.

The material answer to the authoritative question refers to the specific contents of the answer to the substantive question. These contents consist in the most important goods or interests of persons, namely, the generic features of all action. Hence, the substantive answer applies to every agent in all his interpersonal actions, so that it takes precedence over any more specific requirements or conditions of particular kinds of actions or institutions.

The moral principle that serves to ground these three answers to the distributive, substantive, and authoritative questions of moral philosophy is the following precept, addressed to every actual or prospective agent: *Act in accord with the generic rights of your recipients as well as of yourself.* I call this the Principle of Generic Consistency *(PGC)* because it combines the formal consideration of consistency with the material consideration of the generic features and rights of action.[5] Compliance with this principle is categorically obligatory on the part of every agent for the reasons just indicated in connection with the authoritative question. The *PGC* is a principle of the equality of generic rights in that it requires of every agent that he give equally favorable consideration to the rights of each of his recipients to freedom and well-being as he gives to his own generic rights. As will be indicated below, in many contexts the effectuation of this equality requires a system of institutional rules.

We are now in a position to see how the *PGC,* as the supreme principle of morality, imposes certain qualifications on the ethical individualism from which I began. First, this individualism must be egalitarian: all persons must have equal rights to the necessary goods of action. Second, these rights entail certain correlative duties or obligations on the part of all prospective purposive agents, so that the right to freedom that was one of the chief components of the initial ethical individualism must also accommodate various restrictions on freedom. These restrictions or duties, moreover, are positive as well as negative. The generic rights of each purposive agent entail, not only the negative duty of all other agents to refrain from interfering with any agent's having the necessary goods of action, but also the positive duty to help persons have or maintain these goods when they cannot do so by their own efforts and they can be helped at no comparable cost to the agent. Thus, ethical individualism as justified by the *PGC* must be sharply distinguished from egoism. What the *PGC* justifies is a whole system of mutually supportive rights and duties. This system is similar to the "common good" in the distributive meaning distinguished above; but it adds to that meaning the requirement of mutuality, whereby persons not only must refrain from removing from others any of the necessary goods of action but also must help others to obtain these goods when they cannot obtain them by their own efforts. The latter duty often requires a context of institutional rules.

The Justification of Political Obligation

From the above delineation of the form and content of moral obligation, comprised in the *PGC* as the principle of the answers to the three main questions of moral philosophy, there follows a corresponding mandatoriness for political obligation. To see how this is so, we must note that the *PGC* has not only *direct* applications to the actions of individual agents in noninstitutional contexts but also *indirect* applications to the actions of agents that occur within, or are objects of, social rules and institutions. In these indirect applications, the requirements of the *PGC* are imposed in the first instance not on the actions of individual agents but rather on social rules and institutions, which must conform to the *PGC*'s requirements. It is then these rules and institutions whose requirements are imposed, in turn, on the actions of individuals who are subject to these requirements. Thus the *PGC* is here applied to the actions of individual persons only through the mediation of social rules. These rules are morally justified, and the persons who act according to them fulfill their moral obligations, when the rules express or serve to protect or foster the equal freedom and well-being of the persons subject to them.

When social rules and institutions are in this way justified by the *PGC*, their requirements take precedence over the direct applications of the *PGC*. For example, when the umpire in a baseball game declares the batter out, the latter must leave the batter's box, thus experiencing coercion rather than freedom; when the judge sentences the criminal to prison or to a fine, the latter must undergo these losses of well-being and freedom. For such transactions occur in contexts structured by institutional rules; hence, the requirements of such rules, insofar as they are morally justified by the *PGC*, take priority over those of its noninstitutional contexts.

The social rules and institutions that are in this way justified by the *PGC* include three kinds or aspects of political institutions. First, the *minimal state*, consisting in the criminal law and the institutional arrangements for establishing and enforcing it, is justified by the most basic part of the *PGC*'s well-being component. For the rules of the criminal law are instrumentally justified by the *PGC* in that they serve to uphold in certain ways the rights of all persons to such basic components of well-being as life, liberty, and physical integrity, as well as such other important goods as reputation and privacy.

Second, the *supportive state* is also instrumentally justified by the *PGC*, but in a dynamic rather than static way. For, unlike the criminal law, it tries, not to correct or prevent a disruption of an antecedent situation of mutual nonharm, but rather to move toward a new situation, in which equality of well-being is attained or more closely approximated. Under this heading come various provisions for welfare, education, and other goods concerned with relieving severe needs or promoting equality of opportunity. The supportive state's arrangements also include a general context of order that serves to protect and extend well-being through uniform rules that provide for predictability and for impartial resolution of conflicts of interest. Thus, the supportive state contributes protection for the right to well-being by providing various public goods that improve persons' capabilities for action and productive work and by supplying basic goods, such as food and housing, to persons who cannot obtain them by their own efforts.

Third, the *democratic state* is procedurally justified by the freedom component of the *PGC*. For in such a state specific laws and officials are determined by the method of consent, consisting in the equal distribution of the civil liberties in the political process. The democratic state also upholds the civil liberties in all other phases of social action.

These three kinds of state, then, are each justified by the *PGC*, either instrumentally or procedurally. Now, as we have seen, compliance with the *PGC*, and thus acceptance of the moral obligations it imposes, is categorically obligatory for all actual or prospective agents. Hence, since the kinds of state just delineated are themselves justified by the *PGC*, the moral obligations that derive from the supreme principle of morality are also owed to such states by persons living within their territory, so that there is a moral obligation to obey and support them. In this way, political obligation emerges as a species of moral obligation.

The argument to this conclusion may be put somewhat more formally as follows. It has been shown that every prospective agent morally ought to act in accord with the generic rights of all other prospective agents as well as of himself. But obedience to and support of the state and its laws that fulfill the *PGC*'s requirements are conceptually or causally necessary for such action. For such a state serves to protect the generic rights of all persons within its jurisdiction and to bring it about, in various direct or indirect ways, that persons act in accord with one another's generic rights. Therefore, every purposive agent morally ought to obey and support such a state and its laws, which obtain within the territory in which he lives.

It will have been noted that I have used the phrases "moral obligation" and "morally ought" without distinguishing between them. This synonymy is based on the categorical obligatoriness that attaches to moral requirements; I shall have something more to say on this below. But at this point it may be helpful to indicate a connected point about the relation between "moral obligation" and "political (or legal) obligation." It is sometimes held[6] that these are two distinct and parallel types of obligation. But this is a mistake. The point that emerges from my argument, above, is that "Because it is the law" does not, as such, indicate a sufficient ground of obligation; to be sufficient, the law in question must satisfy the institutional requirements of the *PGC* as embodied in the minimal, supportive, and democratic state. From this it follows that moral obligation and political or legal obligation are not parallel modes of obligation, since the latter must derive its justificatory ground from the former. And, for the same reason, they are not even distinct modes of obligation, since political obligation, in order to be genuinely obligatory, must be a mode or species of moral obligation.

The PGC *and Alternative Doctrines of Political Obligation*

I have now briefly given my answer to the problem of how the obligation to obey and support the laws of some state can be morally justified. It will be noted that only some states can meet the conditions of this justification. It must also be noted that the justification I have given leaves open many questions that require further scrutiny. I have justified the institutions of the state and its laws by their serving to protect or secure the rights of persons, the equal distribution of which is required by the supreme principle of morality. This argument assumes that for the fulfillment of this moral function there should be only one state within a given territory, or at least only one state possessing sovereignty. The argument, while leaving open the question of how extensive this territory should be, is compatible both with the existence of historically determinate states embodying various traditions and loyalties and the formation of new states.

In addition to such historical relativity, it must be recognized that different states may vary in the degrees to which they achieve the protection of rights prescribed by the *PGC*. If a minimal state does not equally protect all its members from crime, to what extent does it deserve obedience? What if the minimal state is not, in addition, supportive, because *(a)* it does not provide an adequate context of rules that remove disorder and resolve conflicts of interest or *(b)* it does not promote equality of rights to well-being among all its members? What if a minimal or a supportive state is not also democratic, or a democratic state is not also supportive?

Such questions show that a full answer to the problem of political obligation requires a principled establishment of priorities that take adequate account both of the moral requirements or grounds that underlie political obligation and of historical contexts and possibilities. One important criterion for such priorities, deriving from the *PGC,* is that of the degrees of necessity for action. One moral right takes precedence over another insofar as the good that is the object of the former right is more necessary for action than is the good that is the object of the latter right. This is why, for example, the right not to be lied to must give way to the right not to be murdered when these two rights are in conflict. Similarly, one may hold that when the conditions of a minimal state are in conflict with the conditions of a democratic state, the former conditions should take precedence over the latter because a situation where there is unrestricted bloodshed and wanton killing is more deleterious to the necessary conditions of action than is a situation where the civil liberties are restricted. It must be emphasized, however, as is tragically shown by the current situation in parts of Latin America and elsewhere, that, if such applications of the criterion of degrees of necessity for action are to be rationally justified, the conflict between the two sets of conditions must not be caused or exacerbated by the authorities themselves, nor can the suppression of democracy be justified by appeals to tradition or to conceptions of propriety.

All these difficulties in the application of the criterion of political obligation sketched above still leave firm, however, its basis or ground in the generic rights of persons as these are upheld by the *PGC.* It may help to clarify further the principle's rights-based justification of political obligation if I contrast it briefly with two other kinds of doctrine about political obligation, which I shall call *affirmative* and *negative.* These doctrines hold, respectively, that moral justifications of political obligation can, and cannot, be given. I have already briefly considered the affirmative doctrines, but I shall now look at them again in the light of the justification I have presented here.

There are at least five respects in which the *PGC*'s rights-based justification of political obligation differs from other justification models based on gratitude, fair play, consent, or other criteria. Because of some of these differences, the *PGC,* unlike the other models, can explain why and to what extent there is justification for such infringements of individual rights as conscription. The first difference is that, when the *PGC* provides that political obligation is justified by the state's serving to protect basic rights to freedom and well-being, this justification is not necessarily, or only, backward-looking or retrospective; it may also be forward-looking or prospective. For the justification is based not merely on the fact that the state has protected basic rights in the past and so "deserves" support or obedience in the future; it is also, and primarily, based on the fact that such support is needed in order to enable the state to continue to protect basic rights.

Now there is a contrast here with the justification based on gratitude. For gratitude is owed only for *past* benefits received. Such a retrospective criterion, however, obscures the fact that there would be no political obligation to obey some law if the law in its *present* or *future* operations did not serve to protect rights. The same contrast obtains if political obligation is held to be justified by the duty of fair play where this is construed as assuming equal burdens for *past* equal benefits accepted.

Second, the *PGC*'s rights-based justification of political obligation is not comparative or relative in the way upheld by the justification based on fair play. According to the latter, political obligation is contingent on some persons' first accepting certain restrictions or burdens in order to receive certain benefits which also accrue to other persons, especially the so-called "public goods"; these latter persons are then held to be obligated to take on their fair share of the restrictions or burdens in return for the benefits received. But there still remain the questions whether the latter persons wish to receive these benefits and whether they might not receive them in ways other than those arranged for by the first group of persons. In addition, the stringency or necessity of political obligation is hardly accounted for when the obligation is made contingent on some initial group's acceptance of benefits.

In contrast, the *PGC*'s rights-based justification of political obligation refers directly to each person's having the moral duty to obey rules or laws that are themselves justified by their being instrumental to the protection of the generic rights of all persons. There is indeed a complementary duty of fairness, in that each person not only must obey the laws but also must accept the particular applications of the laws to himself when he comes under their specific provisions. But this comparative duty is derivative from and thus posterior to the rights-based obligation to obey the laws in the first instance.

A third important contrast is that the *PGC*'s rights-based justification of political obligation does not appeal to any presumed optional or voluntary consent. It does not say that persons have obligations to obey the state and its laws because they have voluntarily accepted its benefits and have therefore tacitly consented to its having authority over themselves. The arguments for such voluntary acceptance and tacit consent are weak.[7] Rather, the rights-based justification refers to the state's being needed to protect basic and other rights. Since the argument of the *PGC* establishes that moral obligation is based on practical adherence to and support of the rights to freedom and well-being for all prospective purposive agents, the state's being needed to assure such adherence and support provides a sufficient basis for the moral obligation to obey the state and its laws.

A fourth important contrast is that the *PGC*'s rights-based justification of political obligation refers to *necessary* goods, not contingent ones. The objects of the rights whose protection justifies political obligation are the goods whose possession by agents is the proximate necessary condition of their being able to act either at all or with some chance of success in achieving their purposes. This necessity of the objects explicates and connects with the necessity of the obligation. It is because effective possession of the generic rights is necessary for action that obedience to the state that protects these rights is a necessary moral obligation. In doctrines of political obligation based on consent, gratitude, or fair play, on the other hand, this necessity of the obligation is not explicated, because its grounding in the necessary goods of action is not provided for.

A fifth contrast, finally, is that the *PGC*'s justification of political obligation is grounded in or derived from a moral principle that is inherently rational because violation or denial of it commits one to self-cntradiction. Because of this, political obligation itself emerges as inherently rational and categorically obligatory insofar as the laws and states to which the obligation is owed fulfill the *PGC*'s requirements. The other ways of justifying political obligation can appeal to no such rationality; they ultimately rest either on the vagaries of utilitarian calculation or on intuitions that, because they admit the possibility of rival intuitions, are characterized by arbitrariness and merely assertive dogmatism rather than by any rational finality.

In contrast to the affirmative doctrines, which hold that political obligation can be morally justified, there are negative doctrines, which deny this possibility. I shall briefly consider two such doctrines. Each is based on a king of separatism between morality and politics. One version I shall call *nonmoral separatism*. The exponent of this position concedes that morally justified precepts must be complied with, but he maintains that proper understanding of the problem of political obligation requires abstraction from any moral justification of political authority. Thus he insists that, so far as this problem is concerned, the laws must be viewed as nonmoral. The problem as he conceives it is whether anyone "has a duty to obey the laws of the state *simply because they are the laws*."[8] This "simply because" is designed to present "the laws" as entities that fulfill only the most general positivist criteria, without regard for any moral specification of contents or procedures.

It is no wonder, then, that such a philosopher fails to solve his "problem." Since laws may be egregiously evil in their contents or dictatorially imposed, to demand a justification of a moral duty or obligation of obedience to all laws simply as such is to guarantee failure. This guarantee is compounded when the demand is accompanied by a requirement of individual "autonomy" that exalts freedom of decision with no specification of the content of the decisions that deserve acceptance. In contrast to such nonmoral separatism, the *PGC*'s justification of political obligation requires that the laws have a certain moral content derived from the supreme principle of morality.

A second negative doctrine is based on what I shall call *moral separatism*. The upholder of this doctrine does grant a certain moral content to the laws, but he maintains that, even when the laws have this content, there follows no moral obligation to obey them. The philosopher in question obtains this negative result by construing the word "obligation," as it occurs in "political obligation," in a very restrictive way, so that it is far from coextensive with the whole moral "ought," especially in its categorical, all-things-considered import. In this more specific sense, "obligation" comprises only those moral requirements that derive from voluntary transactions engaged in by agents that are owed to specific persons.[9]

Now I do not deny that the word "obligation" is sometimes used in this more restricted sense. But it is also used in more extensive senses, including the categorical or conclusive "ought." If, however, political obligation is understood to be confined to "obligation" in the restricted sense, then it is quite understandable that the philosopher who uses only this sense has failed to find an adequate basis for political obligation. For voluntary transactions related to specific persons are unable to provide sufficient grounds for the full scope of political bonds where these are viewed as mandatory for all persons within a given state. Such mandatoriness and universality cannot be accounted for on the basis of contingent, voluntary, specific relations or transactions among persons designated by such restricted criteria.

In the system I have outlined above, on the other hand, political obligation derives from the *PGC*, compliance with which is itself morally obligatory in the full-blooded, all-things-considered sense on the part of all actual or prospective agents, because of the logical connection of the generic rights with the necessary goods of action. Since compliance with the *PGC* is categorically obligatory, so too is compliance with the minimal, supportive, and democratic state, since such a state functions for the moral end of securing the *PGC*-based rights of all persons to the necessary goods of action. In this way, political obligation is justified as a species of moral obligation, since the state is internally instrumental to achieving the purpose of the supreme principle of morality.

This position has no difficulty in meeting the "particularity requirement," according to which political obligation must "bind an individual to
one *particular* political community, set of political institutions, etc."[10] It
has been contended that when, as in my doctrine, political obligation is
made to depend on the just quality of a government, "it does not follow
that there is anything *special* about this obligation. I am equally con-
strained by the same moral bond to support every other just government.
Thus, the obligation in question would not bind me to any particular
political authority in the way we want."

The main reply to this contention is given by a consideration that has
already been stated, briefly, above. Political obligation is the obligation to
obey and support the state and the laws that obtain within the territory in
which one lives. There are, then, two conditions, each necessary and
jointly sufficient, for some person's having the obligation to obey the laws
of some state. First, the state must embody the minimal, supportive, and
democratic requirements imposed by the *PGC*, although this condition
may be affected by the variabilities and priorities noted above. Second,
the person must live within the state's territory. (This latter condition also
assumes that there is only one state, as a sovereign unit, within each
politically relevant territory.)

The point of the latter condition is a practical one deriving from the
general justification for the existence of states. I have emphasized, in this
justification, the moral, rights-securing functions of the state. But these
moral functions do not exist in a physical vacuum, in some purely spiritual
fashion. On the contrary, they must operate in relation to persons who are
physically present in a specific physical area. If there were a world-state,
this area would, of course, comprise the whole inhabited earth (and perhaps other planets, if interplanetary travel is developed). But in any
case, the jurisdiction of a state, with the correlative political obligation,
applies within the specific territory in which persons regularly reside. Thus
the problem of political obligation is not merely: Why should one obey the
laws of any state? but rather: Why should one obey the laws of the
territorially circumscribed state in which one lives? Or, alternately: What
is the justification for there being states that claim authority over persons
living within their respective particular territories?

This territorial aspect of political obligation removes the point of questions that might otherwise be raised against the *PGC*'s justification of
political obligation. For example, if some person A lives in state X, which
is minimal but not supportive, should he obey the laws of state X or those
of state Y, which is supportive as well as minimal? Obviously, as long as
he lives in state X, it is to its laws that he is obligated. The persons in state
X do indeed have moral rights to a supportive state as well, as long as

state X is capable of being supportive; and state X is less justified in claiming their obedience than is state Y in claiming the obedience of *its* members. In this way, the *PGC* indicates the goals toward which all states should strive. Nevertheless, the obligation of state X's inhabitants is to obey *its* laws, not those of some other state.

It must also be kept in mind, however, that the minimal state consists primarily in institutions that establish and enforce the criminal law, whose contents are largely the same as the most basic requirements of the *PGC*. Since the minimal state as justified by the *PGC* serves to protect the most basic moral rights for all persons, obedience to it is indeed incumbent on everyone. The moral requirements here at issue are universal in their obligatoriness, not particular, so that the concomitant political obligations are likewise universal in that they are had by all persons. Thus, when citizen A of state X violates the criminal law in state Y, he is rightly subject to state Y's jurisdiction, because the diversities or particularities of nation-states are accidental to the universal applicability of the law in question. At the same time, however, it is because A has committed the violation within the territory of state Y that he is subject to its jurisdiction.

What if state Y has no criminal law that makes A's action punishable? Suppose, for example, A has killed B, a member of a severely oppressed class in state Y. In such a case, state Y is not entitled to obedience from the members of this class at least, for it is not even a minimal state in relation to them. And there is good ground for A's being punished when he returns to state X.

The universality to which I have just referred is not antithetical to the existence of more particularized legal requirements. Just as, in the natural-law tradition, positive law comprises various specifications or particularizations of the universal requirements of natural law, so too in my doctrine there are such relations of positive laws to the *PGC*. Because of the diverse needs of particular times and places, the positive laws of one state may embody different requirements from those of another state without thereby being opposed to the general requirements of justice as propounded in the *PGC*. With the qualification just noted, the jurisdiction of states and the political obligations of citizens are territorially circumscribed; whatever the future prospects of a world-state may be, at the present time and in the forseeable future the practical needs of persons involve their living within distinct states, and it is their laws that persons are morally obligated to obey as the particularized versions of the general moral requirements contained in the *PGC*.

It is a fallacy to assume that the general obligation to obey the *PGC* is incompatible with particular obligations to obey different laws in different states. For this assumption confuses the universality of the *validity* of the principle of morality with the particularity of the *political instrument* for effectuating this principle. Such an assumption is as unwarranted as the parallel idea that the existence of rules of justice that are incumbent on all states is antithetical to the existence of particular, territorially circumscribed sovereign states. As political thinkers at least since Bodin have emphasized, the sovereignty of any state must be limited by the general principles of justice. Hence, the criteria of political obligation may embody universal requirements of justice without violating the "particularity requirement."

Ethical Universalism and Distributive Consequentialism

Let us now return to the question of military conscription. It will be recalled that the question with which I began was whether military conscription can justifiably be imposed on persons in a society like ours. I shall here assume that our society meets the conditions of the minimal, supportive, and democratic state.

Any attempt at even a qualified affirmative answer to this question must take account of the ethical individualist argument presented at the beginning of this essay. Now we have already seen how the *PGC*, because of its indirect applications to social rules and institutions, provides certain qualifications of ethical individualism, as initially sketched above. These qualifications entail that individual rights, including those of life and liberty, do not have the absolute status that my initial argument seemed to ascribe to them. What the *PGC* makes primary, rather, is the whole mutually supportive system of equal rights to freedom and well-being. Sacrifices in the way of military service for the defense of this system are justified if and only if the system cannot be maintained without them. And if the sacrifices are indeed necessary for this purpose, then, in accordance with the *PGC*'s equality of generic rights, they must be imposed as impartially as possible with a view to the indicated objective.

Despite my earlier remarks, made solely within the context of an unreconstructed ethical individualism, there is indeed a parallel between taxation and conscription, despite the much greater sacrifices imposed by the latter. I initially characterized taxation as being justified to the individual taxpayer by a cost-benefit calculation in which the costs of taxes were outweighed by the benefits he personally derived from them. Such an analysis would fail to justify military conscription to most of the individuals subject to it. Viewed in the perspective of the *PGC*, however, taxation is justified more adequately by the contribution it makes, although in a more restricted way than conscription, to the whole mutually supportive system of the equality of generic rights.

The general point may be put as follows. The *PGC* imposes obligations on every prospective purposive agent to respect the generic rights of other persons—their rights to freedom and well-being. This respect entails obeying and supporting the territorially circumscribed sociopolitical system that embodies and makes possible the effectuation of these rights for all persons within the territory in question. In cases of conflict, however, it is the egalitarian-universalist system that takes priority. This subordination of ethical individualism to a certain kind of ethical universalism may be analyzed into three stages, two of which I have briefly mentioned above. First, in justifying both moral and political obligations, the *PGC* already justifies restrictions on the freedom of individuals, since obligations set limits on freedom. Thus, each individual has duties toward other persons correlative with his rights against other persons. Second, the *PGC* embodies not only a purely individualist requirement but also a certain relational or comparative one, since it upholds not merely the generic rights of individuals per se but also an equality of generic rights as between all agents and recipients. Third, the *PGC* upholds this equality, not only in transactions between individuals, but also in the system, including, especially, the state, which exists to protect this equality. In this way, the requirements of the state take precedence over the freedom and well-being of individuals in cases of conflict. But it must be emphasized not only that such conflicts must be avoided whenever possible but also that this priority obtains only when there are indeed genuine and unavoidable conflicts; moreover, the state in question must fulfill the egalitarian-universalist requirements of the *PGC* by embodying the equality of generic rights in a social order or system of mutually supportive rights. The state must in this way serve to protect and support the equality of generic rights for all persons within its territorial jurisdiction.

It follows from these considerations that the generic rights of individuals are not absolute; they are subordinate to the equality of generic rights and to the system that protects this equality. For this very reason, however, a justified state must infringe the rights of individuals as little as possible, and then only when this is needed for preserving and supporting the system as a whole. But the system as a whole exists only for the sake of the equal rights of all its individual members. There is thus a continuum between the ethical individualism described above and the *PGC*'s ethical universalism. For the latter is distributive, not collective; it extends the generic rights to all persons equally and provides the institutional, systematic framework for the equality of generic rights. In this way, the *PGC* supports the values of community and sociality as well as those of individuality and rational autonomy.

The corporate requirements of the *PGC*'s institutional applications can be further clarified by contrasting them with utilitarianism. As we saw above, utilitarianism, requiring that utility be maximized overall, may impose severe sacrifices on the few for the sake of the many. How does this differ from the sacrifices that the *PGC* may impose on individuals in the name of the social values embodied in the minimal, supportive, and democratic state?

There are at least three important differences.[11] First, by virtue of the equality of generic rights, whatever sacrifices the *PGC* may impose regarding the objects of rights must be allocated equally so far as possible. This stands in contrast to an efficiency calculus that looks only to maximizing certain outcomes without regard for their possibly differential impacts on individuals. Second, the *PGC*'s sacrifices must be imposed only for the sake of the generic rights, i.e., the rights to the *necessary* goods of action. This stands in contrast to utilitarianism's concern with goods in general. Although utilitarians sometimes try to show how goods can be weighed in terms of importance, these attempts have incurred notorious difficulties. Third, the *PGC*'s sacrifices are imposed, not to maximize utility indiscriminately, but only to support the equal rights of individuals. The *PGC*'s instrumentalism, whereby the state is justified by its securing the equality of generic rights, is internal rather than external, in that the state as means to an end must embody as far as possible the distributive egalitarianism of the end itself.[12] Hence, unlike utilitarianism, the *PGC* cannot justify sacrificing the necessary goods of individuals to the end of maximizing utility. Both the *PGC*'s means and its ends must embody respect for the equality of generic rights. From this it follows that, other things being equal, a voluntary armed force is preferable to conscription because of the former's provision for freedom.

Another way to put this point about the *PGC*'s instrumentalism is as follows. Part of the *PGC*'s institutional requirements, like the whole of utilitarianism's, are consequentialist in that the moral rightness of social rules and institutions is assayed by their producing certain consequences. Nevertheless, the two types of consequentialism are quite different. It is a mistake to assume, as is often done, that all consequentialism is aggregative in a utilitarian or some other good-maximizing way.[13] There may also be a distributive consequentialism, where the consequences that serve as criterion of the moral rightness of social rules and institutions are assayed not by how much nonmoral good they produce but rather by their serving to promote distributive justice (see *Reason and Morality*, p. 216). The *PGC*'s institutional applications to the minimal, supportive, and democratic state are of this distributive-consequentialist sort, since such a state is justified by its being internally instrumental to securing an equality of generic rights among all its members. But the limits imposed by the internal character of this instrumentalism must be emphasized. And the primary concern is the support of basic rights; the main aim is to see to it that all persons have the necessary conditions of action.

Military Conscription versus Voluntary Military Service

It follows from these premises that military conscription can be morally justified, but only when the equality of generic rights embodied in a morally justified state can be protected in no other way. It is not the case, then, that a state's fulfilling the minimal, supportive, and democratic requirements of the *PGC* is itself a sufficient condition of the moral justifiability of a law it may propound requiring military conscription. Such a law would need a further, independent justificatory scrutiny to check whether the military conscription it calls for is indeed indispensable for protecting the state. But if the answer is affirmative, then the rights protected by the state require legally prescribed duties of individuals to help to maintain that protection. Otherwise, a volunteer force is preferable, because of its greater assurance of the right to freedom.

A counterargument in favor of conscription as against a volunteer military force may be based on the analogy with taxation, mentioned above. Taxes levied to support the state are a burden that is allocated among all the eligible citizens in proportion to their ability to pay. Why shouldn't a similar fair, universal procedure be used for staffing the military forces? There are at least two answers. One is that few persons are likely to volunteer to give the money needed for all the purposes for which taxes must be used, especially when they think that relatively few other persons will contribute. Nor are there, in the tax situation, compensating factors of the sort that can serve to attract suitable volunteers for the military forces, since the financial, educational, and other emoluments invoked for the latter purpose would presumably be already within the reach of possible voluntary taxpayers.

The other answer is that military duties are much more specific than the diffuse purposes for which taxes must be used. Hence, while a general, nonselective procedure must be used to raise taxes, a more selective approach, of the sort embodied in a voluntary military force, is feasible for staffing the military. Thus, while equality of sacrifice is indeed desirable, it could be balanced by providing monetary and other incentives similar to those used to procure workers in other socially necessary but potentially hazardous occupations, such as coal mining and the production of chemicals.[14] Hence a voluntary system—except in conditions where it quite clearly cannot serve the nation's military needs—is preferable.

An important further objection in favor of military conscription is that since the purpose of military service is the protection of the whole society, all its members who are capable of such service ought to perform it or ought at least to be subject to the requirement of performing it when needed. The objection continues that the policy of using a volunteer force equates military service with other types of "careers" and thus obliterates the deep moral distinctions between services essential to the survival of one's society and other occupations and between tasks that threaten one's very life and other far less dangerous functions.

It is more plausible, however, to regard the distinctions emphasized by these objections as differences of degree rather than of kind. Farming, mining, and many other tasks are also vital to the survival of one's society; and if these tasks cannot be performed in some society because of natural limitations of the territory, then other tasks must be performed when possible in order to provide exchange for the needed goods. Yet none of these tasks demands conscription. In addition, as already mentioned, other socially needed tasks besides military service may also be life-threatening. The case remains, then, that a voluntary system of military service is preferable to conscription unless the evidence is quite clear that such a system cannot serve the nation's military needs, themselves estimated on as realistic a basis as possible.

The restrictions just indicated direct attention, of course, to a host of empirical facts and probabilities. I do not have the space here to go into the requisite scrutiny of Soviet intentions and capabilities and their comparison with those of the United States and its allies. Nor can I now examine the extent to which the United States fulfills the requirements of the *PGC*. I wish to emphasize, however, that when phrases like "national defense" and "national security" are used in discussing the United States' and other states' military requirements, the justified use of such phrases must refer back to the moral conditions of the *PGC*. As I noted above, states and societies may satisfy these conditions in varying degrees. It is because and insofar as the sociopolitical system of the United States meets this test that it is worthy of support, including the drastic kind of support embodied in military service.

Notes

1. Alan Gewirth, *Reason and Morality* (Chicago: University of Chicago Press, 1978), esp. pp. 290–327. I have also discussed the problem of political obligation in "Obligation: Political, Legal, Moral" (Essay 11, below), and in "Political Justice," in *Social Justice*, ed. Richard B. Brandt (Englewood Cliffs, N.J.: Prentice-Hall, 1962), pp. 128 ff.

2. See Steven Lukes, *Individualism* (Oxford: Basil Blackwell, 1973), pp. 101–6.

3. For a good recent discussion of some of these answers, see A. John Simmons, *Moral*

Principles and Political Obligations (Princeton, N.J.: Princeton University Press, 1979), chaps. 5–7.

4. See Gewirth, *Reason and Morality,* pp. 18, 19–20, 108–9; "Political Justice," pp. 130–37. See also the excellent discussion of theories of consent in Simmons, *Moral Principles and Political Obligations,* chaps. 3 and 4.

5. The *PGC* has a structure similar to that of the Golden Rule and Kant's categorical imperative. Unlike the latter, however, the *PGC* directly incorporates material components (the generic rights) and not only the formal requirement of universalizability. I have discussed the *PGC*'s differences from the Golden Rule in *Reason and Morality,* pp. 164–71, and in "The Golden Rule Rationalized" (Essay 4, above). The Golden Rule says that an agent should act toward others as he would want them to act toward himself, so that the criterion of the rightness of actions consists in the agent's wishes for himself qua recipient. But these wishes may be opposed both to his recipients' wishes for themselves and to justified social rules. According to the *PGC,* on the other hand, the criterion of the rightness of actions consists in respect for the generic rights that are common to all agents and their recipients; the objects of these rights are the necessary conditions of action, so that they cannot vary from one person to another.

6. See, for example, H. L. A. Hart, "Legal and Moral Obligation," in *Essays in Moral Philosophy,* ed. A. I. Melden (Seattle: University of Washington Press, 1958), pp. 83 ff., and *The Concept of Law* (Oxford: Clarendon Press, 1961), pp. 163 ff.

7. See the texts cited in note 4.

8. Robert Paul Wolff, *In Defense of Anarchism* (New York: Harper & Row, 1970), p. 18 (emphasis in original).

9. See Simmons, *Moral Principles and Political Obligations,* pp. 14–15. Simmons also (pp. 12, 30–31, 37) uses "political obligation" in an expanded sense to include "duties" as well as "obligations" narrowly conceived. This expansion does not, however, help him to avoid his negative conclusion, for at least two reasons. First, he still distinguishes moral obligation, in this expanded sense, from the moral "ought," where the latter signifies conclusive, all-things-considered moral requirements (see his chap. 8, passim). Second, when he discusses (pp. 148 ff.) the "natural duty of justice" as a basis of persons' political bonds, the "duty" he adduces is grounded not in persons' rights to the *necessary* goods of action but, rather, in seemingly arbitrary goods, as in his example of an "Institute for the Advancement of Philosophers" dedicated only to certain *contingent,* dispensable goods.

10. Simmons, *Moral Principles and Political Obligations,* p. 31. The following quotation is also from page 31. In both, the emphases are in the original.

11. I discuss these points more fully in Essay 5, "Can Utilitarianism Justify Any Moral Rights?"

12. On the distinction between internal and external instrumentalism, see *Reason and Morality,* pp. 296–99.

13. For a recent example of this mistaken assumption, see Germain Grisez, "Against Consequentialism," *American Journal of Jurisprudence* 23 (1978): 24 ff.

14. Some of the moral problems of such incentives are discussed in Essay 7, "Human Rights and the Prevention of Cancer."

11
Obligation: Political, Legal, Moral

There is a puzzling complexity in the concept of obligation. It seems tautologically obvious that obligations are obligatory, that "*A* is under an obligation to do *x*" entails "it is obligatory for *A* to do *x*." Since the obligatory is the most stringent of deontic modalities, corresponding to the necessarily true in the sphere of alethic modalities, it follows that fulfillment of one's obligations is normatively unescapable or mandatory. On the other hand, there seem to be obligations which do not have this eminently stringent quality. For example, when two obligations conflict, both cannot be fulfilled; hence, one must either contradict one's previous conviction that both of them were obligations or else give up the idea that all obligations are obligatory, since it seems absurd to regard what is impossible as mandatory. For another example, there are "social obligations" involving various amenities of polite society; since many of these are relatively trivial, their fulfillment can hardly be regarded as mandatory. Still a third kind of case is found in the Fourteenth Amendment to the Constitution of the United States, where, referring to "any debt or obligation incurred in aid of insurrection or rebellion against the United States," it is solemnly declared that "all such debts, obligations, and claims shall be held illegal and void." Here, so far from its being obligatory to fulfill one's obligations, it is instead made obligatory not to fulfill them.

An initial question, then, is: How can obligations be not only obligatory but also trivial, escapable, and even prohibited? Obviously, distinctions must be drawn between kinds or concepts or contexts of obligation. And indeed philosophers have distinguished between perfect and imperfect obligations, between prima facie and actual obligations, between hypothetical and categorical obligations, and so forth. While each of these distinctions is relevant to the contrasts indicated above, I wish to call attention to another distinction which is especially pertinent to the understanding of political and legal obligation.

INSTITUTIONAL OBLIGATIONS

One important concept of obligation is logically tied to the concepts of an institution and a rule. An institution is a standardized arrangement whereby persons jointly pursue or participate in some purposive activity which is socially approved on the ground of its value for society. This arrangement may be solely functional in that it is concerned only with the purposive activity itself, or it may also be organizational in that it is concerned as well with structured groupings of persons associated for pursuing and regulating the activity.[1] Thus if education, religion, and buying and selling are institutions in the functional sense, the corresponding organizational institutions are, among others, schools, churches, and corporations. Indeed, we some-

[1] See such discussions of institutions as B. Malinowski, *A Scientific Theory of Culture and Other Essays* (Chapel Hill: University of North Carolina Press, 1944), pp. 52 ff.; S. F. Nadel, *The Foundations of Social Anthropology* (London: Cohen and West, 1958), pp. 107 ff.

times refer to the latter groups as "organized education," "organized religion," and the like; and we sometimes ask whether a given (organizational) institution has lost its function. In any case, institutions are constituted by rules which define what men are required to do if they are to participate in the respective functions or activities; and these requirements are the obligations which men have qua such participants. Thus, in virtue of the requirements set by the rules constitutive of the institutions mentioned above, men have obligations to teach, to pray or worship, to pay for what they buy, and the like, just as, in connection with such other institutions as promising and marriage, we speak of the obligations persons have to keep their promises and to be faithful to their spouses. I shall refer to such requirements as *institutional obligations.*

It follows from this that institutional obligations are "objective" in that persons who are to participate in institutions must take on the corresponding obligations. This "must" is not moral but logical. It is analogous to the requirements for participating in rule-governed games: if one is to play tennis, for example, then one must hit the ball with one's racket, not with one's bare hands, and so forth. This logical status of institutional obligations should not be obscured by the reference to "purpose" or "function" in the definition of an institution, nor by the fact that institutional obligations operate as constraints or demands on individuals, tying them to performances of acts of certain kinds even in the face of contrary inclinations. Despite these features, the relation of the purpose or function of an institution to its institutional obligations is not primarily a contingent one of end to means but rather is a conceptual one of a definition to its logical components or logical consequences. It is not that action in accordance with institutional obligations comprises the most efficient means to achieving the purpose or goal of some institution, but rather that the obligations are logically required by the very concept of that institution as contained in its constitutive rules. It is in this logical sense that we may say that institutional obligations rest (logically) on reasons which consist in the function or purpose and the corresponding constitutive rules of the institution in question.

Institutions may, of course, change, so that at certain points it may be unclear just what are their constitutive rules and corresponding obligations. Consider, for example, the various changes in religious practices, or in American marriage as depicted in the Kinsey reports. This flexibility does not, however, affect the logical relation indicated above between institutions and obligations. For at such transitional periods questions arise as to whether it is still the same institution, or indeed whether it is then an institution at all, since the aspects of standardization and of social approval are sharply reduced. It remains the case, then, that so long as an institution is defined by constitutive rules, the relation between it and its corresponding obligations is a logical one.

It must also be noted, however, that there is nothing in the concept of an institution, as such, which necessitates either that participation in it be voluntary, or that all participants in it have rights correlative with their obligations, or that the obligations involve equal sacrifices on the part of all. For example, Negro slavery in the Southern United States, sometimes described by its adherents as "the peculiar institution," was an institution in the sense defined above. But while it imposed extreme obligations on the slave, the obligations of the master were minimal, and were in any case sharply curtailed by his ownership relation to the slave.[2] Other examples of such one-sided institutions are suttee, apartheid, the Inquisition, and the jus primae noctis.

The use of the word "obligation" in connection with such institutions may be challenged. It may be contended that "obligation," like "ought," presupposes both "can" and "may not," so that it is illegitimate to speak of a person's having obligations where he has not freely accepted the requirement or status in question and where he is not free to refrain from fulfilling it except at a prohibitive price. Thus it may be urged that the slave, like a man accosted by a gunman, was *obliged* to accede but not that he had an *obligation* to do so. In this connection, however, it is important to note not only the distinction between institutional and moral obligations (to be discussed below), but also the distinction between institutionalized and noninstitutionalized relationships. Since a gunman's domination of his victim, unlike the master's domination of his slave, is not part of a

[2] See K. M. Stampp, *The Peculiar Institution: Slavery in the Ante-Bellum South* (New York: Alfred A. Knopf, 1956), pp. 192 ff.; S. M. Elkins, *Slavery: A Problem in American Institutional and Intellectual Life* (New York: Grosset and Dunlap Universal Library, 1963), pp. 52 ff.

standardized, socially approved arrangement, it does not have the aspects of alleged justification and of formal, stabilized allocation of responsibility that underlie the use of "obligation" to describe the institutional relationship.[3]

DESCRIPTIVE AND PRESCRIPTIVE
OBLIGATION-STATEMENTS

The consideration of such institutions suggests the following consequence: one may, with full consistency, describe and even participate in an institution and fulfill its obligations, without holding that one *ought* to fulfill those obligations. To put it schematically, from "*A* has an obligation to do *x*" there does not logically follow "*A* ought to do *x*."[4] The reason why it does not follow is that the obligation-statement may be a purely descriptive one about what is required by some institution; but the person making the statement may not himself accept the institution or its purposes as right or justified. He may therefore admit that the obligation does in fact exist as part of an institution and yet deny that the obligation ought to be carried out.[5]

We must therefore distinguish between *descriptive* and *prescriptive* obligation-statements. Both kinds of statement as

[3] See, for example, Stampp, *Institution, op. cit.*, p. 206. The slave codes of each slave state "held slaves, as thinking beings, morally responsible and punishable for misdemeanors and felonies."

[4] Such logical disconnection between "obligation" and "ought" has been emphasized, among others, by H. L. A. Hart. See "Are There Any Natural Rights?" *Philosophical Review*, 64 (April 1955), 186; *The Concept of Law* (Oxford: Clarendon Press, 1961), p. 83. Hart does not, however, tie this point to institutional obligations.

[5] See the use of "obligation" in such passages as: "In the British West Indies the achievement of manumission merely involved a release from the obligation to serve a special master. It did not carry with it any new rights. . ." (F. Tannenbaum, *Slave and Citizen: The Negro in the Americas* [New York: Vintage Books, 1946], pp. 93–94).

"The existing Hindoo written law, which is a mixed body of religious, moral, and legal ordinances, is pre-eminently distinguished by the strictness with which it maintains a number of obligations plainly traceable to the ancient despotism of the Family. . ." (H. S. Maine, *Lectures on the Early History of Institutions* [London: John Murray, 1875], pp. 322–23).

"A Henry County, Alabama, landlord required two Negro laborers to sign the following contract before giving them employment: 'That said Laborers shall not attach themselves, belong to, or in any way perform any of the obligations required of what is known as the Loyal League Society. . .' " (K. M. Stampp, *The Era of Reconstruction*, 1865–1877 [New York: Vintage Books, 1967], p. 204).

uttered by a speaker *S* may have the form, "*A* has an obligation (or is under an obligation) to do *x*." In its descriptive sense, however, the statement is used by *S* to indicate that *A*'s doing *x* is required by certain institutional rules, but *S* does not himself endorse or advocate *A*'s doing *x*. There are two possibilities here. One is that *S* in general accepts the relevant institution and its requirements but holds that in this particular case the requirement should not be fulfilled because it conflicts with a more important obligation. The other possibility is that *S* does not accept the relevant institution at all. As an example of the first case *S*, while recognizing that *A* has the obligation to repay on a certain date a sum of money he borrowed, may yet hold that *A* ought not to repay the money on that date because he needs it to buy medicine for his sick child. As an example of the second case *S*, while recognizing that *A,* a South African black person, has certain obligations under apartheid, may yet hold vigorously that the obligations ought not to be fulfilled.

In its prescriptive sense, on the other hand, the obligation-statement is used by *S* to endorse or advocate *A*'s doing *x;* and insofar as *S* regards *A*'s doing *x* as a requirement deriving from the rule of some institution, *S* endorses that rule and institution as well. He may, indeed, endorse the act because of the rule; but then his attitude toward the rule is not merely a descriptive or reportive one but rather one of advocacy or endorsement. In addition, however, *S* may use the statement to endorse *A*'s doing *x* without regard to the act's being required by an institutional rule. For example, he may say to *A,* with solemn emphasis, "It was your moral obligation to come to that poor man's rescue when he was being attacked; in failing to do so, you fell down on your obligation." Here, "obligation" is used as equivalent to "ought," in the sense of what one was required to do as determined by strong justifying reasons.

The failure to take account of this distinction between prescriptive and descriptive obligation-statements has led some philosophers to hold that the correct use of "obligation" is exclusively restricted to what I have called institutional obligations.[6] This view, however, overlooks the fact that "obligation"

---

[6] For a useful corrective, see R. B. Brandt's distinction between "paradigm" and "extended" uses in "The Concepts of Obligation and Duty," *Mind,* 73 (July 1964), 384 ff. The failure to note the distinction between descriptive and prescriptive obligation-statements underlies many attempts to deduce a

may be used in a prescriptive way which lacks the tentativeness or conditionalness characteristic of the concept of an institutional obligation as such. To restrict "obligation" to the institutional context is to make unintelligible both its connection with "obligatory" and the features which are common to descriptive and prescriptive, institutional and moral uses of "obligation." What all uses of "obligation" have in common is the idea of a practical (or task-setting) requirement based on some general alleged justifying reason which can be understood as such, even if not accepted as successfully justificatory, by those who are subject to the requirement. This reason may be some institution with its purpose and rules; but the reason may also consist in quite different considerations, including moral ones.

TENTATIVE AND DETERMINATIVE OBLIGATIONS

The distinction between prescriptive and descriptive obligation-statements leads us to recognize a related distinction between what I shall call *tentative* and *determinative* obligations. A tentative obligation is one that obtains only within a context which has not itself yet received successful justification; it hence does not determine what one's "real" obligations are, that is, what is justifiably required of one, or what one ought to do. A determinative obligation, on the other hand, determines what is justifiably required of one, what one ought to do. Unlike a tentative obligation, it is already justified, and hence does not need to await justification (or disjustification) from some further set of considerations. Determinative obligations, in turn, are of two kinds, *prima facie* and *conclusive*. A prima facie obligation

---

moral ought-statement from a factual is-statement. Such attempts begin from premises which are descriptive obligation-statements (is-statements) to the effect that some person has an institutional obligation; they conclude with a prescriptive obligation-statement to the effect that he ought to fulfill that obligation. This conclusion is a *non sequitur* because it contains an endorsement of the institutional obligation, whereas the premise according to the argument as presented contains no such endorsement. For a recent noteworthy instance of this attempt, see J. R. Searle, "How To Derive 'Ought' from 'Is,' " *Philosophical Review*, 73 (January 1964), 43–58; see also the critique by A. Flew, "On Not Deriving 'Ought' from 'Is,' " *Analysis*, 28 (1964). For a related attempt in connection with the justification of legal obligation, see note 14 below.

is one that ought to be fulfilled unless some other determinative or justificatory obligation has a higher priority in the particular case in question. A conclusive obligation is one where this question of competing priority either does not arise or has already been resolved in favor of the obligation in question; hence, a conclusive obligation determines what one ought to do, decisively and without further question.

In these terms, what is the status of institutional obligations? While a full answer to this question must wait on an explicit discussion of the criteria of justification, the following preliminary considerations can be presented here. We may distinguish two aspects of any institution, its form and its content. Its form is what it has in common with any institution, as indicated by the definition of an institution given above. Its content is the specific kind of institution that it is. Now in respect of its form, the relevant question is: If we consider an institutional obligation simply qua institutional, is it a tentative or a determinative obligation? To answer this question, we must ask another: Do institutions, as such, perform justifiable functions in society? Let us assume that there may be both institutionalized and noninstitutionalized ways of pursuing or participating in the same purposive activities and let us assume also, for the present context, that those activities are themselves justified ones. Does the fact of their being institutionalized itself contribute an important element relevant to justification? One obvious answer to this question is that since the aspect of standardization common to all institutions involves acting in accordance with rules, this provides an important stabilizing element. On the other hand, such stabilization may operate to reduce or even remove spontaneity and innovation, so that an activity which was itself a justified one might be diminished rather than augmented in relevant valuable respects by the fact of institutionalization. We must add to this the consideration that the contents of institutions may themselves be unjustifiable or evil, and a stabilized evil is still an evil. I conclude, then, that institutional obligations, as such, are only tentative, not determinative: the mere fact that an obligation derives from some institution does not, as such, determine what one ought to do. In other words, institutions with their rules and obligations are not, as such, self-justifying; if their obligations are to determine what is justifiably required of persons, the institutions must be justifiable by other considerations.

This question of the justification of institutions may take two
different forms. One is the general question: Why should there
be such an institution at all? Another is the specific question:
Granted that there should be such an institution, why should it
involve such and such a particular arrangement, have such and
such a particular rule? Whether there is any point to asking the
specific question depends on whether or not the general institution admits of variation. In the case of promising, for example, it
seems that only one arrangement is possible: that one keep one's
promises. But in the case of marriage, defined in general terms as
the contractually established and socially recognized cohabitation
of persons of opposite sex, many arrangements are possible, such
as monogamy, polygamy, polyandry, endogamy, exogamy, and so
forth. Both forms of the question of justification can be construed as questions about second-order obligations. For both
forms ask, in the terms presented above, why is there a determinative obligation to have the obligations which, simply as deriving from some institution, are tentative. The determinative obligation derives from reasons which justify that one fulfill the
institutional obligations.

MORAL REASONS

An obvious move at this point is to say that these justifying reasons must be moral ones. Now I think this is true; but it is
important to be clear about its meaning and status in order to
avoid question-begging assumptions. For one thing, men have
often tried to justify institutions and their rules and obligations
by an appeal to such considerations as the national interest, or
the interests of some race, class, or other group, or tradition, or
religion, and so forth. Are all, or any, of these considerations
moral ones? If we answer in the affirmative, then to call a reason
a moral one will mean merely that it is any reason appealed to in
justification of an institution, so that the assertion that institutions must be justified by moral reasons will be an unillumina-
ting tautology. In addition, the question will still remain as to
why *such* reasons should be accepted as succeeding in the task of
justification. If, on the other hand, we say that considerations
like those listed above are not moral ones, then the question will
remain as to what we mean by the considerations or reasons that

we do call moral, and why these should be accorded greater justificatory weight over the others and over institutional obligations generally.

To deal with these questions we must first note that "moral" can be used either in a descriptive sense (in which it is opposed to "nonmoral") or in an evaluative sense (in which it is opposed to "immoral"). Initially, I shall be concerned with the former sense. Now nonmoral rules as well as moral ones may be practical or "action-guiding"; but two differences between them have been held to be especially important. One difference is "formal": a person who upholds a rule or a reason as a moral one regards it as supremely authoritative or of overriding importance, such that it should, in his view, take precedence over all other rules or reasons. The other difference is "material": a person who upholds a rule or a reason as a moral one regards it as being affected with a social interest, in that it bears importantly on furthering the welfare of persons other than himself.[7]

Now there is, of course, no assurance that these two differentiating criteria will always coincide. But even if we were to take them jointly as the criteria of the moral as opposed to the nonmoral, it would still remain the case that considerations of the national interest and the others mentioned above could qualify as moral reasons. Hence, if we hold that institutions must be justified by moral reasons, these considerations would, so far, pass muster as such reasons. There would still remain, then, the question of how we are to choose among them: Which of these moral reasons is morally right or justified?

There is a further difficulty in our project of justifying institutions by moral reasons. It may be contended that morality is itself an institution parallel to such other institutions as law and religion, in that it is a very extensive, socially endorsed arrangement for participating in and regulating a broad range of purposive activities. On this view, moral obligations would them-

---

[7] See W. K. Frankena, "Recent Conceptions of Morality," in H. N. Castaneda and G. Nakhnikian, eds., *Morality and the Language of Conduct* (Detroit: Wayne State University Press, 1963), pp. 1-24; N. Cooper, "Two Concepts of Morality, *Philosophy*, 41 (January 1966), 19 ff. I have discussed the relation between moral and nonmoral "oughts" in "Must One Play the Moral Language Game?" *American Philosophical Quarterly*, 7 (April 1970).

selves be a kind of institutional obligation, and moral obligation-statements, far from representing justificatory reasons superior to those of institutions, would themselves be conditional upon one's acceptance of an institution, morality. Moreover, just as specific legal or religious rules may or may not be accepted as right or justified, so too with specific moral rules.

Now it is true that there are and have been different "positive" or "conventional" moralities in the sense of informal systems of social regulation. But it is also true that these moralities can themselves be evaluated in respect of their moral rightness. This might be interpreted as meaning simply that one code of positive morality is used to evaluate another. Such an interpretation, however, would still leave open the question of which of these positive moralities is right or justified. What this shows is that the concept of morality in the sense of moral rightness is distinct from the concept of morality in the sense of what is upheld as supremely authoritative and welfare-furthering by the rules of one or another institution of positive morality. It is to the former concept, and not to the latter, that appeal is made when the question concerns the evaluation and justification of institutions, including those of the various positive moralities.

By what kinds of considerations of moral rightness, then, are institutions and their rules and obligations to be justified? Let us put the question in the negative: How do we show (or try to show) that an institution is not justified? That is, how do we criticize institutions? We do so, I suggest, by appealing to one or more of three main kinds of consideration: first, that the institution does no good, or does harm, or does more harm than good; second, that even if the institution does good, it is at others' expense, or is wrongly discriminatory, so that the goods which the institution fosters or the harms which it removes are distributed unjustly or unfairly; third, that even if the institution does good and distributes that good fairly, still the institution and its obligations were imposed on the persons subject to them without those persons' consenting or participating in the decision. These three considerations involve reasons, respectively, of welfare, justice, and freedom. The first two considerations are substantive ones bearing on the content of institutional obligations, whereas the third consideration is a procedural one: it concerns the decision-making process whereby men came to be subject to the institution with its rules and obligations.

THE INHERENT RATIONALITY
OF MORAL REASONS

Many questions may, of course, be raised about each of these considerations and about the relations between them. But first I must supplement the above a posteriori approach with an a priori one. The reason for this is that the a posteriori approach still leaves unanswered the question of why these considerations should be accepted as the ones that are to be used in evaluating institutions. After all, the considerations have competitors, such as the national interest and the other grounds mentioned above. What must be shown, then, is that the considerations of freedom, welfare, and justice, as adumbrated above, are superior to their competitors in terms of rightness.

Let us try to make this point more precise. As we have seen, institutional obligations, as such, are not self-justifying, since when the question is raised whether they ought to be fulfilled it must be answered by an appeal to considerations other than the fact that they derive from an institution. Now we seem to have seen the same thing in relation to the competing basic reasons or principles of moral obligation-statements. The question, then, is whether there are any moral principles which are self-justifying. Since moral principles are advanced as basic reasons, another way to put this question is whether any moral principles are inherently rational. For if a principle is inherently rational, then it needs no further reason to justify it and is hence self-justifying.

But what does it mean for a principle to be inherently rational? One traditional answer has been that the principle must be self-evident, in the sense of being seen to be true or correct by immediate inspection or intuition. Such a criterion, however, is open to well-known and well-founded charges of psychologism and dogmatism. The "inherent rationality" which is here in question must be understood in a logical rather than in a psychological sense. Now a necessary condition of all rationality is freedom from self-contradiction. If a principle is self-contradictory, then, entirely apart from any other considerations, it is inherently irrational and self-disjustifying, since it can be

shown to refute itself: it denies what it affirms. If, on the other
hand, a principle is such that its denial is self-contradictory, then
it is inherently rational and self-justifying, since its denial refutes
itself, so that the original principle must stand unchallenged by
any reasons that may be brought against it.

Can any moral principle be shown to be inherently rational in
this sense? The most famous example of such an attempt is
Kant's categorical imperative, according to which the test of the
rightness of a moral rule or maxim is that when generalized it
not be self-contradictory. This test, however, has important difficulties; it would not, for example, rule out the maxim that
deformed children should be left unprotected to die. I wish to
sketch here an argument for a somewhat different principle.
Thus far I have discussed rationality in the logical sense of
freedom from self-contradiction: this is the formal requirement
of rationality. There is also, however, a material requirement, in
that reason takes account of the necessary features of one's
subject matter. Now the subject matter of morality is, primarily,
human action. When human agents act, they do not merely
engage in bodily movements; their action has certain necessary
features which may be summarized as voluntariness and purposiveness. For insofar as men are agents, they initiate and
control their movements (voluntariness) in the light of their
intentions and purposes (purposiveness). This is why human
agents can be held responsible both for their acts and for the
consequences of the acts.

These features of voluntariness and purposiveness are the
maximally general, constitutive conditions of all human action. I
shall refer to them as the *categorial rules* of action, since they
descriptively pertain to the category of human action as such,
and not merely to one kind of act as against another. Whenever a
human agent acts, he necessarily applies to himself these categorial rules: that is, he necessarily acts voluntarily and purposively.

Now suppose one person (the agent) acts on another (the
recipient). I shall refer to this situation as a *transaction*. In
transactions, the agent may or may not apply to his recipient the
same categorial rules that he applies to himself. That is, while
the agent necessarily acts voluntarily and purposively, he may act
toward his recipient in such a way that the latter does or does not
himself participate in the transaction voluntarily and purposively. If the recipient's participation is not voluntary, this means

that the agent has coerced him; if it is not purposive, this means that the agent has harmed him, in that the recipient's own purposes or aims have not been considered or have been frustrated by the agent's action.

It is at this point that the formal aspect of rationality makes connection with the material aspect. If the agent does not apply to his recipient the same categorial rules that he applies to himself—that is, if the agent coerces or harms his recipient—then the agent contradicts himself. For since the recipient, as a potential or prospective agent, is similar to the agent in respect of the categorial rules of action, the agent would be in the position of saying that what is right for him—to participate voluntarily and purposively in their joint transaction—is not right for a relevantly similar person. And this is self-contradictory. Hence, on pain of self-contradiction, the agent logically must accept a principle which may be stated as follows: Apply to your recipient the same categorial rules of action that you apply to yourself. I shall call this the *Principle of Categorial Consistency* (*PCC*), since it combines the formal consideration of consistency with the material consideration of the categorial rules of action. The *PCC* fulfills the requirement mentioned above, that the principle of moral rightness must be inherently rational or self-justifying.[8]

It will be noted that the *PCC* contains the same three components as emerged in my brief a posteriori discussion above of how we justify and criticize institutions. We may now put those components in terms of obligation. According to the *PCC*, men have three basic moral obligations: they must refrain from coercing other persons (freedom); they must refrain from harming other persons (welfare); and they must be impartial as between themselves and other persons when the latter's freedom and welfare are at stake (justice). Indeed, the *PCC* as a whole may be explicated in terms of justice, in that it requires an agent to respect his recipient's freedom and welfare as well as his own. As I have stated them, these obligations are, of course, quite gener-

---

[8] I have presented this argument in somewhat more detail in "Categorial Consistency in Ethics," *Philosophical Quarterly*, 17 (October 1967), 289 ff. For a discussion of the related question of whether the "criterion of relevant similarities" can be so individualized that its application is restricted to a single person, see my "The Non-trivializability of Universalizability," *Australasian Journal of Philosophy*, 47 (August 1969). In my forthcoming book, *Reason and Ethics*, I attempt a full-scale development of the whole argument.

al. The important point, however, is that while their specific application in various contexts must inevitably involve many complexities, this application can nevertheless be made, so that it can be ascertained whether or not the criteria set by the obligations are fulfilled. Because these obligations have been justified by reasons which are inherently rational, they are not only determinative of what men ought to do but are the basis of all other determinative obligations. Hence, if the tentative obligations deriving from institutions are to be determinative, they must meet the criteria set by the *PCC*.

The basis of these determinative moral obligations differs, in respects which are both theoretically and practically important, from that espoused in a pervasive tradition of moral and legal philosophy. This tradition upholds the following interrelated theses: that moral obligations must be "self-imposed";[9] that the only legitimate way to indicate the content of one's moral obligations is to say that one ought to do what one thinks right ("subjective obligation"), not what is right ("objective obligation");[10] that what one ought to do, including whether one ought to obey a law, must be determined by one's own conscience. These theses are often put into a context of "agent morality" rather than "act morality." The former is concerned primarily with the moral goodness of the agent, including the quality of his motivations and their relation to his character,

[9] See, e.g., P. H. Nowell-Smith, *Ethics* (Baltimore: Penguin Books, 1954), p. 210: "The feature which distinguishes moral obligations from all others is that they are self-imposed." This position goes back in modern times at least to Hobbes. See *Leviathan*, ch. 21, ed. M. Oakeshott (Oxford: Basil Blackwell, n.d.), p. 141: ". . . there being no obligation on any man, which ariseth not from some act of his own; for all men equally, are by nature free." The idea that obligations are "self-imposed" is highly ambiguous, it can mean at least three different things: (a) one has no moral obligations until one performs voluntary acts toward other persons; (b) whether one has moral obligations depends on one's voluntary agreements with or promises to other persons; (c) whether one has a moral obligation (including the content of the obligation) depends on whether one accepts it as an obligation, and not merely on what one says or does to other persons.

[10] See H. D. Thoreau, *Civil Disobedience*, in *Selected Writings on Nature and Liberty*, O. Cargill, ed., (Indianapolis: Bobbs-Merrill, 1952), p. 11: "The only obligation which I have a right to assume is to do at any time what I think right." On the distinction between "subjective" and "objective" obligation, see A. C. Ewing, *The Definition of Good* (New York: The Macmillian Co., 1947), pp. 118 ff., and K. Baier, *The Moral Point of View* (Ithaca, N.Y.: Cornell University Press, 1958), pp. 143 ff.

while act morality is concerned rather with the moral rightness of external acts themselves, including within "acts" the agent's intention, his knowledge of relevant circumstances, and his ability to control what he does in the light of his intention and knowledge.[11]

The *PCC* is directly concerned with act morality rather than with agent morality, although it can also be used to evaluate in part the agent's moral character. According to the *PCC,* an agent has basic moral obligations toward his recipient whether the agent agrees to have them or not, and they are obligations to do what is right as determined by the *PCC.* The appeal to conscience leaves unanswered the question whether there are any moral reasons or criteria for the guidance of conscience itself. If there are no such reasons, then there is an obvious danger of arbitrariness and anarchy. But if there are such reasons, then conscience is at most a secondary rather than a primary determinant of moral obligation, since conscience must itself conform to these reasons if it is to be morally right.

The two interrelated ideas of the self-imposition of moral obligations and guidance by one's own conscience are somewhat similar to the freedom criterion adduced above as a component of the *PCC*: that if transactions are to be morally right, then their recipients must participate in them voluntarily. The similarity arises especially when we think of institutions as imposing obligations; for the freedom criterion requires that those who are subject to such obligations accept them freely. Even in this case, however, there are some important differences. The freedom criterion of the *PCC* is advanced not as a definition of moral obligation but rather as a basic theorem about moral obligation, which must itself be proved. Moreover, the freedom criterion, of itself, sets prima facie rather than conclusive moral obligations; as a procedural criterion, it must be supplemented by the substantive criteria of welfare and justice. Hence, whereas exclusive reliance on conscience as the determinant of moral obligations

---

[11] For a good discussion of this distinction, see J. Laird, "Act Ethics and Agent Ethics," *Mind,* 55 (April 1946), 113-132. I have discussed the bearing of the tradition discussed in the text on the relation between legal and moral obligation, in "Some Misconceptions of the Relation between Law and Morality," *Proceedings of the Seventh Inter-American Congress of Philosophy* (Quebec : Les Presses de l'Université Laval, 1967), I, 208. 222.

might be used (and has been used) to justify harmful and unjust acts and institutions, this is not the case with the freedom criterion. While the individual's conscience must be respected, then, because of its relation to his freedom and its importance to his feelings, it should not of itself determine the content of moral obligations.

Another aspect of the basic moral obligations must be briefly considered at this point. It may be objected that the welfare criterion as stated above, requiring merely that one refrain from harming other persons, is too negative, for one might fulfill it by sheer inaction or passivity, and this would make no positive contribution to welfare. The justice criterion, however, puts this point in proper perspective. Specifically, two replies must be made to the objection. First, to refrain from harming other persons requires action rather than inaction whenever one's voluntary or deliberate inaction is harmful to others. The "duty to rescue" is an obvious example of this, but there are also many other such cases in a mass society of interdependent persons.[12] Second, to put the welfare criterion in positive terms, as the obligation to do good or to advance the welfare or interests of other persons, would yield an unmanageable proliferation of obligations. The moral obligation to obey the law is sometimes upheld by such a criterion: law ought to be obeyed because it does great good. But this argument would similarly go to prove

[12] See G. A. Coe, "What Is Violence?" in M. Q. Sibley, ed., *The Quiet Battle* (New York: Doubleday, 1963), p. 48: "For mere non-intercourse, mere refusal to buy and sell, can produce hunger and death just as surely as an embargo by means of warships. . . . For certainly, given the present interdependence of men, we can weaken, distort, and destroy the bodies of our fellows by merely doing nothing." Cf. from a different perspective, the comments of A. Tunc, "The Volunteer and the Good Samaritan," in J. M. Ratcliffe, ed., *The Good Samaritan and the Law* (New York: Doubleday, 1966), pp. 45–46: "From a philosophical point of view, it does not appear possible to distinguish between the man who does something and the man who allows something to be done, when he can interfere. Such a distinction would disregard the liberty of man, his freedom of choice, his creative power, his 'engagement' in the world and among other men. A stone does not bear any liability if a murder is committed beside it; a man does. By his decision not to interfere or to intervene, he participates in the murder." In order to keep clear the distinction between the morally obligatory and moral athleticism or supererogation, this position would have to specify many factual matters about knowledge, ability, and consequences. Nevertheless, when properly interpreted, the position does indicate an important positive application of the welfare and justice criteria.

that men have a moral obligation to support garden clubs, madrigal-singing groups, and the like. If it were replied that the law does more good than any of these, this would subject the obligation to obey the law to a calculus which would jeopardize the stability often alleged as a chief argument for obeying the law. Some of the familiar problems of utilitarianism involved in this issue will be touched on below in connection with legal obligation.[13]

THE MORAL JUSTIFICATION OF INSTITUTIONS

Let us now consider how the *PCC*'s criteria of moral obligation are to be applied in ascertaining whether an institution's obligations are determinative of what men ought to do. To begin, we must note that while the *PCC*'s criteria refer directly to how an agent, a human individual, is to act toward his recipients, there is also a sense in which an institution is an agent. For it operates by imposing obligations on the persons who participate in it, so that the latter are in the position of recipients of the institution's operations. If this seems too metaphorical, however, the same point can be made in terms of human agents. For although many institutions are the results of organic growth rather than of human contrivance, each institution has persons who profit from it or who at least uphold it. Hence, they can be asked the questions set by the *PCC*'s criteria. It must also be noted that individuals and groups often act on other persons in accordance with the rules of institutions. Hence, we can ask whether these actions are in accord with the criteria set by the *PCC*. This is to ask whether the tentative obligations which derive tautologically from the constitutive rules of an institution are also determinative or moral obligations. The application of the *PCC* to test the moral justification of institutions, then, may be made from two different perspectives: from that of the institu-

---

[13] It is not always easy, of course, to distinguish among refraining from harm, preventing harm, and doing good. Formally, it may be said that all cases of preventing harm are cases of doing good, although not conversely. Also, when one is able to prevent harm to other persons and is aware of this, to refrain from harming them requires that one prevent that harm. Further qualifications are needed, however, especially concerning the cost aspects of "able."

tion as agent and from that of the persons who participate in the institution as agents. Let us consider each of these in turn.

From the first perspective, the following questions set by the *PCC* are addressed to an institution or to its upholders: Was the institution freely accepted by the persons subject to it? Would its absence be harmful to their interests or welfare? Does it respect the freedom and welfare of all equally? If these questions are answered in the affirmative, they establish that the institution's obligations are determinative, whereas if they are answered in the negative, then the institution's obligations remain only tentative. But what if one question is answered in the affirmative and another in the negative? With respect to the freedom and welfare criteria which enter, respectively, into the first two questions, one of their underlying assumptions, based on the categorial structure of human action as sketched above, is that men in acting voluntarily intend to fulfill their own purposes and hence to obtain something that seems good to them. In this broad sense, which is the one that figures in the *PCC,* there is no conflict between what men freely choose to do and their interests or welfare, except insofar as the latter may involve means to what men want rather than the wants themselves as ends. As for the justice criterion which enters into the third question above, this may well conflict with the freedom and welfare criteria, in that an institution may be unequal or discriminatory in its relation to persons' freedom and welfare. In such a case, however, it is important to ask whether the inequality is instrumental or final, that is, whether the inequality is used as a means toward increasing freedom and welfare to a point where they come closer to equality for all who are affected or whether, on the contrary, the inequality is accepted as an end of the institution. In the former case, the institution's obligations are determinative; in the latter case, they are not.

Let us now turn to the other perspective from which the *PCC* is to be applied to institutions, that of the individuals who act in accordance with the institutions. Whereas from the first perspective all the individuals who participate in an institution were regarded as recipients of the institution's operations, from this second perspective some of these participants are agents and others recipients, each fulfilling the role set for him by the institution's rules. In this perspective, the specific questions set by the *PCC* are addressed to the agents: Do they, in fulfilling their institutional obligations, coerce or harm other persons or favor the freedom and welfare of some persons at the expense of others? If the answer to any part of this complex question is affirmative, then the persons involved have no prima facie determinative or moral obligation to fulfill their institutional obligations. The significance of this prima facie qualification is related to the reason for distinguishing between the institutional and individual perspectives in asking the questions set by the *PCC*. For it is possible that institutions satisfy the requirements of the *PCC* while individuals who act in accordance with those institutions do not. For example, insofar as a teacher gives a failing grade to a college student, the teacher may be said to harm the student and to act on him against his will; but in so doing, the teacher is acting in accordance with institutional rules (for example, the rules of the college) which are themselves accepted by, and are beneficial to, the students as a whole insofar as they are involved in the functioning of the institution. Hence, the relation of the *PCC* to the acts of individuals and to institutional rules must be put as follows. The obligations which the *PCC* sets for the particular acts of individuals are prima facie rather than conclusive, in that any particular act must be in accord with the *PCC* unless the act is in accord with an institutional rule which is itself in accord with the *PCC*.

The above paragraphs provide, of course, only a very general sketch of the criteria involved in the moral justification of institutions. A fuller account would have to analyze in much greater detail both the criteria themselves and the complex ways in which they may or may not be satisfied by various institutions. Apart from the fact that I attempt such an analysis elsewhere (see note 8), I have tried at least to suggest the logical basis and the general features of the relevant criteria.

THE INSTITUTION OF LAW

Our next step must be to consider how these criteria for the moral justification of institutions are to be applied to law. To begin with, we must note that "law," in the sense in which it is restricted to municipal law, is used with three different kinds of reference. It is used to refer, first, to a general social institution ("law$_1$") common to all societies which have even minimal legal systems; second, to one or another specific legal system ("law$_2$") which may differ from other legal systems in its contents and procedures; and third, to particular legal rules ("law$_3$") which may exist within the same or different legal systems. (These rules are called particular only with respect to their being restricted parts of a legal system; they are general insofar as they deal with classes of acts and persons.) Thus, in the first reference we talk of law as against, for example, religion, as a kind of social institution and as a method of social regulation; in the second reference we talk of United States law, Soviet law, and the like; and in the third reference we talk of the United States income tax laws, and so forth.

When law is called an institution, the reference may be either to law$_1$ or to law$_2$. I shall call these, respectively, the general and the specific institutions of law. And when the question is asked, "Why should one obey the law?" the word "law" may be used with all three kinds of reference. As we shall see, serious confusion is generated by not distinguishing these.

In its most general form, law$_1$ is a second-order institution, in that it provides a certain kind of regulation of other institutions as well as of noninstitutionalized activities. This regulation is concerned with guaranteeing the peace and order or stability which are the necessary conditions—logically and not merely causally—of men's living together in an organized society. To secure these conditions, violence must be controlled and conflicts resolved by antecedently known general rules carrying coercive sanctions, and there must be recognized officials to make, interpret, and execute the rules.

As a general institution, law$_1$ is defined by constitutive rules which determine what is to count as a legal system in general and what men are required to do if they are to participate in such a system and in any society which is regulated by it. In a parallel way, law$_2$ as a specific institution is also defined by more restricted constitutive rules (sometimes called a "constitution") which determine the nature of the specific legal system and what men are required to do if they are to participate in that system and in the particular society which is regulated by it. In both cases, the requirements in question are men's legal obligations, that is, their obligations to obey, respectively, the rules of any legal system as such (law$_1$) and the rules of a specific legal system (law$_2$). According to our previous analysis, however, these legal obligations, insofar as they are institutional obligations entailed by the constitutive rules of a certain kind of institution, are only tentative, not determinative (let alone conclusive). For legal obligations to be determinative of what men ought to do, they, or the institution from which they derive, must be morally justified.

THE MORAL JUSTIFICATION
OF LEGAL OBLIGATION

From failure to distinguish kinds of obligation and kinds of law, it has sometimes been held that it is pointless to ask for a moral justification of legal obligation. Now it is true, but insufficient, to say that an institutional obligation to obey some law$_3$ in a particular society follows from membership in that society with its specific legal system, just as the obligation to obey the rules of some game follows from playing that game.[14] This is insufficient, for since one does not voluntarily undertake membership in a political society in the way in which one undertakes participation in a game, there still remains the question whether there is a rational justification for accepting that the society's legal system should determine what one is to do, either in general or in a particular case. This latter question requires something other than the reiteration of the institutional obligation to obey the law, for it asks about the moral justification of the institution itself or of some part of it. As such, the question may refer to the particular law$_3$ or to the whole legal system (and the society constituted by it); and it may even refer to the general institution of law$_1$. Let us consider each of these in turn.

The moral justification of the general institution of law$_1$ is

14 Cf. T. D. Weldon, *The Vocabulary of Politics* (Baltimore: Penguin Books, 1953), p. 57: "Suppose however the objector goes on to say 'Even if it is the law, I don't see why I should obey it.' The only further comment possible is 'Well, this is Great Britain, isn't it?' The position is indeed exactly parallel to that of the cricketer who asks 'Why should I obey the umpire? What right has he to give me out?' One can answer only by expounding the rules of cricket, the position of the M.C.C., and so on. Beyond that there is nothing to be done except to say 'This is a game of cricket, isn't it?' " For similar positions, see J. R. Carnes, "Why Should I Obey the Law?," *Ethics*, 71 (October 1960), 14 ff., and T. McPherson, *Political Obligation* (London: Routledge and Kegan Paul, 1967), 59 ff.

suggested by the moral overtones of traditional expressions like
the "rule of law" and "due process of law," as well as by repeated
references to law$_1$ as a "minimum ethic,"[15] a "minimum limit of
morality,"[16] having the "minimum content of natural law,"[17] and
so forth. We may explicate these expressions in terms of the
criteria of the *PCC*. With respect to justice, law$_1$ contains general
rules which apply uniformly to all cases falling under them.
With respect to welfare, human life would be difficult or impossible without law$_1$'s stabilizing influence, including its regulation
of violence and conflict. With respect to freedom, law$_1$ enables
men to determine their conduct with intelligent foresight by its
curbing of violence and by making publicly known ahead of time
those areas of conduct to which coercive sanctions are attached.

To the extent to which law$_1$ contains these general features,
there is a prima facie moral obligation to obey it. It must be
noted that law$_1$ here occupies a different status from that which
pertains to institutions generally. I said above that institutional
obligations, as such, are only tentative, not determinative, because the mere fact of institutionalization (which I called the
"formal" aspect of institutions) might be harmful as well as
beneficial to the activities standardized by it. Now law$_1$ corresponds to the formal aspect of institutions insofar as it comprises
simply what is common to all law. But the legalization provided
by law$_1$ has a much stronger justification, especially in terms of
the welfare criterion of the *PCC*, than the institutionalization
provided by all institutions as such. One obvious reason for this
is that law$_1$'s regulation of violence and conflict is more indispensable to human life than are the kinds of stabilization given by
institutions as such. In addition, however, law$_1$ is unique among
institutions because of the other ways in which it is necessary to

[15] G. Jellinek's phrase; see R. Pound, *Law and Morals* (Chapel Hill, N.C.:
University of North Carolina Press, 1926), p. 103.

[16] J. Dewey, in Dewey and J. H. Tufts, *Ethics* (1st ed., New York: Henry
Holt, 1908), p. 467.

[17] Hart, *The Concept of Law*, pp. 189 ff. As I have argued elsewhere, even
such a positivist as Hans Kelsen is unable to avoid attributing to law as such
a basic moral content. See my essay "The Quest for Specificity in Jurisprudence," *Ethics*, 69 (April 1959), 172 ff., and Kelsen, *General Theory of
Law and State*, trans. A. Wedberg (Cambridge, Mass.: Harvard University
Press, 1945), pp. 22 ff., 54 ff., 69; also *What Is Justice?* (Berkeley and Los
Angeles: University of California Press, 1957), pp. 238, 241, 248 ff.

the existence of an organized society, including its provisions for the making of particular laws$_3$ and its enforcement of legal "certainty" or "predictability." Hence, the moral obligation to obey law$_1$ attaches not only to those of its contents which prohibit *mala in se;* it attaches also to those which prohibit *mala quia prohibita* insofar as the latter contents, even though not independently objects of moral obligation, are generically necessary to stabilize an organized society.[18]

The moral obligation to obey law$_1$ is, nonetheless, only prima facie and not conclusive because of considerations deriving from the specific contents of laws. The general features of law$_1$ which justify obedience to it may be specified in immoral ways, and the moral obligations violated by these ways may override the general obligation to obey law$_1$.

It will have been noted that the freedom criterion met by law$_1$ as I stated it above diverges from my earlier statement of that criterion as applied to institutions. Whether persons subject to an institution have freely accepted it is not the same consideration as whether they are enabled to have a degree of freedom by the operation of the institution. The two considerations are, of course, related: they refer to men's effective free choice as figuring, respectively, in the cause and in the effect of institutions. Nevertheless, the issue of freedom in the former respect, that of free acceptance, is insistently raised by the fact that law$_1$, unlike other institutions, does not merely impose obligations but attaches coercive physical or economic sanctions to them. Hence, men are not free to disobey law$_1$ except at the price of punishment. It would be insufficient to try to meet this issue by saying that law is coercive only toward those who want to coerce others, for this would not account for many other coercive contents of law$_1$. There are even more obvious inadequacies in the answer of traditional consent theory that coercive law does not remove freedom because each individual has freely consented to obey the

[18] See in this connection the two ways in which, according to Thomas Aquinas, human laws can be derived from natural law: as deduced conclusions and as specifications, the latter being morally indifferent except insofar as they provide a particular, legally determined way of carrying out the general requirements of natural law (*Summa Theologica*, II, I, Question 95, Article 2).

law$_1$.[19] The most that can be said on this score is, perhaps, that for any legal system to exist there must be some degree of acquiescence in it by a large proportion of the persons subject to it.

Law$_1$, with its coercive sanctions, provides an important example of the distinction drawn earlier between the fulfillment of moral criteria by an institution itself as agent and by individuals who act in accordance with the institution. A judge who punishes a criminal in accordance with law harms him, yet the institution of criminal law itself fulfills the criterion of welfare.

Let us turn to specific legal systems (law$_2$). Every legal system shares the general features and hence the general justification of law$_1$, but adds its own specific features. These, however, can markedly affect the moral quality of the system. With respect to justice, the general rules of the system may be heavily discriminatory against certain groups. With respect to welfare, law$_2$ may stabilize a society to the point of stagnation and promote inefficiency in many other ways, and it may regulate violence by making it legally available to some groups at the expense of others. With respect to freedom, law$_2$ may be dictatorially imposed and may be severely repressive.

It is clear that such a legal system and the society constituted by it do not meet the moral criteria of the *PCC*. It is also clear that insofar as men act in accordance with such a system, their acts too do not meet the moral criteria. Do these points, then, settle conclusively the question of legal obligation, of whether men ought to obey such a legal system in those of its features which are morally wrong? In order to answer this question, we must also take into account the relation of disobedience to the criteria of welfare, freedom, and justice for all the persons affected. Suppose, for example, that one group's disobedience predictably leads to savage reprisals against other groups, or to revolutionary upheavals that disrupt the lives of many other persons. In such a case, the disobedient group might well stand accused of doing harm and injustice, especially if the other groups were themselves not willing to incur the risks involved.

[19] I have previously discussed the principle of consent in "Political Justice," in R. B. Brandt, ed., *Social Justice* (Englewood Cliffs, N.J.: Prentice-Hall, 1962), pp. 128 ff.

On the other hand, where persons and groups are able to ward off an immoral society's harms and injustices without such prohibitive costs, the criteria of welfare and justice make it their moral obligation to do so. To this extent, the persons involved have no moral obligation to obey the laws$_3$ of such a system.

POLITICAL OBLIGATION

It is in connection with questions of this sort that we must come to political obligation in the respect in which it is not the same as legal obligation. Political and legal obligation coincide insofar as the former is the obligation to obey the government or the legitimate political authority; for since this authority rests on law$_2$ and operates through laws$_3$, obedience to the authority is also obedience to law$_{2,3}$. Two plausible redefinitions of political obligation, however, remove this coincidence with legal obligation. One is where political obligation is viewed as referring specifically to the obligations of the governors or rulers of a state. While their regular, official obligation is to act in accordance with the law$_2$, a crisis might arise in which, in order to save the state, they might have to act outside the law.[20] A second, related redefinition of political obligation would refer to the "policy" obligations of all the citizens, rulers and ruled alike, in respect of making or influencing the contents of laws, as against obeying the laws already made. It is this policy sense of political obligation that becomes especially important when we confront the problems of immoral legal systems and the laws$_3$ deriving from them. But as we shall see, such political obligations of active citizenship are also incumbent on citizens of constitutional democracies.

In the general sense in which "policy" is here used, it emerges in the "political life" of individuals and groups who try to influence legislation and government in accord with their self-regarding or public-regarding objectives. Such political life is frequently institutionalized in many formal or informal ways, ranging from political parties and clubs to various other kinds of pressure groups. And, as with the other institutions discussed

[20] Cf. L. Legaz y Lacambra, "Political Obligation and Natural Law," *Natural Law Forum* 2 (1957), 119 ff.

above, these institutions have their constitutive rules and institutional obligations. One kind of political obligation in the policy sense, then, refers simply to these institutional obligations of political groups, that is, the requirements set by the constitutive rules of such groups for the persons who participate in them. For example, the political obligations of lobbyists for the NAM or the AFL-CIO derive from the roles assigned to them by the policies of the respective organizations. Insofar as these political obligations are institutional ones, however, they are only tentative, not determinative; whether they determine what the persons in question ought to do depends on whether the respective institutions and their purposes can meet the rational criteria of moral justification. Thus the basic question of political obligation, as also of legal obligation, is whether or not it satisfies the criteria which would make it a moral obligation. In this context, "moral" refers to the reasons or criteria which are brought to bear in evaluation or justification, while "legal" and "political" refer to the institutions or activities which are adjudged by the criteria. Hence, talk of legal or political obligations may consist in either prescriptive or descriptive obligation-statements, depending on whether or not the speaker is endorsing the acts, policies, or institutions in question. As I have argued above, the correct basis for endorsement is provided by the *PCC*.

LEGAL OBLIGATION IN
A CONSTITUTIONAL DEMOCRACY

The issues of political and legal obligation are sharpened when we consider law_2 in a constitutional democracy. Such a democracy has two main features relevant to its law_2. In its democratic aspect, the legislative officials are elected by universal suffrage, with each person having one vote and the majority vote being decisive; in its constitutional aspect, there are certain constitutionally prescribed restrictions on the contents of the $laws_3$: the civil liberties of speech, press, assembly, and so forth are guaranteed equally for all. These two features constitute what I have elsewhere called the "method of consent,"[21] for they

[21] "Political Justice" (see note 19 above), pp. 137 ff.

provide that each sane, noncriminal adult has the legal right to participate freely in the process which determines who shall have political authority, including the authority to make the laws$_3$. The freedom to participate at this level is the closest that any legal system can attain to the freedom criterion of the *PCC*. For the freedom to participate in determining who shall have political authority must be distinguished from the freedom to determine whether there shall be any political authority or law$_1$ at all, as well as from the freedom to determine whether one shall oneself be subject to that authority. It is sometimes plausible to assume, however, that a person who uses the first of the three freedoms just listed has implicitly given an affirmative answer to the questions accompanying the two other freedoms, which figured centrally in the theory of the social contract.

In addition to this degree of fulfillment of the freedom criterion of the *PCC*, the legal system of a constitutional democracy also fulfills the criterion of political justice, for it gives each person an equal vote and equal rights and liberties for participating in the political process. It has also been a traditional claim of democratic theorists that the system progressively fulfills the criteria of both socioeconomic justice and welfare. For laws$_3$ which emerge through the method of consent will reflect the purposes or interests of those who participate in the method, and since all men have an equal right to participate, this will tend toward an equalization of welfare. The equal protection of the laws, in one interpretation of it, requires, or at least encourages, such equalization. From these considerations it follows that persons who live under the legal system of a constitutional democracy have a moral obligation to obey it.

The actual workings of the system, of course, often fall short of these moral criteria. Great inequalities of social and especially economic power make for drastic inequalities in the ability to participate effectively in the method of consent. Conflicts of actual or perceived interests, based on racial, economic, or ideological grounds, lead some groups to perceive others as enemies and hence to try to deny them important components of welfare and justice. There are also strong differences of opinion, partly based on ideological differences, about the causes of socially important phenomena. As a result of all these factors, the policies which become legalized are sometimes regarded as drastically immoral by sizable groups in the society.

The problem of legal obligation raised by these conflicts may be put in the form of a dilemma. If one obeys certain laws$_3$ of a constitutional democracy, then one does what is morally wrong; if one disobeys those laws$_3$, then one violates the law$_2$ of a constitutional democracy with its relations to freedom, justice, and welfare, and this too is morally wrong. Thus there are two opposed moral obligations, each ultimately based on the same moral criteria: the moral obligation to obey the laws$_3$ not merely because they are laws but because they conform to the law$_2$ of a constitutional democracy, and the moral obligation to disobey laws$_3$ which are harmful, unjust, or violative of the method of consent. To take a current example, many persons have held that there is a moral obligation to disobey the various laws$_3$ accompanying the Vietnam war, especially the draft laws, for the following reasons: (1) the war, with its use of napalm and other lethal weapons, subjects countless numbers of innocent persons to terrible suffering and death, and it does so needlessly, since the United States has no important interest at stake in Vietnam (*welfare criterion*); (2) the draft laws discriminate against those young men who cannot afford to go to college and also against those who seek exemption because of their objection to a particular war for nonreligious reasons, since the draft laws admit as valid ground for exemption only religiously based objections against all wars (*justice criterion*); (3) the war policy was imposed on the American people by deception and manipulation, and without giving the people or their elected representatives a chance to vote on the issue (*freedom criterion*).

CIVIL DISOBEDIENCE

How is this opposition of moral obligations to be resolved? One purported resolution is that of civil disobedience, and I wish to consider some of its claims and problems in the light of the concepts presented in this essay. According to the usual definition, civil disobedience consists in intentionally disobeying some law$_3$ on the ground that it, or a policy related to it, is morally wrong, the manner of disobedience being public, nonviolent, and accepting of the legally prescribed penalty for disobedience. It is to be noted that by this definition civil disobedience purports to resolve the dilemma presented above. For it claims both to disobey the morally wrong law_3 and at the same time to obey the law_2 of constitutional democracy; for in accepting, and not trying to evade, the legally prescribed penalty the civil disobedient shows that he wishes to accept the whole legal order as moral while rejecting one part of it as immoral.[22]

Now if such joint acceptance and rejection are to be rational or coherent, then two kinds of relation between $law_{1,2}$ and law_3 must be excluded. One relation is logical: the relation of the whole legal system to a particular law within the system cannot be a deductive one analogous to the relation between primitive axioms and the theorems they entail, for the denial of any of the theorems logically entails the denial of the axioms and hence of the whole system. The other excluded relation is causal: the existence of the legal system as a viable, effective institution cannot depend on the efficacy of the particular law, that is, on its being universally or generally obeyed. For if the relation were of this kind, then disobedience of the particular law would undermine, or would at least tend to undermine, the existence of the whole legal order. And if this were so, then it would not be rational or coherent to hold that one can both disobey a particular law and accept, let alone respect, the whole legal order.

The first possibility, that of a logical or deductive relation between the whole legal system and a particular law, may seem too far-fetched to merit serious consideration, especially in the light of critiques of the kind made by legal realists. Suppose, however, that we adopt a procedural rather than a substantive interpretation of such a logical relation. Our focus would then be not on the content of the particular law in relation to the content of the whole legal system or of its constitutional principles; rather, it would be on the methods which the system

[22] See M. L. King, Jr., *Why We Can't Wait* (New York: New American Library, Signet Books, 1964), pp. 83-84: "I submit that an individual who breaks *a law* that conscience tells him is unjust, and who willingly accepts the penalty of imprisonment in order to arouse the conscience of the community over its injustice, is in reality expressing the highest respect for *law*" (my italics). See also M. K. Gandhi, *Non-Violent Resistance* (New York: Schocken Books, 1961), p. 60.

requires one to use if one is to be faithful to the system or to operate within it. Clearly, these methods cannot be extralegal ones. Hence, one cannot break a particular law and at the same time claim to be faithful to or respectful of the legal system as a whole. To put it generally, even if one accepts the legally prescribed penalty, one cannot consistently look to a whole legal system to provide one with a justification for disobeying any part of that system, whether the relation of part to whole be conceived substantively or procedurally.[23]

Two partial qualifications of this general point must be noted. First, the legal system as a whole must itself be consistent. For if a legal system S contains two inconsistent rules Ra and Rb, then one may appeal to Ra to justify disobeying Rb. Now in the American legal system there are at least two kinds of inconsistencies which give rise to actual or potential conflicts. One is within the federal Constitution itself, as when the First Amendment's guarantee of freedom of the press conflicts with the Sixth Amendment's guarantee of trial by an impartial jury of the district. The other conflict is when local or state laws are inconsistent with federal laws and ultimately with the Constitution, as was the case with Southern segregation laws. But this latter conflict involved an inconsistency between $laws_3$ and law_2; hence, in such a case to violate a particular law while appealing to the whole legal system was a possibly rational procedure.

If such law-violation is to be called "civil disobedience," however, then a distinction must be drawn between two types, which

---

[23] A doctrine found in various ways in Blackstone, Bentham, and Holmes might be thought to support the position that by accepting the legally prescribed penalty one can violate a law_3 and still respect the law_2. This doctrine assimilates the law_2 to an economic system in that particular $laws_3$ are conceived as having as part of their contents the "prices" attached both for obeying and for disobeying them, punishments of one sort or another being the price of disobedience. This doctrine has the paradoxical result that a person who breaks some law_3 and accepts the penalty (whether willingly or unwillingly) is operating within "the law" just as much as the person who obeys the law. There is, however, a crucial difference in this respect between an economic and a legal system: the alternative of buying or not buying is not analogous to the alternative of obeying or not obeying, for the latter alternative, unlike the former, involves violating a norm based on moral criteria. Hence disobedience, unlike the economic concepts, connotes wrong and guilt. Consequently, the proponent of civil disobedience cannot use this doctrine to support his claim that violation of a law_3 is compatible with respect for law_2.

I shall call *absolute* and *relative*. Absolute civil disobedience consists in disobeying some law$_3$ simply on the ground that it, or a related policy, is morally wrong, without claiming in addition that this law$_3$ or policy is itself illegal or unconstitutional because it violates the law$_2$, that is, some constitutional principle of the whole legal system. Relative civil disobedience consists in disobeying some law$_3$ on the ground that it, or a related policy, is in violation of the law$_2$. Most of the famous cases of civil disobedience over racial issues in the early sixties were of this relative kind—the sit-ins, the freedom rides, the demonstrations for voting rights, and so forth. Hence, scholars have debated whether these cases have been true instances of civil disobedience at all, since they lacked the condition of intentionally disobeying a law; for the protagonists denied that what they were disobeying was legally valid. Whatever one's position on this partly verbal question, it must be noted that relative civil disobedience would not be an issue unless it were in important respects reducible to absolute civil disobedience. For the reason why disobedients objected to certain city or state laws$_3$ as being in violation of law$_2$ was that they regarded the latter as itself morally right, so that ordinances in violation of it were morally wrong. As was suggested above, moral norms are embedded in the constitutional system of American law$_2$ in the guise of concepts like due process, the general welfare, and the equal protection of the laws. Hence, to appeal to one's constitutional rights is at the same time to appeal to one's moral rights of justice, welfare, and freedom.

Even relative civil disobedience, however, still leaves unsettled the question of procedural consistency. Since the legal system itself provides intralegal means both for testing the legal validity of rules and for working to change them, it is not *logically* necessary to violate the rules for this purpose; indeed, it may still seem logically inconsistent to use the procedure of violating the law while claiming to respect it. At this point, however, we must note a second qualification of the general point made above. The inconsistency in question vanishes when not only are alleged laws$_3$ or legal procedures used for ends which are in palpable violation of the law$_2$ of the Constitution, but in addition the legal procedures made available to remove the violations are in fact ineffective because of the prejudice of the authorities and other realities affecting the distribution of power.[24] In such cases it may well be argued that the procedure of civil law violation shows respect for the Constitution by opposing the unconstitutional procedures.

This consideration of effectiveness, which is an empirical matter, brings us to the other, causal relation indicated above as having to obtain between law_2 and $laws_3$ if the claims of civil disobedience were to be coherent. The civil disobedients' violating of $laws_3$ cannot be such as to cause general disrespect for and violation of law_2. The ascertainment of causal relations in social phenomena is, of course, a highly complex affair. It has frequently been claimed that causal responsibility for the riots and other racial violence and lawlessness of the late 1960s rests in

[24] Cf. King, *Why We Can't Wait*, p. 70: "The injunction method has now become the leading instrument of the South to block the direct-action civil-rights drive and to prevent Negro citizens and their white allies from engaging in peaceable assembly, a right guaranteed by the First Amendment. You initiate a non-violent demonstration. The power structure secures an injunction against you. It can conceivably take two or three years before any disposition of the case is made. The Alabama courts are notorious for 'sitting on' cases of this nature. This has been a maliciously effective, pseudo-legal way of breaking the back of legitimate moral protest." For parallel examples of misuse and unequal distribution of political power in the North, see the five-part series of articles by M. W. Newman, "Chicago's Voiceless Ghetto," *Chicago Daily News*, April 29-May 3, 1968. In the first article, Newman writes: "The West Side is a community without real power of any kind—except the power to destroy. The population is overwhelmingly Negro, but absentee white politicians have the power, the votes, the patronage. White businessmen hold the economic reins. . . . Challenging this political system of 'taxation without representation' is dangerous. 'It can get you killed,' said the Rev. Mr. Doss. 'They can hire a black man to do it.' He did not identify the 'they.' "

See, on the other hand, Abe Fortas, *Concerning Dissent and Civil Disobedience* (New York: New American Library, Signet Books, 1968), p. 19: "The events of the past few years in this nation dramatically illustrate the power of the ordinary citizen, armed with the great rights to speak, to organize, to demonstrate. It would be difficult to find many situations in history where so much has been accomplished by those who, in cold realism, were divorced from the conventional instruments of power. Negroes and the youth-generation . . . have caused great events to occur." Mr. Fortas here refers primarily to the advances in civil-rights legislation, and to a lesser extent to the agitation about the Vietnam war. Whether the "ordinary citizen" can obtain the power to effect by legal means corresponding changes in his economic and social conditions is the great question of constitutional democracy in the United States.

important part with the civil disobedience of the earlier 1960s.[25] To the extent to which this claim can be supported by empirical inquiry, it casts further doubt on the doctrine that civil disobedients can coherently violate laws$_3$ while respecting law$_2$.

The conclusions suggested by these considerations are the following. Civil disobedience can never be completely excluded as a morally justified procedure, either in its absolute or its relative form. But a crucial question in ascertaining its justifiability in a constitutional democracy is whether legal methods are actually and effectively available to those who suffer injustices in society. This question is crucial because it asks whether the method of consent which is definitive of constitutional democracy is effective or merely formal. If it is merely formal for the persons who most need its aid, then the institutional legal obligations of constitutional democracy can hardly be made out to be determinative or moral obligations for such persons. Hence, a prime moral obligation of those who uphold the morally justified claims of the method of consent is to seek to make that method and its fruits available to those who are effectively excluded from it. To do this requires an acceptance of the political obligation of active, informed, reformist citizenship.[26]

[25] See the judicious discussion of this claim in F. A. Allen, "Civil Disobedience and the Legal Order," *University of Cincinnati Law Review*, 36 (Winter 1967), 29 ff. The commission appointed by President Johnson to investigate the riots, in listing the causes of "a climate that tends toward approval and encouragement of violence as a form of protest," included "some protest groups engaging in civil disobedience who turn their backs on nonviolence . . . and resort to violence. . . ." *Report of the National Advisory Commission on Civil Disorders* (New York: Bantam Books, 1968), pp. 10-11, 204-205. This statement, however, involves a redefinition of civil disobedience unless it is understood in the sense that groups which formerly engaged in civil disobedience (which by definition is nonviolent) subsequently resorted to violence.

[26] I have discussed some of these problems of civil disobedience more fully in "Civil Disobedience, Law and Morality," *The Monist*, 54 (July 1970).

12
Civil Disobedience, Law, and Morality

Civil disobedience raises difficult problems for most of us because we are neither absolute legalists nor absolute individualistic moralists. As it is usually defined, civil disobedience consists in violating some law on the ground that it or some other law or social policy is morally wrong, and the manner of this violation is public, nonviolent, and accepting of the legally prescribed penalty for disobedience. According to the absolute legalist, civil disobedience is never justified, because he holds that every law, no matter how bad or wrong it may be, ought to be obeyed. According to the absolute individualistic moralist, on the other hand, civil disobedience is always justified, because such a moralist gives absolute priority to the demands of the individual's conscience, so that when anyone's conscience tells him some law or policy is morally wrong, that ought to settle the issue of obedience for the person in question.

Most of us are neither absolute legalists nor absolute individualistic moralists, for we recognize the potential despotism of the former extreme and the potential anarchy of the latter. Since we fall somewhere between these extremes, we face the problem of how to reconcile the demands of moral and legal obligation when they are in conflict. In this essay I want to approach this problem through a critical examination of former Justice Abe Fortas' recent attempt to solve it.[1] Such an examination is called for not only because of Fortas' position at that time on the Supreme Court, but also because his discussion brings out clearly some of the central issues and dilemmas of the relations among civil disobedience, law, and morality.

---

[1] A. Fortas, *Concerning Dissent and Civil Disobedience* (New York: New American Library, Signet Books, 1968). Page references in the text are to this paperback book.

At the very beginning of his book, Justice Fortas writes as follows:

> I am a man of the law. I have dedicated myself to uphold the law and to enforce its commands. I fully accept the principle that each of us is subject to law; that each of us is bound to obey the law enacted by his government.
>
> But if I had lived in Germany in Hitler's days, I hope I would have refused to wear an armband, to *Heil Hitler,* to submit to genocide. This I hope, although Hitler's edicts were law until allied weapons buried the Third Reich.
>
> If I had been a Negro living in Birmingham or Little Rock or Plaquemines Parish, Louisiana, I hope I would have disobeyed the state law that said I might not enter the public waiting room reserved for "Whites."
>
> I hope I would have insisted upon going into the parks and swimming pools and schools which state or city laws reserved for "Whites."
>
> I hope I would have had the courage to disobey, although the segregation ordinances were presumably law until they were declared unconstitutional.
>
> How, then, can I reconcile my profound belief in obedience to law and my equally basic need to disobey *these* laws? Is there a principle, a code, a theory to which a man, with honor and integrity, may subscribe? (pp. 9-10)

In this passage, it will have been noticed, Justice Fortas shows that he is not an absolute legalist, for he says that he hopes he would have disobeyed laws of Nazi Germany as well as the segregation laws of the southern United States. While his language here refers to what he "hopes" he would have done and to his "basic need" to disobey, it seems clear that this hope and need are also "oughts": he hopes he would have disobeyed the laws in question because he believes that he *ought* to have disobeyed them. This "ought," moreover, is a *moral* "ought," as is shown by the fact that Fortas subsequently refers to "the need that sometimes may arise to disobey profoundly immoral or unconstitutional laws," and says that such disobedience is "truly defensible as a matter of social morality" (p. 63).

On the other hand, it also seems clear that Fortas is not an absolute individualistic moralist. What distinguishes such a moralist from other moralists is that the absolute individualistic moralist holds that moral obligations are defined or ascertained simply by the deliverances of his or any other individual's conscience, and that these deliverances are sufficient of themselves, simply because they derive from conscience, to override all other rules or obligations. An opposed kind of moralist is one that I shall call "rational" or "objective," for he holds that the criteria of moral obligation have a definite rational content, so that what is morally right or wrong can be ascertained by an intersubjectively available decision-procedure and not merely by reference to an individual's conscience. The importance of the distinction between individualistic or conscience morality and rational or objective morality consists both in this crucial difference of decision-procedures and in the related fact that the appeal to conscience leaves unanswered the question whether there are any moral reasons or criteria for the guidance of conscience itself. If there are no such reasons, then there is an obvious danger of arbitrariness and moral anarchy. But if there are such reasons, then conscience is at most a secondary rather than a primary determinant of moral obligation, since conscience must itself conform to these reasons if it is to be morally right.

Fortas does not explicitly discuss this distinction between conscience morality and rational or objective morality as rival positions about the status of moral judgments. His use of the word "moral" and related words suggests sometimes the one position and sometimes the other.[2] At certain crucial points, however, he seems to

---

2 Examples of Fortas' objective conception of moral judgments are given in the text below. His subjective conception occurs especially when he is upholding the state's right to punish those who engage in civil disobedience. For example, when he says that he would have been punished if the Supreme Court had upheld the constitutionality of the segregation laws that he hopes he would have violated, he does not characterize the laws as being themselves immoral; rather, he refers to "the deep moral *conviction* that motivated me" and to the assumption "that I profoundly *believe* that the law I am violating is immoral. . . ." Similarly, he describes the civil disobedient as one who "may be *motivated* by the highest moral principles" and, in particular reference to the opponents of the Vietnam war, he says that they have a "deep moral *aversion* to a particular war" (pp. 29, 30, 32, 51; my emphases in each quotation). Such passages suggest that Fortas conceives of moral judgments as reflecting the individual's "conviction" or "belief" or "motivation" or "aversion" rather than as describing objective features of the laws, acts, or policies themselves which are being morally evaluated.

recognize quite clearly the difference between the two positions. He says, for example, with reference to the civil disobedient: "He may be *motivated* by the highest moral principles. . . . He may, indeed, be *right* in the eyes of history or morality or philosophy" (p. 32; my emphases). This distinction between morality as a matter of motivation or conviction and morality as a matter of rightness corresponds to the subjective and objective conceptions of morality. At another point, similarly, Fortas lists "conscience" and "justice" as two *distinct* factors that "impel the white majority to move to rectify an intolerable situation" of the Negroes in America (p. 39). When he refers to the laws that he hopes he would have disobeyed, he calls them "profoundly immoral" and "unjust," and he says that they "are basically offensive to fundamental values of life" (pp. 34, 63). I conclude, then, that in such statements he is claiming to do something more, or other, than merely presenting his own subjective reaction to these laws; he is claiming to make a rational, objective point about the moral status or content of the laws themselves.

Fortas does not, in his booklet, go into the nature of the moral criteria that justify his calling certain laws immoral and unjust. With regard to the laws he cites, however, it would not be difficult to adduce traditional principles of distributive justice which morally invalidate the kinds of discriminations and inequalities to which the Nazi and Southern segregation laws subjected their victims. According to these principles, such laws were unjust because they imposed disabilities and other evils on some persons as against others on grounds that had nothing to do either with their relevant comparative qualities or with the fulfillment of purposes that could be agreed to by all the persons concerned. The inherently rational character of such principles of justice, in turn, could be brought out by showing that they involve the requirement of interpersonal consistency: persons who act on other persons must apply to the latter the same basic rules of action that they apply to themselves. Consistency is involved in this requirement because an agent who applies to his recipient different basic rules from those that he applies to himself is contradicting himself, for he is saying that what is right for one person is not right for a relevantly similar person.[3]

---

[3] I have discussed this consistency requirement more fully in "Categorial Consistency in Ethics," *Philosophical Quarterly*, 17 (1967), 289-99; "Some Comments

It may be held that many moral problems involve more complex factual considerations than those comprised in the discriminatory laws to which Fortas refers, so that it may be more difficult to apply these moral criteria to such problems in a way likely to secure general agreement. I think, however, that such difficulties are usually exaggerated. In any case, it will be sufficient for present purposes to restrict ourselves primarily to the kinds of laws and policies mentioned above.

Just as we saw before that Fortas is not an absolute legalist, so it is also clear that he is not an absolute individualistic moralist nor, indeed, an absolute moralist of any kind. This comes out in such statements as: "I fully accept the principle that . . . each of us is bound to obey the law enacted by his government" (p. 9), and "Any violation of law must be punished, whatever its purpose," even if the law is itself immoral. Fortas also declares that if someone violates an immoral law, then not only should he be prepared to submit to prosecution and punishment for that violation, but "He should even admit the correctness of the state's action in seeking to enforce its laws, and he should acquiesce in the ultimate judgment of the courts" (p. 63).

The question which now arises is this. If Fortas holds that it is indeed the case that some laws are morally wrong, and hence that he himself should have disobeyed them, then how can he also hold that the state is correct in punishing persons for disobeying those laws? How can it be right to violate certain laws if it is also right to punish the violators? For in punishing the violators the state is saying to them: "You ought not to have violated these laws;" but at the same time that Fortas approves of this statement, he is also saying to those same persons: "You ought to have violated these laws." Isn't there a contradiction here?

Moreover, isn't Fortas adopting an immoral position here? As he indicates in upholding civil disobedience of immoral laws, he believes that it is morally right for persons to have violated those laws. But then, in defending the state's position that the persons ought not to have violated those laws, isn't Fortas saying that the violators ought not to have done what was morally right, but ought instead to have done or obeyed what was morally wrong?

on Categorial Consistency," *ibid.*, **20** (1970); and "The Justification of Egalitarian Justice," *American Philosophical Quarterly*, forthcoming.

Before examining in more detail how Fortas' position stands in relation to these charges of inconsistency and immorality, let us note that the difficulties arise because he upholds both civil disobedience with its claim of the primacy of moral obligation and the rule of law with its claim of the primacy of legal obligation. Basically, then, the problem is whether it is either logically or morally possible to uphold both these primacies, as Fortas seems to have tried to do. Various attempts have been made to resolve these conflicting claims of moral and legal obligation by accommodating civil disobedience to the rule of law. It has been held, for example, that civil disobedience is a form of communication protected by the First Amendment; that it is a way of testing the validity or constitutionality of a purported law;[4] and that since the civil disobedient accepts the legally prescribed penalty for violation, this shows that he respects the general rule of law even while violating a particular law.[5] There has also been a proposal that civil disobedience, because of its valuable contribution to society, should be made a separate offense distinct from ordinary crimes, and should be given a lesser penalty.[6]

These suggestions do not, however, enter into Fortas' doctrine to the extent needed to defend it against the charges made above. He rejects the idea that civil disobedience is a constitutionally protected form of communication, and he emphasizes that insofar as someone violates a law in order to test its constitutionality, the state does right in punishing the violator if he loses his test-case. Fortas declares, moreover, that where the right of dissent is legally protected, there is never any justification for the symbolic civil disobedience which, as a pressure tactic, violates a law other than the one directly regarded as immoral. I shall have more to say about this subsequently. But Fortas also asserts that direct civil disobedience is "truly defensible as a matter of social morality" when the laws disobeyed are "profoundly immoral or unconstitutional" (p. 63).

---

[4] H. A. Freeman, *Civil Disobedience* (Center for the Study of Democratic Institutions, 1966), pp. 4-9. See also R. Dworkin, "On Not Prosecuting Civil Disobedience" (*New York Review of Books,* June 6, 1968), pp. 14-21.

[5] M. L. King, Jr., *Why We Can't Wait* (New York: New American Library, Signet Books, 1964), pp. 83-84.

[6] C. P. Colby, "Civil Disobedience: A Case for Separate Treatment," *Wayne Law Review,* 14 (1968), 1165-1180.

This brings us back to our previous questions. How, without falling into contradiction and immorality, can Fortas justify both such civil disobedience and its punishment by the state?

One possible defense against these charges is to distinguish between what is *morally* right or obligatory and what is *legally* right or obligatory. For example, referring to the kind of civil disobedience he upholds, Justice Fortas declares that "a moral (although not a legal) defense of law violation can . . . be urged" (p. 63). Thus, when he says to the civil disobedients, "You ought to have violated those laws," the "ought" in question is a moral "ought," while when he upholds the state's saying to those same persons, "You ought not to have violated those laws," the "ought" in question is a legal "ought." Hence there is no contradiction between the two assertions, for a statement which says that some person *morally* ought to do *x* is quite compatible logically with another statement which says that same person *legally* ought not to do *x*.

This attempt to set up a dualism of legal and moral criteria does not succeed in defending Fortas' position against the charges of contradiction and immorality. For "ought"-statements or statements about what it is "right" to do are practical or action-guiding; they are intended to tell a person who is confronted by two or more alternatives what, all things considered, he should do. But the dualism of legal and moral "oughts" leaves unanswered the question: What should one do when legal and moral requirements conflict? When Fortas tells us that he should have disobeyed immoral laws, he assumes that moral criteria must take precedence over legal criteria. But then he contradicts himself, and he defends what he recognizes to be immoral, when he goes on to uphold the state's claim that he should *not* have disobeyed the immoral laws and that he *should* be punished for the disobedience. Thus the dualism of moral and legal "oughts" does not save Fortas from contradiction when he opposes them to one another in a context which is intended to be practical or action-guiding.

Now if Fortas himself upheld this dualism of moral and legal criteria as his own normative position, he would indeed be a defender of the Machiavellian view that law and politics not only do but also should proceed in complete disregard of moral considerations. But on the contrary, his basic doctrine of law is itself a moral one. He declares that the "duty of obedience to law . . . is a moral as well as a legal imperative" (p. 11), and he defends this moral imperativeness by pointing to the function of law as alone making possible the coexistence of individual liberty and organized society:

> The story of man is the history, first, of the acceptance and imposition of restraints necessary to permit communal life; and second, of the emancipation of the individual within that system of necessary restraints. . . . [This] is true in any organized society. The achievement of liberty is man's indispensable condition of living; and yet, liberty cannot exist unless it is restrained and restricted. The instrument of balancing these two conflicting factors is the law. So we must end as we began, with an acknowledgment that the rule of law is the essential condition of individual liberty as it is of the existence of the state. (p. 59)

On the basis of this statement and other similar ones exalting the rule of law, it might seem possible to construct a second defense of Justice Fortas against the charges of contradiction and immorality. This defense would argue that even if a particular law is itself morally wrong, still the enforcement of that law and the punishment of its violators are morally right because they are in accord with the rule of law, and without that enforcement and punishment the rule of law would in that case lapse. But this would mean the lapse of the most basic moral value, for since the rule of law alone makes possible the reconciliation of that social order without which men cannot live together at all, and that individual liberty without which they cannot live well, the rule of law must take precedence over all other moral values. Thus, in the case of the civil disobedients who disobey immoral laws, when Justice Fortas says to them, "You ought to have violated those laws" and the state says to them, "You ought not to have violated those laws," both "oughts" are moral "oughts," but the state's "ought" takes precedence because of the overriding moral importance of the rule of law. Consequently, there is neither contradiction nor immorality in Fortas' position.

Related arguments to establish the same conclusion could be constructed by using certain distinctions familiar to moral philosophers, especially the distinctions between prima facie rightness and actual rightness and between act-utilitarianism and rule-utilitarianism. An act (such as the act of keeping one's promise) is prima facie right if it is right when considered simply by itself; but it may not be actually right, or right all things considered, that is, after due consideration has been given to all the relevant surrounding circumstances (for example, keeping one's promise may sometimes bring great harm to innocent persons). According to act-utilitarianism, whether a particular act ought to be done must be determined by considering the consequences of that particular act; but according to rule-utilitarianism, whether a particular act ought to be done must be determined rather by considering the consequences of the general performance of that kind of act, that is, the consequences of everyone's acting on the general rule of which the act is an instance.

Applying these distinctions, we might hold that a particular act of civil disobedience may be right according to act-utilitarianism insofar as it does more good than its available alternatives; and it may be prima facie right insofar as it violates an immoral law, since such a law requires that one perform an immoral act. But the act is not actually right, nor right according to rule-utilitarianism, for since the rule of law is the most basic moral value because of its indispensability to organized society, this supplies a contextual consideration which makes the disobedient act in question wrong; and the consequences of general violation of the rule of law are worse than the consequences of maintaining it. Thus when Fortas says to civil disobedients who violate immoral laws, "You ought to have violated those laws," and when he upholds the state's saying to those same persons, "You ought not to have violated those laws," there is neither contradiction nor immorality in this position, because the first "ought" refers to a prima facie duty, or to the utility of the act of civil disobedience taken by itself, while the second "ought" refers to an actual or ultimate duty, or to the utility of the whole morally valuable system of the rule of law.

The trouble with all such arguments is that they come down to that absolute legalism which I mentioned and rejected at the outset, and which we saw was also rejected by Fortas. The arguments would entail, for example, that the morally most important description that can be given of an act is that it is an act of obeying or disobeying some law, so that this description must take moral precedence over—must be regarded as morally more important for determining one's actual conduct than—such other descriptions of the act as that it is an act of killing or otherwise harming innocent persons, or that it is an act which imposes severe hardships on persons solely because of their race or religion, and so forth. This, however, is an absurd consequence, and hence we must reject the premise according to which the rule of law is the most basic moral value.

This premise, with its Hobbesian implication that any legal system, no matter how immoral it may be in its contents or procedures, is morally better than having no legal system at all, is sharply at variance with the view of Locke and the Revolutionary fathers that despotism, no matter how thoroughly buttressed by laws, is worse than anarchy. As for the rule-utilitarian argument, once we begin appealing to consequences we open the door to conclusions opposed to the absolute maintenance of the rule of law. For even if we agree that upholding the rule of law has the best consequences in general, why should the violation of a particular immoral law not be justified if the consequences of *that* violation are better than the consequences of not violating it?

The principle that the rule of law is the most basic moral value does not remove the contradiction which we found in Fortas' position. For since he said that he should have violated immoral laws, without qualifying this by the restriction that they were not really laws, he is still in the position of declaring both that men are morally justified in violating immoral laws and that the state is morally justified in opposing and punishing that violation.

Let us now see whether we can construct a third and more durable defense of Fortas' position against the charges of contradiction and immorality by means of another important distinction. This is the distinction between the rule of law in general or in nondemocratic states and the rule of law in a constitutional democracy. While Fortas' exaltation of the rule of law which I quoted above referred to "any organized society," much of his discussion is taken up with the constitutional structure of the United States. And this structure, he seems to hold, is a profoundly moral one; thus he says of it, "I think it is difficult to find fault with the theory of our system if one believes in the rules of ordered society" (p. 24). He presents, as the chief elements of the system, that each citzen has, first, the guaranteed freedoms of speech, press, and assembly, and hence the right to dissent from and protest against governmental policies; second, the right to vote and to organize with others to try to elect new legislative and executive officials, with the majority vote being decisive; third, the right to bring suit against the state or its officials, and to have the case tried before an impartial court; and fourth, limits on the right to dissent, in that its exercise must not violate laws which prohibit violence, injury, or disturbance of the peace of other persons. Because of the legally guaranteed availability to each citizen of these rights and freedoms of dissent, it is neither necessary nor morally justified that anyone have recourse to illegal methods of social protest or change, like civil disobedience.

On the basis of these elements of the American constitutional system, then, we might hold that Fortas' position is neither contradictory nor immoral, for when he says to civil disobedients who violate immoral laws, "You ought to have violated those laws," this statement is overridden by the state's saying to those same persons, "You ought not to have violated those laws." The former statement is overridden by the latter because the state is acting in accordance with the morally superior elements of the American constitutional system.

A related defense of Fortas' position can be found in his implicit invocation of the generalization principle with its appeal to fairness: if a person claims some right for himself, then he must, on pain of contradiction, concede that other similar persons have that same right. "A person cannot demand of his government or of other people obedience to the law, and at the same time claim a right in himself to break it by lawless conduct, free of punishment or penalty" (p. 33). "Dissent and dissenters . . . must accept dissent from their dissent. And they must give it the respect and the latitude which they claim for themselves" (p. 64). The bearing of this principle on Fortas' own conjoint defenses of violating immoral laws and punishing the violators is that where there is legal protection of the right of dissent and equal freedom to try to change laws, there is implicit acceptance of the general framework of the rule of law as applying impartially to all persons; hence, if someone violates a law, he should accept the penalties prescribed by that framework.

These considerations also provide a more direct way of showing that Justice Fortas' position is not self-contradictory. While he is, indeed, in the position of saying to violators of immoral laws, (1) "You ought to have violated those laws," it is false that his assertion of the correctness of the state's action in punishing the violators puts him in the position of upholding the statement, (2) "You ought not to have violated those laws." What he is saying to the violators, rather, is, (3) "You ought to be punished for violating those laws." Now (3) neither contradicts (1) nor entails (2), for (3) does not bear on the moral rightness or wrongness of the law-violation taken by itself but rather on the moral rightness of punishing the law-violation once it has occurred. This punishment is morally right because of the overriding moral importance of the rule of law in a constitutional democracy. In upholding the punishment as morally justified Fortas is not saying that the specific law-violation was not morally justified, but rather that there is moral justification for maintaining the general procedures of the law in this case as in any other.

That (3) does not contradict (1) may also be shown in other ways. In order to bring a test-case one must violate the law whose validity is being tested; but if one loses the case, then one must accept the punishment: this is what is involved in bringing a test-case. Here, the beliefs that one ought to violate the law in question and that one ought to be punished for the violation, far from being in contradiction to one another, are parts of a single coherent program. More generally, one may consistently uphold both (1) and (3) on act-utilitarian grounds: one ought to violate an immoral law because of the beneficial consequences of that violation, these consequences including not only the public, visible registering of a protest, but also the resultant punishment. For the publicity surrounding the punishment helps call attention to, and hence may lead to the removal of, the immorality one is combating. Thus the law-violator, as well as others, may consistently uphold the rightness both of his law-violation and of his being punished for the violation.

Still another defense of Justice Fortas' position is based on the distinction, which he stresses in another connection (p. 30), between civil disobedience and revolution. The distinction is not merely between nonviolence and violence but, more generally, between acceptance and nonacceptance of the general framework of the rule of law in the society. To maintain that one ought not to be punished for one's illegal act is to uphold the violation not only of the particular law which was directly violated but also of the general legal framework itself. Hence, when Justice Fortas says to the violators, "You ought to have violated that law," he is referring to the particular law; but when he supports the state's punishing the violators, he is referring rather to the general rule of law. Hence, his position is neither inconsistent nor immoral.

These defenses of Justice Fortas' position have many of the same features and shortcomings as the preceding defense in terms of the rule of law in general. He recognizes that even under the American constitutional system there may emerge immoral laws which justify civil disobedience, although it is not entirely clear whether he thinks that all such laws are necessarily also unconstitutional. In any case, since he upholds both civil disobedience to such laws and the state's punishment of the disobedients, his position still incurs the previous charges of contradiction and immorality.

There is, indeed, some cogency in the above-mentioned test-case and utilitarian defenses against the charge of contradiction. But Fortas' justification of the state's action in enforcing its laws is more extensive than these defenses allow. The state's punitive action, as he conceives it, is not merely a utilitarian device; rather, it carries with it the state's evaluation that the persons punished did wrong in violating the law. Since Fortas, in accepting the overriding importance of the rule of law, accepts this evaluation, he cannot consistently also uphold the position that those persons were justified in violating the law.

This inconsistency is not removed by the distinction between civil disobedience and revolution. A person may hold that the state's enforcement of an immoral law is itself immoral, without thereby attacking the enforcement of all laws. More specifically, one may uphold the principles of constitutional democracy in general without thereby giving *carte blanche* to all its particular operations. Hence, Fortas is still left with a contradiction between his conjoint espousal of violating and enforcing a particular immoral law.

Suppose, however, we assume that Fortas escapes this contradiction because his defense of the state's punitive action is only a general utilitarian one. On this interpretation, his statements would not carry any implication of the wrongness of the specific law-violation which is to be punished; his position would rest only on the necessity of having laws and law-enforcement in general for the existence of an organized society. But this would mean that Fortas is concomitantly asserting that certain laws are immoral, that the victims of these laws ought to violate them, and that nevertheless, for general utilitarian reasons, the state ought to punish the violators. This position, however, can be convicted of immorality on two counts: it justifies the existence of immoral societies, that is, societies which rest on immoral laws such as the ones which Fortas cited in his examples of the Nazi and southern segregation laws; and it upholds what is unfair, that the victims of such immoral laws should acquiesce in their enforcement because of the ensuing benefits for the rest of the society. Fortas seeks to evade this latter implication when he writes: "For, after all, each of us is a member of an organized society. Each of us benefits from its existence and its order" (p. 63). The question here, however, is whether the benefits accruing to each of us because of the existence of some legal order, or even of one specific legal order, compensate for the severe disadvantages accruing to some persons as against others under such legal order.

We are left, then, with two conflicting charges of unfairness: Fortas' charge that the civil disobedient claims for himself a right of disobedience which he is unwilling to grant to other persons, and the present charge that Fortas' defense of the state's action in punishing civil disobedients upholds the rule of law at the expense of those who suffer from discriminatory laws. The former charge can be rebutted, among other ways, by pointing out that if the civil disobedient is an absolute individualistic moralist, then he is willing to defend anyone's disobeying the law on conscientious grounds; and if he is an objective or rational moralist, then he will defend civil disobedience on the part of those whose moral claims are rationally justifiable. Legalists, however, whether absolutists or not, will be made uncomfortable by each of these rebuttals; they will feel that even the rational moralist's position leaves the door open to excessive instability, that this can be avoided only by exclusive recourse to legally permitted procedures, and that in a constitutional democracy, with its provisions for dissent as sketched above, these procedures achieve all the moral validity which is either necessary or possible in an organized society.

Now it must be admitted and, indeed, emphasized that the features of the American constitutional system stressed by Fortas give it a great moral superiority over systems which lack these features, and that as a consequence the moral counter-arguments which confront would-be civil disobedients in the United States are much weightier. It is hence worth examining why those counter-arguments are not conclusive. In a statement which I quoted above Justice Fortas said: "it is difficult to find fault with the theory of our system. . . ." He has, then, two kinds of arguments against the justified use of civil disobedience in the United States, one kind bearing on how the theory of our constitutional system is translated into practice, the other bearing on the theory of the system itself. Let us consider each in turn.

His argument from practice may be stated formally as follows: If civil disobedience is to be justified as a method for promoting morally justified social change, then it must be the case that effective intralegal procedures are not available to the persons who need such change. But such procedures *are* available to those persons. Therefore, civil disobedience is not justified as a method for promoting morally justified social change.

The crucial point in this argument is the minor premise. Assuming that there is agreement on the moral aspects of the needs involved, this premise is an empirical one. And Fortas emphatically asserts the empirical claim that such intralegal procedures are available. For example, in an apparent reply to those who might turn to civil disobedience or other illegal methods in their quest for "black power," "student power," and the like, he writes as follows:

> Despite the limits which the requirements of an ordered society impose, the protected weapons of protest, dissent, criticism, and peaceable assembly are enormously powerful. Largely as a result of the use of these instruments by Negroes, the present social revolution was launched: by freedom marches; organized boycotts; picketing and mass demonstrations; protest and propaganda. . . . The events of the past few years in this nation dramatically illustrate the power of the ordinary citizen, armed with the great rights to speak, to organize, to demonstrate. (pp. 18-19)

There are at least two difficulties with this statement. First, the social advances cited by Fortas as proof of the power of legal methods are more fully proofs of the power of illegal methods. For when the Negroes used the instruments he lists to launch their social revolution, they had to go *outside* the laws as they were then interpreted and enforced in the Southern states.

It has often been pointed out that the sit-ins, freedom rides, and other protest activities in the early 1960's were in an important respect not acts of civil disobedience, for the protesters held that the orders they were violating were not valid laws but rather unconstitutional decrees. Nevertheless, these orders did emerge from the duly constituted authorities. We must, then, distinguish between "absolute" and "relative" civil disobedience, the former consisting in disobeying orders which the violators acknowledge to be legally valid although morally wrong, the latter consisting in disobeying orders on the ground that they are not legally valid at all. Now even if all the gains cited by Fortas were obtained only by relative civil disobedience—which is highly doubtful—still the fact is that the procedures used consisted not in following such legally prescribed channels as lawsuits but rather in defying what were then still laws or legal orders, so far as concerns the procedures involved in producing them.

A second difficulty with Justice Fortas' statement is that it is quite unrealistic to hold that the submerged groups whose problems arise precisely because of their powerlessness have the power which he here attributes to them. An expression like "the power of the ordinary citizen" is multiply ambiguous. It may signify the ordinary citizen's legal entitlement to do x, or his effective present ability to do x, or his future potentiality for doing x; and "do x," moreover, may signify either the attempt to do something or the successful achievement of that something. Suppose, now, we ask about the power of an impoverished, poorly educated Negro slum-dweller, singly or in combination, to improve his living conditions marked by rats, low income, poor schools for his children, and the indifference if not the hostility of the authorities. He is, indeed, legally entitled to protest against these conditions; and he may have the future potentiality, granted favorable developments over the next decade or so, to achieve the object of his protest; but, as things now stand, he does not have the effective present ability to achieve this, and in far too many cases he does not have the effective present ability even to try. The following statement in a newspaper article entitled "Chicago's Voiceless Ghetto" is true of most Negro ghettos: "The West Side is a community without real power of any kind— except the power to destory. The population is overwhelmingly Negro, but absentee white politicians have the power, the votes, the patronage. White businessmen hold the economic reins."[7] More generally, the Kerner Commission Report on Civil Disorders declared: "The political system, traditionally an important vehicle for minorities to participate effectively in decisions affecting the distribution of public resources, has not worked for the Negro as it has for other groups."[8]

Such empirical considerations refute the empirical minor premise of Fortas' argument from practice against the justification of both direct and symbolic civil disobedience on the part of the Negroes whose morally justified claims he repeatedly endorses. It must also be noted, however, that the refutation does not necessarily apply to such other civil disobedient groups as college and university students.

Let us now turn to Fortas' argument from the theory itself of our constitutional system. If the system works so poorly for the submerged groups who most need its help, it seems plausible to hold that there is something wrong with the theory of the system itself. Crucial to the theory is the relation between majority rule and minority rights. As we have seen, Fortas stresses, on the one hand, that every citizen has the constitutionally protected right of dissent, and, on the other hand, that the majority decision must be accepted: "The individual must tolerate the majority's verdict when and as it is settled in accordance with the laws and procedures that have been established" (p. 64). But what if the majority is hostile or indifferent to the needs of the minority? The theory of our system, borne out to a considerable extent by American political history, is that minorities equipped with the civil and political freedoms which enable them to press their own interests acquire and use political power and are thereby absorbed into the mainstream of the majority. Competition, bargaining, the pursuit of different group interests in different combinations have the result that there is no permanent "majority" or "minority," but rather a plurality of groups whose members are in the majority on some issues and in the minority on others, with changes occurring frequently.

---

7 M. W. Newman in *Chicago Daily News*, April 29, 1968, p. 1.

8 *Report of the National Advisory Commission on Civil Disorders* (New York: Bantam Books, 1968), p. 287.

The Negroes are the most conspicuous example of a minority that, to a very large extent, has not participated in this process because it has had no competitive or bargaining power to begin with and has been discriminated against by the majority. Other such minority groups are the Indians, the mentally ill, the poor old, and the poor whites. It is a serious defect of the American constitutional system that it does not provide for such relatively powerless minorities the effective power required to press their claims. What is needed, at a minimum, is a governmentally guaranteed forum whereby such disadvantaged groups can persistently and effectively present their case to the affluent majority.

More generally, what is needed is a more affirmative notion of rights. When Fortas emphasizes that "our Constitution protects . . . the rights to speak, to publish, to protest, to assemble peaceably and to participate in the electoral process" (pp. 17, 19), he seems to mean this only in the negative sense that the government will prevent other persons from interfering with anyone's speaking or publishing, and so forth. He does not also mean it in the positive sense that the government will actively assist anyone to publish and to press his grievances. But it is this latter kind of positive right which our system must provide to those who need it most if it is to be true to its own procedural moral ideals. Without such a positive right, submerged groups lack the effective ability to press their claims in public communication by legally available means. Without this ability, it is questionable whether the moral claims of sizeable groups in our society can be fulfilled without recourse to civil disobedience.

One final consideration. It might be held that the difficulties I have found in Justice Fortas' doctrine must really be attributed to the definition of civil disobedience itself. For according to that definition, it will be recalled, the civil disobedient accepts the legally prescribed penalty for disobedience. It might seem, then, that the very concept of civil disobedience is both inconsistent and immoral: inconsistent, in that it requires that the civil disobedient both approve and disapprove the violation of certain laws (the disapproval being evidenced by his acceptance of punishment for the violation) ; immoral, in that his acceptance of the punishment entails his acquiescing in laws which he regards as immoral.

In this respect, Fortas' doctrine is indeed close to that of the upholders of civil disobedience, so that the latter are confronted with similar difficulties.[9] Whether the doctrines are identical, however, depends on the relation between the grounds on which the civil disobedient accepts his punishment and the grounds on which Fortas declares that the civil disobedient "should even admit the correctness of the state's action in seeking to enforce its laws, and he should acquiesce in the ultimate judgment of the courts" (p. 63). The grounds may, however, be different. The civil disobedient may accept the legally prescribed penalty even though he believes that the state ought to have acted differently in his case; his acceptance may be based on the desire to avoid a greater evil to society in respect of its peace and order, or on his wanting to show the depth of his concern over the immorality he is protesting, or on his conviction that the state's enforcement of its laws is justified in general even if not in his particular case, or on the calculation that his goal of removing the immoral law will be best furthered by accepting the penalty. Such grounds do not entail the belief that the civil disobedient ought not to have violated the law in question, so that the definition of civil disobedience is not involved in the contradiction I have attributed to Justice Fortas, arising from his advocacy of the overriding importance of the rule of law.

More generally, it is possible to reconcile acceptance of the rule of law with the principled violation of a particular law by an appeal to moral criteria which would justify both. Such a reconciliation, however, would require that the rule of law be regarded as conditional rather than as absolute. The difficulties I have explored in this essay have arisen in large part from Fortas' contradictory attempt to view the rule of law both as an absolute value and as having only a conditional justification dependent on the conformity of law to moral criteria. While he does indeed give a moral justification of the rule of law, he does not explicitly relate the moral criteria involved in this justification to the moral criteria to which he appeals in upholding the violation of immoral laws. Two conclusions follow from this. If one invokes moral criteria to justify

---

[9] I have discussed these difficulties of the concept of civil disobedience in "Obligation: Political, Legal, Moral," *Nomos* (Yearbook of the American Society for Political and Legal Philosophy) , **12** (1970) , pp. 55-88; see especially pp. 83ff.

an institution, then one must regard the correctness of the institution's operations as contingent on their conformity to those criteria. And if one invokes one set of moral criteria to justify an institution and another set to justify violation of that institution, then a contradiction results unless one can produce some more general principle which makes intelligible the relation between the two sets of criteria.

13
Civil Liberties as Effective Powers

My main concern in this paper is with the distribution of civil liberties in the United States, especially as it bears on their effective exercise in the political process. There is an important moral problem about the fairness of this distribution and hence, by extension, about the fairness of the democratic process itself. This distributive problem is distinct from the problem of the justifiable limits of free speech and other civil liberties—the problem with which American jurists have coped for many decades and philosophers for many centuries, using on the one hand such criteria as "clear and present danger," "preferred position," and "balancing," and on the other such general criteria as "non-harmfulness" and "equal freedom."[1] The two problems are, of course, closely related, among other reasons because the imposition of legal limitations on certain uses of civil liberties may make even more unequal the distribution of those liberties and may hence diminish further the instruments of political protest and dissent which are legally available to disadvantaged groups. Nevertheless, the problem of distribution and the problem of limits are logically distinct. The problem with which I deal in this paper concerns the distribution of civil liberties even in contexts where there is no dispute as to whether their use ought to be legally limited or prohibited. It is important to distinguish this problem from the problem of legal limitation, because the distributive problem poses separate moral issues about the fairness of the democratic process even in respect of those of its methods which are legally and non-controversially open and unlimited for all citizens of the democracy.

I approach this distributive problem through a preliminary analysis of the concept of freedom (or liberty—I use these words interchangeably). Whatever else civil liberties may be, they are liberties or freedoms; and the understanding of this concept should shed light on the conceptual structure of civil liberties. An awareness of this structure, in turn, is important in the context of the democratic process.

I. Freedom as Non-Interference and Power

According to Isaiah Berlin, "I am normally said to be free to the degree to which no man or body of men interferes with my activity. Political liberty in this sense is simply the area within which a man can act unobstructed by others. If I am prevented by others from doing what I could otherwise do, I am to that degree unfree..."[2] Essentially the same definition of liberty is given by E. F. Carritt: "the power of doing what one would choose without interference by other persons' actions."[3] Berlin calls this the notion of "negative freedom," and he contrasts it with a notion of "positive freedom" according to which freedom "consists in being one's own master." It must be noted, however, that even the notion of negative freedom as he presents it, like the definition given by Carritt, contains a positive component as well as a negative one. The negative component is non-interference or non-obstruction by other persons; the positive component is the power or ability to act, and indeed to act as one chooses or wishes.[4] This positive component of power or ability to act is indicated in Berlin's references, in the statements just quoted, to "the area within which a man *can* act" and to "doing what I *could* otherwise do" (emphasis added). The negative and positive components may also respectively be identified to a considerable extent with the traditional distinction between "freedom from" and "freedom to," since the prepositions "from" and "to" here point, respectively, to obstructions and to actions.

An initial question concerns the relation between these two components of freedom. Specifically, can the power to act and non-interference with one's action by other persons be had independently of one another?[5] It is important to distinguish two different interpretations of this question, which I shall call the unqualified and the qualified. The unqualified interpretation asks whether the negative and positive components can exist independently of one another, while the qualified interpretation asks whether the negative and positive components can exist independently of one another *as kinds of freedom*. To answer either interpretation of the question, moreover, the non-interference and the power or ability in question must be specified with respect to some particular action, to which I shall refer schematically as "doing *x*." There is, indeed, a sense in which freedom may be viewed as having no necessary relation to any action at all, as consisting solely in non-interference in the sense of being let alone by others, regardless of whether one wants to do anything. Such being let alone when one wants to be let alone, moreover, has often been rightly regarded as a good in itself. For the purposes of this paper, however, I shall ignore this completely non-actional sense of negative freedom, since the civil liberties, with which I shall be primarily concerned, are freedoms to perform various kinds of deeds or actions.

To return to my initial question, it seems clear that a person may be without interference from other persons as to his doing x, so that his condition conforms to the negative component, while nevertheless he lacks the power or ability to do x, so that his condition does not conform to the positive component. He may, for example, be sitting paralyzed in his room, with no interference or obstruction from other persons so far as concerns his getting up and walking about, and nevertheless he may be unable to get up and walk about. In such a case the person is indeed obstructed or interfered with as to his getting up and walking; but this interference stems not from other persons but from his own physical handicap. But insofar as the negative component is confined to interference by other persons, the paralytic is not interfered with and yet he lacks the ability to walk. This answer to the unqualified interpretation of the question is straightforward enough; it involves no special semantical or evaluative issues.

If, however, we raise the question in the qualified interpretation, a semantical issue about "freedom" does arise. The semantical issue, moreover, also becomes in part an evaluative one: because of the laudatory connotations of the word "freedom," persons want to associate it with policies they favor, as conservatives and liberals, for example, do when they respectively affirm and deny that poor persons in a capitalist society are free to buy what they desire. While it is often difficult to avoid treating evaluative issues as if they were merely semantical ones, clarity can be maintained if we explicitly distinguish the various senses in which the disputed terms are used and if we are careful to follow out the implications of the senses in question.

The paralyzed person in my above example may be said to be negatively free in that he is not interfered with by other persons with respect to his walking about. But, lacking as he does the power to walk about, is he positively free—that is, is he free to walk about? Our strong tendency to say 'no' to this question stems in part from the fact that although the paralytic is not interfered with by other persons, he is interfered with by his own physical condition. But it stems also from the semantics of 'free to do x' which seems to require as a criterion of its application that one be able to do x. Thus it would be at least paradoxical to say of the paralytic that he is *free* to walk about even though he is *unable* to walk about. The avoidance of this paradox requires not an assertion of the 'true' nature or meaning of freedom but rather an awareness that interference with one's actions may come from different sources, and that the non-existence or removal of these interferences with one's doing x is at the same time the acquisition of one's power or ability to do x. For to interfere successfully with a person's doing x is to bring it about that he is at that time unable to do x; hence, to remove the interferences is to remove the disabling factors and hence to enable him to do x. Thus, even on the negative conception of freedom as the nonexistence or removal of interferences, the realization of this conception of freedom is at the same time the attainment of a correlative power or ability. The negative conception of freedom as non-interference hence merges necessarily with the positive conception as power or ability, so that to be free from interference with one's doing x is to have the power or ability to do x.

To insist that the paralytic in my example is free to walk about would be to maintain at all costs, as exclusively correct, the negative definition whereby freedom consists solely in the absence of interference on the part of other persons, so that having the power to do x is not a necessary part of the meaning of "being free to do x." Proponents of this exclusivist position often accuse their opponents of confusing freedom with the quite different concept of power or ability. But that the words "freedom" and "power" do not signify such completely different concepts, and that the meaning of the former includes that of the latter, are suggested not only by considerations like the one just given but also by the tendency of thinkers who wish to distinguish negative and positive liberty to include at least implicit references to power or ability even in their definitions of the negative concept.[6] I conclude, then, that while the negative component of non-interference by other persons can exist without the positive component of power to act (unqualified interpretation of our question), the negative component does not comprise the freedom to act unless there is also the power to act (qualified interpretation of our question).

Let us next consider the reverse situation: can the positive component be had without the negative component? To take first the unqualified interpretation of the question: can A have the power to do x if he is interfered with or prevented by other persons from doing x? To answer this question requires that we distinguish kinds of both power and interference. With respect to power, we must distinguish at least between remote, latent, or passive power and proximate, effective, or active power. A person may have only the remote or passive power to do x, in that his doing x is not entirely beyond his capabilities but it requires that other persons or objects act on him in order to activate his power, so that he then and only then has the proximate or effective power to do x. He has the effective or proximate power to do x if his doing x depends on his own choice so that, given his choice to do x, he does x. It is clear, then, that if a person is interfered with or prevented by other persons from doing x, he may still have the passive or remote power to do x but not the active or effective power to do x. We must also, however, distinguish between two modes of interference: the merely attempted and the successful (only the

latter is usually called "prevention"). The active or effective power to do
x can coexist with attempted but not with successful interference. It must
also be noted, however, that interference may be either negative or positive: it may tend either to prevent the performance of some act or to assist
in its performance. In the present context, it is obvious that the issue
concerns only negative interference.

To take next the qualified interpretation of the question: if A has the
power to do x, is he then free to do x even if he is interfered with or
prevented by other persons from doing x? This is to ask whether the
positive component, consisting in the power to act, is a sufficient and not
merely a necessary condition of the freedom to act. Obviously the same
distinctions that were noted above as to both "power" and "interference" must be applied in answering this question. If a person has the
effective and not merely the remote power to do x, then his doing x
depends on himself alone—his choice to do x is the sufficient condition of
his doing x—so that successful negative interference by other persons
with his doing x is ruled out. Hence the correct position is not that freedom cannot consist in the positive component alone even in the absence
of the negative component, but rather that the positive component, properly interpreted, already includes the negative component, although the
converse is not the case insofar as the negative component is restricted to
non-interference by other persons.

The following argument might be thought to refute the view that the
effective power or ability to do x is a sufficient condition of the freedom to
do x. Suppose a person A is forced or coerced to do x by another person
B. Since A then does x, he at that point has the effective ability to do x.
But, on the view in question, this has the paradoxical result that A is free
to do x even when he does x as a result of coercion by someone else.[7]

There are at least two answers to this argument. One is that the effective power to do x which is a sufficient condition of the freedom to do x
must include the effective power not to do x: it must include the power,
according to one's unforced choice, to refrain from acting as well as the
power to act. The other answer is that the power in question must be
effective in the sense that it depends for its direct effectuation or exercise
on the unforced choice of the person who is said to have the power.
Hence, A does not have the power to do x unless his direct exercise of this
power depends on his own unforced choice, not on his being forced by
some other person to make the choice he does.

Another argument to show that the power to do x cannot be a sufficient
condition or definition of the freedom to do x is the following: Suppose A
has the power or ability to read a certain book; suppose also that he is
prevented from reading the book by other persons. We should then have

to say, paradoxically, that *A* has the freedom to read at the same time that other persons prevent him from reading. This argument is to be answered in much the same terms as the preceding one. In the circumstances as described *A* has only the latent or passive power to read the book, not the active or effective power. The latter includes the absence of successful interference by other persons. To define the freedom to do *x*, then, as the effective power to do *x* avoids both of the paradoxes of freedom here discussed: the paradox of the position that a man who lacks the effective power to do *x* is free to do *x*, and the paradox of the position that a man who is successfully coerced by others to do *x* or to refrain from doing *x* is free to do *x*. On the other hand, the proponents of the exclusively negative definition of freedom cannot avoid the former paradox.

It will be helpful at this point to return to the unqualified interpretation of the question whether the negative component of freedom can be had without the positive component, that is, whether a person can have non-interference with his actions even if he lacks the effective power to act. At least two arguments might be thought to justify a negative answer to this question. One is that actions, insofar as they are genuine actions and not merely physical events or bodily movements, must be controlled or determined by some person or persons. Now if the controller of one's actions is not other persons—so that the negative definition of "freedom" is satisfied—then the controller must be the agent himself—so that the positive definition is satisfied. The reason why the positive definition is satisfied in this latter case is that if a person controls or determines his own actions, then, *a fortiori*, he has the effective power to act, since his control of his actions is an exercise of his power to act.[8] Hence, the negative component of freedom cannot be had without the positive component.

The trouble with this argument is that it assumes the very point at issue: that the person in question is already performing some action. For the only alternatives which the argument considers deal with the control over actions as they occur; this is indicated in the argument's inference from non-control by other persons to control by the agent himself. This inference, however, omits another alternative: that the person in question fails to act because he lacks control over whether he will act, in that he lacks the effective power to act. Obviously, if he is acting, then he has the power to act; but the question still remains whether, while no other person interferes with or controls his doing *x*, he has the power to do *x*. He may lack the power, even though no one interferes with him.

A second argument for a negative answer to our question is that if a person is not interfered with or obstructed in any way in respect of his doing *x*, then he has the effective power to do *x*, since, *ex hypothesi*, there is nothing (such as the paralysis in my earlier example) which obstructs his doing x. The trouble with this argument is that it extends the interferences or obstacles referred to so as to include not only those imposed by other persons but also all the other possible sources of interference or obstruction. But our question bore on whether a person could be without interferences *from other persons* with respect to his doing x and yet be unable to do x. It remains, then, that this question must be answered affirmatively in its unqualified interpretation: there can be the negative component without the positive component, although the negative component taken by itself is not a sufficient condition of the *freedom* to act.

The obstacles or interferences which remove a person's effective power or ability to act, and hence his freedom, may indeed be of many different kinds. They may be internal to the person (consisting in physical or mental ailments, lack of relevant skills or education, and so forth), or external to the person. The external obstacles may include things other than persons (including such natural obstacles as bogs or precipices), or they may be persons other than the one whose ability to act is in question. Interpersonal or social obstacles of this latter sort may be either occurrent, consisting in the direct infliction of interference or obstruction, or they may be dispositional, consisting in the more long-range, institutionalized interferences which are such that, were the person in question to try to do x, he would be prevented from doing it by the standardized arrangements which other persons have established and which they or their successors maintain. In addition, both the occurrent and the dispositional interpersonal obstacles may be either active or passive, in that they may consist either in men's acting or in their failures to act. If, for example, the question is asked whether a slum child is free to learn to read, the obstacles in the way of his learning may be held to consist not only in the institutionalized patterns of poverty and discrimination which effectively prevent him from acquiring the reading abilities in question but also in the inaction of persons who could help to bring about the required institutional changes but who, from inertia or other causes, fail to act toward this end.

These distinctions regarding freedom are important not only in themselves but also with respect to their bearing on the relation between freedom and legislation or governmental action. It has long been recognized that laws may have a double relation to freedom. On the other hand, they may restrict freedom in that, by threatening or inflicting punishment for legally prohibited actions, the laws interfere with the performance of these actions. On the other hand, laws may expand freedom insofar as the actions they prohibit would themselves interfere with the actions of other persons; in such cases, the laws interfere with interferences to action, and hence remove obstructions to action. It has less frequently been noted, however, that laws may have a similar double relation to freedom when the obstacles to action with which the laws interfere are dispositional or institutional rather than occurrent. I shall deal with this relation in the context of civil liberties.

II. Freedom as Effective and Achievemental Powers

According to the above analysis, civil liberties are effective powers to perform or engage in a certain range of actions. The members of this range may be gathered from the Bill of Rights: they include the actions of speaking, publishing, assembling or associating with others, and so forth. For my present purposes it is not important to distinguish between "speech" and "action," since I am not here concerned with the problem of the justifiable limits on speech. In the generic sense, speaking is itself a kind of action. The freedoms to perform or engage in speaking and other kinds of action just mentioned are called "civil liberties" for two closely related reasons: because of the central socio-political importance of this range of actions, and because they are rights guaranteed by government. The crucial initial question concerns the nature of this guarantee.

The First Amendment provides that "Congress shall make no law . . . abridging" the freedoms of speech, press, and assembly. From this it has sometimes been inferred both that the freedoms in question consist simply in governmental non-interference (or non-abridgment) and that the government's guarantee of them consists solely in this pledge of non-interference. We have already seen sufficient grounds for rejecting the former inference: a person is not free to speak, for example, unless he has the effective power to speak; mere non-interference by other persons is not logically sufficient to constitute this freedom, although, of course, for every normal person non-interference from other persons is as a matter of fact a sufficient condition of his having the effective power to speak. As we shall see, however, in the complex political circumstances in which the civil liberties have one of their main fields of application, it cannot be granted that the effective power to speak requires only non-interference on the part of government.

Let us turn to the other inference drawn from the language of the First Amendment, that the government's guarantee of civil liberties consists only in its pledge or obligation not to interfere with their exercise. Doubt is cast on this inference by the fact that when civil liberties are threatened or interfered with by private persons, as when someone making a speech is attacked by persons who disapprove of what he is saying, the law intervenes to protect the speaker's right to talk. Thus the role of govern-

ment in relation to civil liberties is not only the negative one of non-
interference but also the positive one of protecting them from interference
on the part of other persons. It may be contended that the law's intervention to protect the speaker is a defense not of "civil liberties" but of "civil
rights," the distinction between these consisting precisely in the difference between warding off interference from government and from
private individuals. Logically, however, the only difference between the
concept of a liberty and the concept of a right is that the latter adds to the
former a normative element. To say that A is free to do x means, negatively, that no one interferes with A's doing x and, positively, that A has
the effective power to do x; while to say that A has a right to do x means,
negatively, that no one ought to interfere with A's doing x and, positively,
that A ought to have the effective power to do x (so that other persons
ought, if necessary, to see to it that A can do x). Hence, in protecting A's
right to speak against those who would interfere with it, the law protects a
liberty of A which it is legally recognized that he ought to have. And in the
example given, this is a civil liberty of A.

It has long been acknowledged that a chief (although not the sole) basis
of the government's obligation to protect civil liberties is their cardinal
importance for the democratic political process. Unless persons can
speak, write, publish, assemble, and associate without fear of interference
either by other persons or by government, the processes of discussion,
debate, and criticism which are essential to democracy cannot go on. Both
democracy and civil liberties are, indeed, susceptible of a deep kind of
justification which shows them to be inherently rational, in that attempts
to violate them can be convicted of a fundamental inconsistency. The
basis of this rationality is contained in what I have elsewhere called the
Principle of Generic Consistency: Apply to your recipient the same
generic features of action that you apply to yourself. In the present context, however, it is not necessary to go into the complicated philosophic
arguments which bear on these issues.[9] It is sufficient to emphasize that
the essential connection between civil liberties and the democratic political process holds regardless of which version of that process one accepts.
According to one version, the democratic process consists in a search for
the truth concerning those policies which will be most conducive to the
common good (or the public interest); according to another version, it
consists in the pressures exerted by competing groups with a view to the
state's adoption of policies most conducive to their respective group
interests. In either case, democratic political action involves using the
civil liberties with a view to effective advancement of one's views or
interests.

The relation of the civil liberties to democracy is hence a double one.

On the one hand, the civil liberties are "active" in that they consist in forms of action or effective power which function to determine who shall govern; on the other hand, they are "passive" in that they receive protection from those who govern. In both relations, moreover, the theory of democracy requires that the civil liberties pertain equally to every citizen: each citizen has an equal right to participate actively in the democratic process and to be protected by government in that participation. These equalities are susceptible of a rational justification similar to that which I said above could be provided for democracy and the civil liberties; but I shall also omit this here. Before going more fully into what ought to be the passive relations of civil liberties to government, we must examine more carefully the conceptual structure of civil liberties in their active relations. For in this latter respect, as kinds of action which operate in the context of the democratic process, the civil liberties involve some important qualifications in the general concept of freedom as I analyzed it above.

In the preceding section, the freedom to do x was defined as the effective power to do x, and "effective power" was equated with active or proximate power as distinguished from passive, remote, or latent power. A person was said to have the effective power to do x if his doing (or not doing) x depended on his own unforced choice, in that, given his unforced choice to do x, his doing x then occurred, so that he was not prevented from doing x or from not doing x by obstacles either internal or external to himself.

When we try to apply these definitions to civil liberties as they actively operate in the context of the democratic process, it appears that they must be sharply qualified in several respects, especially with regard to the concepts of "doing x" (or action) and of "effective power." Take, for example, freedom of speech, which according to the above account consists in having the effective power to speak. In the context of the democratic political process, speaking is not, like walking, a potentially private act. It is public and social, for it is addressed to other persons, and potentially to large multitudes. It is also teleological, in that it aims at an end other than the mere performance of the action. It is tendentious, in that its aim is to influence other persons as to how they shall think and act with respect to issues of social policy. And to have any realistic hope of succeeding in this aim in the conditions of modern society, political speaking requires abundant economic resources: to hire a hall or at least a sound truck, to buy time on television and space in newspapers or at least leaflets, and so forth. It is true that picketing, marching, demonstrating, sitting-in, and similar activities have at various times been judicially upheld as forms of speech protected by the First Amendment; and these, while of course social in nature and sharing the other characteristics of political speech just noted, may not require such elaborate economic resources. But, as is shown by the development and escalation of civil disobedience during the past decade, such activities are essentially localized and hence may have only a limited impact when wider sociopolitical issues are at stake.

If, then, the effective powers to speak and to publish in which the civil liberties consist have the social, teleological, and tendentious features just noted, and if in the political process the exercise of these powers requires such abundant economic resources if it is to have any chance of success, to what extent do the masses of the poor in our society, or even the bulk of ordinary citizens, have these civil liberties? In answer to this question, it may be held that it is important to distinguish between the concepts of effective *powers* and effective *actions*. According to the definition given above, a person has the effective power to speak if his speaking depends on his own choice, so that, among other things, he is not prevented from speaking by other persons, including the government. On the other hand, even if a person has the effective power to speak, his speaking may not itself be effective in that it does not achieve the goal he intends it to achieve. In other words, we must distinguish between being able to perform an action and succeeding in achieving the aim of that action, where the action is teleological in the sense indicated above. To illustrate this difference, we may distinguish between two different groups with regard to their possession of civil liberties. The members of the first group are prevented from speaking, publishing, and assembling in support of their views or interests. The prevention may come from governmental prohibitions and punishments, or from the threats or coercion of antagonistic private groups. The members of this group lack civil liberties in that they lack the effective power to speak, and so forth, in the social-public and tendentious ways we have seen to be essential to civil liberties in their political application. In contrast to this group, the members of a second group are not prevented from speaking and so forth, but they lack the economic resources required to compete on even terms with members of opposed groups; hence, their actions are not successful: the views or interests which they seek to promote by their speaking and writing do not prevail. Of the members of this group we may say that they do indeed have civil liberties, but that these are not effective, in that, while they have the effective *power* to speak, publish, and assemble, these *actions* of theirs are not themselves effective.

From this distinction it follows that persons may equally have civil liberties, defined as effective powers to speak and otherwise participate in the democratic political process, even if they do not equally have the economic resources to succeed in the aims of their speech. Moreover, these effective powers are good in themselves even if the persons who exercise them do not attain their tendentious objectives. All one need do to verify this is to consider the many groups in totalitarian societies and elsewhere who are legally or otherwise prevented from exercising these powers.

While this distinction is defensible and indeed important, it does not alter the fact that insofar as the actions which comprise the civil liberties are teleological and tendentious, effectively to have these liberties requires not merely the power to speak, publish, and so forth but also the power to succeed in the aims of one's speaking and publishing. I shall refer to the former of these powers as conative and to the latter as achievemental. They specify two different senses in which the civil liberties may be had as effective powers. The achievemental powers are comparative in a way in which the conative powers may not be; for to be able to succeed in one's efforts requires not only the exertion of effort but also a certain relation to possible obstacles or competitors, such that one is able to marshal relevant resources which are superior to those which would otherwise prevent one's success. Although, for a group to have effective achievemental powers, it need not always triumph over its opponents, it is safe to say that if the group never triumphs in relevant respects, then it lacks the effective achievemental powers which are proximately required for success.

In the achievemental sense, the exercise of the civil liberties by various groups is aimed directly at influencing governmental policy in the direction of their views and interests. The stake of the poor in such exercise is especially obvious because of their great and unfulfilled needs in such areas as health, food, education, child-care, and housing. There are wide disparities between the poor and the rich in respect of the distribution of such vital resources. These disparities are rightly decried as unjust, and it is rightly contended that, especially in a country which is still as wealthy as ours, top priority should be given to removing such disparities.

These substantive ends, however, are at once confronted by the procedural questions—questions of means. How, by what methods, should the goal of a greater approach to equal justice be realized, especially in the face of widespread indifference on the part of the more affluent groups? The traditional liberal answer, as my above remarks have suggested, is that the democratic process itself provides the means or methods in question, for this process allows every citizen to press his views and interests in the public forum and to unite with other, like-minded persons in free competition for votes to elect persons who will support the policies advocated by the respective group. In other words, it is alleged that in a democratic society like ours the universal availability of the civil liberties, in what has been called their active relation to government, provides a sufficient basis for confidence that the democratic process will be able to rectify the substantive injustices referred to above.

This answer, however, incurs the difficulty that the democratic process is itself characterized by the same inequalities as characterize the other, substantive aspects of American society. Just as the poor are at the low end of the distribution of other resources, so, largely for that very reason, the poor are at the low end of the distribution of political power, that is, the effective achievemental ability to participate in the political process in such fashion as to influence the outcome of that process in the direction of their own views and interests.[10] For to have this effective achievemental ability in the democratic process requires the use of such means of communication as the press and television, and to command these means of communication to the degree required for success requires superior economic resources. But the poor, lacking those resources, are at a great disadvantage in the political process, despite the fact that their basic needs are the greatest of all.

III. Inequalities in the Democratic Process

In view of these inequalities, what is the status of the claim just mentioned, that the civil liberties provide a sufficient basis for confidence that the democratic process will operate to rectify the injustices of the unequal fulfillment of basic needs caused by the unequal distribution of wealth? It now appears that the civil liberties, as effective achievemental powers, are caught in the same pattern of inequality and injustice as the substantive problems they were supposed to resolve. Hence, to appeal to the civil liberties to remedy the injustices of American society by way of the democratic process is to seek to lift oneself up by one's bootstraps.

These assertions of inequality and injustice, with their use of unanalyzed concepts of the "rich" and the "poor" raise, of course, many complex issues. While the assertions of inequality may be accepted on factual grounds, it may be contended, in particular, that the economic inequalities in American society stem from the differentially effective use which different persons and groups make of their freedom, so that to decry or to try to reduce the inequalities is to threaten the relevant freedoms. It may be added that the inequalities in the effective use of civil liberties are part and parcel of the structure of such individual freedom, so that to try to introduce equality in this area is to interfere with the civil liberties of the persons who have the ability to use them more effectively. More generally, it may be conceded that political power varies with economic power, and that to try to reduce the effects of the latter is to interfere with the legitimate use of the political process on the part of the more advantaged groups.

Although these contentions deserve fuller scrutiny than I can give them here, it can be cogently argued that the unequal distribution of the civil liberties as effective achievemental powers in the political process is unjust in several respects. It fails to correspond to the basic needs of the persons concerned, and indeed it contributes to drastic violations of the basic needs of the poor. The unequal distribution also fails to correspond to the relative merits of the persons concerned, for it can hardly be maintained that all members of the respective groups deserve the markedly differential status they occupy in respect of wealth. Most basically, perhaps, the unequal distribution of the civil liberties as effective achievemental powers is unjust because it fails to correspond to the equal rights of each person to a degree of freedom and well-being consistent with his human dignity as a potential self-determining agent.

The question, then, is whether and how this methodological injustice within the democratic process can be remedied. Here I suggest, as one important possibility, that we turn from the "active" to the "passive" relation of the civil liberties to democratic government. In the passive relation, the various liberties are protected and fostered by government. As we have seen there is a widespread theory, derived in part from the language of the First Amendment and more generally from a traditional conception of freedom, that this passive relation of the civil liberties to government should be only negative, in that government should simply refrain from abridging or otherwise putting obstacles in the way of persons' speaking, publishing, and so forth. This hands-off policy, however, serves to permit the existing distribution of economic resources in the society to work itself out in the political sphere: the political effectiveness of the civil liberties is itself distributed largely in accordance with the existing distribution of economic resources. I suggest, then, that the passive relation of civil liberties to government should also be positive, in that government should affirmatively intervene to remove not only occurrent but also dispositional or institutional obstacles to poor persons' exercising their civil liberties in the democratic process with an effectiveness equal to that of the affluent.

The precise scope and method of such intervention involve, of course, many detailed problems. But one relevant possibility is that the Federal government, recognizing how the inequalities in respect of the effective use of civil liberties drastically mar the conception of procedural justice which we attribute to our political process, would make television time, newspaper space, and the like freely available to groups of the poor, designated by certain methods to be spelled out. These groups would then have at their disposal more regularized methods of public communication than the sit-ins, marches, demonstrations, and near or actual riots which have hitherto been the only means effectively available to them to press their claims of justice in the public forum. What is sought is not an unattainable absolute equality of effective influence for each person in the informal political process leading to the casting of the vote, but rather a closer approach to equality in this area on the part of the economically disadvantaged groups in the society. The aim is to make far more available to such groups the effective ability to press their claims in public communication, and hence to make their civil liberties more nearly equal to those of richer groups as effective achievemental powers toward fulfilling their goals.

At this point, however, we seem to recur to the bootstrap problem that I mentioned before. The sequence of my argument has been, first, that to rectify the substantive injustices of American society it is not enough to appeal to the equal availability of the civil liberties as active procedural determinants in the democratic political process, for those liberties when properly viewed as effective achievemental powers are themselves unjustly distributed. But now, secondly, I have appealed to a positive functioning of government to rectify those procedural injustices. The obvious question that arises here is, of course, that in pushing the situation back to this step, aren't we confronted with the same difficulty all over again? Since it is the operations of the civil liberties which are held to determine the policies and personnel of government, will not those policies and personnel in turn reflect the very injustices of those operations or procedures? It is this question which leads many inquirers to hold that some non-democratic method, such as revolution or violence, must be used to break this circle of injustices, just as Rousseau, to cite an earlier example, appealed to what he called a *législateur* and what we would call a moral-political elite to effect the required transformation.

While this problem of circularity or of the bootstrap is indeed very serious, I suggest that the analysis sketched above indicates ways of resolving it. Two main points are especially important. One bears on a suggestion just made in citing Rousseau. There are already moral forces at work in American society which can be used to help effect the needed procedural and structural changes. I refer in particular to the various public interest groups, like the American Civil Liberties Union, Public Citizen, Common Cause, and other organizations which act, in part, as advocates of the poor. There are also precedents in recent American history, such as the Community Action Programs which had as their purported aims to bring about "maximal feasible participation of . . . the groups served" in coping with their substantive problems of poverty.[11]

The failure of these programs provides instructive lessons for future efforts at increasing for the poor their effective use of civil liberties.[12]

A second main point of the above analysis which bears importantly on the bootstrap problem is the central place of the concept of justice. The bootstrap problem arises when the political process is viewed as a battle of opposed forces each of which seeks to promote its respective interests. On such a view, there is no way of breaking out of the circle whereby the stronger force—which usually means the economically dominant force—carries the day, regardless of the level at which one tries to break the circle. This is, indeed, an eminently realistic view of the political process. There are times, however, when moral considerations of justice may themselves carry great weight in the political process, and thereby help to break the circle wherein economic power is decisive. It may be questioned whether such moral considerations can triumph without the marches, demonstrations, and possibly the civil disobedience whereby the poor bring their claims to the attention of the affluent majority. What is crucially important here, however, is that the claims in question be explicitly advanced and elucidated as claims of justice and not merely of force. Such moral elucidation was strongly influential in bringing about the far-reaching Voting Rights Act of 1965, an act whereby the government took important steps toward equalizing civil liberties insofar as they are directly reflected in the electoral process. I suggest, then, that further progress can be made by calling explicit attention to the unfinished business of justice in respect of the civil liberties as effective achievemental powers in the political process.

As was noted above, governmental action may serve to expand as well as to restrict freedom, by interfering with interferences with men's actions. Since interferences with or obstacles to men's equally effective use of the civil liberties derive largely from their economic inequalities, taxation which reduces the inequality of men's economic resources would help to make less unequal the effectiveness of their use of civil liberties. There are, however, several more direct ways of effecting such civil-libertarian equalization. One, already mentioned, is by making available to groups of the poor, without charge, sufficient newspaper space and television time to enable them to press their views and interests in public forums to a far greater extent than is available to them at present. Another way is to cut down the effectiveness of superior wealth in political communication by sharply restricting the amount of money that can be spent by candidates for office.[13] These and other methods would interfere with the freedom of the rich to maximize the effectiveness of their use of their civil liberties; but by the same token they would increase the freedom or effective power of the poor in this respect.

These methods of equalizing the effective political use of civil liberties may be approached either legislatively or judicially. The legislative approach would be continuous with the attempt made to protect the right to vote on the part of blacks and other minorities in the Civil Rights Acts of 1957, 1960, and 1964 and the Voting Rights Act of 1965. These laws, by prohibiting not only violence but also literacy tests, poll taxes, and other means that had been used to deny the vote to blacks, sought to assure effective equality of voting rights for all citizens. Without disputing the enormous importance of these provisions, a case can be made that the equal right to vote presupposes the equal right to make effective use of one's civil liberties in support of the objects of one's vote, that is, the candidates whose policies one favors. Voting may in this regard be viewed as the culminating act of the political process so far as this involves participation by the ordinary citizen, and the earlier phases of the process, including the use of various methods of communication to influence the voters' views, may exert a strong influence on the direction of that culminating act. The civil liberties are the means, equally guaranteed to all citizens, for using these methods of communication. But if, as is in fact the case, economic inequalities produce drastic inequalities in the ability to make effective use of civil liberties for this purpose, the result is that the effectiveness of the equal right to vote is sharply reduced. Hence, the logic of the various legislative enactments for assuring equality in the right to vote provides a ground for supporting further legislative enactments for assuring equality in the right to make effective use of one's civil liberties in the political process.

There are also grounds for supporting a judicial approach to equalizing the effective use of civil liberties in the political process. The Fourteenth Amendment's provision for equal protection of the laws has been used by the Supreme Court to declare unconstitutional a state's requiring payment of a poll tax as a prerequisite to voting.[14] Citizens are denied the equal protection of the laws if persons with low economic resources are denied equal access to the ballot box with those of higher incomes. It could, I think, be argued with some plausibility that citizens are also denied the equal protection of the laws if persons with higher incomes are allowed to have stronger influence in the political process which culminates in the ballot box. Another, although perhaps less direct, analogue of the judicial intervention here proposed in the political process is found in the various reapportionment cases where the Supreme Court has held that the equal protection of the laws requires that each person's vote count equally with each other person's, so that congressional and state legislative districts must contain numerically equal populations so far as possible.[15] Again, there is justification in arguing that the right to an equally counting vote implies the right to an equally effective use of the legally available influence-producing preliminaries to voting.

In conclusion, I want to connect the suggestions just made with my earlier general discussion of the concept of freedom. The poverty which afflicts sizeable groups in our society and which drastically reduces the effective achievemental power of their civil liberties in the political process derives from a set of humanly-caused institutions which constitute dispositional obstacles to the ability to act on the part of the poor. The positive governmental policies just suggested should be viewed, then, as attempts to expand the freedom of the poor at a crucial point, for their aim is to remove the impact of these obstacles on such groups' effective ability to participate more equally in the democratic process.

My argument in this paper has proceeded within the assumptions of a constitutional democracy, with its framework of legally guaranteed rights and coercive laws emanating from a government whose authority rests on the democratic electoral process. Critics from the side of radical libertarianism will charge that I have gone much too far in the direction of governmental intervention in people's lives, while critics from the side of communism in one or another of its varieties will maintain that I have not gone nearly far enough. Within the confines of the present paper I cannot cope with the details of these criticisms; but I may at least note that the assumptions of each side are morally unacceptable for ultimately the same reason, that they would eventuate directly or indirectly in excessive power—economic or political or both—for some groups over others. On this as well as on other grounds, a constitutional democracy is morally preferable. The urgent task is to deal constructively with its pressing problems of the extent and distribution of freedom and well-being; and the present paper is offered as a contribution to remedying a basic phase of these problems.

Notes

1. For an examination of these general criteria, and especially the principle of equal freedom, see my "Political Justice" (in R. B. Brandt, ed., *Social Justice* [Englewood Cliffs, N.J.: Prentice-Hall, 1962], pp. 141–154), and *Political Philosophy* (New York: The Macmillan Co. 1965), pp. 25–28.

2. I Berlin, *Four Essays on Liberty* (London: Oxford University Press, 1969), p. 122.

3. E. F. Carritt, "Liberty and Equality," *Law Quarterly Review*, vol. 56 (1940); reprinted in A. Quinton, ed., *Political Philosophy* (London: Oxford University Press, 1967), p. 133.

4. For the reference to "wishes" and "choices" in Berlin, see his statements that oppression—the removal of freedom—consists in "frustrating my *wishes*" and that "The sense of freedom, in which I use this term, entails not simply the absence of frustration (which may be obtained by killing desires), but the absence of obstructions on roads along which a man can *decide* to walk" (*op. cit.*, pp. xxxix, 123; my emphasis in each quotation.).

5. Although Gerald C. MacCallum, Jr., in "Negative and Positive Freedom" (*Philosophical Review*, vol. 76 [1967], pp. 312 ff.), denies that there is a useful distinction between negative and positive concepts of freedom, he does not explicitly deal with the questions about their relation which I here discuss.

6. See, for example, F. E. Oppenheim, *Dimensions of Freedom* (New York: St. Martin's Press, 1961), pp. 119; 121: "Our set of definitions leads to another, more controversial implication, namely that X is free to do x, not only if X can do x with impunity, but also if he cannot do x provided this impossibility has not been caused by any particular person or group . . . I realize that one might feel uneasy about calling workers living on starvation wages free to become millionaires, and children whose parents cannot afford to send them to school free to become fully educated. It would, of course, be a poor argument to uphold this interpretation simply because it follows from the proposed definitions."

7. For this argument as well as the following one, see W. L. Weinstein, "The Concept of Liberty in Nineteenth Century English Political Thought," *Political Studies*, vol. 13 (1965), pp. 151–152.

8. Cf. Berlin, *op. cit.*, pp. 131–132: "The freedom which consists in being one's own master, and the freedom which consists in not being prevented from choosing as I do by other men, may, on the face of it, seem concepts at no great logical distance from each other—no more than negative and positive ways of saying much the same thing."

9. I have presented such arguments in "Categorial Consistency in Ethics," *Philosophical Quarterly*, vol 17 (1967), pp. 289–299; "Obligation: Political, Legal, Moral," *Nomos*, vol. 12 (1970), pp. 55–88; "The Justification of Egalitarian Justice," *American Philosophical Quarterly*, vol. 8 (1971), pp. 331–341; and "The 'Is-Ought' Problem Resolved," *Proceedings and Addresses of the American Philosophical Association*, vol. 47 (1974), pp. 34–61.

10. For a recent empirical analysis of the relevant correlations, see Sidney Verba and Norman H. Nie, *Participation in America: Political Democracy and Social Equality* (New York: Harper and Row, 1972), esp. Ch. 20.

11. *Economic Opportunity Act of 1964*, Title II (U.S. Government Printing Office, Washington, D.C.).

12. For two views of this failure, see David Stoloff, "The Short Unhappy History of Community Action Programs," in M. E. Gettleman and D. Mermelstein, eds. *The Failure of American Liberalism: After the Great Society* (New York: Vintage Books, 1971), pp. 232–239; Daniel P. Moynihan, *Maximum Feasible Misunderstanding: Community Action in the War on Poverty* (New York: Free Press, 1969).

13. A step has been taken in this direction by the Federal Election Campaign Act Amendments of 1974 (Public Law 93–443). For a critical discussion, see Marc F. Plattner, "Campaign Financing: the Dilemmas of Reform," *The Public Interest*, No. 37 (Fall, 1974), pp. 112–130.

14. *Harper v. Virginia Board of Elections*, 383 U.S. 663.

15. *Baker v. Carr*, 369 U.S. 186 (1962); *Reynolds v. Sims*, 377 U.S. (1964).

14
Reasons and Conscience:
The Claims of the
Selective Conscientious Objector

Should selective conscientious objectors be exempted from military service? This question asks about the justification of imposing a certain limit on the legal obligation of all draft-age male citizens to perform military service as required by the conscription law. The criteria used in answering this question of justification may be of different kinds, including especially the legal and constitutional standards applied by the Supreme Court in reaching its decisions on the issue. But ultimately the criteria must be moral ones by which those standards and decisions are themselves evaluated. This is true not only on various grounds deriving from the concept of morality, but also because the selective conscientious objector bases his claim to exemption from military service on moral reasons bearing on what he believes to be the moral wrongness of the particular war in which he is asked to fight. Now moral criteria and reasons may themselves be of different kinds. In the following inquiry into the moral justification of the selective conscientious objector's claim, I shall confine myself for the most part to various middle-level principles or criteria on which there is considerable agreement, although some of the main problems arise from conflicts among these criteria. In dealing with such conflicts I shall implicitly appeal to what I have elsewhere called the Principle of Categorial Consistency, which requires, in its individual application, that an agent respect his recipients' freedom and welfare as well as his own, and in its social application, that policies and institutions serve to foster equal freedom and mutual accommodation of wants and purposes among human beings.[1]

I

In order to be clear about the nature and merits of the selective conscientious objector's claim that the law's failure to exempt him from military service in some particular war is morally unjustified, we must distinguish this claim from the claims of three other sorts of social protesters or dissidents: the anarchist, the revolutionary, and the civil disobedient. Although selective conscientious objectors may be anarchists, or revolutionaries, or civil disobedients, in these cases their claims are of a more general nature than those which characterize the selective conscientious objector as such. All four of these types of dissident may be defined in terms of moral opposition to the law, but they differ in respect of the specific reasons on which they ground this opposition, and this difference is reflected in the distinct aspects of law to which they object. To see this, we must note that the word 'law,' even when confined to municipal law, is used with three different kinds of reference which must be carefully distinguished.[2] 'Law' is used to refer (1) to a general social institution which is common to all societies which have even minimal legal systems; (2) to one or another specific legal system which may differ from other legal systems in its contents and procedures; and (3) to some particular legal rule or rules which may exist within the same or different legal systems. I shall indicate these three kinds of reference of 'law' by using the subscripts 1, 2, and 3. Thus, in the first reference ('law$_1$') we talk of law as against, for example, religion or etiquette as a kind of social institution and as a method of social

1. For arguments toward and analyses of this principle, see my "Categorial Consistency in Ethics," *Philosophical Quarterly*, vol. 17 (1967), pp. 289-99; "Obligation: Political, Legal, Moral," *Nomos*, vol. 12 (1970), pp. 55-88; "The Justification of Egalitarian Justice," *American Philosophical Quarterly*, vol. 8 (1971), pp. 331-41; "Moral Rationality," The Lindley Lecture for 1972, University of Kansas.

2. I have previously discussed these distinctions in "Obligation: Political, Legal, Moral" (cited above, note 1), at pp. 74 ff.

regulation, namely, that institution and method which consist in coercively binding and publicly promulgated general rules for regulating violence and other socially important situations. In the second reference ('law$_2$') we talk of United States law, Soviet law, and the like. And in the third reference ('law$_3$') we talk of the United States income tax laws, the conscription law, and so forth.

Now the anarchist, the revolutionary, and the selective conscientious objector are morally opposed, respectively, to law$_1$, to a certain law$_2$, and to a certain law$_3$. Confusion results when these three different bases of opposition are indiscriminately intermingled, as they sometimes are even by otherwise quite intelligent supporters of exempting selective conscientious objectors from military service. Some such supporters, in their zeal to defend selective exemption, take the anarchistic position that there is no moral justification for imposing any legal obligations at all in the sense of coercive requirements set by law$_1$: they hold, indeed, that no governments have any moral right to force people to do things against their will. For example, one writer asserts that "a democratic society should not require its citizens to violate their deeply held principles."[3] If the writer meant this literally, he would not be able to say, as he does a few pages later, that "committed racists" should be forced to pay their taxes even though they object strongly to some uses to which the taxes are put.[4] Since, then, he recognizes that a democratic society is at least sometimes justified in requiring its citizens to violate their deeply held principles, he cannot use an anarchistic opposition to law$_1$ itself as a basis for supporting the exemption of selective conscientious objectors from military service.

Other proponents of such exemption seem to base their views on a revolutionary opposition to our law$_2$ insofar as this consists in the American constitutional system. They hold that the legal compulsion to perform military service is not justified within our present constitutional system because that system is itself morally

3. Michael Harrington, "Politics, Morality, and Selective Dissent," in *A Conflict of Loyalties: The Case for Selective Conscientious Objection* edited by James Finn (New York: Pegasus, 1968), p. 227.
4. *Ibid.*, p. 232.

unjustified. In support of this charge they point, in particular, to the severe inequalities which the system permits in the distribution of economic and political power; and they assert that these are intimately connected with our repressions of foreign national liberation movements in general and with the Vietnam War in particular. (The iniquities of the Vietnam War have, of course, provided the greatest impetus to selective conscientious objection.) While there is, I think, much that is sound in this contention, it is important to be clear about whether one's support of the selective conscientious objector is based on advocacy of revolutionary change of our whole legal system, i.e. our law_2, including its Bill of Rights and its provisions for equal protection of the laws and so forth; or whether one opposes only some $laws_3$ or particular institutions within the whole system. If one opposes our law_2, this would indicate at least a severe qualification of whatever support one might seek from the constitutional provisions for religious freedom, due process, and equal protection which undergird many arguments in support of the selective conscientious objector. This point can be accepted even if one recognizes, as surely one must, the serious gaps between formal constitutional provisions and institutional realities. On the other hand, it is possible, without contradiction, to regard our law_2, or at least basic parts of it, as morally justified while regarding as morally unjustified some particular law_3, such as that which denies exemption from military service to the selective conscientious objector. One obvious reason why there is no contradiction here is that the relation of law_3 to law_2 is not a deductive one: at least our law_2 gives leeway for many different $laws_3$, none of which follow logically from the general framework set by our law_2.

Let us now look briefly at the relation between the selective conscientious objector and the civil disobedient. There are two main potential differences between them, one bearing on what they oppose, the other on how they carry out their opposition. While the civil disobedient, like the selective conscientious objector, is usually morally opposed to a particular law_3, the targets of his opposition may also be broader. They may extend from the whole law_2 of his society to certain official policies or $laws_3$ which he contends are basically illegal because unconstitutional. In the latter case, the civil disobedient, unlike the selective objector, holds that what he opposes is not a valid law_3 at all; familiar examples of this were the segregation ordinances in the South. To be sure, some selective objectors similarly criticized the conscription laws related to the Vietnam War on such grounds, maintaining that the war itself was unconstitutional because not declared by Congress. Still, the basic issues of selective conscientious objection go beyond this particular contention. Moreover, even when the civil disobedient's target is some particular law_3 which he admits to be valid, this may be something other than the law_3 bearing on military service in a particular war which is the specific target of the selective conscientious objector. Examples of these other $laws_3$ include ordinances requiring school attendance and setting school boundaries, income tax laws, eviction orders, civil rights laws, and many others.

In addition to these potential differences as to the laws or policies to which they are respectively opposed, the civil disobedient also differs from the selective conscientious objector with respect to the way in which he carries out his opposition. The civil disobedient, by definition, disobeys either the law to which he objects or some other law, but this is not necessarily true of the selective conscientious objector. The latter may, indeed, refuse the induction into the armed forces which he is legally obligated to accept. But unlike the civil disobedient, he may refrain from making a public issue of this refusal and of the grounds for it; he may also seek to evade the penalty by hiding, emigrating, or other non-public methods; and he may even, with a heavy heart, accept induction. Objection, then, may but need not go so far as disobedience; and when it does, it need not be civil in the sense of accepting the legally prescribed penalty.

Beside these differences in the objects and the methods of the respective protests of the civil disobedient and the selective conscientious objector, there is also frequently a difference in the main justificatory question which is raised about each of them. With respect to the civil disobedient, the main question raised is whether and when his disobedience is itself justified; it is usually taken for granted that the state will proceed to punish him, although recently the justification and degree of this punishment have also been discussed. With respect to the selective conscientious objector, on the other hand, the main question raised has been not whether he is justified in his objection to serving in the particular war he opposes and in carrying out his objection by refusing to serve, but whether the government and the law are justified in not exempting him from this requirement of military service. In other words, in the case of civil disobedience the main justificatory question bears on the protester himself, while in the case of selective conscientious objection the main justificatory question bears rather on the law's requirement about the protester. The chief reason for this difference is that, on the one hand, it is usually held that there is a *prima facie* obligation to obey the law, at least in a constitutional democracy, so that the civil disobedient's refusal to do so requires justification. But on the other hand, it is usually held, at least in our tradition, that conscientious objection to military service deserves respect because of the high value placed on the individual conscience, so that the law's failure to grant this objection is what requires justification. One result of this tradition, however, has been that the specific reasons or grounds for conscientious objection have received very little justificatory scrutiny on their own account. But in the case of the selective conscientious objector, it is precisely these reasons that assume central importance.

Hence, while recognizing that the claims of the civil disobedient, like those of the anarchist and the revolutionary, point to serious problems, I shall focus primarily on the specific issues raised by the selective conscientious objector in respect of a particular law$_3$. Our chief question, then, is this: even if there is a moral justification for the obligations set both by law$_1$, or law in general, and by our law$_2$, the American constitutional system, is there also a moral justification for the obligation set by the particular law$_3$ which requires that selective conscientious objectors not be exempted from military service? At the appropriate point, I shall also consider whether the objector is justified as to his reasons for opposing some particular war.

In order to cope with the issues posed by this question, we must distinguish four main variables that enter into the general area where some person conscientiously objects to performing some legally obligatory action. These variables are, first, the nature of the *action* which persons are legally obligated to perform, and which they object to performing; second, the *conscientiousness* of their objection; third, the *grounds or reasons* on which they base their objections to performing that action; and fourth, the *consequences* of whatever policies are followed in this area, including especially the consequences of legally granting the objection, that is, of legally allowing persons to be exempt from performing the actions which they are otherwise legally obligated to perform, where these consequences are of two main kinds: distributive, involving the distribution of various goods and evils among individual persons, and aggregative, involving the summing of goods or utilities for the society as a whole. I shall refer to these four variables, respectively, as the Action Variable, the Conscience Variable, the Reason Variable, and the Consequence Variable.

The dispute over selective conscientious objection most directly concerns the Action Variable. With respect to this variable, the question is: Is it morally justified that conscientious objectors be exempted from military service only if the actions they object to performing comprise *all* military acts, that is, all participation in war; or is it sufficient if the actions they object to performing comprise only *some* military acts, that is, participation only in some particular war or wars? I shall now develop my answer to this question by considering it within two distinct contexts, one relative or comparative, the other absolute.

II

The relative or comparative context involves the comparison of the selective conscientious objector with the universal conscientious objector. My point here is that if the universal conscientious objector's exemption from his legal obligation to perform military service is morally justified, then so too is the selective conscientious objector's exemption. All the grounds for exempting the former tell also in favor of exempting the latter.

In order to come to somewhat fuller grips with this thesis and with some of the controversial issues it raises, let us look at one of the chief arguments presented by persons who support the universal objector's exemption while opposing the selective objector's exemption. Justice Thurgood Marshall, speaking for the Court in the 1971 Gillette decision, cited the 1967 Report of the National Advisory Commission on Selective Service which opposed exempting the selective objector on the ground that "legal recognition of selective pacifism could open the doors to a general theory of selective disobedience to law, which could quickly tear down the fabric of government," and thus "jeopardize the binding quality of democratic decisions."[5] This argument, it will be noted, focuses on what I have called the Consequence Variable, i.e. on the consequences of exempting the selective objector from military service. And as can be seen from the argument's reference to a "general theory of selective disobedience to law," there is an implicit appeal here to a universalization principle. In terms of this principle, the argument may be stated as follows: If it is right that one person be exempted from some legal obligation on the ground that he is conscientiously opposed to fulfilling it, then it must be right that every other conscientious opponent be exempted on this ground. But if such general exemption from legal obligations were permitted, this would make it impossible to have a society regulated by law. For it is a necessary condition of such a society that laws have universal coercive force in the society, i.e. that all persons in the society be required to obey legal rules even when they conscientiously disapprove of them or oppose them, so long as the rules in question have been established as laws by the constitutionally prescribed procedures. Hence, to drop this requirement of obedience for certain individuals in the face of their conscientious opposition would mean that laws would no longer have universal coercive force: there would be only *selective* obedience to law, and hence also selective *disobedience*. But, the argument continues, this would mean that there would be no law

5. Report of the National Advisory Commission on Selective Service, *In Pursuit of Equity: Who Serves When Not All Serve?* (Washington, D.C.: U.S. Government Printing Office, 1967), p. 50; *United States v. Gillette*, 401 U.S. 459 (1971).

at all, since there would no longer remain the element of coercive-
ness, the requirement of obedience even in the face of vehement
personal opposition or disapproval. But this would be anarchy.
Consequently, it cannot be right that any person be exempted
from his legal obligation on the ground that he is conscientiously
opposed to fulfilling it. Therefore, the selective conscientious objector should not be exempted from his legal obligation to perform military service.

The usual replies given to this argument by proponents of exempting the selective conscientious objector comprise two main
contentions. First, they point out that the argument tells just as
much against the universal conscientious objector to military
service as against the selective objector. For the universal objector also claims, and the conscription laws and the Supreme Court
have upheld his claim, that he should be exempted from fulfilling
a certain legal obligation—that of rendering military service—on
the ground that he is conscientiously opposed to fulfilling it.
Hence, those who present the universalization argument just
cited ought logically to admit that the anarchic consequence they
fear from exempting the selective conscientious objector applies
just as much to the case of exempting the universal conscientious
objector.

How can this contention be dealt with by persons who present
the universalization argument? They can, and do, try to distinguish in various ways between the cases of the universal and the
selective objector to military service, and this primarily in terms
of further aspects of the Consequence Variable. They assert that
it would be more difficult to administer fairly a provision exempting the selective objector than one exempting only the universal
objector; that military morale would suffer much more if selective as well as universal objectors were exempted; and in general
that many more persons would be exempted, thereby weakening
much more the whole coercive structure of democratic law. Thus,
with respect to the antecedent of the universalization argument
as originally stated—"If it is right that one person be exempted
from some legal obligation on the ground that he is conscientiously opposed to fulfilling it, . . ."—those who present the ar-

gument insist that the antecedent, in order to be cogent against
the selective but not the universal objector, must be filled out in
such a way as to take account of these differences, so that the argument must be stated somewhat as follows: If it is right that one
person be exempted from some legal obligation on the ground
that he is conscientiously opposed to fulfilling it, *and* if the exemption can be granted with no unfortunate consequences bearing on the difficulty of fairly administering the exemption, the
lowering of military morale, and the weakening of the whole coercive structure of democratic law from an undue increase in the
number of persons exempted, then it must be right that every
other conscientious opponent be exempted on this ground *so long
as* the unfortunate consequences just mentioned are not likely to
ensue.

This attempt to distinguish between the cases of the universal
and the selective conscientious objector focuses on important considerations, and must be taken seriously. But I think that, by and
large, it does not succeed.[6] There is no reason to think that it
would be more difficult to administer exemptions for the selective
than for the universal objector, or that military morale would
suffer, or that the number of persons exempted would be unduly
increased. The example of Britain, which provides for selective
exemptions, affords confirming evidence for this.[7] In addition, it
must be noted that an increase in the number of persons exempted from the legal obligation of military service would not,
strictly speaking, entail any increase in persons exempted from
the coercive structure of democratic law. The assertion of this entailment rests on a confusion between law_3 and law_2. The selective
objector's exemption from military service would be made by a
particular law_3 which qualifies an antecedent law_3; but such qualification would itself be in accordance with law_2.

6. Thus I agree with David Malament's arguments in "Selective Conscientious
Objection and the *Gillette* Decision," *Philosophy and Public Affairs*, I, 4
(Summer 1972). See also the valuable discussion of this question in Ralph
Potter, "Conscientious Objection to Particular Wars," in Donald A. Gianella,
Religion and the Public Order, No. 4 (Ithaca, N.Y.: Cornell University Press,
1968), pp. 92-95.
7. See Denis Hayes, *Challenge of Conscience: The Story of the Conscientious
Objectors of 1939-1949* (London: George Allen & Unwin, 1949), ch. 5.

One point should be added, bearing on the difficulty of administering exemptions for selective objectors—and this concerns the Reason Variable. By comparison with the universal objector, the selective objector will often have more complex reasons for objecting to military service, based on his specific analyses of particular aspects of our foreign policy, including its history and purposes. These are usually subjects of intense political partisanship, and it may often be difficult for the members of a draft board to hear them out dispassionately. It is this point, among others, that leads opponents of exempting selective objectors to refer to the latter's reasons as being "political," as against "religious" or "moral." But there are at least two confusions in the way in which the Supreme Court has drawn this distinction between the political and the moral. First, it confuses the nature of the *subject-matter* in question—in this case, political or governmental policies and institutions—with the nature of the *judgments* that are made about that subject-matter—in this case, moral judgments. A judgment may be moral, or for that matter, religious, with respect to its motivation or the reasons on which it is based, bearing on considerations of justice and welfare, regardless of whether its subject-matter—that about which it judges—is political, social, or economic institutions, or individual actions, or many other things. In a parallel way, a judgment may be a political one in two quite different respects: first, with respect to the governmental subject-matter about which it makes a judgment; second, with respect to the personal motivations or reasons for which it is itself made. I can make a judgment about a political, i.e. governmental subject-matter without having a personal political motivation in that sense of 'political' in which it refers to partisan purposes of obtaining power or influence over other persons.

A second confusion in the Supreme Court's way of distinguishing between moral and political judgments bears on the interpretation it gives of the moral. The Court, influenced strongly by past traditions of universal objectors, seems to hold that for a judgment about the wrongness of war to be genuinely a moral one, it must be intuitionist or deontological in some very simple way. So soon as reasons for opposing war are introduced of a greater degree of complexity than "my church—or my conscience

—tells me it's wrong," the Court finds that the resulting judgments become political rather than moral. This ignores, of course, the fact that a moral judgment may often be based on a careful examination of facts bearing on the subject-matter which is judged.

I conclude, then, that the opposition to selective exemption which is based on the above universalization argument fails in its attempt to dispose of the first reply given to the argument by proponents of exempting selective conscientious objectors—the reply, namely, that the argument tells as much against the universal as against the selective conscientious objector. But this point, far from leaving the selective objector in the clear so far as concerns the justification of his being exempted from military service, rather puts both him and the universal objector under the anarchic suspicion emphasized by the above universalization argument. For the selective objector is now in the position of placing both himself and the universal objector under the same principle: that it is right that persons be exempted from fulfilling some legal obligation insofar as they are conscientiously opposed to fulfilling it. To ward off the potentially anarchic implication of this principle, proponents of selective conscientious objection offer a second reply, which focuses on the Action Variable—that is, the specific kind of action which they are legally obligated to perform and which they object to performing. They emphasize that there is a drastic difference between the kinds of actions which the legal obligation of military service requires and the kinds required by other legal obligations, including the paying of taxes, the obeying of civil rights laws, and so forth. Military service involves, at least potentially, killing other persons. Nothing of comparable seriousness is involved in the actions required by other legal obligations. Hence, the universalization argument fails, for it does not take account of this decisive difference. Properly stated, the argument should say: If it is right that one person be exempted—not from some or any legal obligation to which he conscientiously objects, but—from the legal obligation to perform military service with its potential killing of other persons to which he conscientiously objects, then it must be right that every other conscientious opponent of performing military service be exempted. Since the exemptions from legal obligation which are here in question are limited in this way to military actions, they do not have the anarchic implications stressed by proponents of the above universalization argument.

This second reply to the universalization argument is sound, but it raises at least three difficulties for the selective objector. First, persons opposed to various other laws, such as civil rights laws, could argue, emphasizing both the Conscience and the Action Variables, that the actions which these laws require of them offend against their conscience as vehemently as military killing offends against the selective objector's conscience. The latter could perhaps answer this by holding that the issue concerns not merely the subjective impact of actions on conscience but rather the objective status of actions. However much racists, for example, are horrified by having to act in accordance with civil rights laws, their horror does not remove the fact that military killing is an infinitely more serious kind of action.

This point raises, however, a second difficulty for the selective objector. If military service involves potential killing, then it also involves potentially being killed. How fair is it, then, that some qualified persons be exempted from this danger while others are not? So far, this difficulty applies, of course, to the universal conscientious objector as well as to the selective objector. In addition, however, it has been held that to make exemptions from military service available to selective objectors would wrongly favor one stratum of the population over other strata, since it would introduce a serious "class bias." For only better-educated young men have the greater specific knowledge and perhaps greater articulateness that would be required in order to make good their claim to exemption on grounds of objecting to a particular war.[8] The implication here is that no comparable expertise or favorable cultural background enters into the exempting conditions for universal conscientious objectors. Now this consideration of fairness is indeed very important. But it applies in a

8. See Michael Walzer, *Obligations: Essays on Disobedience, War, and Citizenship* (New York: Simon and Schuster, 1971), pp. 142 ff.

parallel way to those universal objectors whose consciences have been formed under the influence of a particular religious upbringing not available to other persons. In addition, improving the level of education in the country at large should serve to equalize the abilities relevant to arguing for exemption on grounds of objection to a particular war.

It still remains the case, however, that, by the admission of both the universal and the selective objector (as conveyed by their distinction between killing and other actions), they seek exemption from a danger that goes beyond all others. The universal objector could, of course, meet this point by emphasizing his universal pacifism: he advocates that all military killing cease. The selective objector, however, does not have this way out—and this raises a third difficulty for him. For, unlike the universal objector, he does not object to all wars or to all military killing but only to such killing in certain wars to which he is opposed for moral reasons. Hence, he cannot make opposition to military killing as such the decisive factor in his claim to exemption from military service; this opposition figures only in combination with the reasons for which he objects to the particular war in question. It is this emphasis on more specific reasons which especially distinguishes the selective from the universal objector. Hence, the Action Variable, bearing on the sort of legally obligatory action which he objects to performing, must here be supplemented by consideration of the Reason Variable.

III

It will be best to deal with this point in connection with my second context, the absolute one. I call this context absolute because it does not, like the relative or comparative context, focus primarily on comparing the cases of the selective and the universal objector; it is rather concerned directly with the moral justifiability of exempting the selective objector, especially as this is affected by the moral quality of the war to which he is opposed and of the reasons on which he bases his opposition. In this context, I shall consider two main alternatives: one where the war in question is morally wrong or unjust, the other where it is morally right or just.

It may be contended that these alternatives are too simple, because all wars involve many moral ambiguities, so that it is a matter of more or less rightness and wrongness, not all of one or all of the other. While there is much truth to this, the fact still remains that because of the violent impact of war on human life and liberty, any particular war is morally justified only if there is overwhelming evidence that the most basic rights of freedom and well-being will be jeopardized unless the war is undertaken. Any war for which such overwhelming evidence is not available is not morally justified. Thus, despite all its moral ambiguities, I should hold that World War II was a morally justified war, while on the same ground the Vietnam War was not morally justified.

This criterion of a war's being morally justified bears on the question of intended end, the sort of consideration invoked when one says, "The war is being fought in order to secure x," or "The purpose of the war is to secure x." I am aware of the great complexities which these simple locutions may obscure. There are such questions as: Whose purpose is it? How enlightened, factually and morally, is the reasoning which adopts this war as the means to this purpose? How likely is it that the war will secure x as against some quite different outcome? Should the moral quality of the war be evaluated by reference to the end intended by the ruling authorities or by reference to the probable outcome of the war, especially if these diverge sharply? In addition, where "x" consists, as in my above criterion, in protecting the most basic rights of freedom and well-being, there arise such questions as: Whose freedom and well-being? What if the freedom and well-being of only a small proportion of the inhabitants will be jeopardized? To what degree must they be jeopardized? What is, or must be, the relation between this jeopardy and the preservation of the state as such? How much evidence for such jeopardizing is required? This question of evidence raises the serious issue of who is to determine whether some particular war is morally wrong. If the official procedures of a democratic state are deemed inadequate for such determination, should the convictions of individual citizens be trusted more? The specter of anarchy again arises here.

In reply, I must reiterate the extreme seriousness of war and the consequent requirement that overwhelming evidence be supplied of its necessity to safeguard basic freedom and well-being. This evidence must be intellectually sound, and objective means must be provided for checking this soundness, so that propaganda may be differentiated from fact.

All these questions bear on the crucial relation invoked by the selective conscientious objector: the relation between the moral quality of a particular war, evaluated as suggested above, and his reasons for opposing that war. In order to understand this relation in the present context, we must give further consideration to the connection between the Conscience Variable and the Reason Variable. Originally, the conscription law required that in order to be exempted from military service a conscientious objector had to base his objection on a specific kind of reason, namely, that he was a member of a recognized church or religious sect which explicitly prohibited any resort to physical violence against other persons. This requirement as to the reason for objection was progressively broadened by court decisions so as to consist, first, in belief in God, then in belief in a Supreme Being, then in religious belief, then in "a sincere and meaningful belief which occupies in the life of its possessor a place parallel to that filled by the God of those admittedly qualifying for the exemption . . . ;"[9] and finally, in the 1970 Welsh decision, the Supreme Court held that one's reason for objecting to military service could consist in "deeply and sincerely [held] beliefs that are purely ethical or moral in source and content but that nevertheless impose upon [the individual] a duty of conscience to refrain from participating in any war at any time. . . ."[10]

It is important to note one point about this broadening of the reasons or grounds which conscientious objectors may successfully adduce in claiming exemption from military service. Although the Welsh decision characterizes the exempting beliefs or reasons

9. *United States v. Seeger*, 380 U.S. 176 (1965).
10. *United States v. Welsh*, 398 U.S. 340 (1970).

by the words "purely ethical or moral in source and content," it lays down no specifications as to what that content must consist in, other than an opposition to participating in any war. In particular, normative considerations as to the truth or falsity, or the moral rightness or wrongness, of the objector's beliefs have been explicitly disavowed as a basis for exempting the conscientious objector from military service. As Justice Clark put it in the Seeger decision: "The validity of what he believes cannot be questioned . . . the 'truth' of a belief is not open to question. . . ."[11] This was reiterated by Justice Black in the Welsh decision when he wrote that " 'intensely personal' convictions which some might find 'incomprehensible' or 'incorrect' come within the meaning of 'religious belief' in the Act."[12] On the other hand, Justice Marshall in rejecting the selective objector's exemption in the *Gillette* case, wrote that "under the petitioners' unarticulated scheme for exemption, an objector's claim to exemption . . . might be predicated on a view of the facts that most would regard as mistaken."[13] But Marshall then went on to repeat the words of Clark that "the 'truth' of a belief is not open to question. . . ."

What this means, then, is that exemption from military service is in no way to be affected by the question of the validity or correctness of the Reason Variable, that is, of the factual or moral beliefs which constitute one's grounds or reasons for conscientiously objecting to military service. Indeed, the Reason Variable as having a content distinct from the Conscience Variable has been given up as a requirement for exemption. The only requirement, in addition to an opposition to participating in any war, is that this opposition, whatever the beliefs or reasons on which it is based, must be conscientious. This latter requirement, bearing on what I have called the Conscience Variable, was enunciated by the Supreme Court in what seem to be primarily psychological terms: the emphasis is on the intensity and sincerity with which beliefs are held and on the way in which these beliefs

11. *United States v. Seeger*, 380 U.S. 184, 185.
12. *United States v. Welsh*, 398 U.S. 339.
13. *United States v. Gillette*, 401 U.S. 456-457.

function in the objector's life. Thus the Welsh decision puts the requirement as involving that the individual "deeply and sincerely holds" his beliefs; it says the decisive question "is whether these beliefs play the role of a religion and function as a religion in the registrant's life"; it asserts that the relevant section of the draft law "exempts from military service all those whose consciences, spurred by deeply held moral, ethical, or religious beliefs, would give them no rest or peace if they allowed themselves to become a part of an instrument of war."[14] In his concurrence, Justice Harlan said: "The common denominator must be the intensity of moral conviction with which a belief is held."[15]

This development, in which the requirement of a specific religious content has been dropped, a concern with validity or truth has been disavowed, and a purely psychological requirement has been substituted, has usually been hailed as a strong move in the direction of libertarian enlightenment; and I agree that in many important respects it is. But it has implications which are potentially quite serious for the issue of the moral justifiability of exempting the selective conscientious objector from military service. The point emerges clearly in connection with my absolute context. For this context, like the selective objector himself, views the moral justifiability of exempting him from military service in terms of reasons which determine whether the war in which he is asked to fight is morally right or morally wrong. Thus, where the selective objector emphasizes not only the Conscience Variable but also the Reason Variable as a distinct normative consideration justifying his opposition to a particular war, the Supreme Court emphasizes only the Conscience Variable. Moreover, the selective objector, unlike the Supreme Court, does not have a purely psychological conception of a belief's being a moral one. On the contrary, the objector distinguishes between the moral rightness and the moral wrongness of beliefs, actions, and policies, including wars, in terms of reasons bearing on certain specific contents of each of these. To put it otherwise, for the selective objector moral utterances have not only illocutionary

14. 398 U.S. 339 ff.
15. *Ibid.* 358.

force and perlocutionary effects; they have also certain specific criteria of application which determine for him whether he will apply the words 'morally right' and 'morally wrong' to various objects. But this criterial or objective aspect of moral words is completely rejected in the Supreme Court's test for conscientious objectors because it merges the Reason Variable into the Conscience Variable.[16]

This means that my absolute context, like the selective objector himself, focuses on a variable which is omitted from the Supreme Court's doctrine, namely, the Reason Variable. I shall now go on to consider the two alternatives of my absolute context with due consideration for this variable.

The first alternative is where some particular war is morally wrong, in that the purpose for which it is being fought, as established by the most adequate available evidence, is not to protect basic rights of freedom and well-being but rather to promote national aggrandizement or some similar objective. The thesis I wish to present here is that in such a case it is morally justified that everyone refrain from participating in the war, and *a fortiori* that the selective conscientious objector be exempted from participating in it. I am aware of the problems raised by this position: the war may have been voted for by constitutional democratic procedures, the conscription machinery may be set up by legal processes, and so forth. Nevertheless, as we saw above, the fact that there is a just law$_2$, i.e. a just constitutional system, does

16. This rejection may in fact be less complete than the Court's explicit statements suggest. The Court seems implicitly to incorporate into the meaning or criteria of "religious" and "ethical" or "moral" various conceptions of universalist beneficence, as against their opposites. See, for example, the passage from *Berman v. United States*, 156 F. 2d 381 cited in the Seeger decision: "Surely a scheme of life designed to obviate [man's inhumanity to man], and by removing temptations, and all the allurements of ambition and avarice, to nurture the virtues of unselfishness, patience, love, and service, ought not to be denounced as not pertaining to religion when its devotees regard it as an essential tenet of their religious faith" (380 U.S. 184). See also the passages from letters by Seeger and Welsh cited in the Welsh decision (398 U.S. 338, 342, 343). Nevertheless, directly after citing the passage from the Berman case, Justice Clark went on to say: "The validity of what he believes cannot be questioned . . . the 'truth' of a belief is not open to question. . . ."

not entail that all the particular laws$_3$ made in accordance with that system or law$_2$ are themselves morally right or just. Now in the case of many morally wrong laws$_3$ made within a morally right law$_2$, such as the Prohibition amendment or the income tax laws with their loopholes for the very rich, it may be expedient to obey them for various familiar reasons. But in the case of something as profoundly serious as war, such expediency is overridden because of its drastic impact on basic rights of life and liberty.

The relation of the selective conscientious objector to a morally wrong war is hence of two convergent sorts. Simply as a citizen of the nation engaged in the war, his participation therein is not morally justified. But in addition, since he opposes participating in the war for the reason that the war is morally wrong, and since the war is indeed morally wrong, the selective objector's reasons for claiming exemption from military service are morally correct ones, while the reasons of those who oppose his exemption and who support the war are morally incorrect. The moral rightness of his reasons for refusing to participate hence reinforces the moral rightness of his refusal to participate.

IV

I turn now to the second alternative of my absolute context, where a particular war is morally right in that it is fought in order to protect basic rights of freedom and well-being. Since the selective conscientious objector refuses to participate in the war on the ground that it is morally wrong, this means that he is mistaken so far as concerns his reasons. What we have here, then, is the problem which Aquinas and other scholastics referred to as the "erroneous conscience."[17] It may seem obvious that the selective objector's position here cannot be morally justified, on the principle that it cannot be morally right to oppose what is mor-

17. See Thomas Aquinas, *Summa Theologica*, II, I, qu. 19, art. 5-6. For a recent discussion, see Eric D'Arcy, *Conscience and Its Right to Freedom* (London: Sheed and Ward, 1961). Justice Douglas referred to the concept of the "erroneous conscience" in his dissent from the *Gillette* decision, 401 U.S. 471, n. 5.

ally right. Whatever be the case as to the soundness of this simple principle in general, however, it fails to take account of the specific sort of opposition which is in question. One may, for example, oppose assisting in the implementation of a morally right end because one regards the means of implementation as morally wrong. In the case of the selective conscientious objector, the simple principle may lead one to ignore the specific nature of his reasons for opposing the war and the relation of these reasons to his own moral character. Two possible aspects of these reasons must be distinguished, one empirically factual, the other moral. The selective objector may oppose a morally justified war because he is mistaken about certain empirical facts; he may think, for example, that the war is being fought in order to suppress further some submerged people (a purpose which he correctly holds to be morally wrong), although it is in fact being fought for the opposite purpose. On the other hand, he may oppose the war because he upholds a morally wrong principle; he may, for example, be a racist who holds that the enslavement of black persons is morally justified (and he holds the correct empirical belief that the war is being fought in order to prevent the enslavement of blacks). Now if the objector's opposition to the war is based, as in the first situation, on a reason which is factually false but morally right or at least neutral, then it may still be correctly said that he is here morally good (in respect of his moral character) even though his acts of opposition are morally wrong (in respect of their objective relation to the principles of moral rightness). If, however, the selective objector's opposition to the war is based, as in the second situation, on a reason which is itself morally wrong, then it is the case both that he is morally bad and that his acts of opposition are morally wrong. The moral quality of the selective objector's opposition to the war is hence affected by the quality of his reasons for opposing it.

There are, of course, further possible alternatives here. At one extreme, the selective conscientious objector may be constitutionally incapable of making a morally correct judgment about the war. At the other extreme, he may deliberately uphold a morally wrong principle while knowing or believing that it is morally

wrong. Such cases of moral imbecilism and moral monsterism
may, however, be ignored for present purposes. We are here concerned primarily with cases where a selective conscientious objector opposes a morally right war for morally wrong reasons, where
he believes that what is morally right is in fact morally wrong
and where he is nevertheless capable of distinguishing between
the two. The question is: What bearing does his morally wrong
opposition to the war have on the moral justifiability of exempting him from participating in it?

This question is affected by the distinction drawn by many
moral philosophers between "subjective" and "objective" duty.
The selective objector sincerely believes, on the basis of certain
reasons, that he ought not to fight in some particular war. Now
on the subjective conception of duty, a person really ought to do
or not do what he believes he ought to do or not do; hence, on
this conception, the objector really ought not to fight in the particular war to which he objects. And since a necessary condition
of the fulfillment of this "ought not" is that his request for an
exemption from military service be granted, it follows that he
really ought to be granted the exemption he requests. On the
other hand, his opposition to fighting in the war may really be
morally wrong, because his reasons may be either factually false
or morally wrong or both. But to admit this about his reasons is
to admit that what he believes he ought to do is not conclusive as to
what he really ought to do. Hence, his belief that he ought not to
participate in the war in question may be mistaken, so that it
may be wrong to grant him the exemption he requests.

In order to cut across some of these complexities, I shall here
consider primarily the sort of situation where a particular war is
morally right and a selective objector's reason for not participating in it is morally wrong. This sort of situation has received
almost no attention in the literature[18] by comparison with the
situations where a selective objector opposes a morally wrong

18. See the brief discussions by Geoffrey C. Hazard, Jr., and John de J. Pem-
berton, Jr., in Sol Tax, ed., *The Draft* (Chicago: University of Chicago Press,
1967), pp. 292, 316, 326; and by John Courtney Murray and Paul Ramsey in
Finn, *op. cit.*, pp. 29-30, 33, 37-38, 56-57.

war for morally right reasons, probably because the latter situations are much more frequent. Nevertheless, the former situation raises important questions which deserve consideration both for their own sakes and because they should help us to understand the general merits of exempting selective conscientious objectors from military service.

As an example of such a situation let us suppose that some selective conscientious objector is an anti-black racist, and that his nation, through one of those developments of which history affords some parallels, is undertaking to fight a war to prevent the enslavement of blacks by a potentially invading racist power. Such cases may seem far-fetched, but an understanding of the issues must take account of such hypothetical cases. Nor are they all that hypothetical: during World War II many British Fascists, for example, became selective conscientious objectors who objected specifically, on grounds of conscience, to fighting against the Axis powers.[19] Certain other objections to this example must also be rejected, such as that no racist could have a conscience or could hold his beliefs in the conscientious way required by the conscription law; or that no moral belief, by definition, could be a racist one; or that a racist couldn't possibly be an objector to military service because racism is necessarily connected with militarism, not with anti-militarism; or that the issue of racists who are selective conscientious objectors applies just as much against racists who are universal conscientious objectors. These contentions must be rejected, because racists may indeed have consciences and be quite conscientious and even "fanatical";[20] racism cannot be excluded from being a moral belief unless we define 'moral' in a way different from the Supreme Court, and if we do, there still remains the problem of the racist's conscience;

19. See Hayes, *op. cit.*, p. 52.
20. See, for example, Hannah Arendt's description of Adolf Eichmann: "as for his conscience, he remembered perfectly well that he would have had a bad conscience only if he had not done what he had been ordered to do—to ship millions of men, women, and children to their death with great zeal and the most meticulous care" (*Eichmann in Jerusalem* (New York: Viking Press, 1963), p. 22).

racists may oppose militarism when they regard it as aiding
groups they regard as racially inferior, as for example in the inte-
grated Army of the United States after World War II. As for the
contention that universal conscientious objectors may be racists,
this important difference must be noted: a universal objector
could not logically uphold his opposition to all wars on racist
grounds, since some wars have been fought for racist purposes.

The question to be considered, then, is whether a selective
conscientious objector who opposes a morally justified war for
morally wrong reasons ought to be exempted from participating
in the war. What is crucially involved here is the relation between the Conscience Variable and the Reason Variable. One
frequently upheld libertarian position is that the Conscience
Variable should alone be decisive: if someone conscientiously objects to participating in some war, then he ought to be exempted
from participating in it, regardless of the specific content of his
reasons for objecting to it, and regardless also of the consequences
of granting the objection. His reasons might still be considered,
but only as a clue to his conscientiousness, not with regard to
their objective rightness or wrongness. On this position, absolute
value must be attributed to effective freedom of conscience, including the ability to refrain from doing what one sincerely opposes doing, especially in so serious a matter as military action.

An opposed position on this question focuses on the Reason
Variable, and this from two interrelated viewpoints. One viewpoint confines itself to the objector's own giving of reasons. In
giving these reasons, the objector's attitude is that of a person
who is willing and indeed anxious to engage in a rational dialogue about the objective rightness or wrongness of the war in
question. The objector himself thus invokes not only the Conscience Variable but also, more basically, the Reason Variable:
he claims that he should be exempted from his legal obligation
to perform military service not only because he is conscientiously
opposed to performing it but also because his conscientious opposition is based on valid, indeed conclusive, reasons bearing on
the moral wrongness of the particular war in which he is legally
obligated to fight. He hence makes a claim which purports to be

based on the objective merits of the case, and not only on the depth, sincerity, or intensity of his convictions. Now if, as in the libertarian position, one considers only the Conscience Variable in deciding the question of exemption and ignores the Reason Variable, then one ignores the crucial basis of the objector's claim as he himself envisages it. In effect, he is told that although he bases his claim on a certain reason, and although he has engaged, or wishes to engage, in a dialogue with the government on the basis of that reason, the government has no concern with his reason or with participating in this dialogue. In this perspective, the government's exempting the objector from military service is, in an important sense, not an act of respect for him or for his convictions, since it ignores the chief basis for which he here claims to deserve respect, namely, the specific reasoned content of his convictions.

A second viewpoint focuses on the Reason Variable in terms of the objective merits of its specific content as involving a dialogue which seeks to attain the truth about the moral quality of the war and hence of participation in it. Consider again the objector's claim, now formulated as follows: "I ought to be exempted from participating in this war because it has a certain empirical quality (EQ), and whatever has EQ is morally wrong." Let us assume that the "because" here signifies both necessary and sufficient conditions, and let us also suppose, in accordance with my above example, that the "EQ" here in question consists in fighting to prevent the enslavement of black persons. The objector's claim may hence be reformulated as follows: "If I ought to be exempted from participating in this war, then fighting to prevent the enslavement of blacks is morally wrong." Now for the government to exempt this objector would be for it to accept his antecedent but not his consequent. But insofar as the objector's claim is taken seriously in its own terms, his antecedent should not be accepted, since what he holds it to imply is false. For in his claim as formulated, the falsity of the consequent entails the falsity of the antecedent, so that, in terms of the rational debate which the objector invokes when he gives reasons for opposing the particular war as morally wrong, he must be held to lose the debate. Hence, his claim to exemption must, to this extent, be rejected.

What emerges from the considerations thus far is that to make the Conscience Variable decisive is to hold that the racist selective conscientious objector should be exempted from military service, while to make the Reason Variable decisive is to hold the opposite position. It must be kept in mind, however, that "reason" as so far used has been confined primarily to the objector's own grounds for refusing to participate in a war. Now a person's reasons for believing or doing something may not be rational in the sense of rationally justified; they may not be such as would be acquired by a right use of reason, in that they contain either empirically false but corrigible beliefs or morally wrong principles or judgments which are inconsistent, arbitrary, or otherwise irrational. Hence, in order to ascertain what is rationally justified with respect to the selective objector's exemption, we must go beyond the terms set by his own claims, where he has made the rightness of exempting him depend on the judgment that it is wrong to oppose the enslavement of blacks. Even if, within the racist objector's own terms of rational debate, he must be held to have lost the debate because his judgment is wrong, his terms should not necessarily be the determining ones, since they must themselves be evaluated by broader criteria: factual ones of truth and moral ones of equal freedom and well-being.

Let us consider from John Stuart Mill three points which at least partially embody such relevant criteria. First, the moral wrongness of one's beliefs, such as racist beliefs, should not tell at all against one's freedom to express them. Second, however, insofar as one's beliefs are morally wrong, especially in their bearing on the rights and well-being of other persons, one should not have the freedom to act on them; for example, one should not be free to act out one's racist beliefs in such spheres as enslavement, killing, removal of voting rights, discrimination in public accommodations, and so forth. Now the racist conscientious objector of my above example does not merely claim the right to express his beliefs; nor does he, *qua* objector, necessarily claim the right to act out his beliefs in the positive sense of acting to achieve the blacks' enslavement. Rather, he claims the right to refrain from acting toward the achievement of a condition opposed to his beliefs: he opposes participating in a war to help prevent racist oppression. This, then, is Mill's third point: such refraining is unjustified because it shirks a positive duty:

> There are also many positive acts for the benefit of others, which he may rightfully be compelled to perform; such as to give evidence in a court of justice; to bear his fair share in the common defense, or in any other joint work necessary to the interest of the society of which he enjoys the protection; and to perform certain acts of individual beneficence, such as saving a fellow-creature's life, or interposing to protect the defenseless against ill-usage, things which whenever it is obviously a man's duty to do, he may rightfully be made responsible to society for not doing.[21]

If we were to apply Mill's point to the question of the selective objector, we should have to conclude that exempting him from military service is morally unjustified because he would thereby be permitted to refrain from bearing "his fair share in the common defense" or from "interposing to protect the defenseless against ill-usage." It must be noted, however, that in speaking here of "acts of *individual* beneficence," Mill was not dealing with the broader social-institutional context in which the question of the racist selective objector arises. Nor did he here give any independent consideration to either the Conscience Variable or the Action Variable: the fact that some persons object on grounds of conscience to killing for a cause which they believe to be morally wrong.

Consideration of these variables would strongly affect the question of fairness. We saw earlier that this question may be formulated in at least two ways: (a) Is it fair that some qualified persons be exempted from the danger of being killed in war while

21. *On Liberty*, Ch. 1 (Everyman's Library ed., p. 74). Later in the same paragraph Mill writes that under certain circumstances which "preclude the enforcement of responsibility, the conscience of the agent himself should step into the vacant judgment seat. . . ." This does not, however, affect the present argument.

others are not? (b) Is it fair that better-educated persons have
legally available to them a basis for exemption from military
service (through their selective opposition to a particular war)
when less well-educated persons cannot take equal advantage of
this basis? As with all appeals to fairness, the crucial factor is the
criterion of what one takes to be the relevant quality of the persons between whom one is asked to judge fairly. Now if we take
this criterion from the Action and Conscience Variables, then the
question of fairness would have to be put as follows: Is it fair
that some persons be made to violate their consciences in the most
drastic way possible—by being required to kill other persons for
a cause they deeply believe to be morally wrong—when other
persons are not thus made to violate their consciences? To put the
question in this way is to reemphasize the principle of freedom
of conscience indicated by the Conscience Variable—the same
principle as the general policy of exempting universal conscientious objectors is designed to respect.

Such freedom is, indeed, a determinative even if not a conclusive principle of the rightness of social policy. To call it "determinative" is to say that when a question affecting it arises, it
should determine what social policy should be; but it is not conclusive in that it may be overridden by other principles. As my
above discussions have suggested, considerations of fairness may
point in either direction: both toward exempting and not exempting the selective objector. But the policy upheld by consideration of the Conscience Variable is reinforced by further considerations deriving from the Consequence Variable. It would be
dangerous to let members of draft boards pass on the moral
rightness or wrongness of an objector's reasons for opposing some
particular war (as against judging the conscientiousness of his
objections), for this would open the door to penalizing other men
for unorthodox opinions. In addition, it would do the war effort
no good, and might do it harm, to have in the armed forces men
who are vehemently in disagreement with its aims on grounds
of conscience. Alternative modes of service could be provided
which would remove the extremity of potential killing which
the Action Variable emphasized.

If exempting the racist objector would prove harmful to carrying out the morally right aims of the sort of war mentioned above, then the exemption would not be morally justified. But if, as seems likely, there would not be such harm, then exempting him is morally justified on grounds of respect for freedom of individual conscience. Note, then, that I am not ascribing absolute value to conscience, since its content may be morally wrong in a very drastic way. But the effective freedom of the depth of feeling and belief which it represents is a value which deserves respect if that respect can be given without endangering policies and institutions which are morally right.

It may be helpful if I now summarize the main conclusions of this essay, although, as I have tried to emphasize, the relation of the Reason Variable to the other three variables involves many complexities. I have here argued for three main conclusions. First, if one supports the universal conscientious objector's exemption from military service, then one does not have adequate grounds for opposing the selective conscientious objector's exemption. Second, where the selective objector's reasons for claiming exemption from military service are morally right, in that the war he opposes is morally wrong, it is morally justified that he and all other persons be exempted from supporting the war. Third, where the selective objector's reasons for claiming exemption from military service are morally wrong, in that the war he opposes is morally right, it is still probably justified that he be given the exemption he seeks, although alternative service should perhaps be required. In connection with all three of these conclusions, but especially the last two, justified resolution of the problem requires consideration not only of the selective objector's conscientious convictions but also of the validity or justification of the reasons on which he bases these convictions.

Index

Southern Methodist Univ.   br
JC 571.G44 1982
Human rights :

3   2177   00959   8416